ECCLESIAL EXEGESIS

VERBUM
DOMINI

Nihil Obstat:
Rev. Christopher Begg, S.T.D., Ph.D.
Censor Deputatus

Imprimatur:
Very Reverend Daniel B. Carson
Vicar General and Moderator of the Curia
Archdiocese of Washington
March 10, 2022

The *nihil obstat* and *imprimatur* are official declarations that a book or pamphlet is free of doctrinal or moral error. There is no implication that those who have granted the *nihil obstat* and the *imprimatur* agree with the content, opinions or statements expressed therein.

The paper used in this publication
meets the minimum requirements of
American National Standards for Information Science—
Permanence of Paper for Printed Library Materials,
ANSI Z39.48-1984.

Cataloging-in-Publication Data on file wth the Library of Congress

ISBN 978-0-8132-3522-6 eISBN 978-0-8132-3523-3

Printed in the United States.
Book design by Burt&Burt
Interior set with Minion Pro and Astoria

Ecclesial Exegesis

A SYNTHESIS OF ANCIENT AND MODERN APPROACHES TO SCRIPTURE

GREGORY VALL

The Catholic University of America Press
Washington, D.C.

For Lourdes

Contents

Acknowledgments

Over the twenty-two years during which this book has slowly taken shape, divine providence has sustained me with the love and prayers of many people, beginning with my parents, Robert Vall† and Patricia Vall†, and siblings, Lorrie Miller, Sr. Carrie Vall, CSJ, Martin Vall, and Dr. Patrick Vall. Of the many colleagues and students who have aided my development as a scholar and supported me with their friendship and prayers, I wish in particular to thank Archbishop Gregory Aymond, Fr. John Joseph Bourque, CJC, Fr. J. Edgar Bruns†, Fr. Gregory Fratt, Jordan Haddad, Stephen Hildebrand, Jeremy Holmes, David Liberto, Steven A. Long, Rebecca Maloney, Sr. Maria Veritas Marks, OP, Fr. Francis Martin†, Nathan Mastnjak, Jennifer Morel, Brant Pitre, Matthew Ramage, Msgr. Terry Tekippe†, Michael and Susie Waldstein, and Fr. James Wehner. I owe a special debt of gratitude to Dr. Lorenz Hamburger, apart from whose excellent chiropractic care completing this book would have been physically impossible for me. During the review of the manuscript, the Diocese of Biloxi permanent diaconate formation cohort of 2022 and their wives generously offered many prayers for a successful outcome. In the final stages of the project, John Martino of the Catholic University of America Press supplied wisdom, energy, and patience when I had run out of all three. Editors Gregory Glazov, Fr. Pablo Gadenz, and Jeffrey Morrow have been most encouraging and are kind to include this book in the Verbum Domini series. With his superb copyediting, Claude Hanley has improved my writing and prevented me from publishing dozens of clumsy sentences. Finally, I wish to thank the six people who are dearest to me: my loving wife of twenty-five years, Lourdes Vall; our daughter Teresa and her husband Andrew Maal; and our three sons, Greg, Ezra, and Mark.

Abbreviations

a.	article (in citations of scholastic works)
AB	Anchor Bible
ABD	David Noel Freedman, ed., *Anchor Bible Dictionary*
ABRL	Anchor Bible Reference Library
ANF	Alexander Roberts, James Donaldson, and A. Cleveland Coxe, eds., *Ante-Nicene Fathers*
AYB	Anchor Yale Bible
AYBRL	Anchor Yale Bible Reference Library
Barn.	*Epistle of Barnabas*
BDAG	Walter Bauer, Frederick W. Danker, William F. Arndt, and F. Wilbur Gingrich, *Greek-English Lexicon of the New Testament and Other Early Christian Literature*
c.	chapter (in citations of Aquinas's exegetical works)
CCC	*Catechism of the Catholic Church*
1 Clem.	Clement of Rome, *Letter to the Corinthians* (aka *First Clement*)
corp.	corpus (body of an article in a scholastic work)
DBI	John H. Hayes, ed., *Dictionary of Biblical Interpretation*

Denz.	Heinrich Denzinger, ed., *Compendium of Creeds, Definitions, and Declarations on Matters of Faith and Morals*, 43rd ed.
Did.	*Didache of the Twelve Apostles*
Diog.	*Epistle to Diognetus*
dist.	distinction (in citations of certain scholastic works)
Eph.	Ignatius of Antioch, *Letter to the Ephesians*
HALOT	Ludwig Koehler et al., eds., *Hebrew and Aramaic Lexicon of the Old Testament*
ICC	International Critical Commentary
IDB	George A. Buttrick, ed., *Interpreter's Dictionary of the Bible*
In I Cor.	Thomas Aquinas, *Super I epistolam ad Corinthios*
In II Cor.	Thomas Aquinas, *Super II epistolam ad Corinthios*
In Gal.	Thomas Aquinas, *Super epistolam ad Galatas*
In Heb.	Thomas Aquinas, *Super epistolam ad Hebraeos*
In Ioan.	Thomas Aquinas, *Super evangelium sancti Ioannis*
In Rom.	Thomas Aquinas, *Super epistolam ad Romanos*
JBC	Raymond E. Brown, Joseph A. Fitzmyer, and Roland E. Murphy, eds., *Jerome Biblical Commentary* (1968)
lect.	lecture (in citations of Aquinas's exegetical works)
LSJ	Henry G. Liddell, Robert Scott, and Henry S. Jones, *A Greek-English Lexicon*
LXX	Septuagint

Magn.	Ignatius of Antioch, *Letter to the Magnesians*
MT	Masoretic Text
NABRE	New American Bible, Revised Edition
NICNT	New International Commentary on the New Testament
NJBC	Raymond E. Brown, Joseph A. Fitzmyer, and Roland E. Murphy, eds., *New Jerome Biblical Commentary* (1990)
NPNF[2]	Philip Schaff and Henry Wace, eds., *A Select Library of Nicene and Post-Nicene Fathers of the Christian Church*, Series 2
NRSV	New Revised Standard Version
OTL	Old Testament Library
PG	Jacques-Paul Migne, Patrologia Graeca
Phil.	Polycarp of Smyrna, *Letter to the Philippians*
Phld.	Ignatius of Antioch, *Letter to the Philadelphians*
PL	Jacques-Paul Migne, Patrologia Latina
q.	question (in citations of scholastic works)
Rom.	Ignatius of Antioch, *Letter to the Romans*
sc.	sed contra (pivotal section of an article in a scholastic work)
Smyr.	Ignatius of Antioch, *Letter to the Smyrnaeans*
STh	Thomas Aquinas, *Summa Theologiae*
TDNT	Gerhard Kittel, Gerhard Friedrich, and Geoffrey W. Bromiley, eds., *Theological Dictionary of the New Testament*
TOB	John Paul II, *Man and Woman He Created Them: A Theology of the Body*, cited according to Michael Waldstein's division of the text
WBC	Word Biblical Commentary

Introduction

THE BIBLICAL QUESTION

In every age the people of God must endeavor to interpret and appropriate divine revelation in a manner that is entirely faithful to Scripture and Tradition but at the same time addresses contemporary questions, makes full use of the resources of contemporary thought, and speaks in a way that is intelligible to contemporary minds. This ongoing task requires "a great effort, in terms of both thought and living."[1] At the heart of the particular challenge facing our own age in this regard is "the biblical question." How should believers respond to the discoveries, methods, and theories of modern biblical scholarship, which often shed new light on the pages of Scripture but in the process may also threaten to undermine elements of the Christian faith? What role, if any, should the historical-critical method play in *ecclesial exegesis*—that is, in biblical interpretation that is informed by and informs the life of the Church? Are there other methods or approaches—ancient, medieval, modern, or postmodern—that ought to play a role? What should ecclesial exegesis look like in the twenty-first century?

The historical-critical method, with its diachronic analysis of texts and artifacts, has brought to light long-lost cultures of the ancient Near East, greatly increased our knowledge of the biblical languages, made unprecedented progress in the effort to restore the original texts of Scripture, identified ancient literary devices and genres, placed many biblical passages in their historical context, clarified thousands of obscurities in both

1 Hans Urs von Balthasar, *The Dramatis Personae: Man in God*, vol. 2 of *Theo-Drama: Theological Dramatic Theory*, trans. Graham Harrison (San Francisco: Ignatius, 1976), 193.

testaments, and traced out lines of religious and theological development within ancient Israel and the early Church. In recent decades various synchronic approaches, which concern themselves with the biblical text as a finished product, have given us a deeper appreciation for the literary artistry of the biblical authors and a renewed sense of Scripture's canonical shape and unity. The considerable hermeneutical tension between the older diachronic methods (textual, source, redaction, and form criticism) and the newer synchronic ones (literary, canonical, and reader-response criticism) has been mostly creative, raising important questions about the respective roles of author, text, reader, and community in the act of interpretation, and about the interrelationship between Scripture's historical, literary, and theological dimensions. Some scholars have reasoned, correctly in my opinion, that if one is to avoid both historicism and ahistoricism in the interpretation of Scripture, it is necessary to develop some workable hybrid of the diachronic and synchronic approaches.[2]

While modern biblical scholarship (diachronic, synchronic, and hybrid) has made real gains, it is important to recognize that it does not come equipped with the sort of comprehensive theological hermeneutic that would enable the people of God to take full advantage of the resources that it provides. Despite many attempts to place the historical-critical method on a solid hermeneutical footing, it is not yet entirely clear how an approach to the Bible that is essentially critical can be brought to the service of the word of God—that is, how it might facilitate the sort of inquiry into the mystery of the faith that is proper to the theological endeavor and ought to characterize biblical exegesis as well. In fact, it is safe to say that modern biblical scholarship has been wedded to philosophical presuppositions that present serious impediments in precisely this regard since its inception in the seventeenth century. Among other obstacles, there is a strong prejudice against transcendence and teleology that renders traditional theological categories such as *mystery* and *divine economy* meaningless. If the historical-critical method is to realize its promise for the Church, it must somehow be purged of its false presuppositions and reanimated with new principles. To accomplish this without sacrificing the true genius of the method, which is inseparable from its critical dimension, may prove more difficult than is sometimes supposed.

2 E.g., Ignacio Carbajosa, *Faith, the Fount of Exegesis: The Interpretation of Scripture in Light of the History of Research on the Old Testament*, trans. Paul Stevenson (San Francisco: Ignatius, 2013), 202–19.

Recent decades have witnessed widespread dissatisfaction with historical-critical biblical scholarship, in large part because it is perceived to be, and in many cases in fact is, theologically banal and spiritually sterile. In some circles this dissatisfaction has engendered renewed interest in the precritical exegesis of the Church Fathers, the medieval doctors, and the Reformers. Premodern exegetes were also critical, in the sense that they made discriminating judgments regarding the biblical text,[3] but they did so only after having placed themselves under its authority and under the guidance of the rule of faith. Modern and postmodern exegesis is typically critical in a more radical sense, insofar as it assumes a stance of independence from ecclesial tradition and dogma or even sits in ideological judgment over Scripture itself. Depending on one's point of view, therefore, the label "precritical" need not be taken pejoratively.

Renewed interest in precritical modes of interpretation raises the question of what exactly to make of the exegetical legacy of the patristic and medieval Church. The biblical works of the Fathers and doctors alternately inspire and repel. They are imbued with authentic piety, pastoral concern, and an intimate knowledge of the sacred text, but they are also infected with a virulent strain of anti-Judaism, which renders their exegesis badly distortive in not a few instances.[4] Christian biblical commentators of the patristic and medieval periods amaze us with their broad erudition, but they scandalize us by their almost universal failure to have learned more than a few words of Hebrew.[5] Still, it hardly makes sense to abstain from eating cherries just because they contain pits. Granted that one can easily multiply examples of philological and historical ignorance and of arbitrary and fanciful allegorization among the writings of patristic and medieval exegetes, it would be

3 For example, Origen of Alexandria argued on stylistic grounds that Paul could not have written the Epistle to the Hebrews (Eusebius of Caesarea, *Ecclesiastical History* 6.25), and Thomas Aquinas raised as a serious question whether the book of Job might be a "parable" rather than a narrative of actual events (*Expositio super Iob ad litteram*, prologue).

4 We shall encounter examples of this in chapters 1 and 4 below.

5 Apart from famous exceptions such as Origen and Jerome, or the occasional convert from Judaism, Christian scholars remained largely ignorant of Hebrew throughout the first millennium of Christianity. This began to change in the twelfth and thirteenth centuries, especially in northern France and England, when Christian scholars came into more direct contact with Jewish learning, in some cases through amicable relations with a local rabbi. See Beryl Smalley, *The Study of the Bible in the Middle Ages* (Notre Dame, Ind.: University of Notre Dame Press, 1964), 155 (on Andrew of St. Victor), 190–91 (on Herbert of Bosham), and 338–55 (on the thirteenth-century evidence).

precipitous, not to mention culturally chauvinistic, to suppose that we could for that reason dismiss all precritical interpretation as naïve and outmoded. The modern biblical scholar who invests the intellectual and spiritual capital necessary to become conversant with even a single great work of patristic exegesis, such as Augustine's *De Genesi ad litteram*, will realize how much we stand to learn about the Bible from our ancient predecessors. If we stop to consider, moreover, how deeply rooted traditional Christian exegesis is in the practice of the New Testament authors themselves, how intrinsic it was to the Church's life for the better part of two millennia, and how formative a role it played in the development of liturgy and dogma, we shall recognize that failure on our part to take the patristic-medieval exegetical heritage seriously would sever us from a vital means of access to "the life-giving presence of Tradition."[6] Nevertheless, if enthusiasm for precritical biblical interpretation is to rise above mere nostalgia and antiquarianism and serve the life of the Church in our age, its defects must be squarely faced, its true genius must be recovered, and it must be brought into a living synthesis with modern methods. This too will be a long and arduous project.

The gradual emergence of the historical-critical method from the late seventeenth to the mid-nineteenth century, its period of dominance in the nineteenth and twentieth centuries, and its current malaise have not occurred in isolation from other intellectual developments of the modern world, such as those in the natural sciences, philosophy, historiography, literary theory, sociology, psychology, and political science. On the contrary, the biblical question has played a key role in the intellectual drama of the last half millennium and continues to do so. "Humanism within Christianity is indeed the central theme of our time," wrote Hans Urs von Balthasar, who went on to explain that this theme had emerged largely "as a consequence of the stirring biblical discoveries of recent years."[7] Likewise, Joseph Ratzinger has drawn a close correlation between modern philosophy and the biblical question: "The exegetical problem is identical in the main with the struggle for the foundations of our time."[8] Over a century ago, the Catholic philosopher Maurice Blondel drew attention to the biblical question in his essay

6 *Dei Verbum* 8 (*Traditionis vivificam . . . praesentiam*).

7 Hans Urs von Balthasar, *The Word Made Flesh*, vol. 1 of *Explorations in Theology*, trans. A. V. Littledale and Alexander Dru (San Francisco: Ignatius, 1989), 70–71.

8 Joseph Ratzinger, "Biblical Interpretation in Crisis: On the Question of the Foundations and Approaches of Exegesis Today" (The Erasmus Lecture, 1988), in *Biblical Interpretation in Crisis: The Ratzinger Conference on Bible and Church*, ed. Richard John Neuhaus (Grand Rapids: Eerdmans, 1989), 16.

History and Dogma, and throughout the Modernist Crisis he maintained that Catholic life and thought might actually "profit from the radical effort of criticism and philosophy" and thus contribute to "the laborious parturition of modern consciousness."[9]

These three thinkers are also in substantial agreement as to what constitutes a genuinely Catholic response to the biblical question. According to Ratzinger, Catholic exegesis "cannot simply retreat back to the Middle Ages or to the Fathers and place them in blind opposition to the spirit of the present age. But neither can it renounce the insights of the great believers of the past."[10] In comments evidently directed at Neoscholasticism, Blondel argued that the proper response to Modernism is not "Veterism" and that we must not counter historicism with "extrinsicism," by which he meant a view of revelation that treats it as essentially a matter of propositional truth and thus as extrinsic to the events of sacred history.[11] As for Balthasar, his works contain, somewhat paradoxically, a penetrating critique of modern biblical scholarship alongside a profound appreciation for it. On the one hand, he maintains that speculative theology is threatened by a "kind of paralysis" caused by biblical criticism. On the other hand, he holds that the theologian who knows how to bring modern biblical scholarship into dialogue with the theological tradition stands to gain much. Biblical criticism is "part of the spirit of the age," and "we would be guilty of ingratitude did we not acknowledge how much that was wrongfully neglected in the past is here powerfully reinstated, how much that is essential for a future theology is here made available. The spirit of our age then has its advantages, though it owes its driving force in part to a loss of the power of synthesis."[12] Indeed, it is in large part because Balthasar understood the shortcomings of modern biblical scholarship so clearly that he was able to draw so fruitfully upon it. Still, it was also necessary that he possess within himself the requisite "power of synthesis," and this he must certainly have gained through his immersion in the whole intellectual tradition, ancient, medieval, and modern. Thus, in Balthasar's work we glimpse a living synthesis of "new things and old."[13]

9 Maurice Blondel, *The Letter on Apologetics and History and Dogma*, ed. and trans. Alexander Dru and Illtyd Trethowan (Grand Rapids: Eerdmans, 1994), 32.

10 Ratzinger, "Biblical Interpretation in Crisis," 16.

11 Blondel, *Letter on Apologetics*, 226.

12 Balthasar, *Word Made Flesh*, 97.

13 Cf. Matt 13:52. I am neither a Balthasarian nor an anti-Balthasarian. My point is simply that Balthasar took a solid theoretical position on the biblical question and impressively put it into practice.

The same basic attitude is also found in magisterial documents of the Roman Catholic Church. At least since the promulgation of Pope Pius XII's encyclical *Divino Afflante Spiritu* in 1943, the Magisterium has steadfastly resisted the temptation to choose between the patristic-medieval exegetical heritage and modern biblical scholarship, or to pit them against each other. Though elements of the former constitute serious blind spots, and elements of the latter must be rejected as inimical to the faith, in neither case is the Church willing to throw out the baby with the bath water. On the contrary, even as Pius XII exhorted Catholic biblical scholars not to neglect "any light derived from recent research" (no. 33), he also promoted an "assiduous study" of the Fathers of the Church and of other "renowned interpreters of past ages" and lamented the fact that "such precious treasures of Christian antiquity are almost unknown to many writers of the present day" (nos. 28–29). What Pope Pius seems to have had in mind was a new exegetical synthesis, a "happy and fruitful union" between traditional and modern modes of interpretation (no. 30).

METHOD C

In 1988, nearly half a century after *Divino Afflante Spiritu*, Cardinal Ratzinger delivered his Erasmus Lecture, provocatively titled "Biblical Interpretation in Crisis." The crisis to which he referred was an alleged disjuncture between the historical-critical method of biblical exegesis and the theology, faith, and Tradition of the Church. How might this breach be repaired? The cardinal offered no pat answer. On the contrary, he suggested that "hardly anyone today would assert that a truly pervasive understanding of this whole problem has yet been found which takes into account both the undeniable insights uncovered by the historical method, while at the same time overcoming its limitations and disclosing them in a thoroughly relevant hermeneutic. At least the work of a whole generation is necessary to achieve such a thing."[14]

On the day after the lecture, the cardinal sat down with an ecumenical group of twenty invited theologians and exegetes for an extended conversation about biblical interpretation in the life of the Church, in the course of which Thomas C. Oden, Raymond E. Brown, SS, and Ratzinger himself

14 Ratzinger, "Biblical Interpretation in Crisis," 5–6.

emerged as champions of three decidedly different visions of what ecclesial exegesis ought to look like moving forward. Dr. Oden, a Methodist theologian, had grown disenchanted with the historical-critical method and was convinced that it should be abandoned as a lost cause. In its place he advocated "going directly back" to the reading of the exegesis of the Church Fathers, who model for us how to interpret Scripture with theological clarity and spiritual depth.[15] (Later, Oden would demonstrate the courage of his convictions by serving as the general editor of the 29-volume Ancient Christian Commentary on Scripture.) Fr. Brown, the dean of North American Catholic biblical scholars, spoke in defense of the historical-critical method, but he also stressed the importance of "reading the Scriptures in the context of a believing church, which is the context in which they were written."[16] Cardinal Ratzinger, in order to clarify the nuanced position he had taken in the Erasmus Lecture, now reduced it to a simple tripartite schema: "You can call the patristic-medieval exegetical approach Method A. The historical-critical approach, the modern approach . . . is Method B. What I am calling for is not a return to Method A, but [the] development of a Method C, taking advantage of the strengths of both Method A and Method B, but cognizant of the shortcomings of both."[17]

This proposal was not so much an answer to the biblical question as it was a roadmap to the answer. As the conversation progressed, it became increasingly clear that the future pontiff envisioned a vast, interdisciplinary movement, involving philosophy, theology, exegesis, and hermeneutics, the cooperative effort of many scholars over many years. Well aware that matters were more complex than A–B–C, he employed the schema (in the context of a conversation and possibly off the cuff) for its heuristic value. The term "Method A" cannot refer to a specific methodology but to a set of first principles that unite the work of exegetes as diverse as Origen of Alexandria, John Chrysostom, Bernard of Clairvaux, and Thomas Aquinas. The same is true of "Method B," where the methodological diversity is perhaps even greater. Furthermore, several approaches that do not fall neatly under either Method A or Method B have potentially important contributions to make to a Method C synthesis. These range from the rich tradition of Jewish

15 Paul T. Stallsworth, "The Story of an Encounter," in *Biblical Interpretation in Crisis*, ed. Neuhaus, 113.

16 Stallsworth, 124.

17 Stallsworth, 107–8.

exegesis—ancient, medieval, and modern—to some of the aforementioned synchronic methodologies that emerged as rivals to the historical-critical method in the latter half of the twentieth century (e.g., narrative criticism).

Oden and Brown pushed back vigorously against the cardinal's proposal. Though they agreed on little else, both men felt that such a concerted effort to develop a new hermeneutic would be, at best, a colossal waste of time. Brown dismissively compared it to "the search for the Holy Grail."[18] Ratzinger's Method C proposal was predicated on the conviction that both the historical-critical method and patristic exegesis had real strengths and real weaknesses. Neither Oden nor Brown could accept this premise. According to the former, the historical-critical method was bankrupt, beyond hope of remedy.[19] According to the latter, it was rock solid, based as it was on a strictly historical methodology. It could always be improved upon by greater technical proficiency, of course, but neither philosophy nor hermeneutics had anything to offer it.[20]

If there was common ground among the three men, it lay in the shared conviction that biblical exegesis ought to be more clearly oriented to the life of the Church. Fr. Brown in particular, it seems, had come to the conference in an ecclesial frame of mind. "The Bible is the book of the church," he declared to the ecumenical assembly.[21] He acknowledged that the historical-critical method had borne bad fruit when it had been injected with a dubious philosophy, as in the case of Bultmann's Heideggerian existentialism, or when it had been removed from its proper context—namely, the believing Church—and imported into "a context of hate" by those who wished to destroy the Church.[22] But Brown was convinced that the method itself was sound and required no hermeneutical overhaul.

Cardinal Ratzinger was not deterred, however. In his characteristically incisive manner, he cut to the root of the problem: "It would not be fair to the historical-critical method simply to chastise it because of the faults of its erroneous practitioners. On the other hand, one must ask to what extent its erroneous application is due to *the defects of the method itself*."[23] Fr. Brown

18 Stallsworth, 112.

19 Stallsworth, 113, 126–27.

20 Stallsworth, 138–39.

21 Stallsworth, 123.

22 Stallsworth, 124.

23 Stallsworth, 104. Emphasis added.

could not accept this analysis. He was eager to grant that the historical-critical method was not self-sufficient, that it needed the context of "the teaching church," and that by itself it did not constitute the totality of biblical interpretation.[24] But Ratzinger had posited intrinsic defects in the method, and that was another matter entirely. Brown certainly recognized that the historical-critical method was sometimes misused, but he held that "the problem was not with the intrinsic philosophical foundation of the method itself" but with the erroneous assumptions of the individual scholars who abused it.[25]

In the Erasmus Lecture, Cardinal Ratzinger had identified some of the intrinsic defects that he found in the method.[26] Now, during the colloquium, he made a broad suggestion as to how they might be remedied. He proposed that "we must try to find how to spiritualize the positivistic method and also how to take into account all of the gifts of this method."[27] This brief statement encapsulates Ratzinger's vision for the renewal of ecclesial exegesis. The historical-critical method has something very precious to offer the Church, but it can realize this hope only by being transformed. It must be taken up into a new synthesis and "spiritualized" in the process. An authentic Method C, therefore, can never come about as the result of a mere collaboration or division of labor between Methods A and B. In practice as well as in theory, the two approaches must not remain extrinsic to each other.

Near the end of the colloquium, however, Avery Dulles, SJ, suggested that Method C exegesis should be envisioned as a procedure comprising two quite distinct stages, and he matter-of-factly presented this idea as having the authoritative support of the Second Vatican Council's Dogmatic Constitution on Divine Revelation *Dei Verbum*. The first stage is "technical exegesis"—that is, the historical-critical method—and the second stage is "theological exegesis." Only the latter "builds in certain theological presuppositions"—specifically, taking into account "the whole of Scripture, the whole of church tradition, and the harmony of what the faithful believe."[28] Not surprisingly, Brown eagerly embraced this schema, for it was essentially the same one that he himself had been promoting for years. Biblical

24 Stallsworth, 138, 122.

25 Donald Senior, CP, *Raymond E. Brown and the Catholic Biblical Renewal* (New York: Paulist, 2018), 74.

26 One of these is the "dualism of word and event," which I deal with in chapter 6 below.

27 Stallsworth, "Story of an Encounter," 109.

28 Stallsworth, 145. The last part of this statement is a virtual quotation of *Dei Verbum* 12.

interpretation begins with the historical-critical method, which, operating "neutrally" (i.e., without faith presuppositions), determines what the biblical text *meant* in its original historical context. Only after this has been accomplished do doctrine, theology, and pastoral concern step in. Building firmly on the assured results of the historical-critical method, they tell us what the biblical text *means* for the Church today.[29]

As we shall see in chapter 3 below, this two-stage idea is neither the teaching of *Dei Verbum* nor what Ratzinger had in mind for Method C. If it had been, he would have called his proposal "Method A+B." The whole point of Method C is that Method A and Method B both need to be purified, transformed, and taken up into a tertium quid that is more than the sum of its parts.[30] That is why serious philosophical, theological, and hermeneutical work will be necessary. Unfortunately, it seems that Ratzinger's proposal was doomed to be misinterpreted from the outset.[31] The fact that Dulles, American Catholicism's premier expert in the theology of revelation, could propose the two-stage model of exegesis as an entirely noncontroversial reading of *Dei Verbum* 12 and therefore as the ready-made solution to the quest for Method C gives some indication of what Ratzinger was up against.[32]

29 Raymond E. Brown, SS, *The Critical Meaning of the Bible* (New York: Paulist, 1981), 23–44.

30 According to Pope John Paul II, the historical-critical method can serve as the starting point and "basis" for exegesis, but only after it has been "freed from its philosophical presuppositions or those contrary to the truth of our faith." "Address on the Interpretation of the Bible in the Church," April 23, 1993, in Pontifical Biblical Commission, *The Interpretation of the Bible in the Church: Address of His Holiness John Paul II and Document of the Pontifical Biblical Commission* (Boston: St. Paul Books and Media, 1993), 22.

31 Eventually Ratzinger ceded some ground to the prevailing view. Twenty-two years after the Erasmus Lecture, then-Pope Benedict XVI wrote of the need for two "methodological levels, the historical-critical and the theological," though he quickly qualified this statement: "To distinguish two levels of approach to the Bible does not in any way mean to separate or oppose them, nor simply to juxtapose them. They exist only in reciprocity. Unfortunately, a sterile separation sometimes creates a barrier between exegesis and theology." Post-Synodal Apostolic Exhortation *Verbum Domini* (September 30, 2010), nos. 34–35. Dulles's formulation in terms of two stages suggests such a mere juxtaposition and "sterile separation" inasmuch as it reserves "theological presuppositions" for the second, "theological" stage. As we shall see in chapter 3, Joseph Fitzmyer, unlike his friend Raymond Brown, came to recognize clearly that "presuppositions of faith" must be included from the very beginning of the exegetical process. In my opinion, in any case, Benedict's formulation in *Verbum Domini* 34 is unfortunate, despite the caveats that he adds in no. 35, because it gives the distinct impression that the "historical-critical" method can retain its original identity and even occupy its own "level" in the exegetical process, rather than being taken up into a new synthesis.

32 Dulles had solidified his reputation in this field with the publication of *Models of Revelation* (Garden City, N.Y.: Doubleday, 1983).

This is not to suggest that the interpretation of *Dei Verbum* is simple or obvious. It is a subtler and more carefully nuanced document than *Divino Afflante Spiritu*, being the product of many minds, numerous drafts, and long debate. It is also a far more profoundly theological text, and that by design. *Dei Verbum* is neither the Magisterium's "endorsement of the historical-critical method"[33] nor even merely "the document on the Bible," as thousands of teachers have misinformed their students. It is rather the document in which the council fathers deal with the biblical question obliquely, by placing the Church's teaching about Scripture within the broad framework of the theology of revelation. Their intention, as the constitution's opening paragraph informs us, is to place before the Church and the world "authentic doctrine concerning divine revelation and its transmission" (no. 1). What *Dei Verbum* has to say about Scripture and the proper approach to its interpretation can only be understood in relation to what it teaches us about those two even more fundamental realities.

The impact of modern biblical scholarship on the Catholic Church and the troubling questions that it sometimes raises for believers no doubt constituted one of the major factors compelling the council to take up the onerous task of producing a dogmatic constitution on divine revelation. But whereas Pius XII's encyclical repeatedly makes direct (and mostly favorable) reference to modern tools and methods of biblical scholarship, the council fathers studiously avoid doing so. It may surprise some Catholics to learn that, despite what they have always heard, *Dei Verbum* never actually mentions modern biblical scholarship or the historical-critical method. Not even the oft-cited passage that exhorts exegetes to pay attention to the Bible's various "literary genres" (a patent echo of *Divino Afflante Spiritu*) presents this principle as a distinctively modern concern. Instead, the council fathers place it immediately under a patristic axiom—"in Sacred Scripture God speaks through men in the manner of men"—suggesting that it is a concern rooted in Tradition (no. 12). One must, therefore, look with suspicion on the claim that "the constitution clearly did enshrine the historical-critical method."[34]

By the same token, however, I must admit that if *Dei Verbum* never explicitly refers to modern methods of exegesis, it obviously cannot issue

33 Donald Senior, CP, "Dogmatic Constitution on Divine Revelation *Dei Verbum*, 18 November, 1965," in *Vatican II and Its Documents: An American Reappraisal*, ed. Timothy E. O'Connell (Wilmington, Del.: Michael Glazier, 1986), 127.

34 Ronald D. Witherup, SS, *Scripture: Dei Verbum*, Rediscovering Vatican II (New York: Paulist, 2006), 82.

an explicit call for a synthesis of those methods with the patristic approach to biblical interpretation à la *Divino Afflante Spiritu*. The council fathers' way of handling the biblical question is subtler than that and will therefore require a careful examination (in chapter 3 below). For, in the end, Cardinal Ratzinger's Method C proposal stands or falls with *Dei Verbum*. If the ecumenical council's Dogmatic Constitution on Divine Revelation, a document of the highest magisterial authority and one that is deeply concerned with the role of ecclesial exegesis in the modern world, does not give Ratzinger's idea at least *implicit* support, it matters little that Pius XII's encyclical adumbrated it, that Blondel and Balthasar thought in similar terms, or even that Ratzinger himself, years later as Pope Benedict XVI, promoted the idea in the Post-Synodal Apostolic Exhortation *Verbum Domini* and in the second of his three volumes on the Gospels.[35]

SLOW WORK

In February of 1988, I was studying Semitic languages at The Catholic University of America in the District of Columbia. On one of those bright, crisp days typical of Washington winters, I sat outside the basilica leafing through a copy of the *National Catholic Register* when my eyes fell on an article about the recent Erasmus Lecture conference. It quoted the passage from Cardinal Ratzinger's keynote address that I have cited above, ending with the sentence, "At least the work of a whole generation is necessary to achieve such a thing." This immediately resonated with me. Following a life-changing encounter with Jesus Christ on February 21, 1980, I had been studying the Bible avidly for eight years, attempting to understand the mystery of Christ and his Church, into which I had been baptized as an infant. Along the way, I had experienced both the "undeniable insights" and the "limitations" of the historical-critical method and was eager to be part of the generation that would articulate a "thoroughly relevant hermeneutic" for the sake of the people of God. The Erasmus Lecture became my lodestar, "Method C" my watchword.

A generation has now passed since the Erasmus Lecture, and several promising trends within the world of biblical scholarship have contributed

35 *Verbum Domini* 37 (cf. 32–33); Joseph Ratzinger, *Jesus of Nazareth, Part Two: Holy Week, From the Entrance into Jerusalem to the Resurrection*, trans. Vatican Secretariat of State (San Francisco: Ignatius, 2011), xiv–xv.

to the rapprochement of ancient and modern modes of exegesis. In the late 1990s, for example, the publication of a handful of seminal works by Protestant scholars launched the "theological interpretation" movement.[36] A related development has witnessed an exponential increase of interest in the "reception history" of the biblical text, and new resources have provided readers of Scripture with ready access to the primary sources of patristic and medieval biblical interpretation.[37] Meanwhile, Jewish biblical scholars have fruitfully combined mastery of historical-critical tools with extensive knowledge of the ancient and medieval sources of Jewish exegesis.[38] The fact that non-Catholics have been at the forefront of these movements and that they owe little or nothing to the direct influence of the Erasmus Lecture or the Method C proposal suggests that Ratzinger had put his finger on something that was already germinating in 1988. Other important trends were in full swing by that time, including the canonical approach, narrative criticism of the Bible, and the application of philosophical hermeneutics to the biblical question.[39]

The present volume is my contribution to the ongoing development of an ecclesial mode of biblical exegesis. My progress over the last three decades has been painfully slow, and I had hoped to be much further along by now. Still,

36 Stephen E. Fowl, ed., *The Theological Interpretation of Scripture: Classic and Contemporary Readings*, Blackwell Readings in Modern Theology (Malden, Mass.: Blackwell, 1997); and *Engaging Scripture: A Model for Theological Interpretation* (Oxford: Blackwell, 1998); Kevin J. Vanhoozer, *Is There a Meaning in this Text? The Bible, the Reader, and the Morality of Literary Knowledge* (Grand Rapids: Zondervan, 1998); Francis Watson, *Text and Truth: Redefining Biblical Theology* (Grand Rapids: Eerdmans, 1997).

37 Notable in this regard are two commentary series aimed at providing something like a modern analogue to the *Glossa Ordinaria*: Thomas C. Oden, gen. ed., Ancient Christian Commentary on Scripture, 29 vols. (Downers Grove, Ill.: InterVarsity Press, 2000–2010); and Robert Louis Wilken, gen. ed., The Church's Bible, 5 vols. (Grand Rapids: Eerdmans, 2007–present). Two related series provide entire commentaries and other exegetical texts from the patristic and medieval periods respectively: Thomas C. Oden, Gerald L. Bray, and Michael Glerup, gen. eds., Ancient Christian Texts, 16 vols. (Downers Grove, Ill.: InterVarsity Press, 2009–present); and H. Lawrence Bond, Philip Krey, and Thomas Ryan, gen. eds., The Bible in Medieval Tradition, 5 vols. (Grand Rapids: Eerdmans, 2011–present).

38 Exemplary in this regard are the commentaries of Jacob Milgrom: *Numbers*, JPS Torah Commentary (Philadelphia: Jewish Publication Society, 1990); *Leviticus: A New Translation with Introduction and Commentary*, 3 vols., Anchor Bible 3–3B (New York: Doubleday, 1991–2001).

39 Three seminal works, representing these three trends respectively, appeared circa 1980: Brevard S. Childs, *Introduction to the Old Testament as Scripture* (Philadelphia: Fortress, 1979); Robert Alter, *The Art of Biblical Narrative* (New York: Basic Books, 1981); and Anthony C. Thiselton, *The Two Horizons: New Testament Hermeneutics and Philosophical Description* (Grand Rapids: Eerdmans, 1980).

as our frenetic culture is beginning to discover, there is something to be said for "slow work." Accordingly, from my more mature efforts I have culled nine studies that I hope will demonstrate, both singly and cumulatively, how one might "spiritualize the positivistic method" and release its gifts for the sake of the Church. I have written from a Roman Catholic perspective, but I will be honored if non-Catholic scholars also take the trouble to read my work.

Apart from chapters 3 and 6, which are more theoretical and deductive, the studies in this volume are largely exegetical and inductive. I have tried to allow the hermeneutical issues inherent in the quest for Method C to emerge organically through direct painstaking engagement with the biblical text, the writings of the Fathers and doctors, and modern scholarship. In other words, I have tried to discover Method C by doing Method C. To unite "two quite different types of hermeneutic is an art that needs to be constantly remastered," as Benedict XVI puts it.[40] Recent decades have seen the publication of several helpful works written from a Roman Catholic perspective on the theology of Scripture and the prospects for developing an authentically theological mode of exegesis.[41] These works are for the most part deductive, theoretical, and somewhat thin on actual engagement with the biblical text.[42] If I understand the Erasmus Lecture correctly, there may also be a place in the conversation for a biblical scholar who attempts to "get inside" Method A and Method B by means of concrete exegetical exercises that bring the two approaches into serious dialogue. This may provide the best vantage point from which to discern the strengths and weaknesses of each approach and the possibilities for integrating them.

40 Ratzinger, *Jesus of Nazareth: Holy Week*, xv.

41 In addition to Carbajosa, *Faith, the Fount of Exegesis*, representative titles include: Denis Farkasfalvy, O. Cist, *A Theology of the Christian Bible: Revelation, Inspiration, Canon* (Washington, D.C.: The Catholic University of America Press, 2018); José Granados, Carlos Granados, and Luis Sánchez-Navarro, eds., *Opening Up the Scriptures: Joseph Ratzinger and the Foundations of Biblical Interpretation* (Grand Rapids: Eerdmans, 2008); Jeremy Holmes, *Cur Deus Verba: Why the Word Became Words* (San Francisco: Ignatius, 2021); Luke Timothy Johnson and William S. Kurz, SJ, *The Future of Catholic Biblical Scholarship: A Constructive Conversation* (Grand Rapids: Eerdmans, 2002); and Matthew Levering, *Participatory Biblical Exegesis: A Theology of Biblical Interpretation* (Notre Dame, Ind.: University of Notre Dame Press, 2008).

42 Exceptions in this regard include works by two Catholic biblical scholars: Gary A. Anderson, *Christian Doctrine and the Old Testament: Theology in the Service of Biblical Exegesis* (Grand Rapids: Baker Academic, 2017), and Francis Martin, *Sacred Scripture: The Disclosure of the Word* (Naples, Fla.: Sapientia Press of Ave Maria University, 2006).

The two more theoretical chapters (3 and 6) have been staggered among the exegetical-inductive chapters in order to create a dialogical movement. Also, I have placed the studies that are primarily concerned with the Old Testament (1, 2, 4, and 5) ahead of those primarily concerned with the New Testament (8 and 9), with chapter 7 serving as a bridge. Since chapter 9 deals with the believer's progress from the present life of grace to the future life of glory, it seemed appropriate to place it last. In any case, each chapter can stand on its own, so the reader may tackle them in any order. A précis of each chapter follows.

1. Psalm 22: A Case Study in Method C

This chapter looks at the reception history of an Old Testament passage that has always had an important place in Christianity, in order to bring to the surface some of the respective strengths and weaknesses of patristic-medieval exegesis and historical-critical exegesis. Method A reads the Old Testament Christologically, sometimes to the point of disregarding its context in Israelite history, whereas Method B interprets the Old Testament on its own terms, sometimes to the point of severing its link to the New Testament. Method C integrates these two approaches by discerning the organic connections between Old Testament and New Testament. One such vector of continuity is the piety of the *ʿănāwîm* ("afflicted, humble ones"), which developed in ancient Israel and found its fullness in Jesus of Nazareth.

Originally published as "Psalm 22: *Vox Christi* or Israelite Temple Liturgy?" *The Thomist* 66, no. 2 (2002): 175–200. Used by permission.

2. Yahweh's Repentance and the Immutability of the Divine Will

This essay demonstrates how ecclesial exegesis (Method C) can lead to a proper understanding of Old Testament passages that speak anthropomorphically of Yahweh's "repentance" (or nonrepentance). Augustine and Aquinas, who serve as representatives of Method A in this chapter, bring astute exegetical observations and insights to the table, while Method B tools of narrative criticism enhance our appreciation for the literary artistry and theological sophistication of the biblical authors. The frequent supposition that one must choose between the immutable God of dogma and the biblical God who acts in history turns out to be a false dilemma.

3. Two Trajectories in the Reception of *Dei Verbum*

This historical study first examines the respective interpretations of *Dei Verbum* by Raymond Brown and Joseph Ratzinger, from the 1960s to their meeting at the Erasmus Lecture conference in 1988. Next, it looks at the hermeneutical works of Brown's longtime collaborator Joseph A. Fitzmyer, SJ, who distanced himself from Brown's two-stage model ("meant" and "means") and took up a position somewhat closer to Ratzinger's by insisting that one must engage the historical-critical method from the start with the "presuppositions of faith." Fitzmyer's understandings of Sacred Tradition and the spiritual sense of Scripture, on the other hand, appear to be in tension with the teaching of the dogmatic constitution. The chapter concludes with a close reading of *Dei Verbum* 12, which supports Ratzinger's contention that the council fathers of Vatican II were in effect calling for a Method C synthesis.

Originally published as "Ratzinger, Brown, and the Reception of *Dei Verbum*," *Josephinum Journal of Theology* 23, no. 1 (2016): 205–26. Used by permission.

4. The Sabbath Precept in the Divine Pedagogy

This chapter studies a commandment at the very heart of Yahweh's covenant with Israel in order better to understand the divine pedagogy and the relationship between the literal sense and the spiritual sense of Scripture. The standard patristic view of the Sabbath precept, which is marred by a bias against Judaism, emerged in the second century and attained its classic expression in the works of Augustine. Thomas Aquinas's dual conviction that every precept of the Mosaic law has a literal "reason" and that "the law was our pedagogue unto Christ" led to a major breakthrough in the Church's understanding of the Sabbath precept and its place in the Decalogue. It also makes possible a unified ecclesial exegesis of the Sabbath precept according to the four senses of Scripture.

5. The Knowledge of God in Israel's Prophetic Literature

This exegetical essay examines the topic of "knowledge" (*dáʿat*) in the books of Samuel, Kings, and Hosea. A first section considers five prose narratives involving the preclassical prophets Samuel, Elijah, and Elisha, in which the Hebrew verb *yādaʿ* ("to know") has a programmatic significance. A second section examines the leitmotif of "knowledge of God" (*dáʿat ʾĕlōhîm*) in the poetic oracles of the classical prophet Hosea. A final section employs philosophical categories drawn from the work of Terry J. Tekippe in order to disclose the nascent epistemology of faith that is operative in these texts. I develop the thesis that the prophetic "knowledge of God" is a primordial mode of knowledge.

Originally published as "An Epistemology of Faith: The Knowledge of God in Israel's Prophetic Literature," in *The Bible and Epistemology: Biblical Soundings on the Knowledge of God*, ed. Mary Healy and Robin Parry (Colorado Springs: Paternoster, 2007), 24–42. Used by permission of Authentic Media, Ltd., Milton Keynes, UK.

6. Word and Event: A Reappraisal

This theoretical and systematic essay responds to Cardinal Ratzinger's call for a fresh assessment of "the relationship between event and word." I begin with an example of how "the dualism of word and event," which Ratzinger identifies as a characteristic problem of modern thought, manifests itself in historical-critical biblical scholarship. The remainder of the essay sketches out Scripture's own theological vision of the unity of word and event, considering in turn: creation and the *imago Dei*; language and truth; God's word in human events; time, narrative, and history; and the Christ event and the Gospels. This chapter takes us near the philosophical and theological heart of the Method C project.

Originally published in *Nova et Vetera* 13, no. 1 (2015): 181–218. Used by permission.

7. Man Is the Land: The Sacramentality of the Land of Israel

This wide-ranging study argues that the land of Israel is a "sacrament," taking its point of departure from the poetry of Karol Wojtyła, who enigmatically states that "man is the land." This mystery is rooted in the order of creation, manifests itself in the bond between the people of Israel and their land in the Old Testament, and is truly present in Christianity through the incarnation of the Word and the glorification of Christ's (Israelite) humanity. I offer corrective nuances to the thesis that Israel's "territorial realism" has been "spiritualized" in the New Testament. Properly understood, this spiritualization is not a matter of exchanging physical realities for immaterial ideas. Already in the order of creation and in Israel's covenant with Yahweh, the land itself serves as the bearer of spiritual realities in a variety of ways. This sacramentalization of the land of Israel makes a quantum leap in the Christ event, but material reality is never left behind. In a true sense, the land of Israel has been taken up into the Christian mystery, and this spiritualization, while unique and unprecedented, is fully in continuity with the Old Testament mystery of Israel's covenant with Yahweh.

Originally published in *John Paul II and the Jewish People: A Jewish-Christian Dialogue*, ed. David G. Dalin and Matthew Levering (Lanham, Md.: Rowman & Littlefield, 2008), 131–67. Used by permission.

8. Psalms and Christ Event in the Epistle to the Hebrews

This exegetical study examines the way the author of the Epistle to the Hebrews cites and comments on Psalms 8:5–7 and 40:7–9, in Hebrews 2:5–9 and 10:5–10 respectively. In each case, he discovers a succinct narration of the Christ event in the words of the psalm, such that psalm and Christ event are mutually illuminating. For each psalm passage, I consider the original Hebrew, distinctive features of its Greek rendering in the Septuagint, and how the Greek author of the Epistle to the Hebrews takes advantage of these distinctive features. As both passages are concerned with the human body of Jesus Christ, I draw upon insights of Gregory of Nyssa, Thomas Aquinas, and Pope John Paul II—ancient, medieval, and modern representatives of Sacred Tradition—to shed light on this reality.

9. The Goods of Grace and Glory: Filial Adoption in Romans 8

This final exercise in Method C brings Thomas Aquinas's *Super epistolam ad Romanos* into dialogue with a major modern commentary, Douglas Moo's *Epistle to the Romans*, in order to explore the apostle Paul's teaching about the two-stage realization of the gift of "filial adoption" (υἱοθεσία), which, according to Thomas, admits us to "the goods of grace and glory" (cf. Rom 8:15, 23). Thomas's commentary sheds light on the relationship between filial adoption and the infusion of grace and charity, but it leaves Paul's teaching on "sanctification" (ἁγιασμός) insufficiently illuminated. To fill this lacuna, I turn to Thomas's discussion of the increase of charity in *Summa Theologiae* II-II, question 24, and then return to Paul's epistles to expound the dynamics by which the believer makes progress toward the consummation of filial adoption in glory. In particular, I attempt to account for the accent that Paul places on the role of bodily suffering in the Christian life.

Originally published as "*Ad Bona Gratiae et Gloriae*: Filial Adoption in Romans 8," *The Thomist* 74, no. 4 (2010): 593–626. Used by permission.

MISCELLANEA

Finally, a few miscellaneous remarks are in order.

At numerous places throughout this book I refer to the *divine pedagogy*, a concept that has roots in the New Testament (Gal 3:24–25) and the writings of Irenaeus of Lyons. Noting that the Old Testament contains "some things that are imperfect and provisional," *Dei Verbum* associates this principle with God's dealings with Israel under the old covenant, in a passage that also speaks of this period as one of "preparation" for the advent of Christ (no. 15). The *Catechism of the Catholic Church* explains that it was characteristic of the divine pedagogy of the Old Testament period for God to reveal himself to Israel "gradually" and thus to prepare humanity "by stages" to receive his definitive self-revelation in Jesus Christ (no. 53). This principle of gradual revelation under the old covenant provides a locus within Tradition where historical-critical theories concerning Israel's religious development can be assessed from a properly theological point of view. Although the principle of divine pedagogy holds great explanatory power with respect to those Old Testament laws, institutions, beliefs, and practices that do not seem to measure up to the gospel, one should be careful not to invoke it glibly, lest we underestimate the theological acuity of the Old Testament authors.

Since I also make occasional reference to the *Priestly School* as coauthors and compilers of Genesis and Exodus, I shall briefly state my position on the question of the authorship of the Pentateuch. Overwhelming linguistic, literary, and historical evidence indicates that the Pentateuch was written by multiple authors several centuries after the time of Moses. While I do not accept the classic Documentary Hypothesis (JEDP), *some* aspects of that theory have borne scrutiny rather well and thus provide building materials for a revised working hypothesis. These aspects include a basic threefold distinction between Priestly passages, Deuteronomic passages, and passages that are neither Priestly nor Deuteronomic. The idea that there once existed a "Priestly document" that was written to stand on its own, however, should be rejected in favor of the recognition that the Priestly School composed a redactional narrative framework into which older "pre-Priestly" materials (formerly identified as J and E) could be inserted and properly showcased. The Priestly School was thus the curator of much early Israelite tradition and was responsible for giving the first four books of the Bible something approximating their canonical shape.[43] This alternative hypothesis leads to a higher valuation of the Priestly School from both a literary and a theological point of view than one typically finds in conjunction with the Documentary Hypothesis.

Except where otherwise indicated, the *translations* of Scripture, other ancient and medieval texts, and *Dei Verbum* are my own. The exceptions are mostly in chapter 1. When citing the protocanonical books of the Old Testament, I follow the chapter and verse enumeration of the Hebrew Masoretic Text, which is also followed in the New American Bible, Revised Edition. Some other translations, including the Revised Standard Version, follow the Septuagint's enumeration of verses (though not necessarily of chapters). In the Psalter, the RSV does not assign a verse number to the superscript (e.g., "A Psalm of Asaph"), and so, for psalms that have a superscript, the verse numbers in the RSV are usually one digit lower than in my citations. Outside the Psalter, such divergences are sporadic, and I have noted them where they occur. Most of these involve citations of the book of Hosea in chapter 5.

43 This is essentially the position taken by Frank Moore Cross nearly half a century ago in *Canaanite Myth and Hebrew Epic: Essays in the History of the Religion of Israel* (Cambridge, Mass.: Harvard University Press, 1973), 293–325.

CHAPTER ONE

Psalm 22: A Case Study in Method C

At the 1988 Erasmus Lecture conference in New York City, as we have seen, Joseph Cardinal Ratzinger encouraged biblical scholars and theologians to work toward a suitable "Method C" synthesis of the historical-critical approach to biblical interpretation (Method B) and the more theological and spiritual approach characteristic of traditional or precritical exegesis (Method A).[1] One of the most important points of contrast between traditional exegesis and historical-critical exegesis concerns the interpretation of the Old Testament and its relationship to the New Testament. Method A reads the Old Testament Christologically, sometimes to the point of disregarding its context in Israelite history, whereas Method B interprets the Old Testament on its own terms, sometimes to the point of severing its link to the New Testament.[2] Method C, I suggest, would integrate these two approaches by discerning the genuine organic connections between Old Testament and New Testament.[3]

For this to occur, the New Testament's own Christological interpretation of the Old Testament must not be regarded as merely one among many

1 Stallsworth, "Story of an Encounter," 107–8. Cf. Ratzinger, "Biblical Interpretation in Crisis," 1–23.

2 This is not to suggest that all Method B exegetes have been unaware of this danger. For a bibliographic essay on twentieth-century attempts to articulate the relationship between Old Testament and New Testament, see Henning Graf Reventlow, *Problems of Biblical Theology in the Twentieth Century* (Philadelphia: Fortress, 1986).

3 Ratzinger speaks elsewhere of the "inner continuity and coherence of the Law and the Gospel" and of the "inner continuity of salvation history." *Many Religions—One Covenant: Israel, the Church and the World*, trans. Graham Harrison (San Francisco: Ignatius, 1999), 36, 68.

possible "readings." It is rather the hermeneutical key that discloses the inspired logic of the Old Testament. Christ is the telos on which the divinely orchestrated trajectories of the Old Testament's various component parts converge. But these theological and spiritual trajectories of the Old Testament cannot be discerned on the basis of the telos alone. The exegesis of a given Old Testament text must be allowed to unfold according to principles and categories intrinsic to that text. This unfolding will be aided by historical and literary-critical tools and procedures but must not be hampered by positivist or historicist presuppositions and goals.[4] The Old Testament is to be read on its own terms but also under the guiding light of Christ. In the end these two will be found to be one and the same, since "the Spirit of Christ" was already present to Israel prior to the incarnation, exercising an influence upon the authors of the Old Testament and preparing Israel for Yahweh's eschatological kingdom (1 Pet 1:10–11).

The book of Psalms presents a unique challenge in this regard. No other book of the Old Testament has been so thoroughly assimilated by the Christian tradition, yet there are few books of the Bible for which the respective exegetical conclusions of Method A and Method B diverge so widely. This has been especially true for the past one hundred years or so, during which Psalms scholarship has been dominated by the form-critical approach of Hermann Gunkel. As Brevard Childs notes, because form criticism clarifies the original sociological and liturgical context of the various psalms, it makes the Church's traditional use of the Psalter seem "highly arbitrary and far removed from the original function within ancient Israel. With one stroke Gunkel appeared to have rendered all pre-critical exegesis of the Psalter invalid."[5] Childs goes on, however, to note that this situation has, somewhat paradoxically, made Christian scholars anxious to reconcile the two approaches and "bridge the gap between critical exegesis and the actual faith of the church."[6]

Psalm 22 presents an interesting case in point. It is frequently quoted or alluded to in the New Testament, and it is treasured in Christian tradition as a unique prophetic witness to the passion of Christ. Historical-critical

4 As Francis Martin notes, "there is a difference between getting behind a text in order to use it as a source for the history of early Christianity and as a norm for judging the meaning of the text (historical criticism), and the historical and philological study that facilitates the communicative effort of the text itself. The first makes the text a servant of extraneous preoccupations, the second seeks to serve the text." *Sacred Scripture*, 34.

5 Childs, *Introduction to the Old Testament*, 510.

6 Childs, 511.

exegesis poses a serious challenge to this traditional view, but Christian scholars who practice historical-critical exegesis seem eager in the case of Psalm 22 to account for, if not to justify, its use in the New Testament. The remainder of this article will examine Psalm 22 as a case study for Method C exegesis, in hope of offering a modest contribution to a much larger project.[7] I shall consider, first, the Method A interpretation of Psalm 22 as the *vox Christi* ("voice of Christ"); second, the Method B attempt to locate this psalm in an Old Testament Israelite context; third, various attempts to reconcile this Old Testament setting with the New Testament use of Psalm 22; and, fourth, a Method C attempt to describe the organic connection between the psalm in its Old Testament context and Jesus's quotation of it from the cross (Matt 27:46; Mark 15:34).

METHOD A: *THE VOX CHRISTI*

While the New Testament quotes or alludes to a small handful of verses from Psalm 22, the Church Fathers take the process to its logical conclusion by referring the entire psalm to Christ's death and resurrection. But the Fathers do far more than this. They do not treat Psalm 22 as a typological foreshadowing, nor is the reference to Christ understood to be the psalm's spiritual sense. Rather, in Psalm 22 the Fathers hear the *vox Christi*, the very words of Christ as he prays to the Father upon the cross, and this is treated as the psalm's literal sense.

The Fathers assume that King David was the human author of Psalm 22, but they demonstrate no desire whatsoever to locate the psalm in David's life or in any other Old Testament context. David is merely a mouthpiece through whom "the prophetic Spirit speaks in the name of Christ."[8] He is "the king and prophet who spoke these words" but "endured none of these sufferings."[9] It is important to note that this interpretation was forged in an apologetic context. For Justin Martyr, Tertullian, and Lactantius alike, it

7 According to Ratzinger, "at least the work of a whole generation" will be required to achieve a Method C synthesis. "Biblical Interpretation in Crisis," 6.

8 Justin Martyr, *First Apology* 38. Translation: Justin Martyr, *Writings of Saint Justin Martyr*, ed. and trans. Thomas B. Falls, Fathers of the Church 6 (New York: Christian Heritage, 1948), 74. According to Athanasius, Psalm 22 "tells the manner of the death from the Savior's own lips." *Ad Marcellinum* 7. Translation: Athanasius, *The Life of Antony and the Letter to Marcellinus*, ed. and trans., Robert C. Gregg, Classics of Western Spirituality (New York: Paulist, 1980), 105.

9 Justin Martyr, *First Apology* 35. Translation: Falls, *Writings of Saint Justin*, 72.

is not enough to ignore the Old Testament context of Psalm 22; they must emphatically deny that it even has one. If Trypho the Jew or Marcion of Pontus can refer this psalm to David or another Israelite, its authority as a unique prophetic witness to Christ may be doubted. But the apologists argue that this is impossible. "David himself did not suffer this cross, nor did any other king of the Jews."[10] Rather, Psalm 22 contains "the entire passion of Christ, who was even then prophetically declaring his glory."[11]

Two commentators of the Antiochene School challenged the *vox Christi* interpretation and sought an Old Testament context for Psalm 22. Diodore of Tarsus and his student Theodore of Mopsuestia hold that this psalm describes the afflictions suffered by David during the revolt of Absalom.[12] It is spoken "by the person of David," not "by the person of the Lord."[13] Diodore grants that the psalm contains certain "partial likenesses" to the passion of Christ, but these do not disrupt the basic "plan" (ὑπόθεσις) of the psalm taken as a whole.[14] He notes how one detail after another "fits David" better than it "fits the Lord,"[15] but even those details that "ended up" fitting the Lord's passion first "happened historically" to David.[16] Theodore's interpretation is, if anything, even stricter. Christ merely borrowed a line from Psalm 22 to speak of his own sufferings, and this in no way justifies taking the psalm as such to refer to him.[17]

This Antiochene exegesis of Psalm 22, however, stood no chance of dislodging the *vox Christi* interpretation. The latter found an authoritative voice in Augustine and was widely disseminated via the popular *Expositio Psalmorum* of Cassiodorus.[18] Meanwhile Diodore and Theodore were condemned as heretics.

10 Tertullian, *Adversus Marcionem* 3.19. Translation: *ANF* 7:158. Cf. Justin, *Dialogue* 97; Lactantius, *Divine Institutes* 4.18.

11 Tertullian, *Adversus Marcionem* 3.19. Translation: *ANF* 7:158.

12 Diodore of Tarsus, *Commentarii in Psalmos* 21.1; Theodore of Mopsuestia, *Expositionis in Psalmos* 21.1. On the authorship of the former work, see *Diodori Tarsensis Commentarii in Psalmos*, vol. 1, *Commentarii in Psalmos I-L*, ed. Jean-Marie Olivier, Corpus Christianorum Series Graeca 6 (Turnhout: Brepols, 1980), lxxiii–cviii.

13 Diodore, *Commentarii in Psalmos* 21.1.

14 *Commentarii in Psalmos* 21.1, 19.

15 *Commentarii in Psalmos* 21.2b.

16 *Commentarii in Psalmos* 21.19.

17 Theodore, *Expositionis in Psalmos* 21.1.

18 According to Augustine, in Psalm 22 "the passion of Christ is . . . plainly recited as if it were a gospel." *Ennaratio in Psalmos* 21.2.2. According to Cassiodorus, "the Lord Christ speaks

At the same time, Cassiodorus's detailed exposition has the unintended effect of exposing three serious weaknesses in the traditional interpretation. First, passages that do not seem appropriate on the lips of Christ are given strained interpretations. For example, how can the celibate Christ speak of "my seed" (v. 31)? Cassiodorus answers that "seed" here refers to "the works which he revealed on the earth at the time of his incarnation."[19] Second, over this exposition of the literal sense, an equally arbitrary interpretation of the spiritual sense is sometimes superimposed. On the line, "my tongue cleaves to my jaws" (v. 16), Cassiodorus comments: "His *tongue* denotes the apostles as preachers, who cleaved to Christ's jaws in maintaining his commands."[20] Third, and most critical for our purposes, the *vox Christi* interpretation forces Cassiodorus to deny Old Testament Israel its rightful place in the psalm. The phrase "seed of Israel" (v. 24) must be interpreted so as to refer to Christians.[21] Indeed, Israel only figures into the psalm as the enemies of Christ. The "calves" and "fat bulls" who surround the psalm's speaker (v. 13) "are clearly the Jewish people."[22]

Thomas Aquinas's exposition of Psalm 22 is more sophisticated and less arbitrary than Cassiodorus's. For example, Thomas relates the phrase "my tongue cleaves to my jaws" (v. 16) to Christ's silence during his passion (citing Ezek 3:26 in support), an interpretation that goes back to Justin Martyr.[23] This seems preferable to the comment of Cassiodorus cited above. In the end, however, Thomas's exposition serves to confirm the authority of the *vox Christi* interpretation with its inherent limitations.[24] Thomas is emphatic

through the whole of the psalm," and thus "it appears not so much as prophecy, but as history." *Expositio Psalmorum* 21.1. Translation: Cassiodorus, *Explanation of the Psalms*, vol. 1, *Psalms 1–50*, ed. and trans. P. G. Walsh, Ancient Christian Writers 51 (Mahwah, N.J.: Paulist, 1990), 216.

19 Cassiodorus, *Expositio Psalmorum* 21.32. Translation: Cassiodorus, *Explanation*, trans. Walsh, 233.

20 *Expositio Psalmorum* 21.16. Translation: Cassiodorus, *Explanation*, trans. Walsh, 224.

21 *Expositio Psalmorum* 21.25. Translation: Cassiodorus, *Explanation*, trans. Walsh, 230. It is perfectly legitimate to find references to the Church in the Psalter when it is read according to the spiritual sense, but such spiritual exegesis must be built upon a solid interpretation of the literal sense.

22 *Expositio Psalmorum* 21.13. Translation: Cassiodorus, *Explanation*, trans. Walsh, 222. It is easy to see how such an interpretation might encourage anti-Judaic attitudes rather than an appreciation for Israel's place in salvation history.

23 Aquinas, *In Psalmos Davidis Expositio* 21.12; Justin, *Dialogue* 102–3.

24 Initially, Thomas seems to acknowledge a level at which the words of the psalm bear some relation to David's trials, while these in turn symbolize the sufferings of Christ. *In Psalmos*

that the psalmist speaks "in the person of Christ praying" (*in persona Christi orantis*)[25] and that the reference to Christ's passion is the psalm's "literal sense" (*sensus litteralis*).[26] Thus Psalm 22 is still effectively denied an Old Testament context.

But along with its patent weaknesses, the Method A interpretation of Psalm 22 has certain strengths. First, it takes seriously the foundational New Testament insight that the "Spirit of Christ" was already present to Old Testament Israel, "bearing witness in advance to the sufferings destined for Christ and the glories to follow" (1 Pet 1:11).[27] Second, it does justice to the facts that Christ himself takes up this prayer and makes it his own precisely at the most pivotal moment in salvation history, and that the passion narratives in all four Gospels contain quotations of or allusions to Psalm 22.[28] In other words, the *vox Christi* interpretation respectfully follows a seminal intuition regarding this psalm, one that can be traced back to the apostolic Church and indeed to the Lord Jesus himself—who, we should remember, was a Jew and thus ought to have had some idea what the psalm meant.[29]

Finally, by listening to Psalm 22 as a prayer offered by Christ during the extremity of his suffering, the more astute of the Method A exegetes are able to disclose something of this text's remarkable spiritual quality. Thomas, in particular, shows a real feel for the psalm's poetic texture when he comments on its imagery. For example, the phrase, "like water I am poured out" (v. 15), suggests to him a complete effusion of life. "If oil is poured out, some remains in the vessel, and if wine is poured out, at least some aroma remains in the

---

Davidis 21.1. In practice, however, Thomas only carries this two-level approach through his explanation of the psalm's superscription, after which he never again mentions David.

25 *In Psalmos Davidis* 21.20.

26 *In Psalmos Davidis* 21.1.

27 According to John H. Reumann, this verse alludes to Psalm 22 "as a whole." "Psalm 22 at the Cross: Lament and Thanksgiving for Jesus Christ," *Interpretation* 28, no. 1 (1974): 41.

28 Matt 27:35, 39, 43, 46; Mark 15:24, 29, 34; Luke 23:34–36; John 19:24, 28.

29 With respect to the question of historicity, it seems more likely that Jesus actually quoted the opening line of Psalm 22 from the cross than that it was placed on his lips by the early Church or the evangelists, though the point is disputed. In the cautious estimation of Raymond E. Brown, the historicity of this logion is "a possibility not to be discounted." *The Death of the Messiah, From Gethsemane to the Grave: A Commentary on the Passion Narratives in the Four Gospels*, ABRL (New York: Doubleday, 1994), 1088. Reumann concludes his treatment of the question as follows: "In short, we find the *evidence and arguments for genuineness* in the logion of Mark 15:34 to *fall short of definite proof* that Jesus said it" ("Psalm 22 at the Cross," 57). But how could one ever hope to find definite proof in such a case?

vessel. But from water nothing remains."[30] On the other hand, "Upon you was I cast from the womb" (v. 11) suggests total dependence on God and thus "the perfection of hope."[31] Taken together, these two comments adumbrate an important insight into Psalm 22—namely, that this prayer illustrates dramatically how an exalted hope may be present in the midst of the deepest desolation, indeed how total reliance on God can only be perfectly realized through an experience of Godforsakenness. And as one recent commentator has noted, this juxtaposition of complaint and trust, which is characteristic of the entire psalm, is already found *in nuce* in its opening line. The one who complains of being forsaken by God still calls upon Yahweh as "my God, my God."[32] The line quoted by Jesus, then, is an epitome of the psalm's spirituality.

METHOD B: THE OLD TESTAMENT CONTEXT

Like the Antiochene School, modern historical-critical exegesis strives to locate Psalm 22 in its proper Old Testament context. But unlike Diodore and Theodore, Method B commentators reject the idea that this context is to be found in the life of King David.[33] Indeed, since the advent of the form-critical method in the early twentieth century, the tendency has been to locate most psalms not "in particular historical events, but in the cultic life of the community."[34] Accordingly, Psalm 22 is said to have been composed for use in the temple liturgy.[35] It begins as a prayer of lament and petition (vv. 2–22) to be offered by "persons who were severely sick and threatened by death."[36] It continues with a jubilant hymn of praise "in the midst of the assembly" (vv. 23–27), and it concludes with an exalted eschatological vision of universal homage to Israel's God (vv. 28–32).

30 Aquinas, *In Psalmos Davidis* 21.11.

31 *In Psalmos Davidis* 21.7.

32 J. Clinton McCann, Jr., "The Book of Psalms: Introduction, Commentary, and Reflections," in *New Interpreter's Bible*, ed. Leander E. Keck (Nashville: Abingdon, 1996), 4:762.

33 Hermann Gunkel rejects Davidic authorship on the basis of Psalm 22's relatively late vocabulary and its advanced theology, for example, the anticipated conversion of the gentiles in vv. 28–29. *Die Psalmen*, 5th ed. (Göttingen: Vandenhoeck & Ruprecht, 1968), 94.

34 Childs, *Introduction to the Old Testament*, 509.

35 James L. Mays, *Psalms*, Interpretation (Louisville: John Knox, 1994), 106.

36 Peter C. Craigie, *Psalms 1–50*, WBC 19 (Waco, Tex.: Word Books, 1983), 198.

Scholars variously explain the abrupt transition between verses 22 and 23. Many hold that the petitioner received an "oracle of salvation" from a temple functionary at precisely this point.[37] Others (correctly, in my opinion) question the grounds for such an assumption.[38] In any case, Psalm 22 is "the basis of a liturgy, in which the worshiper moves from lament to prayer, and finally to praise and thanksgiving."[39] As we shall see, this dynamic and dramatic character of the psalm and the "movement" of prayer that it is designed to engender are crucial to understanding its theology and spiritual function. Psalm 22 has a sort of "plot" in which something "happens."[40]

Of particular concern to Method B scholars has been the liturgical and theological identity of the psalm's speaker, the "I" who laments, petitions, and praises God. Having already swept aside the patristic-medieval view that the speaker is Christ and the Antiochene view that he is David, early form critics also rejected the traditional Jewish view, which held that the "I" represents Israel as a collective, and maintained that the speaker is simply an individual Israelite.[41] This does not mean that Psalm 22 originated with the sufferings of a particular Israelite, but simply that it was composed for and made available to any suffering Israelite who might come to the temple to petition Yahweh. This is part of a more general form-critical trend, which views the sufferings described in the individual laments throughout the Psalter as stereotypical, like those described in other ancient Near Eastern laments.[42]

Other scholars, however, were quick to point out that Psalm 22 seems to differ from other laments in precisely this regard. Its extremely graphic images suggest a physical suffering so severe and a spiritual trial so intense that one can hardly think of an "ordinary member" of the Israelite community. For Hans-Joachim Kraus, the speaker is "an archetypal figure," and

37 Hans-Joachim Kraus, *Psalms 1–59: A Continental Commentary*, trans. Hilton C. Oswald (Minneapolis: Augsburg, 1988), 298; Reumann, "Psalm 22 at the Cross," 44; Craigie, *Psalms 1–50*, 200; McCann, "Book of Psalms," 763.

38 Rudolf Kilian, "Ps 22 und das priesterliche Heilsorakel," *Biblische Zeitschrift* 12, no. 2 (1968): 172–85.

39 Craigie, *Psalms 1–50*, 197.

40 Mays, *Psalms*, 108.

41 E.g., Gunkel, *Psalmen*, 94. For the traditional Jewish view, see Rashi, *Rashi's Commentary on Psalms 1–89 (Books I–III) with English Translation, Introduction and Notes*, ed. Mayer I. Gruber, South Florida Studies in the History of Judaism 161 (Atlanta: Scholars Press, 1998), 126.

42 Childs, *Introduction to the Old Testament*, 519; John Barton, "Form Criticism (OT)," *ABD* 2:840. A. A. Anderson describes Psalm 22 as containing "more or less stereotyped language." *Psalms 1–72*, New Century Bible Commentary (Grand Rapids: Eerdmans, 1981), 185.

in Psalm 22 "the 'archetypal affliction' of Godforsakenness is being suffered in a mortal sickness."[43] Still other scholars returned to something akin to the traditional Jewish interpretation. For Alphonse Deissler, the speaker of Psalm 22 represents Israel, and this explains why he possesses both collective and individual traits.[44] Earlier, Charles Briggs had compared the sufferer of Psalm 22 with the figures of Mother Zion in the book of Lamentations and the Servant of Yahweh in Isaiah 40–55. In all of these texts, individual sufferings are "combined with national experiences." The speaker of Psalm 22 is thus taken to be an "idealized" representation of the early postexilic remnant harassed by neighboring nations.[45]

Without turning Psalm 22 into an historical allegory, as Briggs virtually does, we might still locate it within certain theological developments of the exilic and early postexilic periods. Indeed, several twentieth-century commentators associate Psalm 22 with *ʿănāwîm* piety, a spiritual development that finds its earliest articulation in Zephaniah (seventh century BC), comes to classic expression in Lamentations 3 (sixth century BC), and encompasses a large number of psalms.[46] In verses 24–27, the speaker of Psalm 22 addresses a group of *ʿănāwîm* ("afflicted, lowly, humble ones"), whom he also refers to as his "brethren." In verse 25, he calls himself an *ʿānî* (functionally, the singular of *ʿănāwîm*) and refers to his suffering as *ʿĕnût* ("affliction"), a cognate noun. Kraus is correct to reject the notion that we are dealing here with a distinct "religious party" or faction in ancient Israel.[47] Nevertheless, the *ʿănāwîm* are "brothers . . . in a religious sense," a group constituted by a shared "theological spiritual identity."[48]

43 Kraus, *Psalms 1–59*, 294. Similarly, Mays describes the speaker as "a special case of the type" or "prototypical." *Psalms*, 108.

44 Alphonse Deissler, *Le Livre des Psaumes 1–75*, Verbum Salutis 1 (Paris: Beauchesne, 1966), 111.

45 Charles A. Briggs and Emilie G. Briggs, *A Critical and Exegetical Commentary on the Book of Psalms*, vol. 1, ICC (Edinburgh: T&T Clark, 1906), 190–91. It is precisely this interpretation that Gunkel rejected (*Psalmen*, 94–95), presumably because it connects a psalm of individual lament to specific historical events, a procedure opposed to the canons of form criticism.

46 The classic treatment is Albert Gelin, PSS, *The Poor of Yahweh*, trans. Kathryn Sullivan, RSCJ (Collegeville, Minn.: Liturgical Press, 1964), which refers Psalm 22 to this movement at p. 84. Hans-Joachim Kraus's survey of the theme of the "poor" in the Psalter, *Theology of the Psalms*, trans. Keith Crim (Minneapolis: Augsburg, 1986), 150–54, is valuable for its rigorous methodology but reductionist in some of its conclusions.

47 Kraus, *Theology of the Psalms*, 153.

48 Mays, *Psalms*, 111.

The *ʿănāwîm* are those who "fear" and "seek" Yahweh (vv. 24, 27). By also calling them "the seed of Jacob" and "the seed of Israel" (v. 24), the psalmist does not mean to suggest that Israel according to the flesh and the *ʿănāwîm* are coterminous groups. Rather, the *ʿănāwîm* are thus identified as "the true Israel."[49] As James L. Mays puts it, the *ʿănāwîm* are "thinking and speaking about themselves and their relation to God in a way that is beginning to redefine what it means to be Israel."[50]

This is a crucial point. Mays has indicated, in a more satisfactory way than Briggs, the manner by which the speaker of Psalm 22 might be said to represent Israel. For Briggs the representation takes place on a literary plane, by a sort of symbolism or allegory. The sufferer of Psalm 22 *stands for* Israel. As Gunkel notes, this is problematic, since the speaker also addresses other pious Israelites.[51] Who, then, would *they* represent? But for Mays the sufferer of Psalm 22 is an *ʿānî*, indeed the "prototypical" member of the *ʿănāwîm*, and it is only qua *ʿānî* that he represents Israel. That is, the *ʿănāwîm* are those who most fully assume the true identity and vocation of Israel, and the sufferer of Psalm 22 most fully manifests the spiritual character of this group. Thus, "the figure in the psalm shares in the corporate vocation of Israel."[52]

THE SEARCH FOR A SYNTHESIS

There is a consensus among historical-critical commentators that Psalm 22 is not predictive of the passion and resurrection of Christ. It is neither "prophetic" nor "messianic."[53] This conclusion is based on form criticism, which observes that, in terms of genre, Psalm 22 is neither a prophetic oracle nor a royal psalm. Thus, it was not "intended" to be a prediction of the sufferings and subsequent glory of Christ.[54] Such an interpretation would seem to sever Psalm 22 from its New Testament use and its Method A interpretation.

But some scholars maintain that this discrepancy between traditional exegesis and form-critical analysis only forces one to consider the

49 Mays, 111.

50 Mays, 111–12.

51 Gunkel, *Psalmen*, 94.

52 Mays, *Psalms*, 113.

53 Gunkel, *Psalmen*, 94; Deissler, *Psaumes 1–75*, 111; Kraus, *Psalms 1–59*, 301; Anderson, *Psalms 1–72*, 185; J. Clinton McCann, Jr., *A Theological Introduction to the Book of Psalms: The Psalms as Torah* (Nashville: Abingdon, 1993), 169.

54 Anderson, *Psalms 1–72*, 185.

relationship between Psalm 22 and the gospel passion narratives from new angles. Kraus looks for the "inner connections" between the two and finds them in the "archetypal" character of the psalm and of the afflictions it describes. Jesus's praying of Psalm 22 on the cross indicates that he "identifies himself with the entire fullness of suffering."[55] Similarly, Claus Westermann holds that Christ "has descended into the depths of human suffering of which the psalm speaks."[56] Thus, according to A. A. Anderson, "the real point of contact between the psalmist and Christ is the reality of suffering and faith, not simply the poetic language."[57]

This Method B effort to locate the true continuity between Old Testament and New Testament at the level of extratextual "reality" rather than at the level of language or concepts provides a promising point of synthesis with Method A. Thomas Aquinas teaches that while the literal sense of Scripture is a matter of words signifying "things" (that is, realities), the spiritual sense is a matter of these same things having a signification of their own. Thus, for example, "the things of the old law signify the things of the new law."[58] One might posit, then, that the *words* of Psalm 22 refer to Old Testament realities—namely, the suffering of Israel's *'ănāwîm* and their "habitual, trustful recourse"[59] to Yahweh (the literal sense)—and that these realities themselves, not the words of the psalm as such, "signify" in some manner the sufferings of Christ and his recourse to the Father on the cross (the spiritual sense).

Precisely there is the rub, however. What could *signify* mean in such a statement? If the Israelite author of Psalm 22 does not seem to have intended his text to be predictive, how can we imply that the Old Testament realities of which Psalm 22 speaks have a proleptic and not merely coincidental correspondence to New Testament realities? Method A would presumably make appeal at this point to divine inspiration, noting that God is author of both Sacred Scripture (the words) and sacred history (the "things"). But Method B exegetes seem reluctant to do the same.[60] Deissler, writing in the 1960s,

55 Kraus, *Psalms 1–59*, 301; cf. Craigie, *Psalms 1–50*, 202.

56 Claus Westermann, *The Living Psalms*, trans. J. R. Porter (Grand Rapids: Eerdmans, 1989), 298; cf. Deissler, *Psaumes 1–75*, 112.

57 Anderson, *Psalms 1–72*, 185.

58 Aquinas, *STh* I, q. 1, a. 10. See also the discussion of Eric Auerbach's distinction between figural and symbolic interpretation in Martin, *Sacred Scripture*, 54–55.

59 Gelin, *Poor of Yahweh*, 84.

60 Briggs may imply a divine purpose in the composition of Psalm 22. For him, however, we are not dealing with Old Testament realities signifying New Testament ones but with an Old Testament "ideal" or "concept" that somehow "prepares" for the historical experience of

employed the then-popular notion of *Heilsgeschichte* ("salvation history") in order to link Psalm 22 to Jesus Christ, in whom salvation history reaches its "culminating point." But while such categories seem to imply at least some sort of divine providence over history, Deissler insists that Psalm 22 is "not a prophetic text, and still less a prediction."[61]

Perhaps this is merely to agree with Thomas that the signification of the realities of sacred history goes beyond the signification of the mere words of the biblical text. On the other hand, we may be glimpsing a problem inherent in Method B. How can historical-critical exegesis, with its tendency toward positivism, accommodate a developed notion of divinely directed and revelatory history, much less a truly operative notion of biblical inspiration? Does Method B have trouble with the idea of inspiration precisely because it does not have an adequate philosophy of history or, for that matter, of human action? In other words, is the failure to perceive or allow for a "vertical dimension" of events the cause of Method B's failure to allow for a "vertical dimension" of texts?[62]

Perhaps the observation, valid in itself, that the literary genre of Psalm 22 is not prophetic or messianic serves as a smoke screen. Is Method B capable of proclaiming *any* Old Testament text of *any* genre to be truly predictive of New Testament events? And if not, how can it continue to appeal to "salvation history" in order to find the "real connection" between Old Testament and New Testament? Not surprisingly, the notion of *Heilsgeschichte*, in the sense of God's salvific self-disclosure in real history, has been dying a slow death in biblical scholarship in recent decades. Thomas L. Thompson, for example, maintains that the term *Heilsgeschichte* is to be retained only in the sense of "a form of theologically motivated *Tendenz* in Israel's view of its past." As "a concept of revelation" or "a view of the history of Israel itself as salvific," it has been "largely discredited."[63]

Jesus. The author of Psalm 22 "idealises the sufferings of Israel" and presents pious followers of Yahweh with "a comforting conception of a divine purpose in their sufferings." Briggs goes on to suggest that "this ideal was *designed* to prepare the minds of the people of God for the ultimate realisation of that purpose of redemption in a sufferer [Jesus] who first summed up in his historical experiences this ideal of suffering." He concludes that Psalm 22 is "in this sense" messianic (*Psalms*, 192, emphasis added). Designed by whom? Briggs does not say.

61 Deissler, *Psaumes 1–75*, 111.

62 For the relationship between these two, see Martin, *Sacred Scripture*, 36.

63 Thomas L. Thompson, "Historiography (Israelite)," *ABD* 3:209. Thompson uses the German word *Tendenz* here as a technical term, denoting "a dominating point of view or purpose influencing the structure and content of a literary work." *Merriam-Webster*, s.v. "*tendenz* (*n.*)," accessed October 15, 2021, https://www.merriam-webster.com/dictionary/tendenz.

Many recent commentators on Psalm 22, while not subscribing to this position explicitly, seem to have accepted its terms implicitly. They view the connection between the psalm and Christ's passion not in terms of a divinely directed and salvific sequence of events but entirely as a matter of interpretive hindsight. According to Peter C. Craigie, for example, Psalm 22 is "not messianic in its original sense or setting," but "it may be *interpreted* from a NT *perspective* as a messianic psalm." Thus, in the hands of the evangelists it "takes on the *appearance* of anticipatory prophecy."[64] For Patrick D. Miller, Psalm 22 provided the early Christians with "interpretive clues to the meaning of the passion" and thus served as a "hermeneutical guide."[65] Similarly, J. Clinton McCann states that the psalm supplied the evangelists with "a rich resource . . . for articulating the meaning of both the cross and the resurrection."[66]

These statements are true as far as they go, but they do not go far enough. Is there not the risk of reducing everything to interpretation? As long as we speak only of how the psalm is interpreted from a New Testament perspective and do not demonstrate the appropriateness of this interpretation from an Old Testament perspective, a Christological reading of the psalm will appear arbitrary or merely imaginative. A yawning chasm will remain between the testaments, and no synthesis between Method A and Method B will have been achieved.

METHOD C: THE ORGANIC CONNECTION

The single most important point of contact between Old Testament Israel and the New Testament Church is, of course, Jesus of Nazareth himself.[67] This observation has a special pertinence to our discussion of Psalm 22. Jesus's use of this classic *ʿănāwîm* prayer from the cross is consistent with the overall Synoptic presentation of his relationship with the Father,[68] which

64 Craigie, *Psalms 1–50*, 202, emphasis added.

65 Patrick D. Miller, *Interpreting the Psalms* (Philadelphia: Fortress, 1986), 109. Cf. Mays, *Psalms*, 106.

66 McCann, *Theological Introduction*, 173.

67 N. T. Wright has challenged the validity of the way New Testament scholarship has tended so to distance Jesus both from Israel and from the Church that he seems neither rooted in the former nor in any way responsible for the latter. See *Jesus and the Victory of God*, vol. 2 of *Christian Origins and the Question of God* (Minneapolis: Fortress, 1996).

68 The Lord's Prayer and the Beatitudes are classic expressions of *ʿănāwîm* piety. In Matt 11:29, Jesus identifies himself as "meek and humble of heart."

is one of profound intimacy[69] and complete dependence—traits that are by no means lacking even from the Johannine portrait. In fact, the Markan and Matthean "My God, my God" discloses the same essential spirituality as the Lukan "Into your hands" and the Johannine "I thirst," which are also drawn from the Psalter.[70] In other words, we have a range of witnesses supplying the basic contours of the Israelite piety of the historical Jesus. They indicate that in his hour of trial he prayed as one of the *ʿănāwîm*.[71]

As we have seen, for some scholars the essential link between Psalm 22 in its Old Testament context and Jesus's use of it on the cross is the reality of human suffering, generically speaking, and Jesus's profound participation in this reality. But it would be a grave mistake to minimize or omit from consideration the Israelite context of the sufferings described in Psalm 22 and the Israelite context of Jesus's own sufferings. If Jesus enters into human suffering, he does so as an Israelite who enters into Israel's sufferings. Indeed, by taking up the prayer of the *ʿănāwîm* he identifies himself as one who has assumed and is living out Israel's true identity and vocation. To appreciate this, we must return once more to the Old Testament context of Psalm 22 and examine certain aspects of the *ʿănāwîm* piety that it embodies.

First, what is most distinctive of, and fundamental to, the Israelite context of Psalm 22 (and the rest of the Old Testament) is revelation. The *ʿānî* does not use the expression "my God" to refer to his personally chosen image for unknowable transcendence, but to call upon Yahweh, the savior of Israel. The *ʿānî* is a member of a community of faith that extends from "our ancestors" (v. 5) down through the present generation and to future generations (vv. 31–32). The sarcasm of those who ridicule him betrays their antagonism toward this faith (vv. 8–9), so that we might even say that the *ʿānî* is, in a

69 According to Brown, because Jesus feels forsaken on the cross, he "no longer presumes to speak intimately" to God as "Father" but uses "my God," which is "the address common to all human beings." *Death of the Messiah*, 1046. In my opinion, this view does not take sufficient account of the fact that Jesus is taking up the words of a sacred text. In any case, while the feelings of abandonment may be very real, the words "My God, my God" hardly suggest a diminishment of intimacy (as Brown himself acknowledges in n. 41 on the same page).

70 Naturally, there are differences in presentation. In Luke and John, Jesus is more composed and decisive, both in the garden and on the cross, than he is in Mark and Matthew. The Lukan "Into your hands" (Luke 23:46) is taken from Psalm 31 (v. 6), which, like Psalm 22, embodies an individual's act of trust in the midst of affliction and persecution. The Johannine "I thirst" (John 19:28) may allude to Psalm 22:16 (Thomas Worden, "My God, My God, Why Hast Thou Forsaken Me?" *Scripture* 6, no. 1 [1953–54]: 15), while it also echoes Pss 42:2–3; 63:2; 69:4.

71 So Barnabas M. Ahern, CP, preface to Gelin, *Poor of Yahweh*, 8 (implied by Gelin himself on p. 87); cf. Mays, *Psalms*, 114.

sense, persecuted for the word of God. Through this ordeal the *'ānî* will gain a deeper understanding of who Yahweh is and will bear witness to God's "name" (v. 23).

Second, the *'ānî* is one who is keenly aware of his total, lifelong dependence on God. Yahweh is, as it were, the midwife who pulls him "from the womb" (v. 10) and the undertaker who lays him "in the dust of death" (v. 16). And for the entire intervening period he is "thrown upon" God (v. 11). It is true that all human beings are in fact utterly dependent on God, but those who are seriously afflicted, poor, or denied justice are more likely to *recognize* this utter dependence.[72] Their "troubles drive them to rely on Yahweh alone." They are mocked for this very thing. They flee to take refuge in "the precincts of the sanctuary" and "with great intensity . . . turn to God."[73]

Third, God allows the *'ănāwîm* to experience vulnerability. This is described in extreme terms in Psalm 22, where the *'ānî* is stripped of his clothes, bound hand and foot, surrounded by his enemies, and stared at (vv. 17–18). Equally striking are the images by which the *'ānî* speaks of his intense physical pain (vv. 15–16). They suggest his keen awareness of his mortality. The image of water being poured out, for example, recalls the proverbial saying of the wise woman of Tekoa: "We all must die—like water spilled on the ground, which cannot be gathered up again" (2 Sam 14:14). This is the ultimate vulnerability, and it presents the ultimate spiritual trial—for, to Old Testament Israel, death *means* estrangement from God.[74]

The crucial question is how the sufferer will respond to all of this. It is not affliction itself that makes one an *'ānî*, but the manner in which one undergoes affliction.[75] Every affliction calls for an act of trust, and the most severe afflictions will prove whether or not one is a true *'ānî*. To bring one's

72 Kraus names such traits as characteristic of the "poor" in the Psalms but then cautions: "These features of social justice should not be transformed too readily into a religious or spiritual interpretation." *Theology of the Psalms*, 152. Certainly there is a risk of over-spiritualizing the term *'ănāwîm*, but is it not equally mistaken to under-spiritualize it? Does Kraus not make the same error as those whose interpretation he criticizes, insofar as he fails to realize that, at least in this case, concrete circumstances and spirituality are inseparable?

73 Kraus, 152.

74 This traditional view, represented by texts such as Psalm 88, gave way only very gradually to personal hope for postmortem union with God. Such hope may be hinted at in a few relatively early texts, such as Psalm 73 (part of the psalms of Asaph, which seem to have been written in the sixth century BC), but it is most clearly articulated in texts from the second or first century BC, such as Daniel 12, 2 Maccabees 7, and Wisdom 1–5.

75 Mays, *Psalms*, 112.

affliction to the temple and to take up this prayer is itself an act of faith; it is to choose to let oneself be guided through the experience of trial by the words of a liturgy.

Psalm 22 is a model *ʿănāwîm* prayer. "To use it was to set oneself in its paradigm."[76] The prayer is designed to lead the sufferer through a process. This process begins with a frank acknowledgement of feelings of abandonment, an articulation of the experience of Godforsakenness. The profound emotions of a spiritual trial are released as the sufferer laments his deplorable condition; he feels like "a worm and not a man" (v. 7). But the genius of this prayer is that it helps the lamenter to be brutally honest with God while remaining within a framework of faith, intimacy, and reverence. Words of lamentation and complaint are interwoven with words of petition and even praise. Furthermore, by phrasing his complaint as a question ("Why have you forsaken me?") the sufferer opens himself to an answer.

The turning point of the psalm and the decisive moment in the liturgy come with verses 20–22. This passage places the divine name upon the sufferer's lips, followed by a string of confident and very personal petitions ("Hasten to help me . . . Rescue my soul . . . Save me"). These words call for a great act of faith on the part of the lamenter, commensurate to the severe trial through which he is passing. If he is allowing himself to be led by the words of the liturgy, he will begin to experience a real change at this point, an interior renewal. Before circumstances change there must be a change of attitude and a renewal of commitment. Otherwise, the affliction will not have served its purpose as a means of purification and deepening of trust.

Next, the psalm leads the worshiper into a hymn of praise. Whereas he formerly was "the reproach of mankind and despised by the people [of Israel]" (v. 7), he now experiences renewed fellowship with other Israelites, especially his fellow *ʿănāwîm* (vv. 23–27), and he proclaims the kingship of Yahweh over the gentiles (vv. 28–31). His mockers had assumed that his severe affliction was a sign of God's displeasure and distance, and he himself had been tempted to draw the same conclusion. But now, aided by the words of the psalm and under the influence of the spirit of prayer of which the psalm-liturgy is a vehicle, he recognizes that God has not "hidden his face" but has "listened" to his cry for help. Moreover, he realizes now that Yahweh is not the sort of God who "despises" or "detests" the "affliction of an afflicted one" (*ʿĕnût ʿānî*, v. 25).

76 Mays, 106.

In some respects, this last point is the most significant theological claim in the entire psalm, and it may help us to locate Psalm 22 in the larger context of Israel's theological development during the exilic and early postexilic periods. In particular, I have in mind the simple but profound insight that affliction, far from necessarily indicating divine disapproval or the condemnation of sin, may often be "the painful means chosen by God to lead man to total surrender, to a form of denudation in His presence, to a dramatic purification of faith," as Albert Gelin so aptly expresses it.[77] This truth (which finds a variety of articulations in Lamentations, Job, Isaiah 40–55, Genesis, and the Psalter) became a key element in postexilic Israel's new awareness of her true identity and vocation. At least some Israelites came to understand that it would not be through a glorious renewal of the Davidic-Solomonic Empire that Israel would realize its destiny as "a light to the nations" (Isa 42:6). On the contrary, only a humble, docile remnant could inherit "the everlasting covenant, the sure promises made to David" and thereby assume David's vocation to be "a witness to the peoples" (55:3–4). Those who accept this call to be the "Servant of Yahweh" constitute the true Israel.

Something of how suffering and witness are connected may be indicated in the remarkable final verses of Psalm 22, where the universal dimensions and eschatological orientation of Yahweh's kingship are proclaimed. Apparently it is precisely Yahweh's saving action on behalf of the *ʿānî* that the gentiles are to "remember" and on the basis of which they will "turn to Yahweh" and come under his rule (v. 28; cf. v. 31).[78] Thus, none of the sufferings of Israel's least ones—of all those anonymous *ʿănāwîm* who prayed in the spirit if not the actual words of Psalm 22 down through the centuries—are permitted to fall through the cracks of historical contingency. Rather, they are all gathered up into the divine plan of salvation, which not only extends to "the ends of the earth" (v. 28) but mysteriously unfolds in history in such a way as to encompass both those who have already "gone done into the dust" (v. 30) and those who are "yet to be born" (v. 32). God's universal salvific will is forever founded on his particular historical dealings with Israel.

Psalm 22, then, gives postexilic Israel a way of praying that prepares her for the eschatological kingdom of Yahweh. It teaches Israel that she will discover her true identity and fulfill her vocation insofar as she lives and prays as the *ʿănāwîm*. It may even imply (though not so clearly as Isa 55:3–4) that the

77 Gelin, *Poor of Yahweh*, 45–46.

78 So Mays, *Psalms*, 112–13; cf. Gelin, *Poor of Yahweh*, 86–87.

ʿănāwîm will replace the Davidic monarchy as the instrument through which Yahweh will usher in his universal reign. Thus, while it does not contain the word or concept "messiah," it refers to that which is truly messianic. As Mays expresses it, the *ʿānî* of Psalm 22 participates in "the corporate vocation of Israel and the messianic role of David."[79]

On the cross Jesus took Psalm 22 upon his lips as an Israelite who had lived his life as an *ʿānî* and who now faced his ultimate trial. Finding himself surrounded and mocked for his trust in God, and seeing his clothes divided among his assailants, the particular appropriateness of this psalm must have impressed itself upon him. He prayed the opening line of Psalm 22 both to express the depth of his suffering and desolation and to make a solemn act of trust in God.[80] In other words, this psalm presumably helped him to *pray through* his trial, just as it was designed to do. As he experienced the total vulnerability of having his hands and feet nailed to the cross,[81] as his arms and legs were wrenched at the joints, and as he felt the life pour out of him like water, what other prayer in the entire tradition of his people could have served him so well?

But it is clear that Jesus did not see himself as just another Israelite, or even as just another *ʿānî*. By habitually calling upon God as "Father" throughout his ministry, Jesus had indicated that he embodied Israel's unique filial relationship to God (see Exod 4:22; Hos 11:1), and indeed that he himself was the true Israel.[82] Moreover, he was convinced that his own suffering and death would usher in the eschatological kingdom of God. Nor is it implausible to suggest that meditation on Psalm 22 had played a part in his coming to this conviction. As the quintessential *ʿānî*, Jesus would live out Israel's spiritual destiny.

N. T. Wright has made a strong case that the historical Jesus, already during his ministry and especially in his final trip to Jerusalem, not only considered himself the Messiah but quite deliberately acted out a messianic drama.[83] Wright demonstrates how Jesus derived his understanding of

79 Mays, *Psalms*, 113.

80 I agree with Brown that it is unlikely that Jesus recited the entire psalm from the cross (*Death of the Messiah*, 1087n129), but it is not unreasonable to suppose that in praying its first line he had in mind the psalm's "whole meaning" (Gelin, *Poor of Yahweh*, 87).

81 Regarding verse 17b ("they have bound [?] my hands and my feet"), see Gregory Vall, "Psalm 22:17b: 'The Old Guess,'" *Journal of Biblical Literature* 116, no. 1 (1997): 45–56.

82 Roch Kereszty, O. Cist, "God the Father," *Communio* 26 (Summer 1999): 260–65.

83 Wright, *Jesus and the Victory of God*, 477–611.

messiahship from the Scriptures and notes how remarkably well Psalm 22, with its pattern of suffering and restitution, matches "Jesus' mindset, aims and beliefs."[84]

This raises the possibility that Jesus quoted Psalm 22 not only for his own sake but for the benefit of the witnesses surrounding him, as a final, albeit cryptic, proclamation of his identity and of the salvation-historical significance of what he was at that moment undergoing. If so, the misapprehension of his words by some of those present (Matt 27:47–49; Mark 15:35–36) appears tragically ironic, whereas the New Testament use of Psalm 22 as an interpretive key to the passion shows itself to be a matter of fidelity to the Master's dying words.

Accordingly, Psalm 22 reveals that Jesus's passion was the ultimate act of *ʿănāwîm* piety. As he hung upon the cross and poured out his life, Jesus made a conscious and deliberate decision to entrust himself to God. He did this, moreover, with all his Israelite "brethren" (v. 23) and "all the clans of the nations" (v. 28) in mind. Jesus experienced fully humanity's alienation from God, and in the midst of this very experience he rendered God perfect devotion on humanity's behalf. Because of who Jesus is, and because of the intensity of his love for God and neighbor, his act of humble submission is salvific for all human beings, provided they conform themselves to his way of relating to God—that is, provided they too become *ʿănāwîm*.

A Method C study of Psalm 22 can increase our appreciation for the epiphanic quality of Jesus's death on the cross. This is the single act in all of history by which the inner life of the Blessed Trinity is most fully revealed, and Jesus's quotation of Psalm 22:2 (like his other "last words") discloses an interior dimension of this theandric act. Far from indicating that the Father had turned his back on the Crucified, Jesus's praying of Psalm 22 (or even its first line) would have confirmed his abiding intimacy with the Father and assured him that God "does not despise or detest the affliction of an afflicted one" (v. 25).

At the same time, Jesus's quotation of Psalm 22:2 expresses human spiritual desolation, and this fact must not be swept aside with facile explanations. The paradox of desolation in the midst of unbroken communion can, however, be illuminated through meditation on the incarnation, in conjunction with a Method C interpretation of Psalm 22. The communion of divine knowledge and love that the Son has with the Father in the Holy Spirit from

84 Wright, 600.

all eternity is now (from the first moment of the incarnation) lived in and through a concrete humanity.[85] Thus, after having related to the Father for thirty-some years by means of a somatically based human intellect, imagination, and will (all mysteriously united to his divine personhood), on the cross Jesus experienced the violent rending asunder of the body-soul unity.[86] Psalm 22 accents the somatic dimension of such a spiritual trial in typically Hebraic fashion. The dissolution of those bodily members that symbolize spiritual capacities is described poetically in the most concrete of terms.

> My heart has become like wax,
> melting within my breast;
> my palate is dry like a potsherd,
> my tongue cleaves to my jaws;
> you lay me in the dust of death. (vv. 15b–16)

For all of us, death involves a surrender of the human faculties by which we have related to God throughout our lives. It is thus the ultimate spiritual trial and life's culminating opportunity to make a perfect act of faith, hope, and love. Death, therefore, is itself a paradox, since that which came into the world because of sin (Rom 5:12) has by grace become our last and best chance to reverse our first parents' usurpation of the Creator's authority over their lives by rendering ourselves back to God. Of course, this transformation of human death has been effected precisely by Christ's self-offering on Golgotha, by which he consecrated his humanity (in solidarity with all humanity) perfectly to the Father. But in Psalm 22 we see Israel already participating—by prophetic anticipation and however imperfectly—in Christ's passion.

CONCLUDING REMARKS

By describing Psalm 22's function as a model prayer of postexilic *'ănāwîm* piety and relating this function to Jesus's own use of this psalm, I have attempted to demonstrate something of the organic continuity between

85 "The Son of God ... communicates to his humanity his own personal mode of existence in the Trinity" (*CCC* 470). "His humanity appeared as 'sacrament,' that is, the sign and instrument, of his divinity and of the salvation he brings: what was visible in his earthly life leads to the invisible mystery of his divine sonship and redemptive mission" (no. 515).

86 Christ's body and soul each remain united to the Word, and the body-soul unity was to be reestablished and glorified through the resurrection (*STh* III, q. 50, aa. 2–3).

Old Testament and New Testament. But if this exercise is to contribute to the development of the "thoroughly relevant hermeneutic" for which Cardinal Ratzinger has called,[87] it must be said that we are not dealing here with a clever appropriation of an Old Testament text on the part of Jesus or the early Church, nor with a spontaneous evolution of religious ideas and experiences. Rather, I discern in both the composition and the intended use of Psalm 22 a divine directedness and forward-leading intentionality at work in Israel's history. In accord with Method A, I wish to take quite seriously the New Testament's claim that the preincarnate Word was already active among Old Testament Israel.

At the same time, I would not restrict this activity to isolated moments of textual inspiration. According to Method A, Christ spoke through David, but what he says through David in Psalm 22 is disconnected not only from David's own life but from Israel's broader historical experience. For Method B, by contrast, Christ has nothing to do either with the composition of Psalm 22 or with its use by Israel during the Old Testament period. Rather, either Jesus, the early Church, or both drew upon the psalm as a resource or interpretive guide in order to *make* sense out of Jesus's passion and death. The remarkable similarity between Psalm 22 and the passion narratives, contemporary exegetes imply, must be due to some combination of historical contingencies, Jesus's self-interpretation, and the evangelists' intertextual hermeneutic. The one conclusion that Method B would seem to wish to avoid is that Psalm 22 was actually composed *for* Jesus—that it is in any real sense prophetic, predictive, or messianic.

My proposal is not merely that God was involved in the composition of Psalm 22 but that the "Spirit of Messiah" (1 Pet 1:11) guided and inspired the entire process by which *'ănāwîm* piety developed in Israel, a process that takes in not only the inspired composition of Psalm 22 but also its intended use. Moreover, this process was part and parcel of the broader "divine pedagogy" by which the Blessed Trinity was teaching and forming Israel and preparing her for the advent of the Messiah.[88] When the Messiah came, he was led, in his humanity, to an understanding of Israel's true identity and vocation—and

87 Ratzinger, "Biblical Interpretation in Crisis," 6.

88 Gelin, *Poor of Yahweh*, 74; *CCC* 53. This position has something in common with, but should not be confused with, social theories of inspiration. It is important to maintain a technical and restrictive sense for the word *inspiration*, one which pertains specifically to the Holy Spirit's involvement in the composition of the sacred text itself.

therefore to an understanding of his own identity and vocation—by the liturgical and spiritual traditions that he himself, in his preexistent divinity, had formed among his people and by the very Scriptures that he had likewise inspired.

CHAPTER TWO

Yahweh's Repentance and the Immutability of the Divine Will

In book 12 of the *Confessions*, Augustine of Hippo gives classic expression to the doctrine of the immutability of God's will. The divine substance, he reminds us, "is in no way altered by time," nor is God's will "separate from his substance":

> Consequently, he does not will one thing now and another thing later, but once and for all and forever he wills all things that he wills. Not again and again, nor now this, now that; nor does he will afterwards what he did not will before, nor does he not will what he previously did will. For that sort of will is mutable, and nothing mutable is eternal; but our God is eternal.[1]

Reading the Old Testament in light of this doctrine, one can hardly fail to be puzzled by a whole series of texts that speak of Yahweh's "repentance." In more than a dozen different passages widely distributed throughout the Hebrew Bible, the verb *niḥam* (the Niphal stem of the verbal root *nḥm*) has the sense "to regret, repent, change one's mind," and has Yahweh the God of Israel as its subject.[2] In several of these passages this sense of *niḥam* is reinforced by the verb *šûb*, meaning "to turn back" from a course of action,

1 Augustine, *Confessions* 12.15.

2 Gen 6:7; Exod 32:12, 14; 1 Sam 15:11, 35; 2 Sam 24:16; 1 Chron 21:15; Jer 18:8, 10; 26:3, 19; 42:10; Joel 2:13–14; Amos 7:3–6; Jonah 3:9–10; 4:2; Pss 90:13; 106:45. Even many of the passages that speak of Yahweh *not* repenting on a given occasion imply that on other occasions he *does* repent: Jer 4:28; 15:6; 20:16; Ezek 24:14; Zech 8:14. Exceptional in this regard are Num 23:19 and 1 Sam 15:29, and possibly Ps 110:4 (all of which will be discussed below). In Deut 32:36 and Ps 135:14, the verbal root *nḥm* in the Hithpael stem may have a similar meaning to the Niphal stem, and it clearly means "to repent" in Num 23:19. On the other hand, the Niphal stem seems to mean "to be moved to pity" in Judg 2:18.

again with Yahweh as the subject.[3] Sometimes Yahweh repents of a course of action that he has already undertaken (1 Sam 15:11), but more often he turns back from a course of action that he has only proposed to undertake (Exod 32:14). Merciful God that he is, he tends to repent of punishments threatened (Jer 18:8), but he may just as well repent of blessings promised (18:10). In fact, in a few passages he threatens a punishment and then promises that *this time* he will not repent (Ezek 24:14). Still, on the whole, the divine repentance texts accent Yahweh's mercy. In two postexilic passages the phrase "repents of evil" has been appended to the classic description of God's merciful character. Yahweh is "merciful and compassionate, slow to anger and abounding in steadfast love, and repents of evil" (Joel 2:13; Jonah 4:2).[4]

The difficulty presented by these passages is not simply that most of them appear to fly in the face of the doctrine of divine immutability, specifically the immutability of God's will, but that they do not seem, even when taken on their own terms, to present a unified canonical picture in this regard. Most of them speak of "repenting" as something that Yahweh is free to do whenever he wills, but two passages state categorically that Yahweh *does not repent*. The first of these is Numbers 23:19, where the prophet Balaam declares,

> God is not man, that he should lie,
> nor a son of man, that he should repent.
> When he has spoken, will he not do it?
> Does he make a promise and not uphold it?

Not surprisingly, when Thomas Aquinas addresses the question of whether or not God's will is mutable, representative Old Testament passages referring to God's having repented are quoted in the objections, but Numbers 23:19 is the authority cited in the *sed contra* (*STh* I, q. 19, a. 7).

This intracanonical tension comes to a head in 1 Samuel 15, where Yahweh's emphatic statement, "I repent that I have made Saul king" (v. 11), is closely followed by Samuel's patent echo of Balaam's words: "Moreover, the Everlasting One of Israel neither deceives nor repents, for he is not man that

3 Exod 32:12; Jer 4:28; Joel 2:14; Jonah 3:9; Pss 90:13. Elsewhere *šûb* is used (without *niḥam*) to refer to Yahweh's "turning back" from his fierce anger: Deut 13:17 (RSV 13:18); Josh 7:26; 2 Kgs 23:26; cf. Jer 4:8; Hos 14:5 (RSV 14:4).

4 The formula "merciful and compassionate, slow to anger, and abounding in steadfast love" (with slight variations) also occurs at Exod 34:6 (cf. Num 14:18); Pss 86:15; 103:8; 145:8; and Neh 9:17. The shorter formula "merciful and compassionate" is found at Ps 111:4; 2 Chron 30:9; Neh 9:31; Sir 2:11; and Jas 5:11. *Prayer of Manasseh* 7 echoes Joel 2:13 and Jonah 4:2.

he should repent" (v. 29). Just a few verses later, the narrator compounds our perplexity by concluding the chapter with this summary: "And Yahweh repented that he had made Saul king over Israel" (v. 35).

In this chapter I hope to demonstrate how ecclesial exegesis can lead us to a proper understanding of the Old Testament passages that speak in terms of Yahweh's repentance or nonrepentance, while it also provides an authentic way to deal with the tensions that these passages engender both within the canon of Scripture and between biblical exegesis and dogmatic theology. Augustine and Aquinas, who will serve as representatives of Method A in this chapter, will bring some helpful observations and crucial insights to the table. For the most part, I shall supply the Method B contribution and the Method C synthesis myself, although I shall cite linguists and exegetes for support on technical matters. In particular, I shall employ the skills of narrative analysis, which has become such an important component of biblical exegesis over the past forty years and has greatly enhanced our appreciation for the literary artistry and theological sophistication of the biblical authors. This literary perspective is crucial for negotiating the interface between biblical exegesis and dogmatic theology.

I have chosen the present topic not only because it makes for an interesting study in ecclesial exegesis but also because it is of real theological importance. Some contemporary theologians and biblical scholars feel that we must choose between the immutable God of dogma and the biblical God who acts in history. This turns a true tension into a false dichotomy. The exegetical and theological issues here are many and complex, extending far beyond the dozen or so passages of Scripture that speak in terms of Yahweh's repentance or nonrepentance. These passages nonetheless form one important part of the puzzle, and they deserve a careful reading.[5]

Rather than attempt to discuss all the relevant passages, I have chosen a small handful of foundational texts from the Pentateuch and the Deuteronomistic History (i.e., Joshua to 2 Kings). First, I shall examine Genesis 6:5–8,

5 Matthew J. Ramage's treatment of our topic, *Dark Passages of the Bible: Engaging Scripture with Benedict XVI and Thomas Aquinas* (Washington, D.C.: The Catholic University of America Press, 2013), 28–29, 160–61, underestimates the literary sophistication and theological depth of the biblical texts as well as the exegetical skill of Augustine. Furthermore, Ramage overlooks Num 23:19 and 1 Sam 15:29, creating the false impression of a dichotomy between biblical thought and ecclesial dogma. For a more careful literary-theological reading of some of the divine "repentance" texts (which, however, likewise ignores Num 23:19 and 1 Sam 15:29), see Anderson, *Christian Doctrine*, 23–38.

where Yahweh "repents" of having created man. To interpret this text within its canonical context, it will be helpful also to consider some aspects of the Priestly Heptaemeron, or narrative of the seven days (Gen 1:1–2:3), as well as the establishment of the Noachian covenant in the aftermath of the flood (8:20–9:17).[6] Second, I shall look at Exodus 32–34, where Yahweh threatens to exterminate his chosen people due to their apostasy with the golden calf, then "repents" of this course of action when Moses intercedes for them, and lastly grants Moses a deeper revelation of his mercy. Third, I shall briefly consider Balaam's declaration in Numbers 23:19 and then somewhat more fully treat 1 Samuel 15. Finally, I shall draw a few theological conclusions.

GENESIS 6:5–8

In order to view our first passage in proper canonical focus, it will be helpful to begin with a few observations about Genesis 1:1–2:3. The Priestly Heptaemeron presents God's creation of the world as an action that is intelligent, free, and successful. A God who can create simply by speaking things into being knows what he wants and gets it, immediately. "God said, 'Let there be light,' and there was light" (1:3). The words by which God creates light, *yəhî 'ôr*, express intelligible content, the thoughts of the divine mind. Creation is the rational act of an intelligent God. These same words also express volition. The Hebrew verbal form *yəhî* ("let there be") is a third-person volitive, or jussive.[7] God commands light to exist. In this, he acts in freedom. He is neither compelled to create nor hindered from doing so.[8] Moreover, his word is efficacious. The close verbal correspondence between God's creative word, *yəhî 'ôr* ("let there be light"), and the narration of its immediate result,

6 On the Priestly School, see the brief discussion toward the end of the introduction to this volume.

7 Biblical Hebrew employs three classes of volitive verb forms, one for each grammatical person: the cohortative (first person), the imperative (second person), and the jussive (third person). See Paul Joüon, SJ, *A Grammar of Biblical Hebrew*, trans. and rev. Takamitsu Muraoka, Subsidia Biblica 14 (Rome: Pontifical Biblical Institute, 1993), 125 (§40b).

8 Unlike other cosmogonies or creation narratives, even some within the Old Testament itself (e.g., Ps 89:10–12), Genesis 1 contains no hint of a divine struggle against the forces of chaos. As Franz Josef Haydn expresses so beautifully at the beginning of his oratorio *Die Schöpfung*, the first two verses of Genesis evoke a scene of great serenity, into which the words "Und es ward Licht" ("And there was light"; 1:3) erupt with power and majesty.

wayhî 'ôr ("and there was light"), suggests that what God says happens, with no remainder, no trial and error, and no surprises.[9]

The Priestly author further indicates the success of God's act of creation by solemnly declaring that "God saw that the light was good" (1:4). This phrase becomes a refrain throughout the chapter (vv. 10, 12, 18, 21, 25), culminating in the notice: "And God saw all that he had made, and behold, it was very good" (1:31). This is of great importance to our topic. A God possessing intellect and will just might, after all, be malevolent; but a God who calls into being what is emphatically "very good" is not only intelligent and free, but wise and loving. Moreover, the fact that God himself is said to recognize the goodness of what he has made leads the reader to expect that this God will not anytime soon regret having made it. We ought to anticipate such an outcome least of all in the case of man, the creature whom God, with manifest intentionality, has fashioned to his own image and likeness (1:26–27). Surely the biblical God would not, in the manner of the Mesopotamian deity Enlil, send a deluge upon the earth to destroy humanity.[10] He must be more committed to his creation than that.

In this way the Priestly narrative of creation has set us up for a surprise when, just a few chapters later, we read these words.

> And Yahweh saw that the evil of man was great upon the earth, and that every inclination of the thoughts of his heart was only evil all the day. And Yahweh repented that he had made man on the earth, and he was grieved to his heart. And Yahweh said, "I shall wipe out man, whom I have created, from the surface of the ground—from man to beast, to creeping things, to the birds of the sky—for I repent that I have made them. But Noah found favor in the eyes of Yahweh. (Gen 6:5–8)

After such a promising start, how could things have gone so wrong, so quickly?

The appropriate reader response would not be to lay the blame for this with Yahweh, as if he really were acting rashly like Enlil. After all, the Heptaemeron led us to expect far better *from man*, who in the intervening chapters has shown himself distrustful, disobedient, disingenuous, easily angered, fratricidal, bigamous, petty, and vengeful. No, the above passage from Genesis

9 "The exact echoing of the command here emphasizes the total fulfillment of the divine word." Gordon J. Wenham, *Genesis 1–15*, WBC 1 (Waco, Tex.: Word Books, 1987), 18.

10 See Jack P. Lewis, "Flood," *ABD* 2:798–99.

6 is clearly intended to evoke sympathy for Yahweh, whose good intentions and best efforts have been so badly repaid. Still, there is considerable tension between the creation narrative of Genesis 1:1–2:3, where God seems so completely in control, and the passage presently under consideration, where he appears to be more in the mode of reacting and taking desperate measures.

Having reached this part of the biblical story in book 15 of *The City of God*, Augustine pauses to guide his readers through this difficult passage from Genesis. In order to appreciate his exegesis, however, we must first cite the specific portion of the biblical text on which he is commenting and do so according to the Latin text that he is using—namely, a form of the Old Latin translation.

> And God considered that he had made man on the earth, and he reconsidered. And God said, "I will destroy man, whom I have made, from the face of the earth; from man to cattle, and from creeping things to fowl of the sky; for I am angry that I have made them." (Gen 6:6–7, Old Latin)[11]

In this ancient translation of the biblical text the problematic anthropomorphisms of the original Hebrew have been muted or otherwise altered. In place of the statement that God "repented" and "was grieved to his heart," we read that he "considered" and "reconsidered." This sounds like a more purely rational act, without any connotation of emotive remorse or deep sorrow. Note that the reference to God's "heart" has been removed entirely. Where the Hebrew text has God himself say, "I repent," the Old Latin has him say, "I am angry." The latter is a strong anthropomorphism, though a very common one in Scripture. Thus, in the translation from which Augustine quotes, some impression of divine "emotion" remains, but the specific idea

11 This is my translation of Augustine's citation of the biblical text in *De civitate Dei* 15.24 (*Et cogitavit Deus, quia fecit hominem super terram, et recogitavit; et dixit Deus: Deleam hominem, quem feci, a facie terrae, ab homine usque ad pecus et a repentibus usque ad volatilia caeli, quia iratus sum, quoniam feci eos*). The Old Latin was a translation of the Greek Septuagint (thus a translation of a translation) made in the second century AD for Latin-speaking Christians in southern Gaul and North Africa. By the time of Augustine and Jerome, it existed in numerous recensions and had been badly corrupted in the process of transmission, so that any two manuscripts were likely to differ from each other significantly. Fortunately, Augustine often quotes in full the passage on which he is commenting. See Ernst Würthwein, *The Text of the Old Testament: An Introduction to the Biblia Hebraica*, trans. Erroll F. Rhodes, 2nd ed. (Grand Rapids: Eerdmans, 1995), 91–94; and Eva Schulz-Flügel, "The Latin Old Testament Tradition," in *Hebrew Bible/Old Testament: The History of Its Interpretation*, vol. 1, *From the Beginnings to the Middle Ages (Until 1300)*, ed. Magne Sæbø (Göttingen: Vandenhoeck & Ruprecht, 1996), 645–50.

of repentance and regret has been removed. This does not, however, mean that Augustine is wholly ignorant of what the Hebrew text says. In particular, he is clearly aware that, in Genesis 6 and elsewhere, Scripture refers to God's having "repented."[12]

The essential difficulty of the passage remains in any case. In either translation, Scripture here seems to contradict the doctrine of divine immutability. To deal with this problem, Augustine first dissuades his readers from taking the biblical anthropomorphisms at face value. We should not suppose that Scripture is ascribing human passions to God. Above all, we must not construe statements about the Lord's "reconsideration" (or "repentance") to mean that the divine will actually ever changes. Augustine writes: "The anger of God is not a disturbing emotion of his mind, but a judgment by which punishment is inflicted upon sin. His thought and reconsideration also are the unchangeable reason which changes things; for he does not, like man, repent of anything he has done, because in all matters his decision is as inflexible as his prescience is certain."[13]

Having explained a text that says that the Lord "reconsidered" (or "repented") by saying that the Lord "does not repent of anything," Augustine senses that some hermeneutical justification of his exegesis may be in order. Accordingly, he adds:

> But if Scripture were not to use such expressions as the above, it would not familiarly insinuate itself into the minds of all classes of men, whom it seeks access to for their good, that it may alarm the proud, arouse the careless, exercise the inquisitive, and satisfy the intelligent; and this it could not do, did it not first stoop, and in a manner descend, to them where they lie.[14]

12 This is evident from *De civitate Dei* 14.11 (*tropica locutione in scripturis etiam paenituisse legitur Deum*) and from the allusion to Num 23:19 and 1 Sam 15:29 in *De civitate Dei* 15.25 (*neque enim sicut hominem, ita Deum cuiusquam facti sui paenitet*). By the time he wrote books 14 and 15 of *De civitate Dei* (AD 418), Augustine had studied the book of Genesis with avid interest for over thirty years (beginning with *De Genesi contra Manichaeos*, written circa AD 388) and, though he knew virtually no Hebrew and had never attained proficiency in Greek, he had become familiar with many of the differences between the Hebrew Proto-Masoretic Text and the Greek Septuagint. He had gained this knowledge in part by way of exegetical tradition and in part by comparing the Old Latin (a translation of the Septuagint) to Jerome's fresh Latin rendering of the Hebrew (i.e., the nascent Vulgate). The phrases *paenituit eum* ("he repented") and *paenitet enim me* ("for I repent") in Jerome's translation of Gen 6:6–7 would not have escaped Augustine's notice.

13 Augustine, *De civitate Dei* 15.25. Translation: Saint Augustine, *The City of God*, trans. Marcus Dods (New York: Modern Library, 1950), 515.

14 *De civitate Dei* 15.25. Translation: Augustine, *City of God*, trans. Dods, 515.

Augustine's argument here rests on two principles that have been part of the Church's hermeneutical heritage from the patristic period up to *Dei Verbum* and beyond. First, he makes explicit appeal to the "condescension" of Scripture—that is, the way God comes down to speak to us at our level. In Sacred Scripture God adopts human modes of discourse because it is to human beings that he addresses himself,[15] and for the omniscient God to speak to human beings in human words—even to the most intelligent human beings in the most sophisticated human words—must of necessity be an unimaginable "stooping" and "descending to them where they lie." In this respect Scripture's mode of communication may even be said to be analogous to the Word's descent in the incarnation.[16] Augustine's contemporary, John Chrysostom, popularized this principle under the Greek term συγκατάβασις, to which Latin *condescensio* corresponds precisely.[17] Second, Augustine makes an implicit appeal to the canonical principle, according to which each passage of Scripture should be read in light of the whole.[18] When he asserts that God "does not, like man, repent of anything," he is patently evoking Numbers 23:19 and 1 Samuel 15:29 and is allowing these categorical statements to guide his interpretation of Genesis 6:5–8. With the aid of these two principles Augustine plausibly asserts that when Scripture refers to Yahweh's "reconsideration" (or "repentance") it is actually referring to "the unchangeable reason which changes things."[19]

Earlier in *The City of God*, Augustine anticipated the whole problem of the Old Testament's references to divine "repentance" and proposed as its solution that in these passages Scripture speaks "by means of a figurative expression" (*tropica locutione*) and "with reference to man's expectation, or the order of natural causes."[20] In other words, in such cases Scripture speaks not only in a human mode of speech but from a temporal, human perspective. Presumably, then, the passages that categorically deny that Yahweh

15 Augustine, *De Trinitate* 1.12; cf. *Dei Verbum* 12.

16 *Dei Verbum* 13.

17 See Sten Hidal, "Exegesis of the Old Testament in the Antiochene School with its Prevalent Literal and Historical Method," in *Hebrew Bible/Old Testament*, ed. Sæbø, 559–60; and M. M. Mitchell, "Chrysostom, John," in *Historical Handbook of Major Biblical Interpreters*, ed. Donald K. McKim (Downers Grove, Ill.: InterVarsity Press, 1998), 31–32.

18 This is one of the "rules" (*regulae*) of interpretation included in *Dei Verbum* 12.

19 *De civitate Dei* 15.25. Translation: Augustine, *City of God*, trans. Dods, 515. Cf. *De civitate Dei* 17.7 and Augustine, *Ennarratio in Psalmos* 131.11.

20 *De civitate Dei* 14.11. Translation: Augustine, *City of God*, trans. Dods, 457.

repents are speaking from the divine and eternal perspective. This proposal, too, is plausible and potentially helpful. Later in this essay, taking my lead from a comment made by Thomas Aquinas, I shall pursue the idea that some passages of Scripture speak with reference to the order of natural causes and their temporal unfolding while others speak more absolutely and from the perspective of divine omniscience. For the moment, however, it is fair to broach the question of *why* Scripture might sometimes speak one way and sometimes the other.

It is Augustine's failure to pose this question with regard to Genesis 6:5–8 that leaves the reader unsatisfied. Assuming for the sake of argument that Scripture is *not* here asserting that God's will really changes—least of all with regard to his decision to create man—what, positively, *is* the inspired author asserting by saying, "Yahweh repented that he had made man on the earth"? After all, if Scripture can "familiarly insinuate itself into the minds of all classes of men" in Numbers 23:19 by saying that "God is not man, that he should lie, nor a son of man, that he should repent," why can it not speak in similar terms here in Genesis 6:5–8? Better yet, why mention the confusing idea of divine repentance (or reconsideration) at all? What if the sacred author had simply written this: "And, verily, the LORD knew from the beginning that man would sin and corrupt his way upon the earth, and he had determined in the counsel of his heart to send a flood upon the earth in the days of Noah, in order to punish man for his evil ways." That would express, in simple language understandable to all classes of men, just what Augustine takes from this passage, while avoiding the dangerously misleading idea of divine repentance.

Actually, my whimsical rewriting of Genesis 6:5–8 omits a great deal of what is expressed in the inspired text. All I have really done is to put Augustine's interpretation of the passage into biblical diction in order to make a point. The deficiency in Augustine's comment is that he tells us what the text *does not mean* without really telling us what it *does* mean, apart from stating the obvious—namely, that the flood was "a punishment inflicted upon sin." It is not often that Augustine leaves himself open to the charge of having given a reductive exegesis of Scripture, but that may be the case here. In order to go deeper, we must note two ways in which Genesis 6:5–8 differs from all other "divine repentance" passages found in the Old Testament.

First, Genesis 6:5–8 spells out the anthropomorphic implications and emotional overtones of the Hebrew verb *niḥam* ("to repent"). After stating that "Yahweh repented that he had made man on the earth," the sacred author adds that "he was grieved to his heart." The verb translated "was grieved" (*'āṣab*) elsewhere expresses an intensely personal emotion, as for example when David grieves for his son Absalom (2 Sam 19:3; RSV 19:2), and here in Genesis 6 this sense of the verb is reinforced by the phrase "to his heart." In such a context, one might justifiably translate *niḥam* "to regret." The pathos engendered by these words is still further intensified when the author allows us to listen in on Yahweh's interior monologue, which ends with the words "for I regret that I have made them."

Let us assume for the moment that, metaphysically speaking, Augustine is correct to say that "the anger of God is not a disturbing emotion of his mind." That very consideration compels us to ask why the inspired Hebrew authors seem to go out of their way to represent Yahweh's response to human sin as if it *were* a disturbing emotion, such as anger, grief, or, regret. If such anthropomorphic language is Scripture's way of insinuating itself into our minds, what exactly is it insinuating?

Broadly speaking, Sacred Scripture employs anthropomorphic language in order to indicate that God is personal, that he has created human beings to enter into a covenantal relationship with him, and that he cares deeply about that relationship. That is why, when Israel sins, Yahweh seems to take it personally.[21] Note, for example, the plaintive tone of Yahweh's words in these oracles of the classical prophets:

> What am I to do with you, Ephraim?
> What am I to do with you, Judah?
> Your love is like a morning cloud,
> like the dew that goes early away. (Hos 6:4)
>
> My people, what have I done to you?
> Or how have I wearied you? Testify against me! (Mic 6:3)
>
> I have raised and reared them as my children,
> but they have rebelled against me. (Isa 1:2)

Israel's sins are not merely infractions of the rules but personal acts of rebellion against a loving and concerned father, a father who is hurt by this rebellion. The moral law that Yahweh imposes on Israel and the rest of humanity is not an arbitrary set of restrictions but a revelation of the heart of God. Thus, when the thoughts of man's "heart" are only evil all the day, Yahweh is grieved "to his heart."

21 As this applies to the present passage, see Gerhard von Rad, *Genesis: A Commentary*, trans. John H. Marks, 3rd ed. (London: SCM, 1972), 117–18.

The second feature that makes Genesis 6:5–8 stand out among the divine repentance texts is the apparent incompleteness of God's repentance in this case. When Yahweh repents of having made Saul king, a new king is anointed forthwith (1 Sam 15:35–16:1). When he repents of the punishment that he threatened to inflict upon Nineveh, the city is spared (Jonah 3:10). But in the present case, the Creator's repentance or regret that he has created man on the earth leads to the strangely ambiguous, even paradoxical, event of the flood. This event is both the reversal of creation and the renewal of creation, simultaneously judgment and mercy, the destruction of all life and the salvation of a remnant.[22] Has God repented, or not?

A key to the passage may be that God's will seems to be running in two directions simultaneously, but somehow without contradiction. Yahweh's "repentance" of having made man on the earth is as complete, as utterly devastating, as it could possibly be without actually annihilating the human race; and yet the deliverance that he mercifully provides is, in a sense, still more complete, inasmuch as it grants humanity a new lease on life. Mankind is not simply spared so that it might continue on its present course but is given a fresh opportunity to live out its original vocation. Genesis 6:5–8, which is one of the Bible's most sobering statements about universal human sinfulness, ends on a hopeful note: "But Noah found favor in the eyes of Yahweh" (6:8). In and through this exceptionally "righteous" man (6:9) and his descendants, the human race is set on a course that will lead to faithful Abraham and the whole history of Yahweh's covenant with Israel. By sending the flood, God indicates his total opposition to human sin, but by saving Noah and his family he manifests his unfailing commitment to, and his irrevocable purpose for, creation in general and humanity in particular.

Near the end of the flood narrative, we come upon a passage that is clearly intended to hark back to the text we have been considering:

> Noah built an altar to Yahweh, and he took from all the clean livestock and from all the clean birds and offered burnt offerings on the altar; and Yahweh smelled the soothing aroma, and Yahweh said to his heart, "I shall never again curse the ground on account of man, though the inclination of the heart of man is evil from his youth. Nor shall I ever again smite all living things as I have done. As long as the earth abides, seedtime and harvest, cold and heat, summer and winter, day and night shall not cease." (8:20–22)

22 Claus Westermann, *Genesis 1-11: A Commentary,* trans. John J. Scullion (Minneapolis: Augsburg, 1984), 475–76.

Once again we find references to the human heart, the divine heart, and Noah's acceptance before God, but this time in reverse order.

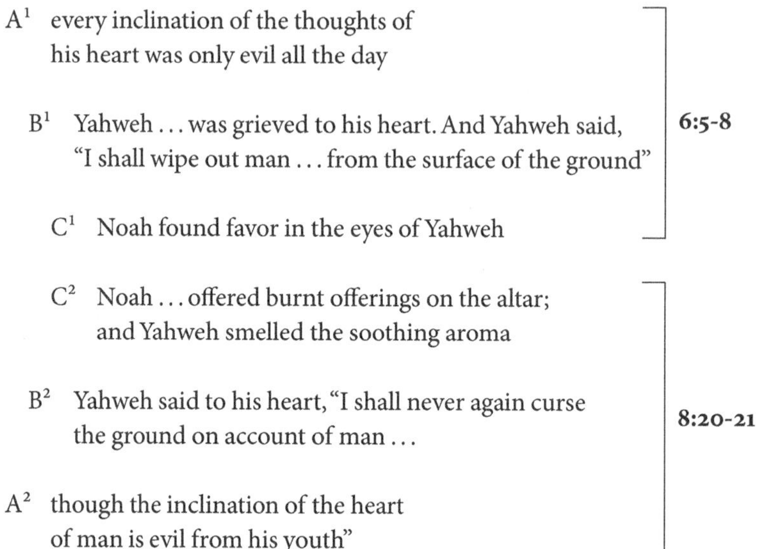

A^1 every inclination of the thoughts of his heart was only evil all the day
B^1 Yahweh . . . was grieved to his heart. And Yahweh said, "I shall wipe out man . . . from the surface of the ground"
C^1 Noah found favor in the eyes of Yahweh
6:5-8
C^2 Noah . . . offered burnt offerings on the altar; and Yahweh smelled the soothing aroma
B^2 Yahweh said to his heart, "I shall never again curse the ground on account of man . . .
A^2 though the inclination of the heart of man is evil from his youth"
8:20-21

This chiastic echo highlights three salient facts about the postdiluvian situation. First, man's heart remains unchanged, his thoughts still inclined toward evil. No remedy has been found for the moral malady that brought on the flood (A^1–A^2). Second, something has nevertheless "taken place" in the heart of God. His disposition toward man has changed from grief to good pleasure, from the determination to destroy to the promise to preserve (B^1–B^2). Third, the acceptability of Noah and his offering has in some manner been instrumental in bringing about this "change" in the heart of God. The favor that Noah found in God's eyes seems to have prompted the saving provision of the ark in the first place, and his burnt offering after the flood seems to have "soothed" God's sorely aggrieved heart (C^1–C^2).

The sacred author has used daringly anthropomorphic language at both ends of the flood narrative in order to approach the great mystery of divine freedom and its interaction with human freedom. Yahweh's "repentance" or "regret" about having made man (6:6–7), taken on its own terms, seems to represent a decisive departure from his original plan for creation and for man in particular. Furthermore, it represents something real in the heart of God, something the sacred author describes as "grief." Moreover, this divine sorrow does not remain merely interior to God but is *acted upon* when Yahweh sends the flood. The human race and the other species of living creatures are saved, but not by means of an abrogation of Yahweh's determination to bring about "the end of all flesh" (6:13).

One could of course speak of a mitigation of punishment, but perhaps we come closer to the true theological sense of the flood narrative by saying that salvation comes about *through* destruction, not in spite of it. In his sovereign freedom and in his acceptance of the one man who pleases him, Yahweh finds a way to punish sin more or less definitively, even while his saving mercy transcends his judgment in and through the very act of judgment! Paradoxically, Yahweh repents of having created man while he also somehow reaffirms his commitment to his original plan for creation, and even takes that plan to a new level, through the very event by which he expresses his regret. This may be the best way to account for the paradox that in the flood narrative the divine will seems to run in two opposing directions simultaneously.

To probe this paradox further, we must touch briefly on the biblical concept of "covenant" (*bərît*), which makes its first canonical appearance in the context of the flood narrative (6:18; 9:8–17). Broadly speaking, a covenant is a solemn agreement under oath between two parties that establishes a relationship based on loyalty and mutual obligations.[23] Leaving aside covenants between two human parties (e.g., 21:22–32), I shall mention three salient characteristics of those covenants that Yahweh makes with human beings and specify their pertinence to the present case. The first such characteristic is that, while Yahweh always takes the initiative in establishing a covenant, in many cases he does so in response to some human virtue (e.g., Num 25:10–13). In all cases, moreover, he looks for trusting obedience in his covenant partner (e.g., Exod 19:5–6). In this regard, Noah is exemplary. He finds favor with Yahweh even before the covenant is established (Gen 6:8–9) and displays unswerving obedience throughout (6:22; 7:5, 9, 16).

The second salient characteristic of biblical covenants is that Yahweh makes a covenant with an individual and his "seed," such that the individual in some sense represents and embodies the people who will descend from him. Here the whole mysterious, sacramental relationship between the particular and the universal in the divine economy comes into view. The

23 For an overview of this important biblical theme, see George E. Mendenhall and Gary A. Herion, "Covenant," *ABD* 1:1179–1202.

covenant with Noah is the extreme case in this respect. God establishes a covenantal relationship with Noah, his family, all the creatures with them in the ark, *and* with their descendants after them "for endless generations" (9:12). This is how it is possible for God to bring judgment upon sinful humanity while simultaneously establishing an "everlasting covenant" with all humanity and all living creatures (9:16). This is how a covenant between God and one righteous man can in principle bring redemption to the whole race and even to the whole of creation.

The third salient characteristic of biblical covenants is that devotion and constancy are of the essence of the covenant. "Steadfast love and faithfulness" (*ḥésed weʾĕmet*) are the covenantal virtues par excellence. Though these terms are not found in Genesis 6–9, the flood narrative does manifest a unique sort of fidelity in the heart of God the Creator. It is largely through this fidelity that what we call the immutability of the divine will is revealed. It is not a static or mechanical immutability but the immutability of one who is supremely loving and loyal.

Next, we need to consider the specific role of the Noachian covenant within the covenantal economy, when the latter is viewed qua revelation of the divine immutability. According to Priestly theology, Yahweh establishes a series of four major covenants: (1) with Noah, his descendants, and all living creatures (Gen 9:8–17); (2) with Abraham and his descendants (17:1–21); (3) with the people of Israel at Sinai (Exod 19:5; 34:27–28); and (4) with Phineas and his descendants, who will serve God as priests (Num 25:10–13). Canonically, this series of four is continued by the later covenants, most prominently the Deuteronomic, the Davidic, and the "new covenant." Each covenant, moreover, builds on and incorporates into itself any previous ones, so that ultimately there is really one covenant, unfolding in stages, just as there is one unified economy of redemption.

As the first in the series, the Noachian covenant is foundational for the rest and discloses the true reciprocity between the order of creation and the order of redemption. Creation must be preserved from the threat of sin in order to provide the theater in which the drama of redemption will be played out, while the whole history of redemption is necessary to bring creation to its divinely intended goal. The first covenant thus manifests one vital aspect of the whole series. By means of the covenantal history of redemption, Yahweh will uphold the order of creation and fulfill his purpose for creation over against the dire threat posed by human sin. Note that in the narration of the flood's immediate aftermath (Gen 8:20–9:17), where the word *bərît* is used seven times, there is an accent on the order and stability of creation as the manifestation and sign of God's constancy, combined with reminders that man's "heart" stands in need of redemption. In a word, the covenant is that by which God will both maintain and redeem his creation. That is why Yahweh's covenantal dealings with Israel and humanity always involve judgment and mercy.

The covenantal dynamics of judgment and mercy—and the concomitant mystery of divine freedom and human freedom—are paradigmatically on display in the flood narrative. Already here, in the context of the first stage of the covenant, Scripture locates the great mystery of freedom not only in the interplay between the divine will and human wills (where we would expect to find it) but also in a sublime and ineffable anguish within the heart of God itself. The language of divine regret and grief, and above all the fact that the threatened punishment of the deluge is not averted but actually carried out, indicates how deadly serious the Creator is about the problem of moral evil residing in the human heart. On the other hand, this same language of regret and grief strongly suggests that things cannot really be put right (in God's heart) by means of total destruction. If God were merely angry, even supremely angry, his heart might well be satisfied by uncreation, but that is not where the text of Scripture places the accent. Indeed, in the original Hebrew, the flood narrative never explicitly mentions divine "wrath" or "anger." Instead, it says that God "regretted" having made man and "was grieved to his heart" (6:6). These expressions bespeak a heart that is in some sense torn between two alternatives, offended by the moral evil that has spoiled creation but longing for the wayward creature who is responsible for this catastrophe.

This longing of the divine heart fixes itself upon "a man blamelessly righteous among his contemporaries" (6:9) and determines to establish a covenant with him and—through him and his family and the animals that join them in the ark—with all creation (6:18). When the flood waters crest above the mountain tops and every living being that has not entered the ark perishes, God "remembers" the righteous man and all the representatives of creation that are with him in the ark (8:1) and thus "remembers" his purpose for creation. When the flood waters recede, the "soothing aroma" of this man's offering alters, or at least plays a part in altering, the disposition of God's heart toward all of creation, despite the fact that "the inclination of the heart of man is [still] evil from his youth" (8:20–22). Thereupon, God himself reminds the reader that he "made man in his own image"; he reaffirms his primordial blessing of man ("be fruitful and multiply"); and, by enacting the first of his covenants, he formally commits himself to maintaining the order of creation (9:1–17).

If this is so, however, we must be careful not to confuse the order of creation with the order of redemption. The Priestly authors have a profound appreciation for the intimate relation between these two, but they do not encourage us to view creation itself as the first covenant in the series. In their meticulous account of the seven days (1:1–2:3) they studiously avoid referring to God's creation of man or of any other creature as establishing a "covenant," reserving the term *bərît* for the four covenants mentioned above. Obviously, the covenant with Noah has an especially close connection to creation and to God's purpose for man and creation, but we miss the whole point of this connection if we collapse creation itself into a covenantal scheme, as is sometimes done.

After the flood waters recede, Yahweh still bemoans the fact that "the inclination of man's heart is evil from his youth." No remedy has been found for the moral evil that brought on the flood in the first place. In the same breath, however, Yahweh solemnly declares "to his own heart" (*'el libbô*) never again to bring a curse upon the earth (8:21). Rather, he reaffirms the primal blessing of man and binds himself to his creation by an everlasting covenant (9:1–17). Yahweh's repentance and the severity of the flood indicate that human sin is a grave problem that will need to be dealt with sooner or later, while the rescue of a remnant of humanity through the building of the ark represents a merciful deferral of final judgment until a remedy for sin should be found.

According to the literal sense, then, the flood narrative indicates the need for a remedy for sin and God's commitment to find such a remedy. Interpreted according to the spiritual sense, however, the flood prefigures the remedy itself. In closing this section, I shall merely mention some highlights along the early trajectory of this traditional interpretation. Already in Second Temple Judaism, the flood was interpreted as a great "purification" of the earth.[24] Building on this idea, the apostle Peter (writing with the assistance of Silvanus) identified the sacrament of baptism—in which we are "saved through water" and enter into Christ's Church through his paschal mystery—as the "antitype" of the flood.[25] Near the end of the first century, Clement of

24 James L. Kugel, *The Bible as It Was* (Cambridge, Mass.: Belknap Press of Harvard University Press, 1997), 118–19.

25 1 Pet 3:18–22; cf. 5:12.

Rome referred to the flood as a cosmic "regeneration" (παλιγγενεσία) and hinted that the ark itself is a type of the Church and that "the living creatures who entered it in concord" prefigure all those who enter the Church in peace (*1 Clem.* 9.4). These pregnant suggestions gave rise to more elaborate allegorical interpretations among the Church Fathers. Augustine, for example, noting that the dimensions of Noah's ark are proportionate to a man's body as he lies supine, interpreted the ark as a type of the body of Christ, both the historical body in which he passed through the waters of death, as it were, and his ecclesial body. The door in the side of the ark prefigures the wound in Christ's side, from which come the sacraments of initiation.[26]

EXODUS 32–34

We turn now to Exodus 32–34 and begin once again by placing our text in its canonical context. God has revealed himself to Moses as Yahweh, delivered the Israelites from bondage, brought them to himself at Sinai, given them the moral law in the form of the Decalogue, and entered into a solemn covenant with them (Exodus 1–24). The sacred authors repeatedly note that he has done all this in fidelity to his promises to Abraham, Isaac, and Jacob.[27] In a characteristically programmatic passage, the Priestly authors imply that, while the exodus inaugurates a decisive new stage in the unfolding of God's self-revelation, there is in fact one unified divine plan, which comprises creation and a series of covenants (6:2–8). Already according to a much older text, the archaic Song of the Sea, this plan involves Yahweh's guidance of his people through the wilderness to the land of Canaan, where he will "plant" them and establish his sanctuary forever (15:13–18).[28]

As interpreted by the theologians of the Priestly School, this early tradition means that Yahweh himself will relocate from Mount Sinai to Mount Zion by means of a portable sanctuary. In Exodus 25–31 (a Priestly

26 Augustine, *De civitate Dei* 15.26. For a fuller discussion of the biblical typology of the flood in ancient Judaism and early Christianity, see Jean Daniélou, SJ, *From Shadows to Reality, or Sacramentum Futuri: Studies in the Biblical Typology of the Fathers*, trans. Wulstan Hibberd (London: Burns & Oates, 1960), 69–112.

27 Exod 2:24; 3:16–17; 6:2–8.

28 The Song of the Sea (Exod 15:1–18) is often judged to be one of the oldest portions of the Pentateuch, composed in archaic Hebrew poetry. See Brian D. Russell, *The Song of the Sea: The Date of Composition and Influence of Exodus 15:1–21*, Studies in Biblical Literature 101 (New York: Peter Lang, 2007), who argues for a date circa 1150 BC.

composition if ever there was one), Moses receives from Yahweh a detailed set of instructions for building the wilderness tabernacle. In another programmatic passage, Yahweh indicates the function of this tabernacle:

> I shall meet there with the children of Israel, and it will be consecrated by my glory.... And I shall dwell in the midst of the children of Israel, and I shall be their God. And they will know that I am Yahweh their God, who has brought them forth from the land of Egypt in order to dwell in their midst—I, Yahweh their God. (Exod 29:43–46)

It is by means of the wilderness tabernacle, then, that Yahweh will travel in the midst of Israel until they and he arrive at their permanent home in Canaan. This is but a Priestly specification of a basic theological truth that permeates the book of Exodus with its layers of tradition and redaction: Yahweh delivers Israel from harsh "servitude" (*ʿăbôdâ*) in Egypt in order that they may "serve" or "worship" (*ʿābad*) him, the one true God.[29]

By the time we arrive at Exodus 32, therefore, the trajectory and goal of the divine plan have been laid before us with admirable clarity.[30] But alas, while Moses is on Mount Sinai receiving divinely revealed instructions for how God is to be worshipped, Aaron and the people are at the base of the mountain indulging in a time-honored but, for all that, false and degraded form of worship.[31] Yahweh turns to Moses and thunders:

> Go down! For *your* people, whom *you* brought up from the land of Egypt, has acted corruptly.... I have seen this people, and behold, it is a stiff-necked people. Now then, let me be, that my wrath may burn against them and I may annihilate them; and I shall make *you* into a great nation. (32:7, 9–10)

After everything that has transpired from the call of Abram (Genesis 12) to the inauguration of the Sinai covenant (Exodus 24), suddenly Yahweh seems ready to give up on Israel. He appears ready to scrap Plan A in order to start from scratch with Moses, who would then become a sort of new

29 Exod 1:13–14; 2:23; 3:12; 4:22–23; 5:9–11; 6:5–9; 7:16; etc.

30 This clarity is destroyed by the unfounded hypothesis that Exodus 19–40 should be read as a "dischronologized narrative," according to which the instructions for building the wilderness tabernacle (chapters 25–31) were given to Moses *subsequent to* the golden calf incident. Scott W. Hahn, *Kinship by Covenant: A Canonical Approach to the Fulfillment of God's Saving Promises*, AYBRL (New Haven: Yale University Press, 2009), 143–52.

31 On the cultic background, symbolism, manufacture, and worship of the golden calf, see John R. Spencer, "Golden Calf," *ABD* 2:1065–69.

Abraham. One can hardly avoid the impression that Yahweh is acting capriciously, even erratically, here. The careful reader, however, will recognize that Yahweh is in fact testing Moses. On the one hand, he discourages Moses's intercession for the people ("let me be") and encourages him to think rather of his own glory ("I shall make you into a great nation"). On the other hand, it is Yahweh who hints at the very possibility of intercession and who in doing so makes the outcome of this crisis dependent in part on Moses.[32] By referring to Israel as "your people," moreover, he indirectly invites Moses to consider his own responsibility for the people, even as the same jarring phrase ought to alert him to the enormity of what Yahweh is proposing. Rhetorically, Yahweh's speech places Moses squarely between two options: to act as a true leader on behalf of his people, or to abandon them and think of himself.

Moses passes the test with flying colors. He understands clearly that Yahweh has made a firm commitment to Abraham, Isaac, and Jacob, and that by means of the exodus event he has claimed the people of Israel as his "special possession" (19:5).

> And Moses appeased the face of Yahweh his God, and he said, "Why, O Yahweh, should your wrath burn against *your* people, whom *you* brought forth from the land of Egypt with great power and a strong hand.... Turn back from your blazing wrath, and repent of the harm you would do to your people. Remember Abraham, Isaac, and Israel, your servants, to whom you swore by your own self, saying to them, 'I will multiply your seed like the stars of the sky; and all this land, about which I have spoken to you, I shall give to your seed, and they will inherit it forever.'" And then Yahweh repented of the harm which he had said he would do to his people. (32:11–14)

Moses places the immediate crisis within the framework of God's overarching purpose, which reaches back to his oath to Abraham and forward to Israel's everlasting inheritance of the promised land. He recognizes how utterly unfitting it would be for Yahweh, however sorely provoked, to abandon this grand design. Nor will he cooperate in Yahweh's apparent attempt to abdicate responsibility for the people and the exodus event. Instead, he

32 Brevard S. Childs, *The Book of Exodus: A Critical, Theological Commentary*, OTL (Louisville: Westminster, 1974), 567. Medieval Jewish commentators such as Saadia Gaon, Rashi, and Abraham ibn Ezra likewise held that "God's declaration was meant to encourage Moses to pray for his people." Israel Drazin and Stanley M. Wagner, *Exodus: Onkelos on the Torah, Understanding the Bible Text* (Jerusalem: Gefen, 2006), 221.

turns the phrase "*your* people, whom *you* brought forth from the land of Egypt" right back around at Yahweh and reminds him of his solemn oath to the patriarchs.[33] As for the crass appeal to self-interest contained in the words, "and I shall make you into a great nation," Moses treats it as unworthy of a response.

It is crucial to note that Yahweh here "repents" of a course of action that—while strictly justifiable—would, if carried out, represent a significant modification of what he has already revealed to be his master plan. In other words, the motif of divine repentance in the present passage runs almost in the opposite direction of the first passage that we examined. Whereas in Genesis 6 divine repentance seemed to place Yahweh's master plan in jeopardy, here in Exodus 32 it represents recommitment to that master plan. In the latter case divine repentance, far from reflecting fickleness, actually indicates steadfastness of will.

This does not, however, mean that Yahweh is merely bluffing when he tests Moses by threatening to disown his people and scrap Plan A. Israel's proclivity for idolatry, manifested in the manufacture and worship of the golden calf, represents a real problem, an objective impediment to God's plan. The golden calf incident is not simply a teachable moment. Even after Moses has appeased Yahweh's face and turned back his blazing wrath, the latter informs him that Plan A needs to be modified. Yahweh will spare Israel and will send them on to their destination, but he will not be going along with them. Instead, he will send his "angel" before them (32:34; 33:2). Yahweh explains the rationale for this change of plans: "I cannot go up in your midst, for you are a stiff-necked people, lest I annihilate you on the journey.... Were I to go up in your midst even for one moment, I would annihilate you" (33:3, 5). An all-holy God cannot travel in the midst of a sinful people. It simply will not work—at least not unless some special provision is made.

At this point we would do well to consider a passage from Thomas Aquinas's *Super epistolam ad Hebraeos*. Thomas comments on Hebrews 6:17, which reads: "God, willing to demonstrate more abundantly to the heirs of

33 It is misleading, however, to say that Moses "categorically denies any degree of ownership over this people" (Anderson, *Christian Doctrine*, 27). His insistence on Yahweh's ownership of the people (32:11) by no means implies a denial of his own responsibility for them as their divinely commissioned leader. Indeed, throughout the remainder of chapters 32–34 Moses exhibits a strong sense of personal responsibility for Israel, in contrast with Aaron's pitiful attempt to lay full blame for the manufacture of the golden calf at the feet of the people (32:21–24).

the promise the immutability of his counsel, interposed an oath."[34] The oath to which the author of Hebrews here refers is precisely the one mentioned by Moses in Exodus 32:13, the oath which Yahweh swore "by himself" to Abraham, Isaac, and Jacob. In his comment Thomas wishes to explain why Scripture sometimes seems to present God's will as changeable but at other times explicitly indicates that it is unchangeable, the very issue with which we are concerned.

Thomas notes that created effects that proceed from God can be considered in two ways: according to "the very procession of things," or according to "the counsel of God by which such a procession is caused." The former is mutable but the latter "altogether immovable." Now, in Scripture "the Lord sometimes pronounces something according to what the order and procession of things demands."[35] Thomas gives an example. When Yahweh, through the prophet Isaiah, tells King Hezekiah that he should put his house in order because he is about to die (Isa 38:1), he is not fibbing or bluffing but speaking the truth. Hezekiah actually has "a progressive infirmity," which will indeed claim his life if it is allowed to run its course. Yahweh, of course, foreknows that he will intervene and heal Hezekiah, granting him another fifteen years of life, but he speaks truly about the present trajectory of things when he says that the king is about to die. On the other hand, Thomas continues, Scripture sometimes speaks of the course of things according to the counsel of God by which it is caused, and "of this God never repents." Here Thomas cites Isaiah 46:10: "My counsel shall stand, and all my will shall be done." Finally, Thomas notes that "whenever the Lord swears something under oath, it is a prophecy of predestination, which is indicative of the divine counsel; and such a promise is utterly immutable."[36]

Applying this insight to Exodus 32–34, we can say that when God declares that he would annihilate the Israelites if he were to go up in their midst, he is speaking "according to what the order and procession of things demands." Israel's sinfulness is a real impediment to God's dwelling in their midst, and something must be done about it. On the other hand, Moses correctly intuits that when Yahweh swore an oath "by himself" to the patriarchs, he was taking the long view and declaring his unchangeable purpose.

34 Aquinas, *In Heb.*, c. 6, lect. 4. Translation: Thomas Aquinas, *Commentary on the Epistle to the Hebrews*, trans. Chrysostom Baer (South Bend, Ind.: St. Augustine's Press, 2006), 138.

35 *In Heb.*, c. 6, lect. 4.

36 *In Heb.*, c. 6, lect. 4.

But what about Yahweh's offer to send an angel to guide Israel to the land of Canaan? Might this not be the provision by which he will alter "the very procession of things" in order to remove the impediment and preserve his unalterable oath to the patriarchs? The proposal sounds like an eminently reasonable compromise. But Moses is not taking the bait. In the canonical unfolding of the narrative, the promise of a guiding angel was already made back in Exodus 23:20–23, but there the emphasis was on the intimate connection, the virtual identity, between Yahweh and his angel: "My name is within him" (23:21). In the present case, by contrast, Yahweh is clearly proposing that the angel take his place: "I shall not go up in your midst" (33:3). And that makes all the difference. Having been shown the heavenly pattern of the tabernacle on the mountain,[37] and having learned the purpose of the tabernacle (29:42–46), Moses realizes that any compromise that would result in Yahweh's not traveling in the midst of Israel would actually gut the master plan of its most essential and glorious feature. With magnificent sincerity, the lawgiver prays:

> Behold, you say to me, "Lead this people up," but you have not made known to me whom you will send with me. And you have said, "I know you by name, and you have found favor in my eyes." Now then, if indeed I have found favor in your eyes, let me know your way, that I may know you, in order that I may find favor in your eyes. And see that this nation is *your* people. (33:12–13)

This brings us to Exodus 33:14, the verse that Jacob Milgrom plausibly identifies as the centerpiece of a massive chiasmus stretching from Genesis to Joshua, the dramatic hinge upon which the entire Hexateuchal narrative swings.[38] It is one of the shortest verses in the Old Testament, a mere five Hebrew words: *wayyōʾmar pānay yēlēkû wahăniḥōtî lāk*, "And then he said, 'My face [i.e., presence] will go [with you], and I shall give you rest [i.e., bring you to the place of rest, the holy land].'" These words represent a distillation of the divine plan to its essence. But because the statement is elliptical and ambiguous—in Hebrew the pronoun "you" is singular, which could refer to Moses alone—and because there is so much riding on it, Moses presses for a clarification of Yahweh's intent:

37 Exod 25:40; 26:30; 27:8; cf. Wis 9:8; Heb 8:5.

38 Milgrom, *Numbers*, xviii.

> If you are not going, do not send *us* up from this place. For how then will it be known that I have found favor in your eyes, *I and your people*? Is it not in your going with *us*, so that *we* may be distinguished from all the people who are upon the face of the earth? (33:15–16)

Here especially, Moses's sense of solidarity with and responsibility for the people of Israel is evident. Yahweh's reply is equally poignant: "This thing too, which you have spoken, I shall do. For you have found favor in my eyes, and I do know you by name" (33:17).

So, Moses has passed part two of the test, and Yahweh has again repented of tinkering with his own plan. Things will go forward according to Plan A. The tabernacle will be built according to the pattern shown Moses on the mountain. The cloud of glory will come to rest upon it, and the Israelites, together with their divine fellow traveler, will set forth from Mount Sinai. Incorporating the rational and free instrumentality of his prophet into the mystery of divine providence in a strangely wonderful manner, God has manifested the steadfastness of his own will and his unwavering commitment to the grand design that is the divine economy of creation and redemption. The narrative of Exodus 32–34 indicates that the Bible's anthropomorphic language of "repentance" need not betoken the mutability of God's will, much less divine caprice.

God's plan will go forward, but the real, objective impediment of Israel's sinfulness remains. Just as it is still the case after the flood and after Noah's acceptable offering that "the inclination of man's heart is evil from his youth" (Gen 8:21), it remains true even after Moses's successful intercession that Israel is "a stiff-necked people" and that the all-holy God can go in their midst only if he forgives their "iniquity and sin" (Exod 34:9). It is in this connection that Moses is granted a deepened revelation of the divine name, one that accents Yahweh's merciful character.

> Yahweh, Yahweh, a God merciful and compassionate, slow to anger and abounding in steadfast love and faithfulness, keeping steadfast love for thousands, taking away iniquity and transgression and sin; yet he by no means pardons, but visits the guilt of parents upon children and grandchildren to the third and fourth generation. (34:6b–7)

It is vitally important to understand correctly the phrase "yet he by no means pardons" (*wənaqqēh lō' yənaqqeh*). Its function is not rhetorical, as if to mitigate, soften, or walk back the exuberant description of Yahweh's merciful love that precedes it. If anything, it deepens and strengthens this description by indicating that when Yahweh "takes away" sin he is not content merely to pardon and grant amnesty. He does not deal with sin by pretending that it never happened. Rather, he is so merciful that he wishes to root out sin and deliver his people from its grip. This involves a long historical process of discipline and chastisement, allowing his people to experience some of the consequences of their sin ("to the third and fourth generations") in order to bring them to their senses and lead them to repentance.[39]

On the basis of this divine mercy, the Sinai covenant is solemnly restored (34:10–28), but the renewed form of the covenant, as presented by the Priestly theologians, will contain an elaborate battery of offerings and purificatory rites, comprising the book of Leviticus with its centerpiece, the ritual of Yom Kippur (16:1–34). As Milgrom explains, the sins committed by Israel cause a certain "contamination" to build up gradually in the tabernacle. This creates a dangerous situation, for the friction between divine holiness and human sinfulness can spark an outbreak of wrath. The annual rite of Yom Kippur amounts to a yearly "decontamination" of the sanctuary, reducing this friction and permitting Yahweh's presence to remain with Israel for another year.[40] From a New Testament perspective, we might say that the wilderness tabernacle manifests God's will to dwell in the midst of his people and even a certain imperfect and provisional realization of that divine purpose—inasmuch as it gives Old Testament Israel a dignified and meaningful way to worship the true God—while Yom Kippur represents "a yearly reminder of sins" (Heb 10:3) and a certain imperfect manifestation of God's commitment to deal with sin, ultimately to provide a definitive expiation for sin that does more than merely "pardon."

NUMBERS 23:19 AND 1 SAMUEL 15

Within the all-encompassing and utterly immutable counsel of God, the lawgiver and protoprophet Moses has exercised instrumental causality through his prayer of intercession. He has not changed the eternal will of

39 This interpretation of the phrase *wənaqqēh lōʾ yənaqqeh* is strongly suggested by the use of the same idiom in Jer 30:11 and 46:28, where "chastising in justice" is explicitly indicated as the opposite of "pardoning."

40 Jacob Milgrom, *Leviticus 1–16: A New Translation with Introduction and Commentary*, AB 3 (New York: Doubleday, 1991), 253–61, 1009–84. Cf. David P. Wright, "Day of Atonement," *ABD* 2:72–76.

God, but he has played a role in altering "the very procession of things" in a manner that is already built into God's master plan. The authors of Exodus wish us to marvel at the greatness of this man and the dignity of his prophetic office. Though Moses boldly commands Yahweh to "turn back" from his blazing wrath and to "repent" of the harm he has threatened to do (32:12), he is not in fact setting his own will in opposition to the divine will. Far from it! The secret to his intercessory power lies precisely in his intimacy with Yahweh, his love for Israel, and his commitment to God's master plan.

Absolutely none of this is understood by Balak, king of Moab, who thinks that he can simply hire Balaam the prophet to slap a curse on Israel, as if the prophet possessed such authority: "For I know that he whom you bless is blessed, and he whom you curse is cursed" (Num 22:6). As much as Balaam would like to accept the fee that Balak offers to pay him for his services, he recognizes that Yahweh has blessed Israel with a blessing that no prophet can revoke (23:20):

> God is not man, that he should lie,
> nor a son of man, that he should repent.
> When he has spoken, will he not do it?
> Does he make a promise and not uphold it? (23:19)

With each of his four oracles, Balaam is able to see farther into the future of Yahweh's plan for Israel. In the final oracle he foresees the dawning of the Israelite monarchy—"a star shall come forth from Jacob, and a scepter shall rise out of Israel" (24:17)—and the destruction of Amalek (24:20). The role of the prophet, the rise of the monarchy, the destruction of Amalek, and the nonrepentance of Yahweh—this combination of motifs anticipates our final text, 1 Samuel 15.

When King Saul sins by failing to carry out fully the *ḥērem* against Amalek,[41] the word of Yahweh comes to the prophet Samuel: "I repent that I have made Saul king." Upon hearing this, "Samuel became angry, and he cried out to Yahweh all night long" (1 Sam 15:11). The narrator does not tell us *at whom* Samuel directs his anger or *why* he cries out to Yahweh all night long. Unquestionably, the prophet is displeased with King Saul, but there is

41 The noun *ḥērem* and the cognate verb *ḥāram* (in the Hiphil stem) refer to the devotion to Yahweh of persons and property, via destruction, in the context of holy war. See Marvin H. Pope, "Devoted," *IDB* 1:838–39; and Horst Dietrich Preuss, *Old Testament Theology*, 2 vols., OTL (Louisville: Westminster John Knox, 1995), 1:136–37.

good reason to suppose that he is also upset with Yahweh. Recall that the prophet was very much opposed to the idea of instituting a monarchy in the first place and acceded to the people's demand only after Yahweh had talked him round to it (8:1–22). By unmistakable signs of providence, Yahweh brought Samuel and Saul together and directed the former to anoint the latter (9:1–10:16). The prophet came to regard the institution of monarchy as God's will for Israel (12:12–15) and, by the time of the war with Amalek, had become deeply attached to Saul, having a personal and professional stake in his kingship. Later, the narrator will tell us more than once how Samuel "grieved" over Saul's fall from divine favor (15:35; 16:1).

Connecting the dots, then, we may suppose that Samuel is deeply upset at Yahweh's "repentance." If a prophet spends an entire night "crying out" (*zāʿaq*) to God, we may assume that he is attempting to influence God's thinking.[42] In this case, we can be fairly sure that Samuel is trying to convince Yahweh to let Saul have just one more chance. Yahweh has given up on Saul, but Samuel is not quite ready to do the same. The prophet spends the night pleading with Yahweh *to repent of his repentance*, as it were. By morning, however, Samuel has resigned himself to Yahweh's decision and accepted it as irrevocable.

Later that day, Samuel meets up with Saul and confronts him (15:13–14). After several lame attempts to plead his own innocence, Saul has a confession wrung from him. He finally admits that he fears the people and that he has obeyed them rather than Yahweh (15:15–24). This confession has no real effect on the course of events, however. Saul's fate is sealed. Yahweh has repented of making him king and will not repent of this repentance. The real issue in this scene is whether Samuel will exercise enough prophetic fortitude to uphold Yahweh's decision by withdrawing his public support for the young king. This he must do over against his own deep personal desire to give Saul another chance and Saul's desperate pleas for the prophet to go with him to the sacrifice at Gilgal and to honor him in the presence of the elders of Israel (15:25–26, 30). When Samuel physically turns away from Saul and starts to leave, Saul grabs hold of his robe skirt and tears it (15:27). Recognizing this as a prophetic sign, Samuel takes the opportunity to place Yahweh's rejection of Saul in a broader prophetic framework: "Yahweh has torn the kingship of

42 The verb *zāʿaq* (or its biform *ṣāʿaq*) most often means to "cry out" (whether to God or man) for help, justice, or deliverance. But in several cases a prophet "cries out" to Yahweh with a specific complaint about some punishment that Yahweh has set in motion, attempting to turn Yahweh back from this undesirable course of action (e.g., Num 12:13; Ezek 9:8; 11:13).

Israel away from you today and will give it to your neighbor, who is better than you" (15:28). This statement obviously looks forward to the kingship of David, who will be anointed in the next chapter.

Then, in the last words he will ever speak to Saul this side of the grave, Samuel adds: "Moreover, the Everlasting One of Israel neither deceives nor repents, for he is not man that he should repent" (15:29). This is the lesson that the prophet learned during that long night of crying out to God. Yahweh's decision to give up on Saul is part of a single, overarching divine plan for Israel. There is nothing ad hoc or capricious about it. Viewed from *within* human temporality and the flow of history, however, this plan includes some abrupt twists and turns that may at first be difficult to accept as God's will. When Yahweh tells Samuel, "I repent that I have made Saul king," this is as much as to say, "this turn of events is my will, Samuel, and you need to accept it as such." Likewise, when the narrator tells us that "Yahweh repented of making Saul king over Israel" (15:35), he wants to reassure us that "this thing was from Yahweh." These two statements use the Hebrew *perfect tense* to indicate God's will according to "the very procession of things."[43] But Samuel's statement in verse 29 takes us outside the temporal flow for a moment, in order to view the matter from the side of God's eternity. Here the Hebrew *imperfect tense* is used with the negative adverb *lōʾ* in order to deny categorically that Yahweh *ever* repents; in other words, to affirm the immutability of the divine counsel.[44] The use of the otherwise-unattested divine title *nēṣaḥ yisrāʾēl*—"the Everlasting One of Israel"[45]—reinforces this eternal perspective. The author of 1 Samuel 15 skillfully plays these two types of affirmation off each other.[46]

43 The use of the perfect tense in vv. 11 and 35 might be analyzed as the "ingressive perfective." Yahweh has entered into the state of regretting that he ever made Saul king. See Bruce K. Waltke and Michael O'Connor, *An Introduction to Biblical Hebrew Syntax* (Winona Lake, Ind.: Eisenbrauns, 1990), 483 (§30.2.3b).

44 This use of the Hebrew imperfect, to express categorical denial, is the negative counterpart of the "habitual" imperfect. See Waltke and O'Connor, 506 (§31.3e).

45 This phrase is usually translated "the Glory of Israel" (RSV, NRSV, NABRE), primarily on the basis of 1 Chron 29:11, where *nēṣaḥ* is found between two words that mean "splendor" in a list of divine attributes. In dozens of other biblical passages, however, *nēṣaḥ* means something like "everlastingness" (e.g., Jer 15:18; Amos 1:11; Pss 13:2; 16:11; 74:3; Isa 34:10), just as it does in the Qumran Scrolls. P. Kyle McCarter Jr. therefore favors the translation "Israel's Everlasting One." *1 Samuel: A New Translation with Introduction, Notes & Commentary*, AB 8 (Garden City, N.Y.: Doubleday, 1980), 268.

46 According to McCarter, the "contradiction" between verses 11 and 29 is so "blatant" that we should probably regard the latter statement as "a late addition to the text . . . penned by a

In the words of Hans Urs von Balthasar, the Old Testament "gives the impression that God can change" when "a partial situation (partial, because Israel is journeying along its pilgrim path) is confronted with the totality of the [divine] plan," such that "refractions occur," whereas in fact, "the only thing to change is our perspective."[47]

CONCLUSION

In each of the first two narratives that we have examined, human sin threatens to thwart the divine plan, but Yahweh acts in mercy to preserve his original plan through the instrumentality of a man who has "found favor in his eyes."[48] In the first case, Yahweh institutes a covenant with Noah and all creation, and this covenant seems to take God's commitment to his original plan to a new level. Though sin is not yet dealt with as such, it is becoming clear that Yahweh will not allow sin to have the last word. The divine plan for creation will go forward on the new level of "covenant."

By the time we come to the second narrative, the covenant has advanced two key steps, through Yahweh's oath to the patriarchs and the giving of the law. While Moses obviously understands that Israel has broken the covenant by worshipping the golden calf, he does not flinch when Yahweh threatens to scrap his plan for Israel or at least to modify it significantly. Moses intercedes on the basis of Yahweh's long-term commitments, and the renewal of the covenant that takes place in Exodus 34 is accompanied by a deepened revelation of the divine name and character. Yahweh is a God of mercy and compassion, steadfast love and faithfulness. Through a history of fidelity to his own covenant, the Old Testament God is revealing, stage by stage, the truth that will later come to be understood in more properly metaphysical terms as "the immutability of his counsel" (τὸ ἀμετάθετον τῆς βουλῆς αὐτοῦ, Heb 6:17).

---

redactor to whom the suggestion of divine change of mind was unacceptable." *1 Samuel*, 268. Since nothing else in chapter 15 points to such a redactional layer, however, the validity of this hypothesis depends entirely upon the modern scholar's assumption that the two statements really are incompatible. This assumption, in turn, reflects a failure to appreciate the biblical author's capacity for literary sophistication and theological nuance.

47 Balthasar, *Dramatis Personae*, 279, 284.

48 On the parallels between Genesis 6–9 and Exodus 32–34, see R. W. L. Moberly, *At the Mountain of God: Story and Theology in Exodus 32–34*, Journal for the Study of the Old Testament Supplement Series 22 (Sheffield: JSOT Press, 1983), 91–92.

In 1 Samuel 15, this dimension of divine mercy and the progress of the covenant is less immediately apparent but present nonetheless. Here it is helpful to note that the categorical statement about divine nonrepentance in verse 29 immediately follows upon the prophetic announcement that Yahweh will give the kingship to Saul's "neighbor, who is better than [him]." This is our first hint that Yahweh will not be choosing one king after another, only to repent of choosing them. He has found David, son of Jesse, "a man after his own heart" (13:14), and with this man and his descendants he will establish an irrevocable covenant based on his own steadfast love.[49]

None of this betokens an inclination on God's part to ignore or merely to remit human sin. On the contrary, while revealing his steadfast love and mercy, Yahweh is concurrently revealing, step by step, that he has a plan to deal definitively with the problem of sin. As the covenant goes forward, he will continue to punish and chastise Israel, in particular the house of David, for their infidelities, but he will never withdraw his steadfast love (2 Sam 7:14–15; Ps 89:31–34). Ultimately, the unique priestly offering that will take away sin and impart the grace of the new covenant will be revealed in fulfillment of the promises made to the patriarchs, the people of Israel, and the house of David, and in accord with a single master plan. In each generation, on the day when the new Davidic king took the throne in place of his father, he was addressed with this ancient oracle: "Yahweh has sworn, and he will not repent: You are a priest forever, in the order of Melchizedek" (Ps 110:4). As Thomas Aquinas teaches us, "Whenever the Lord swears something under oath it is a prophecy of predestination, which is indicative of the divine counsel; and such a promise is utterly immutable."[50]

49 2 Sam 7:11–16; 23:5; Ps 89:20–38.

50 Aquinas, *In Heb.*, c. 6, lect. 4. Translation: Aquinas, *Commentary on the Epistle to the Hebrews*, trans. Baer, 138.

CHAPTER THREE

Two Trajectories in the Reception of *Dei Verbum*

In a 2012 essay on the Dogmatic Constitution on Divine Revelation *Dei Verbum*, Pauline Viviano, a longtime member of the Catholic Biblical Association, reminisces about "those heady exciting post-Vatican II days" when she was a graduate student and scholars such as Raymond E. Brown, SS (1928–1998), Joseph A. Fitzmyer, SJ (1920–2016), and Roland E. Murphy, OCarm (1917–2002), were in their prime. For Viviano, the significance of *Dei Verbum* lies first and foremost in the ecclesiastical sanction it gave to historical-critical interpretation of the Bible.[1] She recounts how, over the years, she has found most students and parish groups receptive to historical-critical exegesis, but also how she has become gradually aware of an undercurrent of opposition to modern methods of exegesis within Catholicism. At first, "these attacks were few and far between," but during the pontificate of Benedict XVI there was a "backlash against Vatican II," and "fundamentalism" made inroads into the Catholic Church.[2]

Strikingly, the only author whom Viviano identifies for his involvement in this backlash is Pope Benedict himself. She finds fault in particular with the exegetical approach taken in the multivolume *Jesus of Nazareth*, where the pope first declares the historical-critical method "indispensable" but then goes on to apply to the Gospels an exegetical procedure that amounts to "a return to the spiritual interpretation of the early church fathers which," according to Viviano, "renders the contributions of historical-critical

1 Pauline A. Viviano, "Fighting Biblical Fundamentalism," in *Vatican II: 50 Personal Stories*, ed. William Madges and Michael J. Daley (Maryknoll, N.Y.: Orbis Books, 2012), 142.

2 Viviano, 142.

scholarship null and void, and, thus, dispensable."[3] Viviano closes her essay with the wish that Catholic biblical scholars will "remain faithful to the spirit of Vatican II."[4]

Viviano's reading of Benedict's work is inaccurate and unfair. She is, of course, within her rights to disagree with his exegetical and hermeneutical opinions, particularly in the case of *Jesus of Nazareth*, which claims no magisterial authority. As the pope writes in the foreword to the first volume, "everyone is free, then, to contradict me."[5] It is inaccurate, however, to say that his exegesis of the Gospels renders historical-critical scholarship null and void. Indeed, it would be difficult to find a single page in any of the volumes of *Jesus of Nazareth* that does not reflect the profound influence of modern biblical scholarship. When Benedict does occasionally draw elements of patristic exegesis into his argument, they are carefully woven into an interpretive framework that is well informed by historical-critical research.

The exegetical approach on display in *Jesus of Nazareth* represents an attempt to put into practice a hermeneutic that Joseph Ratzinger developed over the course of nearly half a century. This hermeneutic involves purifying the historical-critical method of its positivism so that it can be of service to a deeper rationality, the sort of rationality that is truly commensurate with an inspired text and divinely revealed realities. As Pope Benedict explains, biblical scholarship must "see itself once again as a theological discipline, without abandoning its historical character. It must learn that the positivistic hermeneutic on which it has been based does not constitute the only valid and definitively evolved rational approach; rather it constitutes a specific and historically conditioned form of rationality that is both open to correction and completion and in need of it."[6] The crucial insight here is that the historical-critical method is itself historically conditioned and thus cannot be the final measure of the historical witnesses to divine revelation. It has a vital contribution to make, to be sure, but it can only fully do so when it has been transformed by the light of faith and brought into a new

3 Viviano, 143. Cf. Joseph Ratzinger, *Jesus of Nazareth: From the Baptism in the Jordan to the Transfiguration*, trans. Adrian J. Walker (New York: Doubleday, 2007), xv. Viviano offers a similar criticism of Benedict's Post-Synodal Apostolic Exhortation *Verbum Domini*, in "Fighting Biblical Fundamentalism," 143.

4 Viviano, 143.

5 Ratzinger, *Jesus of Nazareth: From the Baptism*, xxiv.

6 Ratzinger, *Jesus of Nazareth: Holy Week*, xiv–xv.

hermeneutical synthesis with the Church's ancient exegetical tradition. Then, "the great insights of patristic exegesis will be able to yield their fruit once more in a new context."[7]

It is with this last point in particular that Viviano takes issue, for she appears to consider patristic exegesis incompatible with the historical-critical method. This position reflects the fact that Viviano belongs to a Catholic exegetical school that has developed its own hermeneutic over the same half century. According to this school, the historical-critical method has simply transcended precritical exegesis and stands in no need of essential modification. It can be enhanced and supplemented by still more modern methodologies, such as narrative criticism or sociological criticism, but it remains the inviolable foundation for Catholic biblical interpretation and the measure by which all other approaches are to be assessed. As for the spiritual or allegorical exegesis practiced by the Church Fathers, it served a pastoral function in an age that did not yet enjoy the benefits of the modern method, but any attempt to revive it for our own day would be retrogressive.[8]

These two approaches reflect two different trajectories in the reception of *Dei Verbum*. Dr. Viviano represents what may be called the Brown-Fitzmyer trajectory, after its two most prominent spokesmen. According to this school of thought, self-described "centrist" Catholic biblical scholars have been carrying out the mandate of *Dei Verbum* successfully for decades by using the historical-critical method "responsibly."[9] According to the Ratzinger-Benedict trajectory, on the other hand, the historical-critical method must be taken up into a new hermeneutical synthesis if we are truly to put into practice the exegetical principles of *Dei Verbum*. In the opinion of Pope Benedict, this is "a task that unfortunately has scarcely been attempted thus far."[10]

The conflicting claims here are quite extraordinary. According to Benedict, two generations of Catholic biblical scholars, however much potentially valuable research they have produced, have scarcely begun to put into practice the principles of *Dei Verbum*, all the while thinking that they have.

7 Ratzinger, xv.

8 Pauline A. Viviano, "The Senses of Scripture," in *The Word of God in the Life and Mission of the Church: Celebrating the Catechetical Year 2008–2009* (Washington, D.C.: United States Conference of Catholic Bishops, 2008), 2.

9 Raymond E. Brown, SS, Joseph A. Fitzmyer, SJ, and Roland E. Murphy, OCarm, eds., *The New Jerome Biblical Commentary* (Englewood Cliffs, N.J.: Prentice Hall, 1990), 1168 (*NJBC* 72:9); Raymond E. Brown, SS, *Biblical Exegesis and Church Doctrine* (Mahwah, N.J.: Paulist, 1985), 8.

10 Ratzinger, *Jesus of Nazareth: Holy Week*, xv.

Pauline Viviano's countercharge is no less remarkable: Joseph Ratzinger—*peritus* at the council, coauthor of a major commentary on *Dei Verbum*, President of the Pontifical Biblical Commission for twenty-four years, and Supreme Pontiff for nearly eight years—has been at the center of a dangerous backlash against Vatican II and encourages a method of exegesis that verges on fundamentalism.[11]

At stake here is the correct interpretation of *Dei Verbum* and the implementation of its prophetic vision for the life of the Church. What does *Dei Verbum* teach about the nature of divine revelation and the relationship between Scripture and Tradition, and what implications does this teaching have for Catholic biblical hermeneutics? Does the historical-critical method require any essential modification if it is to be incorporated into a comprehensive theological-ecclesial approach to exegesis? And what value, if any, does the patristic-medieval exegetical tradition hold for Catholic exegesis and theology in the twenty-first century?

To begin to tease out answers to these questions I shall trace the two trajectories through the postconciliar period and offer a running commentary and critique, proceeding in the following five steps. First, I look at two works of Fr. Ratzinger from the 1960s, in which he expounds *Dei Verbum*'s teaching on revelation per se and Sacred Tradition, two aspects of the dogmatic constitution that the council fathers considered central but which Catholic biblical scholars tend to neglect insofar as they view *Dei Verbum* as "the document on Scripture." Second, I turn to two relatively early works of Fr. Brown in which he directly addresses the topic of biblical hermeneutics and clarifies his own understanding of the place of historical-critical exegesis in the life of the Church. Third, the hinge of my study is a brief account of the 1988 Erasmus Lecture colloquium, at which Cardinal Ratzinger issued his call for a hermeneutical synthesis of the ancient and modern approaches to Scripture and Fr. Brown expressed his strong objections to this proposal. Fourth, I consider the hermeneutical works of Fr. Fitzmyer, who after the Erasmus Lecture took up the hermeneutical mantle from Brown and modified the latter's more problematic proposals in ways that brought him a little closer to the position of Ratzinger. Fifth, I conclude with a close reading of *Dei Verbum* 12, to determine whether or not that key passage adumbrates the sort of hermeneutical synthesis that Ratzinger envisioned.

11 While Viviano does not explicitly accuse Benedict of "fundamentalism," he is the only person whom she singles out for criticism in an essay entitled "Fighting Biblical Fundamentalism."

Before proceeding with this agenda, however, I wish to clarify the rationale for my choice of subject matter. I have chosen to focus on the Brown-Fitzmyer and Ratzinger-Benedict trajectories because they are influential, clearly articulated, and take us to the heart of the interpretation of *Dei Verbum*, not because I suppose them to be the only significant trajectories. In terms of the reception of *Dei Verbum*, one could identify influential Catholic scholars and schools of thought both to the "right" of Ratzinger and to the "left" of Brown.[12] With regard to the former, Viviano is not mistaken to suppose that from the start there have been pockets of conservative resistance to the full vision of *Dei Verbum* and that such resistance has increased in recent years. Her error lies in associating Pope Benedict's approach to exegesis with this resistance.[13] With regard to the latter, Brown gloried in the label "centrist" because he was criticized not only by traditional Catholics, who found him too liberal, but also by progressive Catholics, who found him too conservative. But whereas Brown's public disagreements with more liberal scholars generally remained substantive and civil, even if they included some sharply worded exchanges, criticism from the far right was frequently ill-informed, reactionary, and mean-spirited.[14] I have no desire to add to that injustice. Moreover, while conservative criticism of Brown has generally focused on

12 For example, an approach to *Dei Verbum* that is decidedly more conservative than Ratzinger's is found in the works of Scott W. Hahn, who has succeeded Brown as the most influential Catholic biblical scholar in North America. Hahn's disproportionate focus on the phrase "without error" in *Dei Verbum* 11—and the implicit equation between "truth" and "factual accuracy" whereby he interprets that passage ("For the Sake of Our Salvation: The Truth and Humility of God's Word," *Letter & Spirit* 6 [2010]: 21–45, at 33)—tends to rule out of court the sort of difficult questions regarding the relationship between "word" and "event" that Ratzinger considers so essential to the quest for a new hermeneutical synthesis. See chapter 6 in this volume. An example of the reception of *Dei Verbum* that is far more radical than Brown's is found in the feminist hermeneutics of the influential Catholic scholar Elisabeth Schüssler Fiorenza, who proposes that the Bible is no longer to be regarded as an authoritative "source" of revelation but as a "resource" for feminism. "Women's experience in their struggle for liberation" replaces the Bible as the "normative authority" and starting point for theology. Indeed, the very notion that the Bible is the word of God is "an archetypal oppressive myth that must be rejected." *Bread Not Stone: The Challenge of Feminist Biblical Interpretation* (Boston: Beacon, 1984), 14, 13, 10.

13 Viviano may have been influenced in this regard by the fact that Scott Hahn had recently devoted an entire book to Pope Benedict's "biblical theology," in which he emphasizes points of ostensible commonality with his own approach. Scott W. Hahn, *Covenant and Communion: The Biblical Theology of Pope Benedict XVI* (Grand Rapids: Brazos, 2009).

14 For examples of these two tendencies, see Senior, *Raymond E. Brown*, 190–92 and 206–7, respectively.

certain of his exegetical conclusions, I wish to examine the hermeneutical foundation of his work as he himself presents it. Key aspects of this hermeneutic, as both Ratzinger and Fitzmyer seem to have recognized, are deeply problematic inasmuch as they cut directly against the grain of *Dei Verbum*. The corrective offered by Fitzmyer, though not entirely successful, represents a significant improvement and helps to bring into focus some of the most basic issues involved in the development of an authentically ecclesial exegesis.

TWO EARLY WORKS OF JOSEPH RATZINGER

In June of 1963, the month that saw the death of Pope John XXIII and the election of Pope Paul VI, Fr. Joseph Ratzinger assumed the Chair of Dogmatic Theology and History of Dogma at the University of Münster and delivered an inaugural lecture on "Revelation and Tradition."[15] This lecture gives us a good feel for the perspective that the young *peritus* would soon bring to his work at the ecumenical council. The thesis of the inaugural lecture is that the Western Church's preoccupation since the Reformation with the question of the material sufficiency (or insufficiency) of Scripture amounts to "lingering over a relatively superficial symptom" of a much deeper issue—namely, "the way the word of revelation uttered in Christ remains present in history and comes to man."[16]

Drawing on an insight of Karl Barth, Ratzinger explains that revelation in the proper sense is to be located not merely in texts and meanings, but in extratextual realities—in the whole historical economy of words and deeds by which God has revealed himself, and above all in the person and event of Jesus Christ. Revelation is a reality to which Scripture bears witness, and therefore it cannot simply be identified with Scripture or the meaning of Scripture.[17] In the definitive sense, Jesus Christ himself *is* revelation, and therefore only Christ is "sufficient."[18] Once this is clearly understood, and only then, can we begin to consider how revelation is *made present* in

15 Karl Rahner and Joseph Ratzinger, *Revelation and Tradition*, trans. W. J. O'Hara, Quaestiones Disputatae 17 (New York: Herder & Herder, 1966), 26–49; here cited from Joseph Ratzinger (Pope Benedict XVI), *God's Word: Scripture—Tradition—Office*, trans. Henry Taylor (San Francisco: Ignatius, 2008), 41–67.

16 Ratzinger, *God's Word*, 50, 41.

17 Ratzinger, 51–52.

18 Ratzinger, 56.

Scripture and Tradition, whereas a failure to grasp this point will inevitably reduce the content of revelation to some combination of the merely noetic and the merely mystical, with disastrous consequences for the whole quest for a proper biblical hermeneutic.

Next, Ratzinger turns to the question of Tradition. He notes that it is not simply doctrines but "the entire mystery of Christ's presence" that is transmitted in Tradition.[19] He also emphasizes the pneumatological and hermeneutical aspects of Tradition. The Holy Spirit makes the living Christ present to the Church in such a way that Tradition is not merely the Spirit-guided interpretation of texts or ideas, but the Church's ongoing assimilation of the mystery of the person and event of Christ through various interconnected modalities of presence, such as Scripture, proclamation, sacraments, and works of charity.[20] The Spirit's "interpretation" of the mystery of Christ in the life of the Church, moreover, parallels Christ's own interpretation of the economy of the Old Testament during his life on earth.[21]

In this connection, Ratzinger sketches out a helpful schema for viewing the relationship between the Old and New Testaments, as well as the relationship between Scripture and Tradition, in light of the historical perspective opened by modern scholarship. Historical-critical exegesis discloses "an Old Testament theology of the Old Testament" by allowing us to read Israel's sacred writings in their historical context and on their own terms, and we discover that already within the Old Testament there are "overlapping layers" of interpretation, because "old texts are reread and reinterpreted in the light of new events."[22] Alongside this intra-Old Testament theology, there is "a New Testament theology of the Old Testament," which, while it is distinct from the former, continues its inner dynamic on a new level by offering a new interpretation of God's self-revelation to Israel in light of the Christ event.[23] In parallel fashion, historical-critical research discloses both "a New Testament theology of the New Testament," by permitting us to read the writings of the apostolic age in their historical context and on their own terms, and a distinct "ecclesial theology of the New Testament"—that is, the interpretation of these same texts provided by ecclesial Tradition. The latter

19 Ratzinger, 63.

20 Ratzinger, 58.

21 Ratzinger, 65.

22 Ratzinger, 60.

23 Ratzinger, 60–61.

is certainly not identical with the former, but neither is it the result of the imposition of an extrinsic principle (such as "Hellenism"). Historical-critical exegesis itself shows us that "the ecclesial process of interpreting what has been handed down" begins within the New Testament itself, with the result that there is an organic connection between intra-New Testament theology and ecclesial Tradition.[24]

Two remarks about this schema are in order. First, it is crucial to view it in light of Ratzinger's most basic point—namely, that revelation per se is to be located in extratextual realities, not in texts and meanings. Otherwise, we risk reducing the deep levels of continuity between Old Testament and New Testament, and between Scripture and Tradition, to an "intertextual hermeneutic" that is merely the product of the ancients' literary-religious imagination and ideology. Second, we should note how, in this early work of systematic theology, Ratzinger views the potentially unsettling perspectives opened by historical-critical scholarship not as a threat but as an opportunity to deepen our understanding of the mystery of the faith.

Shortly after the close of the council, Ratzinger coauthored a major commentary on *Dei Verbum* with fellow *periti* Alois Grillmeier, SJ, and Béda Rigaux, OFM.[25] For present purposes, we must confine ourselves to a few of Ratzinger's keenest observations bearing on the historical-theological background of the dogmatic constitution, the proper hermeneutic for understanding its relationship to the teaching of earlier ecumenical councils, and its distinctive concept of divine revelation and Tradition.

With regard to the dogmatic constitution's background, Ratzinger identifies three catalysts in the preconciliar period that led to *Dei Verbum*. The first of these is a renewed theology of Tradition, which had roots in the thought of Johann Adam Möhler, John Henry Newman, and Maurice Blondel, and which crystalized in the works of Yves Congar just prior to the council.[26] As we shall see, this enrichment of the theology of Tradition is of vital importance for a proper understanding of *Dei Verbum*. The second

24 Ratzinger, 61–62.

25 Joseph Ratzinger, Alois Grillmeier, SJ, and Béda Rigaux, OFM, "Dogmatic Constitution on Divine Revelation," in *Commentary on the Documents of Vatican II*, vol. 3, *Declaration on the Relationship of the Church to Non-Christian Religions, Dogmatic Constitution on Divine Revelation, Decree on the Apostolate of the Laity*, ed. Herbert Vorgrimler (New York: Herder & Herder, 1969), 155–272. Hereafter cited as *Commentary*. Except were otherwise indicated, the sections cited below were authored by Ratzinger.

26 Ratzinger, *Commentary*, 155–57, 184.

catalyst is the impact of the historical-critical method on Catholic biblical scholarship. Ratzinger views the historical-critical method quite positively, but he recognizes that its proper integration into ecclesial exegesis and theology presents a real "theological problem" to which much careful work must be devoted.[27] The third catalyst is "the biblical movement," which had already "brought about a . . . new attitude to Scripture" in the Catholic world.[28] Since Ratzinger treats the biblical movement as a third catalyst, distinct from the second, he obviously does not think that historical-critical exegesis deserves all the credit for this enrichment of Catholic life and thought. He views the biblical movement as a much broader phenomenon, closely interwoven with the patristic movement, the liturgical movement, and the ecumenical movement. His perspective on the preconciliar matrix of *Dei Verbum* is thus wider and richer than those of Brown and Fitzmyer, who tend to ignore the first catalyst altogether, while collapsing the third into the second.[29] In other words, for Brown and Fitzmyer the historical-critical method is *the* catalyst for *Dei Verbum*, and *Dei Verbum* is essentially an endorsement of the historical-critical method.

On the basis of later statements made by Ratzinger, we may identify three basic ways to interpret the documents of Vatican II and to understand their relationship to the teaching of earlier ecumenical councils: (1) a hermeneutic of rupture and open-ended progress, (2) a hermeneutic of dynamic but faithful continuity, or (3) a hermeneutic of minimalism and ecclesiastical positivism.[30] In the case of *Dei Verbum*, the question of the proper hermeneutic for

27 Ratzinger, 157–58.

28 Ratzinger, 158–59.

29 See Joseph A. Fitzmyer, SJ, *The Interpretation of Scripture: In Defense of the Historical Critical Method* (New York: Paulist, 2008), 3–6; and Raymond E. Brown, SS, *The Critical Meaning of the Bible* (New York: Paulist, 1981), ix.

30 Near the beginning of his "Christmas Address to the Roman Curia," December 22, 2005, Pope Benedict briefly discussed "two contrary hermeneutics" in the reception and implementation of the documents of Vatican II, one of "discontinuity and rupture," the other of "continuity" and "reform." I have added the third hermeneutic on the basis of Cardinal Ratzinger's references to "a merely positivistic and rigid ecclesiasticism" and "ecclesiastical positivism" at the Erasmus Lecture conference. Ratzinger, "Biblical Interpretation in Crisis," 6; Stallsworth, "Story of an Encounter," 118. An example of this third hermeneutic is Scott Hahn's insistence that, because a footnote to *Dei Verbum* 11 cites the section of Leo XIII's encyclical that contains the statement about "the dictation of the Holy Spirit" excluding error from the biblical text "absolutely" (*Providentissimus Deus*, Denz. 3292), the phrase *sine errore* ("without error") in *Dei Verbum* 11 must mean no more and no less than Leo's statement (Hahn, "For the Sake of Our Salvation," 33–37). While Hahn grants that *Dei Verbum* 11 includes "a new emphasis on

interpreting the conciliar documents merges in a striking fashion with the actual doctrinal content of the document in question. In other words, how one interprets the documents will depend in large measure on one's prior understanding of "divine revelation and its transmission" in the life of the Church (no. 1).[31] Not surprisingly, Ratzinger embraces the second of the three hermeneutical options, dynamic but faithful continuity. His reading of *Dei Verbum* is informed by a diachronic analysis of the conciliar process that produced it, but it is at the same time guided by the conviction that the Holy Spirit assures both vitality within the Tradition and essential fidelity to it. The text of *Dei Verbum* is "the result of many compromises," Ratzinger explains, but it is not merely that. The dogmatic constitution "combines fidelity to ... tradition with an affirmation of critical scholarship, thus opening ... a path that faith may follow into the world of today."[32] The council fathers did not abandon the teaching of Trent or Vatican I, but neither did they "mummify" it. True fidelity to Tradition requires "a constantly renewed appropriation."[33] This exemplary hermeneutic has characterized Ratzinger's reception of *Dei Verbum* throughout his career, from *peritus* to pontiff.

According to Ratzinger, the great achievement of *Dei Verbum*, above and beyond the two previous ecumenical councils, is to present a more comprehensive and dynamic concept of divine revelation. For example, where the fathers of Vatican I had spoken of God's revelation of "himself and the eternal decrees of his will," the fathers of Vatican II had chosen the phrase "himself and the mystery [*sacramentum*] of his will."[34] Ratzinger explains: "Instead of the legalistic view that sees revelation largely as the issuing of divine decrees," *Dei Verbum* gives us a more "sacramental view, which sees law and grace, [and] word and deed ... within the one comprehensive unity of the mystery."[35]

---

the Bible's salvific purpose" (36), he rejects any notion that the conciliar formulation invites further reflection on what constitutes "error," especially if that reflection includes inductive considerations drawn from exegesis or genre analysis of biblical texts (34). Cf. Scott W. Hahn, *Letter and Spirit: From Written Text to Living Word in the Liturgy* (New York: Doubleday, 2005), 187–89n14.

31 Translations of passages from *Dei Verbum* are my own.

32 Ratzinger, *Commentary*, 164.

33 Ratzinger, 164–65.

34 Ratzinger, 171. Cf. *Dei Filius* 2; *Dei Verbum* 2.

35 Ratzinger, *Commentary*, 171.

Dei Verbum's salvation-historical view of the divine economy, with the person and event of Jesus Christ as its centerpiece, is able to take positive account of the gradual theological development that historical-critical scholarship has made undeniably manifest both within the biblical period and within ecclesial Tradition. God's gradual revelation to Israel through the prophets is pedagogy and preparation for his definitive self-revelation in Christ, while the history of the Church entails a gradual unfolding and assimilation of this mystery, to culminate in the parousia. The Christ event is thus both "end" and "beginning." As the centerpiece in God's master plan, it is the τέλος ("end, goal") toward which ancient Israel's history builds and the ἀρχή ("beginning, principle") from which the Church's history unfolds. Theological and doctrinal development within the Church "cannot surpass what has taken place in Christ, but it must attempt to catch up with it gradually."[36] Ratzinger's notion of "catching up" guards against any misreading of *Dei Verbum* 8—"Tradition makes progress . . . understanding grows . . . the Church advances" (*Traditio proficit . . . crescit perceptio . . . Ecclesia tendit*)—in terms of modernistic evolutionism or ecclesiopolitical "progress."

At the same time, this more comprehensive and dynamic concept of revelation freed the council fathers from a narrow intellectualism or verbalism. Ratzinger writes:

> The point is certainly not to play off the theology of salvation history against word theology, but in place of a narrowly doctrinal conception of revelation, as had been expressed in the Tridentine word theology, to open up a comprehensive view of the real character of revelation, which—precisely because it is concerned with the whole man—is founded not only in the word that Christ preached, but in the whole of the living experience of his person, thus embracing what is said and what is unsaid, what the Apostles in their turn are not able to express fully in words, but which is found in the whole reality of the Christian existence of which they speak, far transcending the framework of what has been explicitly formulated in words.[37]

Properly understood, none of this diminishes the intellectual character of the act of faith or the importance of verbal proclamation and written dogma. Rather, it enhances these elements by placing them within a fuller account

36 Ratzinger, 175.

37 Ratzinger, 182.

of revelation. In the last analysis, there can be no dualism of word and event when the entire economy of revelation receives its definitive recapitulation through the personal entrance of the Logos into creation and history.[38]

In this way *Dei Verbum* "provides an essentially new starting-point for the question of tradition," one which was urgently needed in light of "our deeper knowledge of the problem of historical understanding."[39] Ratzinger notes that, unlike their forebears at Vatican I, the fathers of Vatican II chose not to adopt Vincent of Lérins's overly sharp distinction between understanding and dogma—or, together with it, his attempt to locate the constancy of the faith within dogmatic formulations as such—for this no longer seemed the proper way to approach the whole problem of how to define the authentic content of Tradition and defend its "historical identity and continuity."[40] I may venture to add that, properly understood, *Dei Verbum*'s notion of "the vivifying presence of Tradition" (no. 8), building on the comprehensive, dynamic, and Christocentric concept of revelation described above, is the antidote to two types of positivism: (1) a historicism that, merely by amassing incontrovertible evidence of doctrinal development, appears to refute the existence of anything that can meaningfully be called *depositum fidei*, and (2) an ecclesiastical positivism that resorts to contrived and implausible harmonization in order to defend the immutability of Catholic dogma.

It is only from this vantage point, moreover, that we can begin to appreciate why the dogmatic constitution, not once but twice, commends "the study of the holy Fathers" precisely in the context of fostering the Church's advance toward a more profound understanding and actualization of Sacred Scripture (nos. 8 and 23). Ratzinger readily recognizes the implications here for the whole question of how best to integrate modern biblical scholarship into ecclesial exegesis and theology: "To separate Scripture from the total tradition of the Church leads either to biblicism or modernism or both. For, given the way the human mind works, it would not result in a more immediate relation to Scripture, but would rather allow itself to be fitted into one's own particular intellectual tradition."[41] In other words, if one neglects or rejects

38 Ratzinger, 177.

39 Ratzinger, 181, 188.

40 Ratzinger, 187. Cf. Vincent of Lérins, *Commonitorium* 23 (PL 50:668a); *Dei Filius* 4 (Denz. 3020). Ratzinger mistakenly speaks as if the fathers of Trent had also cited Vincent's formula. He may be thinking of Pius IX's Bull *Ineffabilis Deus* (Denz. 2802).

41 Ratzinger, *Commentary*, 267.

Tradition as the proper milieu for biblical interpretation, one will inevitably replace it, consciously or unconsciously, with some other hermeneutic or philosophy. Therefore, the notion that one can employ the historical-critical method in a "neutral" manner, without presuppositions, is a chimera. Can one find a more succinct and incisive diagnosis of the essential failure of modern biblical scholarship?

THE HERMENEUTICS OF RAYMOND BROWN

While Ratzinger, Grillmeier, and Rigaux were working on their commentary, Fathers Raymond Brown, Joseph Fitzmyer, and Roland Murphy were busy producing a volume that would sell hundreds of thousands of copies and have a massive impact on how *Dei Verbum* would be received throughout the English-speaking world and beyond. For two generations of Catholic theology students and seminarians *The Jerome Biblical Commentary* (1968), or its successor *The New Jerome Biblical Commentary* (1990), has been required reading and, more importantly, a vivid symbol of the implementation of *Dei Verbum* by centrist biblical scholars.[42] Of particular interest for present purposes is Fr. Brown's 1968 topical article on "Hermeneutics," which is largely occupied with the question of the "literal" and "more-than-literal" senses of Scripture.[43]

Here, Brown describes the history of Christian biblical interpretation as a long struggle to the death between allegorical and literal exegesis. The former dominated the patristic period and "ran riot" through much of the Middle Ages. Over the centuries, schools that favored the literal sense and developed scholarly tools for discovering it occasionally "rose to the surface like islands in the sea" only to be swamped by the returning tide of allegorical exegesis, until the rise of the historical-critical method and the final "triumph" of literal exegesis in the nineteenth and twentieth centuries.[44] In *Dei Verbum* "Vatican II gave its approval to biblical criticism," and Catholic biblical scholarship finally came of age.[45] Brown acknowledges that some

42 Raymond E. Brown, SS, Joseph A. Fitzmyer, SJ, and Roland E. Murphy, OCarm, eds., *The Jerome Biblical Commentary* (Englewood Cliffs, N.J.: Prentice Hall, 1968). Cited as *JBC* with chapter and section number(s).

43 *JBC* 71:1–102.

44 *JBC* 71:37–45.

45 *JBC* 71:46.

allegorical and typological exegesis of the patristic period was relatively "sober" and restrained, but he adamantly opposes any attempt to revive the "symbolic exegesis" of the Church Fathers for our own time. The real value of spiritual exegesis in the precritical period was that it "let the Scriptures speak to a contemporary situation." We should attempt to do this too, but "in a truly modern way," not by imitating a symbolism that is no longer meaningful.[46]

This raises the question of what sort of "more-than-literal" exegesis, if any, might be valid for our day. Brown mentions in passing Krister Stendahl's distinction between what the biblical text "meant" in its original historical context and what the text "means" to believers today. Historical criticism gives us access to the former but cannot by itself disclose the latter.[47] This distinction between *meant* and *means* was to become increasingly important to Brown's own approach over the next couple decades.

In the 1968 version of "Hermeneutics," Brown devotes fifteen paragraphs to the so-called *sensus plenior*, the topic of his 1955 dissertation.[48] This "fuller meaning" of Scripture is "intended by God but not clearly intended by the human author" and thus takes us beyond the realm of what historical-critical interpretation can provide access to. The *sensus plenior* emerges when the Old Testament is read by the New Testament authors in light of the "further revelation" that they enjoy in Christ, or when the words of either testament are read by the Church's dogmatic tradition in light of "development in the understanding of revelation."[49] There is a tacit acknowledgement here that the historical-critical method is unable by itself to deal with either the problem of the relationship between Old Testament and New Testament or the closely related problem of the relationship between Scripture and Tradition. Specifically, it cannot justify in terms of "literal sense" the way the New Testament authors interpret the Old Testament, or the way the liturgical, theological, and dogmatic tradition interprets either testament. Hence, the need for some "more-than-literal" sense.

Brown strives mightily to put his theory on an objective footing by proposing criteria for distinguishing between real instances of *sensus plenior* and cases of mere "accommodation" (i.e., transposing a biblical text into

46 *JBC* 71:47.

47 *JBC* 71:49. Cf. Krister Stendhal, "Biblical Theology, Contemporary," in *IDB* 1:418–32.

48 *JBC* 71:56–70. Cf. Raymond E. Brown, SS, *The Sensus Plenior of Sacred Scripture* (Baltimore: St. Mary's University, 1955).

49 *JBC* 71:57.

a foreign context for illustrative or rhetorical effect), insisting that there must be "homogeneity" between the *sensus plenior* and the literal sense *as determined by historical-critical exegesis*. But the whole discussion only demonstrates how impossible it is to do this, at least within the hermeneutical framework that Brown has adopted. According to Brown, we must look to the New Testament authors, the Church Fathers, and magisterial pronouncements for authentic instances of the *sensus plenior*, but even such authorities are not decisive, since all of the above frequently indulge in accommodation as well. Indeed, in Brown's opinion "the majority" of the New Testament's citations of the Old Testament and "the overwhelming majority of the liturgical and patristic citations of Scripture" do not meet the criteria for a "valid" *sensus plenior*.[50] At this point one begins to wonder whether a theory that yields such meager results is worth the trouble. Apparently Brown wondered too, for in the 1990 version of "Hermeneutics" the treatment of the *sensus plenior* would be reduced to three paragraphs.[51]

The failure of the *sensus plenior*, and of Brown's whole quest for a "more-than-literal" sense that is in real continuity with the literal sense, lies in large part in his quasi-intellectualist view of revelation, a view that runs very much against the grain of *Dei Verbum*. Throughout the 1968 version of "Hermeneutics" Brown speaks of revelation in terms of "meanings" that are intended by the human author or God, or both, and are able to be discovered in the words of Scripture. His thinking about revelation seems virtually untouched by *Dei Verbum*'s teaching that the economy of revelation "is realized in deeds and words intrinsically interconnected" (no. 2) and that Jesus Christ "perfected revelation by fulfilling it through his whole presence and self-manifestation" (no. 4).

If, therefore, we wish to discern the deep continuity between what the Bible "meant" and what it "means," we must view Scripture as a mode of presence, not merely as a container of encoded "meanings." According to *Dei Verbum*, Scripture must be read "together with Sacred Tradition" (no. 24)—that is, within the whole mystery by which "the Church, in her doctrine, life and worship, perpetuates and transmits to all generations all that she herself is, all that she believes" (no. 8). Read this way, Scripture makes present not simply "meanings" but realities, the deeds and words by which God has revealed himself in history—above all, in the person and event of Jesus Christ. As we have seen, by 1963 Fr. Ratzinger already recognized that

50 *JBC* 71:63–65.

51 *NJBC* 71:49–51.

what was most fundamentally at issue in the council fathers' deliberations over *Dei Verbum*, and what had been at issue in the Western Church since the Reformation, was the question of *how* God's definitive self-revelation in Christ remains present throughout the Church's history.[52] Unless we address this issue squarely and bring the resources of the entire philosophical and theological tradition to bear upon it, we have no chance of rendering modern biblical scholarship theologically and spiritually fruitful, no chance of making it serviceable to the word of God.

The problems that can already be seen budding in the 1968 version of "Hermeneutics" are in full bloom in Brown's 1981 book, *The Critical Meaning of the Bible*, a remarkable little volume in which he stakes out what he takes to be an unassailable and exclusive claim for historical-critical exegesis in the life of the Church. Brown's first task is to explain what it means to call the Bible "the word of God." He informs us at the outset that in tackling this important question he will have no recourse to philosophy, to historical theology, or to systematic theology. Instead, he will confine himself to "an outlook gained from biblical criticism."[53] This a priori orientation to the question, which Brown makes no attempt to justify, puts him in an enviable position. He can profess that he "fully accept[s] the Roman Catholic doctrine of the Bible as the word of God" while eschewing any consideration of what twenty centuries of Fathers, doctors, popes, councils, and ordinary Christians have understood that doctrine to mean.[54] In other words, he does not mind *calling* the Bible "the word of God," so long as he is free to "rethink critically" how that phrase is to be understood, in effect redefining it from his chosen vantage point.[55]

According to Brown, the phrase "word of God" cannot mean a word that God has spoken or continues to speak, for "God does not speak." In fact, "technically God does not think, has never had an idea, and makes no judgments."[56] The phrase "word of God," accordingly, has two parts. "Word" refers to the strictly human dimension of Scripture, and "of God" refers to the divine dimension. To call the Bible "the word of God in human words" is therefore "tautological," since the phrase "word of God" by itself already

52 Ratzinger, *God's Word*, 41.

53 Brown, *Critical Meaning* (see n. 29 above), 5.

54 Brown, 3, 5.

55 Brown, 2.

56 Brown, 3.

implies that the words of Scripture are human words—strictly human words. This is self-evidently the case since "only human beings use words."[57]

At the same time, Brown does not deny to God all power to communicate, nor does he remove divine communication entirely from the Bible. In fact, while rejecting the formulation "word of God in human words," Brown himself calls the Bible "a divine communication in human words."[58] So, what is the difference? Initially it appears that Brown is merely trying to get away from a crassly verbal model of revelation and a "dictation" model of biblical inspiration. "God did not actually speak words (external or internal)" to the prophets or the other authors of Scripture, he informs us.[59] But at this point—just where many theologians would affirm that phrases such as "word of God" and "God spoke" are used analogically (and not merely metaphorically)—Brown takes us in a very different direction.[60]

For all intents and purposes, Brown confines "revelation" to the phenomenon of prophecy. The entire Bible is inspired, he tells us, "but only some parts of the Bible transmit revelation"—namely, those parts where there is a more or less explicit claim that a divine communication has been received and is being transmitted.[61] Such divine communications cannot really have taken the form of words—for God does not speak—but they do constitute some sort of nonverbal divine "message" that has been given verbal expression by the human authors. When we read an oracle from the book of Jeremiah, "the message is the message of God, but the words are words of Jeremiah." Likewise, Pentateuchal laws are "human formulations of a less specified revelation of divine moral demand."[62] The quasi-intellectualist understanding of revelation that Brown worked with in the 1968 version of "Hermeneutics" has been reduced here even further to a vague psychological model.

Brown does not spell out what he means by "less specified" revelation, nor does he seem to realize that such a qualification hardly gets him around the whole problem of mediation. Any communication of the divine "message" to the prophet must come in a form that the human psyche can receive.

57 Brown, 21.

58 Brown, 23.

59 Brown, 4.

60 Michael Maria Waldstein, "*Analogia Verbi:* The Truth of Scripture in Rudolf Bultmann and Raymond Brown," *Letter & Spirit* 6 (2010): 116.

61 Brown, *Critical Meaning*, 7–8.

62 Brown, 9–10.

In the words of Thomas Aquinas, "whatever is received into something is received according to the mode of the recipient" (*STh* I, q. 75, a. 5, corp.). If Brown cannot imagine God granting the prophet an inner locution in human words, why should it be any less problematic for God to grant a mystical vision, an illumination of the intellect, an aesthetic feeling, or a vague intuition of moral truth?

None of this concerns Brown, however. What does concern him is to drive a wedge between divine revelation and its merely human verbal "expression" in Scripture. "My chief concern here," he tells us, "is the extent to which the inspired Bible is a time-conditioned word, marked by the limitations of human utterance."[63] A few pages earlier, he remarks: "This is no minor issue, because if God did not actually speak words (external or internal), one must admit clearly and firmly that every word pertaining to God in the history of the human race, including the biblical period, is a time-conditioned word, affected by limitations of human insight and problems."[64]

Even in the case of Jesus's own words, Brown opines, "it is dubious that one encounters an unconditional, timeless word spoken by God."[65] The implication seems to be that God's own eternal and unconditioned Logos cannot truly come to us in and through that which is human and temporal—and this from a scholar who wrote an acclaimed two-volume commentary on the fourth Gospel.[66] It is true, of course, that human words are time-conditioned. Indeed, they are conditioned by any number of contingencies. The pertinent question is not whether they are conditioned but whether, and in what ways, they may *participate in* the one absolute Word of God. If we wish to gain any clear sense of what it means to call the human words of Scripture "word of God," our starting point must be to recognize, with Thomas Aquinas, that the eternal Logos is the primordial "fountain" from which "all other words are derived," the "one absolute Word, by participating in which all persons who have a word are called speakers."[67]

But because Brown, for whom such speculations of philosophy and systematic theology are of no consequence, remains utterly convinced that "God

63 Brown, 14–15.

64 Brown, 4.

65 Brown, 12.

66 Raymond E. Brown, SS, *The Gospel According to John*, 2 vols., AB 29–29A (Garden City, N.Y.: Doubleday, 1966–1970).

67 Aquinas, *In Heb.* c. 4, lect. 2; *In Ioan.* c. 1, lect. 1.

does not speak," the fact that human words are time-conditioned apparently means that they cannot transcend human limitations. He sees here two major ramifications for our view of Scripture. The first is that we must "shift to an *a posteriori* approach to inerrancy" and grant that the Bible contains, not only scientific and historical inaccuracies, but "religious errors" as well.[68] The formulation of *Dei Verbum* 11, *sine errore*, presents no obstacle here, provided one recognize the "compromise nature" of this document. Disclosing his unedifying view of the conciliar proceedings, Brown suggests that "it became a matter of face-saving that in the revisions and in the final form of the Constitution the ultraconservatives should have their say." In interpreting the documents of Vatican II, Brown implies, we are free to sift out such "conservative older formulations" and attend to the "more open recent formulations."[69] This is a textbook example of the hermeneutic of rupture and open-ended progress in the reception of *Dei Verbum*.

The second ramification—and this seems to be the main point of *The Critical Meaning of the Bible*—is that the task of establishing what the time-conditioned human words of Scripture *meant*, whether in their original historical context or in their somewhat later canonical context, is the exclusive purview of historical-critical biblical scholarship.[70] It is dangerously misleading, Brown warns, to suppose that ecclesiastical authorities have told us, or can tell us, what the Bible *meant*. He writes, "to the best of my knowledge the Roman Catholic Church has never defined the literal sense of a single passage of the Bible."[71] In the few instances where an ecumenical council *seems* to have done so, he explains, we are actually only dealing with "an interpretation of the general thrust of the [New Testament] for the life of the Church."[72]

It is only at the level of what the Bible *means* for today that "church authority" exercises its prerogative of "authentically interpreting" the Bible.[73]

68 Brown, *Critical Meaning*, 17.

69 Brown, 18.

70 According to Brown, "we go beyond the literal sense when we move from the meaning of the book in itself to the meaning that the book has when it is joined to other books in the canon of Scripture" (30), but this "canonical sense" still belongs to what the Bible "meant" in the historical past and is thus subject to the judgment of historical-critical scholarship (35).

71 Brown, 40.

72 Brown, 40.

73 Brown, 37. Cf. *Dei Verbum* 10, 12.

For all intents and purposes, Brown restricts the authority of the teaching office to the definition of doctrines, and in his judgment, doctrines seldom depend on matters of historical fact. Apart from affirming the central events of Jesus's life, the Magisterium has no real competence in historical matters. Hence Brown's dictum: "The Church is the ultimate judge of faith and morals; historical criticism is the criterion of history."[74]

How far does the "criterion of history" extend? Brown stresses that the Church's "dogmatic formulations are historically conditioned and sometimes need to be reformulated" and that in this process "exegetes should have a consultative role."[75] By itself this is little more than a restatement of *Dei Verbum* 12, which grants biblical exegetes a significant role in the "preparatory study" by which the judgment of the Church "matures." The problem is that Brown's understanding of how this process should play out is built on a shaky foundation, not on the "genuine doctrine of divine revelation and its transmission" that the council fathers set forth (no. 1). Throughout *The Critical Meaning of the Bible*, Brown uses "tradition" as a generic term for radically time-conditioned elements of the Church's historical existence, rarely betraying any sense that we are dealing here with something sacred, much less of intrinsic divine authority. As we have seen, Brown has a pejorative view of the patristic-medieval exegetical tradition and is entirely unwilling to grant it a voice in establishing what our exegetical method should be today. We have also seen him make a deliberate decision not to consult the philosophical and theological tradition with regard to what it means to call the Bible "the word of God." Thus, the object of study is defined, and the correct approach to studying it is determined, on the basis of a method that is simply assumed to supply its own foundation.

According to Fr. Brown, critical biblical scholarship plays the "benevolent role of challenging the Church and moving it slowly but ultimately to what it should be."[76] "It has the power to serve as the conscience of the Church" and "has only begun to have its impact on the Catholic Church scene."[77] Because the findings of historical-critical exegesis sometimes have "shocking implications, at least upon initial impact," it is necessary that scholars establish a "working partnership" with ecclesiastical authorities in order to strike the

74 Brown, *Critical Meaning*, 39.

75 Brown, 81; cf. 61.

76 Brown, 82.

77 Brown, 81.

right balance between "the need to investigate new questions honestly" and "pastoral care for the faithful."[78] Now more than ever, the teaching office is "supremely important," for it establishes the "boundaries" of orthodoxy that provide unity in the midst of change.[79] Centrist biblical scholars will be careful to operate within these boundaries, where, Brown reassures them, there is "plenty of room to think."[80] Those anxious for change must guard against impatience, remembering that "eventually authority will go along with the majority on many issues; for that is part of the dynamism of the consultative system."[81] Brown readily acknowledges that the Church has defined its dogmas "with divine guidance" but in the same breath reminds his readers of the "conditioned value" of all dogmatic formulations.[82] Ultimately everything is subject to criticism, except the "criterion of history" itself.

It goes without saying that Raymond Brown's insistence that "God does not speak" flies in the face of Scripture and Tradition. Notwithstanding his confidence that "most centrist Catholic theologians" would agree with him,[83] his interpretation of the phrase "word of God" is highly idiosyncratic. Nor is he deterred by the fact that the council fathers have gone out of their way to describe divine revelation, and Scripture itself, as God's speech. It is arguably the dominant leitmotif of *Dei Verbum*, as the following pastiche of citations demonstrates:

> And thus, through this revelation the invisible God, out of the abundance of his love, speaks [*alloquitur*] to men as to friends (no. 2).... After God had spoken [*locutus est*] in many and varied ways through the prophets, "in these last days he has spoken [*locutus est*] to us in a Son" (no. 4; cf. Heb 1:1–2).... And thus God, who spoke [*locutus est*] of old, uninterruptedly converses [*colloquitur*] with the bride of his beloved Son (no. 8).... For Sacred Scripture is the speech of God [*locutio Dei*] inasmuch as it is consigned to writing by the inspiration of the divine Spirit (no. 9).... But since in Sacred Scripture God has spoken [*locutus sit*] through men in the manner of men (no. 12) ... with God himself speaking [*loquente*] to them through the mouths of the prophets (no. 14) ... [the Scriptures] make the

78 Brown, 117.

79 Brown, 37, 94.

80 Brown, 87, 94.

81 Brown, 116.

82 Brown, 61.

83 Brown, 21.

> voice [*vocem*] of the Holy Spirit resound in the words of the prophets and apostles.... For in the sacred books, the Father who is in heaven lovingly meets his children and engages them in conversation [*cum eis sermonem confert*] (no. 21) . . . that [the Church] may incessantly feed her children with the divine utterances [*divinis eloquiis*] (no. 23).... Therefore, let them gladly approach the sacred text itself, whether in the sacred liturgy, which is dense with the divine utterances [*divinis eloquiis*], or in devout reading.... But let them remember that prayer ought to accompany the reading of Sacred Scripture, that there may be a conversation [*colloquium*] between God and man (no. 25).

As Michael Waldstein puts it, Brown's redefinition of the phrase "word of God" is "a violently simple and impatient solution [to] the complex problem of the truth of Scripture."[84] The correct starting point for dealing with this problem is precisely opposite the one that Brown has chosen. That is, we should begin by affirming that God *does* speak. He speaks his Logos eternally. By that same Logos, he has spoken the world into being and "gives human beings a perpetual witness to himself in created things" (*Dei Verbum* 3). To man he has granted a unique share in the light of the divine intellect in the form of linguistic rationality (λόγος), so that there might be a *colloquium* between God and man. "In many partial and varied ways" God spoke to Israel through the prophets, and in the fullness of time he revealed himself definitively in his incarnate Logos (Heb 1:1–2; John 1:14). All this and more must be taken into account if we wish to give serious thought to what it means to affirm that the Bible is "the word of God." Scripture must be viewed as an integral element within the entire economy of revelation, and above all, it must be placed in its proper relation to the centerpiece of that economy, the person and event of Jesus Christ.[85] To borrow a phrase used by Francis Martin, Scripture is the word of God by virtue of its "economic participation."[86]

The "analogy of the word" (*analogia verbi*) just sketched out is foundational to the teaching of *Dei Verbum*,[87] but Brown excludes it a priori when

84 Waldstein, "*Analogia Verbi*," 108.

85 Gregory Vall, *Learning Christ: Ignatius of Antioch and the Mystery of Redemption* (Washington, D.C.: The Catholic University of America Press, 2013), 27–33.

86 Martin, *Sacred Scripture*, 241.

87 See *Dei Verbum* 3–4 and 13. Benedict XVI discusses the *analogia verbi* in relation to Scripture in *Verbum Domini* 7.

he makes a deliberate decision to confine his thinking to "an outlook gained from biblical criticism."[88] This choice, as Waldstein explains, is but one reflex of an even more basic a priori judgment—conscious on the part of the thinkers who gave modern thought its basic orientation but imbibed in a largely unreflective manner by the rest of us:

> All who reflect about their Christian faith in the modern age experience the pressure of the scientific picture of the world or, more exactly, of the choices and philosophical premises implicit in that scientific picture. These premises, which lie in the voluntaristic nominalism of William of Ockham and the choice of mathematical mechanics as the master science of nature by Bacon and Descartes, destroy the metaphysics of analogy and participation required for understanding the *analogia verbi*.... Structures of plausibility and intellectual customs are slowly built up by this pressure and Enlightenment prejudices thereby achieve the status of the self-evident.[89]

Brown thinks that it is a relatively simple matter to practice the historical-critical method sans Enlightenment prejudices, which he regards as "regrettable accretions rather than as intrinsic principles of the method." He facilely supposes that, as long as one avoids "skepticism about the transcendent" and does not deny the possibility of miracles, presuppositions are not a live issue.[90] In fact, however, Brown's entire argument in *The Critical Meaning of the Bible* is fraught with deeply flawed presuppositions. Foremost among these is the assumption that the mode of rationality operative in the historical-critical method is self-validating and beyond criticism or intrinsic improvement, at least with respect to the access it gives us to "the human element in the word of God."[91] In other words, Brown treats the historical-critical method as the one phenomenon that has somehow mysteriously escaped historical conditioning. It thereby places the interpreter on an epistemological perch overlooking the flux of history, enabling him or her to sit in judgment on all things historical.

This working assumption requires Brown to ignore the scientific, philosophical, religious, and political milieu in which the historical-critical method developed. And recognizing that this is the case helps to account

88 Brown, *Critical Meaning*, 5.

89 Waldstein, "*Analogia Verbi*," 97, 121.

90 Brown, *Critical Meaning*, 25.

91 Brown, 26.

for an otherwise inexplicable lacuna in Brown's historical narrative of the triumph of literal exegesis over spiritual exegesis. He passes over the founding of the historical-critical method almost entirely, without a word either about the role played by the seventeenth-century philosophers (Hobbes, Spinoza, and Locke), or about the seminal figures of the crucial eighteenth century (Collins, Reimarus, Semler, Michaelis, Herder, and Kant). In fact, Brown's account reduces this entire formative period of 150 years to two sentences about one man, the Oratorian priest Richard Simon (1638–1712), whom Brown identifies as "a prophet before his time and the first of the modern biblical critics."[92] This dubious claim has encouraged other members of the centrist school to treat the historical-critical method as originating "primarily" in the nineteenth century—viewed as the age of "scientific study" and historical objectivity—and to ignore its roots in the Enlightenment and in certain responses to the Enlightenment, such as Romanticism and historicism.[93]

THE ERASMUS LECTURE

In January of 1988, the two scholars whose hermeneutics we have been considering in this chapter crossed paths in New York City, when Joseph Cardinal Ratzinger delivered his Erasmus Lecture and then sat down with Fr. Raymond Brown and nineteen other scholars for an ecumenical colloquium on the Bible in the life of the Church.[94] In the introduction to the present volume, we took a brief look at what is arguably the most significant and enduring aspect of this event—namely, Cardinal Ratzinger's call for a Method C synthesis and the icy reception that this proposal received from Fr. Brown. Now that we have gained a better sense of the approach to Scripture that each of these men brought to the conference, we can expand our view of Ratzinger's proposal and better appreciate why it brought him into conflict with Brown in particular. Toward the end of the Erasmus Lecture, the

92 *NJBC* 71:42.

93 E.g., Witherup, *Scripture*, 100.

94 Primary sources for this event include Ratzinger, "Biblical Interpretation in Crisis"; Stallsworth, "The Story of an Encounter"; and Raymond E. Brown, SS, "Addenda," in Neuhaus, *Biblical Interpretation in Crisis*, 37–49. Other redactions or translations of the Erasmus Lecture include: Joseph Ratzinger, ed., *Schriftauslegung im Widerstreit*, Quaestiones Disputatae 117 (Freiburg: Herder, 1989), 15–44; Granados, Granados, and Sánchez-Navarro, eds., *Opening Up the Scriptures*, 1–29; Ratzinger, *God's Word*, 91–126.

future pope implicitly but nonetheless unmistakably singled out Brown's *The Critical Meaning of the Bible* as a perfect example of how a well-intentioned biblical scholar can build his whole approach to Scripture on deeply flawed presuppositions that lie at the core of the historical-critical method. But before taking up that point, I would like to consider a passage found much earlier in the lecture, where Ratzinger calls for "a criticism of criticism." In recent years this phrase has been quoted frequently but perhaps not always with an adequate understanding of what it means in context.

Many Christians who would like to see biblical exegesis restored to a mode that is theologically orthodox and spiritually fruitful suppose that the core problem with the historical-critical method is that it is overly critical. In particular, they find its practitioners far too ready to call into question traditional views about the date and authorship of most books of the Bible and to cast doubt on the complete historicity of its narrative portions. The application of a critical method to a sacred text strikes them as fundamentally misguided. This is not, however, the diagnosis given by Cardinal Ratzinger in the Erasmus Lecture. Instead, he suggests that the basic problem with modern exegesis is that *it has not been critical enough*, specifically, that it has not called into question its own philosophical foundations: "What we need might be called a criticism of criticism. By this I mean not some exterior analysis, but a criticism based on the inherent potential of all critical thought to analyze itself. We need a self-criticism of the historical method which can expand to an analysis of historical reason itself."[95]

This important passage, which is much more than a rhetorically clever turning of the tables, deserves careful consideration. Correctly interpreted, it offers no encouragement to those who would like to make short work of the historical-critical method. It is relatively easy to criticize the historical and philosophical foundations of modern exegesis if one begins with the premise that the whole thing has been a tragic mistake.[96] Many critics of historical-critical exegesis naïvely cling to the old, cherished assumptions. They claim, for example, that it has not been sufficiently demonstrated that Moses did not author the Pentateuch, or they insist that it is possible to harmonize the narratives of the four Gospels on the level of strict facticity, thus denying any real literary license to the evangelists. But such reactionary

95 Ratzinger, "Biblical Interpretation in Crisis," 6.

96 This is the tenor of Paul Cardinal Taguchi, "Sacred Scripture and the Errors of the 'New' Exegesis," *Letter & Spirit* 6 (2010): 383–400.

critics can provide no more than an "exterior analysis" of modern exegetical methods. Only those who, by struggling to bring the method to the service of faith, have glimpsed its potential for real greatness—which lies precisely in its critical dimension—and who, along with Pope Pius XII, have arrived at the conviction that the many discoveries and technical tools of modern biblical scholarship have come to us "not without the provident counsel of God,"[97] are able to view the method *from within* and contribute to the "self-criticism" of which Ratzinger speaks.[98]

Ratzinger views the problem posed by modern biblical exegesis as part and parcel of the basic problem of modernity itself—namely, the search for "foundations" that is characteristic of our age.[99] Modern thought cannot simply reverse its course but must press forward, deepening and purifying its critique of human reason through the recovery of aspects of the wisdom of the past. The search for a suitable exegetical approach lies near the center of this larger quest. This is why Ratzinger envisions the self-critique of the historical-critical method broadening into "an analysis of historical reason itself."[100]

Here I would remind the reader of four other planks in Ratzinger's platform, all of which were discussed in the introduction to this book. First, patristic, medieval, and Reformation exegesis (Method A) must be "brought into the discussion," but there can be no question of a "retreat" that sets precritical exegesis "in blind opposition to the spirit of the present age."[101] Second, Ratzinger is not looking merely to supplement the historical-critical method (Method B) by appending to it an extrinsically related theological "step."[102] Rather, the historical-critical method must be transformed as it is taken up into a new synthesis of ancient and modern modes (Method C).[103] Third, one of the keys to accomplishing this synthesis will be the effort "to

97 Pope Pius XII, Encyclical *Divino Afflante Spiritu* 12, my translation.

98 Exemplary in this regard is Martin, *Sacred Scripture.*

99 Ratzinger, "Biblical Interpretation in Crisis," 16.

100 Ratzinger, 6.

101 Ratzinger, 22, 16.

102 Taken out of context, the reference to a "further step" in the last paragraph of the Erasmus Lecture (Ratzinger, "Biblical Interpretation in Crisis," 23) may seem to suggest such a thing, but in context it clearly refers not to an additional exegetical step but to a hermeneutical step that would bring the faith of the Church into the very act of reading and interpretation from the outset.

103 Stallsworth, "Story of an Encounter," 107–8.

find how to spiritualize the positivistic method and also how to take into account all of the gifts of this method."[104] Positivism is in the DNA of the historical-critical method and is therefore not easily removed, but the exegete whose mind is illumined in prayer and who immerses himself or herself in Sacred Tradition, including the works of the Fathers and doctors, will little by little gain new instincts for how to use the tools and procedures of the historical-critical method theologically and spiritually. Fourth, according to Ratzinger, a Method C synthesis can only come about through much philosophical, theological, and hermeneutical labor. To achieve such a thing will require "the attentive and critical commitment of an entire generation."[105]

Although Cardinal Ratzinger paid Fr. Brown several warmly respectful public compliments during the course of the two-day conference, there can be little doubt that in the following passage he takes dead aim at *The Critical Meaning of the Bible*: "Thus the exegete should not approach the text with a ready-made philosophy, nor in accordance with the dictates of a so-called modern or 'scientific' worldview, which determines in advance what may or may not be. He may not exclude a priori that (almighty) God could speak in human words in the world."[106] As we saw above, this is precisely how Brown laid the foundation for his entire program—his vision, one might even say—for how modern biblical scholarship will "move" the Church.

Brown bristled at the suggestion that the foundations of the historical-critical method need to be probed philosophically and theologically, and frankly admitted that he distrusted philosophy.[107] To Brown's thinking, no new hermeneutical synthesis is necessary because the foundation for exegesis has already been supplied by "an outlook gained from biblical criticism."[108] The historical-critical method must be given free rein to determine what the biblical text *meant*, apart from any consideration of ecclesiastical tradition, liturgy, or doctrine. These criteria are brought into play only when it comes to saying what the text *means* for believers today.

104 Stallsworth, 109.

105 Ratzinger, "Biblical Interpretation in Crisis," 16.

106 Ratzinger, 19. Note the curious use of parentheses in Ratzinger's text, as if he could not decide whether or not to include a patent verbal allusion to the (ironic) title of the first chapter of Brown's book: "The Human Word of the Almighty God" (*Critical Meaning*, 1–22).

107 Brown, "Addenda," 47.

108 Brown, *Critical Meaning*, 5.

About the time of the Erasmus Lecture, Brown was revising "Hermeneutics" for the *New Jerome Biblical Commentary* (1990) and had recruited Sandra M. Schneiders, IHM, to contribute an account of the "literary turn" that biblical scholarship had taken in the two decades since the publication of the original *Jerome Biblical Commentary* (1968), followed by a brief survey of structuralism, deconstructionism, rhetorical criticism, narrative criticism, and sociological criticism.[109] Brown was careful to file all these approaches under "More-Than-Literal Senses," thus guarding the turf of the historical-critical method.[110] But it was doubtful whether the proponents of these new methods would all grant the obvious implication—namely, that they do not pertain to the literal sense of Scripture and thus have no direct bearing on what the text *meant* in its original historical context. In any case, to one extent or another each of these methods presented itself as an alternative to the historical-critical method, or at least as a challenge to its hegemony. In the tidy world of the *New Jerome Biblical Commentary*, each new method had a seat at the table—but not at the head of the table. Catholic biblical scholarship would carry on peaceably under the leadership of the historical-critical method. In fact, however, the real world of biblical scholarship, Catholic and non-Catholic, was in upheaval in the late 1980s. The situation cried out for a new hermeneutical synthesis.

As we saw in the introduction, Brown was not the only conference participant to balk at Ratzinger's Method C proposal. Thomas C. Oden, who for some years had been advocating a return to "classical Christianity," took exception to the Catholic cardinal's warning against a "retreat" to patristic exegesis. To Oden's mind, a direct line of retreat was exactly what the situation called for. Modern Christians could recover a fruitful approach to exegesis simply by immersing themselves in the writings of the Church Fathers. No intervention of philosophy was necessary.[111] Thus, while Oden and Brown were backing different horses, they shared a strong distaste for the sort of intensive philosophical and hermeneutical project that Ratzinger deemed necessary, and neither was well disposed to a rapprochement between the ancient and modern exegetical approaches.

The German cardinal, finding himself under attack on two fronts, politely stood his ground. The essential idea of the Erasmus Lecture had been on his

109 *NJBC* 71:55–70.

110 Brown, "Addenda," 48. Note the major subject heading above *NJBC* 71:30.

111 Stallsworth, "Story of an Encounter," 113.

mind for decades. We have seen adumbrations of it in the Inaugural Lecture (1963) and the *Commentary* (1967). Likewise, in *Eschatology* (first published in 1977) he writes that "only by listening to the whole history of interpretation can the present be purified by criticism and so brought into a position of genuine encounter" with the biblical text.[112] In *Principles of Catholic Theology* (first published in 1982) he develops this point forcefully by noting:

> No satisfactory conclusion can be reached if we place a vacuum between ourselves and the Bible and try to forget that the Bible comes to us by way of history. Only by acknowledging history can we transcend it. If we try to ignore it, we remain entangled in it; we cannot possibly read the Bible in a way that is truly historical however much we may seem to be applying historical methods. In reality, we remain bound to the horizon of our own thinking and reflect only ourselves.[113]

Above all, Ratzinger was convinced that *Dei Verbum* itself points us in the direction of a new synthesis of the historical-critical and patristic-medieval approaches to exegesis.[114] I shall test that thesis in the last part of this chapter.

THE HERMENEUTICS OF JOSEPH FITZMYER

While Cardinal Ratzinger's Method C proposal does not seem to have had a significant impact on Raymond Brown's thinking, the Erasmus Lecture nonetheless marks a watershed for the Brown-Fitzmyer trajectory. During the twenty-year period from 1968 to 1988, it was primarily Brown who articulated the hermeneutical stance of centrist Catholic biblical scholarship in North America, but in the two decades following the Erasmus Lecture it was Brown's close friend and longtime collaborator Joseph Fitzmyer who wore the hermeneutical mantle. By the late 1980s, the American Jesuit was alarmed

112 Joseph Ratzinger, *Eschatology: Death and Eternal Life*, trans. Michael Waldstein, 2nd ed. (Washington, D.C.: The Catholic University of America Press, 1988), 24.

113 Joseph Ratzinger, *Principles of Catholic Theology: Building Stones for a Fundamental Theology*, trans. Mary Frances McCarthy (San Francisco: Ignatius, 1987), 152.

114 Ratzinger, *God's Word*, 96–98. He went even further in 1993, asserting that *Dei Verbum* "provided us with a synthesis, which substantially remains, between the lasting insights of patristic theology and the new methodological understanding of the moderns." Joseph Ratzinger, Preface to *The Interpretation of the Bible in the Church: Address of His Holiness John Paul II and Document of the Pontifical Biblical Commission*, by The Pontifical Biblical Commission (Boston: St. Paul Books & Media, 1993), 28.

at the way the historical-critical method, whose hegemony over the world of Catholic biblical scholarship had gone virtually unchallenged during the first two decades after the council, had recently "come under fire" on multiple fronts. Many wished to replace it with a "postcritical approach," such as rhetorical, narratological, structuralist, or feminist criticism. Others, fewer in number, were calling for "a return to precritical interpretation," especially patristic interpretation.[115] Of particular concern was Cardinal Ratzinger's Method C proposal, which to Fitzmyer looked like a dangerous combination of both tendencies.[116]

Esteemed by centrists as one who "incarnates the spirit of *Dei Verbum*,"[117] and having served on the Pontifical Biblical Commission (under Cardinal Ratzinger's presidency) since 1984, Fitzmyer was well positioned to respond to these threats and lost no time in doing so. In 1989 he published a programmatic article in *Theological Studies*, entitled "Historical Criticism: Its Role in Biblical Interpretation and Church Life."[118] Over the next several years, Fitzmyer invested considerable energy in drafting, interpreting, and popularizing the Biblical Commission's 1993 document, *The Interpretation of the Bible in the Church*, which he clearly viewed as a unique opportunity to bestow quasi-magisterial status on the centrist interpretation of *Dei Verbum*.[119] In 1994 he published *Scripture, the Soul of Theology*, the most complete account of his hermeneutics.[120] Finally, in 2008 he gathered several essays, including the 1989 article, in *The Interpretation of Scripture: In Defense of the Historical-Critical Method*.[121]

Fitzmyer begins the *Theological Studies* article with a sketch of the history of the historical-critical method, tracing its roots back to classical

115 Fitzmyer, *Interpretation of Scripture*, 59; and *Scripture, the Soul of Theology* (New York: Paulist, 1994), 7.

116 Fitzmyer, *Scripture, the Soul of Theology*, 34–38.

117 Witherup, *Scripture*, x.

118 Joseph A. Fitzmyer, SJ, "Historical Criticism: Its Role in Biblical Interpretation and Church Life," *Theological Studies* 50, no. 2 (1989): 244–59; here cited from Fitzmyer, *Interpretation of Scripture*, 59–73.

119 Pontifical Biblical Commission, *Interpretation of the Bible*; Joseph A. Fitzmyer, SJ, *The Biblical Commission's Document 'The Interpretation of the Bible in the Church': Text and Commentary*, Subsidia Biblica 18 (Rome: Pontifical Biblical Institute, 1995); Fitzmyer, *Interpretation of Scripture*, 74–85.

120 See n. 115 above.

121 See n. 29 above.

Alexandrian philology and the critical techniques sometimes employed by Origen, Augustine, and Jerome. He implies that the exegesis of the Church Fathers is to be valued precisely insofar as it anticipates elements of modern methodology. Fitzmyer acknowledges that the Reformation agenda, Enlightenment rationalism, and German historicism all "tainted" the use of the historical-critical method during its formative period. Still, he maintains that the method is "per se neutral."[122] Here he makes an important distinction between the method itself, which he views as a set of "philological tools and techniques," and "exegesis," which comprises the tools of the method *plus* the presuppositions with which they are employed by a given scholar.[123] In this way he can assert the neutrality of the method without suggesting that it has ever actually been employed in an entirely neutral manner.

Nor does Fitzmyer view the neutral application of the method as an ideal to be pursued. Indeed, the central point of the article is that the historical-critical method not only can be but should be employed with the presuppositions of faith. These include (1) that "the text being critically interpreted contains God's Word set forth in human words," (2) that it was "composed under the guidance of the Spirit," (3) that it is "part of a canon" that "has been given by God for the edification and salvation of his people," and (4) that "it is properly expounded only in relation to the Tradition that has grown out of it."[124] When these presuppositions are operative, the historical-critical method, notwithstanding its checkered past, "becomes a *properly oriented* method of biblical interpretation."[125]

This program for how the historical-critical method should be taken up into the life of the Church represents a marked improvement over Brown's and in important respects is actually closer to Ratzinger's. Fitzmyer is clearly talking about how the method is to be employed in order to discover what the biblical text *meant* in its original historical context. Faith presuppositions are not to be held in abeyance until after we have made this determination and are ready to ask what the Bible *means* for the believer. When the method has been "properly oriented" through the "plus" of the faith presuppositions listed above, its tools and techniques are not employed as ends in themselves but "only to achieve the main goal of ascertaining what the biblical message

122 Fitzmyer, *Interpretation of Scripture*, 62, 66–69.

123 Fitzmyer, 68.

124 Fitzmyer, 68.

125 Fitzmyer, 69.

was that the sacred writer of old sought to convey—in effect, the literal sense of the Bible."[126]

While Brown and Fitzmyer always stood shoulder to shoulder against their common foes and were of one mind on most issues, important differences between them emerge here. Fitzmyer explicitly rejects the dichotomy between what the Bible *meant* and what it *means*, insisting on the "homogeneity" of the two.[127] Properly oriented historical-critical exegesis of the biblical text "leads to the discovery of its religious and theological meaning" and thus "assists the Church in its ongoing life, by helping it to uncover the essence of the revelation once given it—the meaning of the Word of God in ancient human words."[128] Here and elsewhere, Fitzmyer employs the formula "Word of God in human words." Unlike Brown, he obviously does not consider it tautologous. In fact, in Fitzmyer's hermeneutics there is a kind of immediacy among God's communicative intention, the human author's communicative intention, and the "essence of revelation" that nourishes the life of Christians today.

One might object that Fitzmyer can be so sanguine about all of this because he is hermeneutically naïve. To be sure, he seems not to recognize the enormous complexity and real difficulty of the problems surrounding the historical mediation of divine revelation, problems for which Brown had resorted to such a drastic solution. But if Fitzmyer has in effect distanced himself from the thesis of Brown's 1981 *The Critical Meaning of the Bible* and taken up a position not too different from the one Brown had occupied in 1968, that should hardly be counted against him. Sometimes the best way out of a blind alley is to retrace one's steps.

Fitzmyer's hermeneutical naïveté is more troublesome vis-à-vis the specific problem of modern historical understanding. In its broad outlines, the position that he takes with regard to how we should deal with the flawed presuppositions that have plagued historical-critical exegesis is not all that different from what Ratzinger proposes. To abstract from the method-as-practiced a set of philological "tools and techniques" that are "per se neutral" and then to employ these tools and techniques with a series of presuppositions of faith sounds very much like an attempt to "spiritualize the positivistic method" à la Ratzinger.[129] But whereas Ratzinger suggests that "at least the

126 Fitzmyer, 69.

127 Fitzmyer, *Scripture, Soul of Theology*, 81; *Interpretation of Scripture*, 89.

128 Fitzmyer, *Interpretation of Scripture*, 69, 72.

129 Fitzmyer, 68–69; cf. Stallsworth, "Story of an Encounter," 109.

work of a whole generation is necessary to achieve such a thing,"[130] Fitzmyer seems to think that he has already completed the job more or less by himself. He tosses aside the Erasmus Lecture's critique of the historical-critical method—which focuses on Bultmann's radical subordination of event to word—as nonapplicable to the present generation of scholars, who he assures us are neither enamored with Heideggerian existentialism nor guilty of Bultmann's excesses.[131] Like Brown, Fitzmyer fails to recognize that in Bultmann Ratzinger is merely pointing to a conspicuous instance of how modernity's fact-value dichotomy has infected biblical scholarship. Bultmannianism may be passé, but the dichotomy itself is as deep-seated as ever. Unfortunately, and perhaps not coincidentally, the same naïveté is reflected in the Biblical Commission's 1993 document, which tells us that at some unspecified point in the past the historical-critical method "was freed from external prejudices," and that "for a long time now scholars have ceased combining the method with a philosophical system."[132]

Not surprisingly, then, Fitzmyer is no more enthusiastic than Brown was about Ratzinger's call for a philosophical probing-to-the-depths of the very mode of rationality embodied in the historical-critical method, a criticism of criticism itself. When Fitzmyer discusses new methods such as rhetorical criticism, narrative criticism, and canonical criticism, he readily grants that they represent "refinements" and perhaps even "serve to correct" the historical-critical method, but he adds apodictically that "none of them is a substitute for the fundamental method, and none can be allowed to replace it."[133] This assertion is presented as self-evident, in need of no justification whatsoever. Is modern historical criticism, then, so fundamental that no deeper mode of historical rationality can be imagined to exist? Is it so fundamental that even the presuppositions of faith are in effect added on top of it as extrinsic principles? As long as these questions have not been addressed, how can we be sure that the "tools and techniques" that Fitzmyer has abstracted from the method-as-historically-practiced are truly "per se neutral"?

Another problem area—indeed, the Achilles heel of Fitzmyer's hermeneutics—is his working understanding of Tradition. The last item on

130 Ratzinger, "Biblical Interpretation in Crisis," 6.

131 Fitzmyer, *Scripture, Soul of Theology*, 36–37; *Interpretation of Scripture*, 67–68.

132 Pontifical Biblical Commission, *Interpretation of the Bible*, 41.

133 Fitzmyer, *Interpretation of Scripture*, 69.

his list of faith presuppositions is that the biblical text is "properly expounded only in relation to the Tradition that has grown out of it."[134] Inasmuch as he is speaking here about expounding the *literal sense*, he accords Tradition a greater scope and more ground-level exegetical influence than Brown does, and to that extent he is on the right side of *Dei Verbum*. The problem is that Fitzmyer consistently refers to Tradition as that which "has grown out of" Scripture or "springs from" Scripture, formulations that tend to reduce Tradition to the *Wirkungsgeschichte* ("history of effects") of the biblical text.[135] In a word, Tradition is "Scripture interpreted."[136] These statements are misleading because they yield only a partial truth. To describe Tradition as biblical interpretation does, of course, indicate one of its most important dimensions, for the whole of the Church's life is in a sense an "exegesis" of Scripture.[137] But in the same breath we must add that it is equally true that Scripture springs from Tradition, is encompassed and canonized by Tradition, and is carried down the ages on the current of Tradition.[138]

Fr. Fitzmyer was a superb New Testament scholar, and he knew as well as anyone that the apostle Paul drew upon the earliest Christian tradition in recounting the institution of the Eucharist and the death, burial, resurrection, and appearances of Christ, and that Paul even used technical terminology for "receiving" and "transmitting" tradition.[139] Fitzmyer likewise knew that Luke the evangelist drew upon a wealth of early tradition about Jesus and the apostles in composing his Gospel and the Acts of the Apostles.[140] Fitzmyer chooses not to recognize such early tradition as Tradition in the technical sense, however, because he wishes to limit the latter to postbiblical dogma,

134 Fitzmyer, 69.

135 Fitzmyer, *Interpretation of Scripture*, 13; *Scripture, Soul of Theology*, 63 (n. 12), 72.

136 Fitzmyer, *Scripture, Soul of Theology*, 72.

137 Yves Congar, *The Meaning of Tradition*, trans. A. N. Woodrow (San Francisco: Ignatius, 2004), 87, 90, 127.

138 On the teaching of *Dei Verbum* concerning the relationship between Scripture and Tradition, see Albert Vanhoye, SJ, "The Reception in the Church of the Dogmatic Constitution *Dei Verbum*," in *Opening Up the Scriptures*, ed. Granados, Granados, and Sánchez-Navarro, 105–112.

139 Joseph A. Fitzmyer, SJ, *First Corinthians: A New Translation with Introduction and Commentary*, AYB 32 (New Haven: Yale University Press, 2008), 435–36; 545–46; 408–9; cf. 1 Cor 11:23–26; 15:3–7; 11:2.

140 Joseph A. Fitzmyer, SJ, *The Gospel According to Luke: Introduction, Translation, and Notes*, 2 vols., AB 28–28A (Garden City, N.Y.: Doubleday, 1981–1985); *The Acts of the Apostles: A New Translation with Introduction and Commentary*, AB 31 (New York: Doubleday, 1998).

viewed as the Church's interpretation of Scripture. Following Karl Rahner, moreover, Fitzmyer accepts the Lutheran distinction between Scripture as the *norma normans non normata* and Tradition as the *norma normata*, and he goes as far as to say that "Tradition is nothing more than 'a legitimate unfolding of the biblical data.'"[141] In all this, he appears determined to subordinate Tradition to Scripture and to pass this off as the teaching of *Dei Verbum*.

In actual fact, the council fathers have gone out of their way to present Sacred Tradition as primordial. Scripture and Tradition issue "from the same divine wellspring" and "are to be received and venerated with the same pious devotion and reverence" (no. 9). True, the dogmatic constitution does say that "the Magisterium is not above the word of God, but serves it" (no. 10), but this statement must not be wrenched from its context and made to support the erroneous notion that *Dei Verbum* subordinates Tradition to Scripture. The passage in question begins with the assertion that "Sacred Tradition and Sacred Scripture constitute one sacred deposit of the word of God," and it goes on to explain that the Magisterium serves the word of God when it "draws forth from this one deposit of faith everything that it proposes to be believed as divinely revealed" (no. 10). In other words, the "word of God" that the Magisterium serves comprises both Scripture and Tradition in inseparable unity. The council fathers subordinate the Church's teaching office as such to Scripture and Tradition, but they by no means subordinate the content of Tradition to the authority of Scripture.[142]

Furthermore, when Fitzmyer speaks of "Tradition" as the normative context for biblical interpretation, he has in mind "the dogmatic Tradition," not the exegetical tradition as such.[143] *Dei Verbum*, by contrast, presents Sacred Tradition as comprehensive. It encompasses "all that [the Church] herself is and all that she believes" (no. 8). As Fitzmyer surely realized, this teaching on Sacred Tradition has important implications for biblical interpretation, which are spelled out later in the document. The Catholic exegete must attend to "the living Tradition of the whole Church" (no. 12), not simply to established dogmas. In particular, the dogmatic constitution encourages "the study of the holy Fathers" as a way to "advance daily toward

141 Fitzmyer, *Interpretation of Scripture*, 13. Cf. Karl Rahner, *Concerning Vatican Council II*, vol. 6 of *Theological Investigations*, trans. Karl H. Kruger and Boniface Kruger (Baltimore: Helicon, 1969), 92.

142 On the interpretation of this passage, see Vanhoye, "Reception in the Church," 105.

143 Fitzmyer, *Interpretation of Scripture*, 100.

a deeper understanding of the Sacred Scriptures" (no. 23). Therefore, the council fathers by no means limit the content of Tradition to dogmatic propositions, for that would have the effect of collapsing Tradition into Magisterium. Fitzmyer's attempt to circumscribe Tradition in this way is foreign to the whole tenor of *Dei Verbum*.

In sum, we might say that, while Congar, Ratzinger, and *Dei Verbum* all espouse a thick notion of Tradition, Fitzmyer—under the influence of Karl Rahner and, indirectly, Lutheran theology—works with an attenuated concept of it. This reductive notion of Tradition is, moreover, closely related to Fitzmyer's cautiously minimalistic concept of the "spiritual sense" of Scripture. For the most part, he identifies the spiritual sense as the literal sense read with proper Christian presuppositions. As far as the living practice of contemporary exegesis is concerned, this means that a "properly oriented" use of the historical-critical method yields a literal sense that is innately theological and spiritually nourishing. "In reality, this spiritual sense of Scripture is nothing other than the literal sense intended by the inspired human author."[144]

Beyond this, Fitzmyer grants that in Christian dogma and liturgy the Christological reading of the Old Testament constitutes "an *added* spiritual sense."[145] He strictly limits this "added" spiritual sense of the Old Testament to instances that can be confirmed by Scripture itself—that is, by the New Testament's use of the Old Testament—and he permits no further extrapolation from these. The "individual interpreter" has no authority to invoke this "added" sense "in the explanation of any biblical text whatsoever."[146] The contemporary Catholic exegete is thus reduced to using the historical-critical method, with faith presuppositions, to discover a literal sense that is theologically vital and thus "spiritual." Patristic exegesis is admired exactly insofar as it attempted and accomplished something like this with the tools available to it. In such cases, patristic exegesis "rightly functioned."[147]

The Church Fathers went astray, however, when they took passages out of context and produced "multifarious symbolic and allegorical meanings."

144 Fitzmyer, *Scripture, Soul of Theology*, 63.

145 Fitzmyer, 65.

146 Fitzmyer, *Interpretation of Scripture*, 97. Here Fitzmyer includes the "added" spiritual sense of the Old Testament under the *sensus plenior*, much as Brown does in the 1968 version of "Hermeneutics."

147 Fitzmyer, *Scripture, Soul of Theology*, 67–68; *Interpretation of Scripture*, 78.

Such interpretive practices "are not of the essence of the spiritual sense and run 'the risk of being something of an embarrassment to people of today.'"[148] The medieval schema of four senses, which Fitzmyer finds scarcely coherent, is little more than the byproduct of the unfortunate patristic tendency to "oscillate" between literal and spiritual exegesis.[149] To Fitzmyer's thinking, it would be misguided and retrogressive to attempt to revive any of this for the contemporary life of the Church. He reminds his readers that "it was precisely in reaction to the medieval multiple senses of Scripture" that the modern historical-critical method was developed.[150]

Fitzmyer's critique of allegorical exegesis and the fourfold schema is superficial and dismissive. He targets the oft-quoted couplet of Augustine of Dacia—*Littera gesta docet, quid credas allegoria, / moralis quid agas, quid speres anagogia* ("The letter teaches deeds; allegory, what you are to believe; / the moral, what you are to do; anagogy, what you are to hope")—which he sets up as a straw man and discards as "problematic."[151] The couplet is, of course, little more than a mnemonic device and by itself can hardly be expected to disclose the real genius of the patristic-medieval approach, something that Henri de Lubac accomplishes only over the course of several long volumes.[152] Fitzmyer occasionally cites these volumes in his footnotes, but he never engages de Lubac's arguments or theses. It is true that the vast corpus of patristic and medieval exegesis contains much that is arbitrary, quaint, and unworthy of imitation ("a lot of junk," as de Lubac himself admits), but the patient collector of its occasional gems slowly comes to realize that here the Church possesses a real treasure, a unique set of insights into "the internal logic of the Christian mystery."[153] A modern scholar is within his rights to criticize the schema of the four senses, but not to trivialize it. The mere fact that spiritual exegesis plays an integral role in the greatest theological

148 Fitzmyer, *Interpretation of Scripture*, 93 (cf. Pontifical Biblical Commission, *Interpretation of the Bible*, 101); Fitzmyer, *Scripture, Soul of Theology*, 65.

149 Fitzmyer, *Scripture, Soul of Theology*, 71; *Interpretation of Scripture*, 94–95.

150 Fitzmyer, *Scripture, Soul of Theology*, 37–38.

151 Fitzmyer, *Interpretation of Scripture*, 94; cf. *Scripture, Soul of Theology*, 67.

152 Henri de Lubac, *History and Spirit: The Understanding of Scripture according to Origen*, trans. Anne Englund Nash (San Francisco: Ignatius, 2007; first published 1950); and *Medieval Exegesis: The Four Senses of Scripture*, 3 vols., trans. Marc Sebanc and E. M. Macierowski (Grand Rapids: Eerdmans, 1998–2009; first published 1959–1964). The fourth volume of the French edition has never been translated into English.

153 De Lubac, *Medieval Exegesis* 2:211.

synthesis of the first millennium—namely, that of Augustine of Hippo—might discourage one from doing so.

If de Lubac demonstrates anything in *Medieval Exegesis*, it is that the allegorical-mystagogical approach to Scripture, crystalized in the schema of the four senses, is inextricably woven into the whole fabric of first-millennium exegesis and theology and therefore cannot be dismissed as an aberration or mere excrescence. One cannot commend only that in patristic and medieval exegesis which appears to anticipate the historical-critical approach, that which seems relatively "sober" to us, while rejecting out of hand everything that does not readily conform to our sensibilities or mode of rationality. There is, to be sure, no question of taking over the patristic approach wholesale and without further ado importing it into the twenty-first century. A process of winnowing and sifting must take place, not only in the case of Method B but also in the case of Method A. But we shall never arrive at a true Method C synthesis if our critique of Method A involves little more than haling it before the tribunal of Method B. Rather, we must make an honest effort to get inside Method A, to appreciate it on its own terms and discover its real genius. Only then shall we be in a position to separate the wheat from the chaff.

DEI VERBUM 12 AND METHOD C

Pauline Viviano accepts Raymond Brown's sharp distinction between *meant* and *means*, and she even considers it an acceptable substitute for the traditional distinction between literal sense and spiritual sense.[154] She deems it beyond dispute that to practice exegesis according to Brown's centrist model is to interpret the Bible "in conformity with the directives of Vatican II," while she views Pope Benedict XVI's attempt to integrate elements of patristic exegesis into his interpretation of the Gospels as part of a "backlash against Vatican II."[155] All of this must be called into question. While Brown's hermeneutical works doubtless constitute a sincere attempt to develop an approach to exegesis that is beneficial to the life of the Church, we have found this approach to be deeply at odds with the teaching of *Dei Verbum*. Joseph Fitzmyer's hermeneutic represents a significant improvement but

154 Viviano, "Senses of Scripture," 4.

155 Viviano, "Fighting Biblical Fundamentalism," 142–43.

nevertheless suffers from a deficient concept of Tradition and a similarly truncated notion of the spiritual sense. Most seriously, both authors fail to realize that the historicist mode of rationality at the heart of the historical-critical method is itself historically conditioned and thus in need of critique. The central point of the Erasmus Lecture has escaped them.

The hermeneutic of Joseph Ratzinger/Pope Benedict XVI, on the other hand, is born of a profound knowledge of the theological tradition and an intimate acquaintance with the text of *Dei Verbum* from its very origins. It represents the true, prophetic vision of the council and is in no sense reactionary or ultraconservative. Indeed, it is Ratzinger, rather than Brown or Fitzmyer, who marks out a path to the future for Catholic biblical scholarship. In concluding this chapter, I shall demonstrate that Ratzinger's Method C proposal is not some pet theory but is right in step with the teaching of the dogmatic constitution. I shall focus on paragraph 12—which, as Ratzinger recognizes, is the key text in this regard[156]—and give special attention to what it means to interpret Scripture "in the Spirit in which it was written."

The introductory sentence of *Dei Verbum* 12 stresses the inseparable unity between God's speaking in Scripture and Scripture's human mode of speech (*pace* Brown). It begins by invoking the Augustinian principle that "in Sacred Scripture God speaks through men in the manner of men [*per homines more hominum*]."[157] This axiom suggests a kind of common ground between modern exegetes and (some of) their ancient forebears—namely, a concern with the human character of biblical discourse.[158] But for Origen, Chrysostom, and Augustine this concern never becomes an end in itself. Accordingly, the council fathers assert that it is the exegete's duty "carefully to investigate what the sacred writers really intended to signify," and in the same breath they indicate that the telos of this investigation is "to perceive what God willed to communicate to us" by the human authors' words (no. 12).

The next four sentences unfold a hermeneutical perspective that approximates one of the central concerns of the historical-critical method—namely,

156 Ratzinger, *God's Word*, 96–98.

157 The council fathers cite *De civitate Dei* 17.6 somewhat freely and out of context. Augustine makes a similar point more explicitly in *De Trinitate* 1.12: "For the Scriptures speak by means of no other kind of usage than that which is found among human beings, since it is expressly to human beings that they speak" (*Neque enim aliquo genere loquuntur scripturae quod in consuetudine humana non inveniatur quia utique hominibus loquuntur*).

158 In Augustine's case this is especially evident in *Confessions* 11–13 and throughout *De Genesi ad litteram*.

that in order to discern the human author's intention, the exegete must pay careful attention to, "among other things [*inter alia*], literary genres" and "those customary and native modes of thinking, speaking, and narrating that prevailed in the times of the sacred writer" (no. 12). This passage unmistakably evokes Pius XII's encyclical *Divino Afflante Spiritu* (1943), which Brown and Fitzmyer celebrate as the "Magna Charta" of modern Catholic biblical scholarship.[159] By comparison to the encyclical, however, the conciliar text represents a rather cautious and merely implicit endorsement of modern methods. After all, attention to literary genres and ancient modes of thinking is hardly the sum and substance of the historical-critical method. With scholarly methods constantly evolving, the council fathers wisely chose neither to commit themselves to too many particulars of modern methodology, such as source criticism or form criticism, nor to exclude these out of hand. The phrase *inter alia* leaves the matter open for further consideration.

With this passage, which evokes a hermeneutical perspective akin to that of the historical-critical method, the council fathers juxtapose a second hermeneutical perspective in the form of three principles that are more characteristic of patristic exegesis. The exegete must take into account (1) "the content and unity of the whole of Scripture," (2) "the living Tradition of the whole Church," and (3) "the analogy of faith." As Ratzinger notes, these principles are in considerable tension with the guiding spirit of historical-critical exegesis, which revels in the discontinuities within the Bible, attempts to emancipate exegesis from ecclesiastical Tradition, and by no means presupposes the objective unity and coherence of the Christian faith.[160] According to Ratzinger, moreover, the tension within the conciliar text is itself instructive, for it indicates that the two perspectives cannot be combined easily or without significant modification to both. If their true "complementarity" is to be disclosed, it must be "by means of this antithesis" between them.[161]

This reading of *Dei Verbum* 12, while insightful, is perhaps unduly influenced by Ratzinger's quasi-Hegelian tendency to think in terms of thesis, antithesis, and synthesis. If there is an "antithesis" here, it is not within the conciliar text as such but between the two historical phenomena of ancient exegesis and modern exegesis. The text of *Dei Verbum* itself is marked by a gentle tension between two sets of principles *that have already been distilled*

159 *JBC* 72:6; cf. Fitzmyer, *Interpretation of Scripture*, 3.

160 Ratzinger, *God's Word*, 97–98; cf. *Principles of Catholic Theology*, 135–37.

161 *Principles of Catholic Theology*, 136.

from these two approaches. The argument of paragraph 12 assumes that these two sets of principles are fully compatible, but it also implies that it would be easy for the exegete to attend to one set to the neglect of the other. The proper way to relate the two hermeneutical perspectives to each other is indicated by way of a striking parallelism between the respective introductions to the two sets of principles.

Parallel Introductions in *Dei Verbum* 12

CONJUNCTION	
Since, however [*Cum autem*],	But, since [*Sed, cum*]
PATRISTIC AXIOM	
in Sacred Scripture God has spoken through men in the manner of men,	Sacred Scripture is also to be read and interpreted in the same Spirit in which it was written,
GOAL OF EXEGESIS	
in order to perceive what God has willed to communicate,	in order to draw forth correctly the sense of the sacred texts,
DUTY OF EXEGETE	
the interpreter of Sacred Scripture must attentively investigate . . .	one must attend no less diligently to . . .

The *conjunctions* contribute to a dialectical rhythm that runs through the whole of chapter III (nos. 11–13), between considerations that pertain, alternately, to the divine and to the human character of the biblical text. Thus, the postpositive *autem* that stands at the head of paragraph 12 serves to present the first set of principles, which bears upon the human mode of biblical discourse, as a kind of counterpoint to paragraph 11, which deals with Scripture's divine inspiration. Likewise, the word *sed*—which is the structural center of paragraph 12, as Ignace de la Potterie demonstrates[162]—presents the second set of principles as a kind of qualification to the first set.

162 Ignace de la Potterie, "Interpretation of Holy Scripture in the Spirit in Which It Was Written (*Dei Verbum* 12c)," in *Vatican II: Assessment and Perspectives Twenty-Five Years After (1962–1987)*, vol. 1, ed. René Latourelle (New York: Paulist, 1988), 236.

The fact that each set of principles is introduced by a *patristic axiom* is of obvious importance for the present inquiry. Insofar as paragraph 12 implies a kind of endorsement of the historical-critical method (a partial truth that needs to be carefully qualified), we must recognize that the identification of literary genres—or any other modern "tools and techniques" we may wish to employ—must be practiced not simply within the "boundaries" of Catholic dogma but under the positive guidance of those luminous principles that gave patristic exegesis its unique sort of access to the Christian mystery as that mystery is present to the Church in the modality of Sacred Scripture.

We have already considered the significance of the first axiom, which is from Augustine and deals with the human mode of God's speaking in Scripture. The second axiom, which comes from Jerome (who learned it from Origen), teaches us that "Sacred Scripture is to be read and interpreted in the same Spirit in which it was written" (no. 12). This clause, which was inserted into the text of the dogmatic constitution at the eleventh hour, places the various exegetical principles in a new light and gives them a deeper significance.[163] Apart from this patristic axiom, which accents the pneumatological character of the interpretive act, one might be tempted to suppose that paragraph 12 portrays exegesis as a matter of sheer criteriology, or methodology in the strict sense.

Jerome's axiom indicates that the mind of the exegete must come under the influence of an action of the Holy Spirit that is analogous to the action of "the same Spirit" upon the mind of the ancient human author. It is insufficient merely to interpret Scripture with "presuppositions of faith," though these are, of course, necessary. Authentically theological exegesis flows from the interpreter's interior life and living contact with the divinely revealed realities to which Scripture bears witness. In the words of Denis Farkasfalvy: "The interpreter aims not to reach a merely intellectual comprehension of the text but to experience the reality about which the text speaks, and thereby to encounter God, the ultimate speaker in each biblical passage."[164]

This spiritual, even mystical, experience creates a "deep communion" and "mysterious unity" between ancient author and modern reader.[165] This

163 De la Potterie, "Interpretation of Holy Scripture," 251–54; Alois Grillmeier, "Chapter III," in *Commentary*, 225–26.

164 Denis Farkasfalvy, O. Cist, *Inspiration and Interpretation: A Theological Introduction to Sacred Scripture* (Washington, D.C.: The Catholic University of America Press, 2010), 130–31.

165 De la Potterie, "Interpretation of Holy Scripture," 244.

does not, however, mean that the hermeneutical gap can be bridged by an experience that is merely subjective and individualistic, for that which is genuinely pneumatological or charismatic is always also fully ecclesial and grounded in the rule of faith. Ancient author and modern reader belong to the same pilgrim people of God, are carried along by the current of the same Tradition, and are put in touch with the same realities by the Holy Spirit. Their fellowship across time is thus historical in the deepest sense of the word. The spiritual and ecclesial life of the interpreter places him or her within the living Tradition, where the reading of Scripture becomes genuinely mystagogical.

The "sense" (*sensus*) that the interpreter is to "draw forth" from the sacred text is not merely its "meaning" or "message" in the modern sense, a configuration of ideas decoded from the words. It is rather a shared understanding of divinely revealed realities. The ancient author shared this understanding with the believing community to which he belonged (whether ancient Israel or the early Church), and under the inspiration of the Holy Spirit he consigned it to writing, giving it a new, objective, and enduring mode of presence within the life of the people of God. To draw forth the *sensus* of any passage of Scripture rightly—that is, to interpret the text "in the same Spirit in which it was written"—is to participate in that "supernatural sense of the faith" that belongs to the people of God as a whole.[166]

Fr. Fitzmyer refers to the term "spiritual sense" as a "weasel word" because "it is not always used in a univocal way."[167] His solution is to use the term in two ways but to keep these sharply distinct. First, as we have seen, he identifies a "spiritual sense" that is "nothing other than the literal sense" when this is discovered through the employment of the historical-critical method with presuppositions of faith. Second, he speaks of an "added" spiritual sense that constitutes a closely circumscribed Christological interpretation of the Old Testament.[168]

To a certain extent, Fitzmyer's usage here parallels that of the patristic-medieval exegetical tradition, which speaks of biblical interpretation as "spiritual" in two distinguishable but closely related ways. First, for the Fathers and doctors, an interpretation is "spiritual" when it is not "carnal"—that is, when it does not reflect a merely human understanding of the things spoken

166 Cf. Vatican Council II, Dogmatic Constitution on the Church *Lumen Gentium* 12.

167 Fitzmyer, *Scripture, Soul of Theology*, 62–63; cf. *Interpretation of Scripture*, 91.

168 Fitzmyer, *Scripture, Soul of Theology*, 63–65.

of in the biblical text. This can apply even to exegesis of the literal sense. In *De Genesi ad litteram*, for example, Augustine confines himself to an interpretation of the literal sense but reminds his readers that "we must first drive from our minds the carnal notions that people entertain about creation."[169] Second, and more commonly, exegesis is "spiritual" when it goes beyond the literal sense to the allegorical, tropological, and anagogical senses.

Unlike Fitzmyer, however, the Church Fathers are not interested in sharply distinguishing between these two uses of the word "spiritual." Rather, they slide back and forth from one to the other almost imperceptibly. This is not because they use "spiritual sense" as a weasel word but because they use it analogically—that is, to refer to things that participate in each other. Exegesis of the literal sense is "spiritual" (that is, noncarnal) when the interpreter comes, through the signification of the words of Scripture, to a divinely granted understanding of the *realities* to which those words refer. As for the "spiritual sense" that goes beyond the literal sense, it is not an "additional" meaning of the *words* but is the unfolding of deeper dimensions of signification (allegorical, tropological, and anagogical) that lie hidden within the *realities* to which Scripture (literally) refers.[170] The *sensus litteralis* and the *sensus spiritualis* thus interpenetrate and participate in one another.[171]

According to Augustine, the interpreter of Scripture should strive to discern what the human author "meant" (*sensit*)—that is, what he wanted the reader to "understand" (*intellegere*).[172] What the author wants us to understand, however, is not merely a meaning or message, but "divinely revealed things" (*divinitus revelata*, cf. *Dei Verbum* 11). One can never arrive at such an understanding by the mere application of a rational method, even if that method has been "properly oriented" by the addition of "presuppositions of faith"—at least, not so long as these presuppositions are expected to function as rational criteria, as mere ideas that must be factored into the process by which we decode the "meaning" or "message" of Scripture. Rather, Scripture must be "read and interpreted in the same Spirit in which it was written" (no. 12). This is why Augustine prays for a grace correlative to that given to the sacred author: "You, who granted to that servant of yours to speak these things, grant also to me to understand them."[173]

169 Augustine, *De Genesi ad litteram* 4.8.

170 Thomas Aquinas distills the patristic tradition in this regard in *STh* I, q. 1, a. 10.

171 De Lubac, *Medieval Exegesis*, 2:26.

172 Augustine, *Confessions* 12.30; 12.23; cf. *De Genesi ad litteram* 1.21.

173 *Confessions* 11.3 (*et qui illi servo tuo dedisti haec dicere, da et mihi haec intellegere*).

In 1993, Pope John Paul II felt it necessary to recall this principle for the benefit of Fr. Fitzmyer and the other members of the Pontifical Biblical Commission:

> Indeed, to arrive at a completely valid interpretation of words inspired by the Holy Spirit, one must first be guided by the Holy Spirit; and it is necessary to pray for that, to pray much, to ask in prayer for the interior light of the Spirit and docilely to accept that light, to ask for the love that alone enables one to understand the language of God, who "is love."[174]

Recognizing that it can be difficult to determine with confidence the human author's intention, but that our understanding of the realities to which Scripture refers must in any case be in conformity with the faith of the Church, Augustine articulates a prioritization of hermeneutical values. Faced with a plurality of interpretations that are in conformity with Catholic faith, "we should choose above all that which appears certain to have been meant by the author we are reading." If this cannot be determined, we should at least select an interpretation "that the context of Scripture does not impede and that harmonizes with sound faith." If consideration of the context arrives at inconclusive results, we should by all means be careful to interpret in a way that does not depart from the rule of faith.[175] Ideally, then, exegesis should accord with the *voluntas scriptoris*, the *circumstantia scripturae*, and the *regula fidei*.[176] When there is uncertainty about the first of these criteria, as is often the case, one should strive for conformity with the second and the third. When even the second criterion cannot be met, the interpreter must at least adhere to the third.

In this passage from *De Genesi ad litteram*, Augustine is concerned with exegesis of the literal sense, but he lays a solid foundation for interpretation of the spiritual sense as well. For unless the exegete comes to a "spiritual" (that is, not merely human) understanding of the realities to which Scripture literally refers, how can he or she go on to unfold the deeper dimensions of these realities? While Augustine specifies his hermeneutical criteria and even prioritizes them, his hermeneutic is not merely criteriological.

174 Pope John Paul II, "Address on the Interpretation of the Bible in the Church," in Pontifical Biblical Commission, *Interpretation of the Bible*, 19–20. Punctuation modified.

175 Augustine, *De Genesi ad litteram* 1.21; cf. 4.1.

176 That is, the human author's communicative intention, the context within the canonical narrative of Scripture, and the ecclesial rule of faith.

Similarly, in *Dei Verbum* 12 the council fathers lay out a unified set of hermeneutical principles for discerning the literal sense, but in such a way as to lay the foundation for exegesis of the spiritual sense as well. In its essential principles, the hermeneutic of *Dei Verbum* is patristic and especially Augustinian, but it also incorporates elements of the historical-critical approach. The two patristic axioms that are quoted in paragraph 12—namely, that in Scripture God has spoken *per homines more hominum* ("through men in the manner of men"), and that we must interpret Scripture *eodem Spiritu quo scripta est* ("in the same Spirit in which it was written")—are decisively important for achieving a proper synthesis of all these elements along the lines of the Method C envisioned by Joseph Ratzinger.

Elsewhere in the dogmatic constitution, the council fathers seem to invite the Church to rediscover the patristic-medieval approach to Scripture, including exegesis of the spiritual sense. For example, this tradition is repeatedly evoked in chapter IV, on the Old Testament. The economy of the old covenant was instituted, in part, in order to "signify by various types" the advent of Christ and of his kingdom. In the books of the Old Testament "the mystery of our salvation lies hidden." Indeed, in inspiring both testaments, God arranged things in such a way that "the New lies hidden in the Old, and the Old is made manifest in the New" (nos. 15–16). Similarly, toward the end of the document, when the council fathers describe the study of Scripture as the "soul" of theology, they seem to have in mind something that goes beyond exegesis of the literal sense, for it is a question of "searching out, under the light of faith, the whole truth hidden in the mystery of Christ" (no. 24). Finally, as we have seen, the dogmatic constitution explicitly recommends "the study of the holy Fathers" in the context of fostering the Church's advance toward a more profound understanding of Scripture (no. 23).

This point, however, must not be stated one-sidedly. The section on the Old Testament (chapter IV, nos. 14–16) has also been profoundly influenced by the perspectives of modern exegesis, and the section on the New Testament (chapter V, nos. 17–20) even more so. The widespread notion that *Dei Verbum* amounts to an "unabashed endorsement of the historical-critical method"[177] must not be countered with the equally mistaken idea that it is advocating a "return" to the patristic approach. The entire dogmatic

177 Donald Senior, CP, "Dogmatic Constitution on Divine Revelation *Dei Verbum*, 18 November, 1965," in *Vatican II and Its Documents: An American Reappraisal*, ed. Timothy E. O'Connell (Wilmington, Del.: Michael Glazier, 1986), 127.

constitution weaves together patristic and historical-critical perspectives on Scripture, and it is this above all that points us in the direction of a Method C synthesis. As Ratzinger never tires of pointing out, achieving such a synthesis is a vast and complex multidisciplinary undertaking that has hardly begun. The *ressourcement* of patristic exegesis is but one piece in the puzzle, albeit a crucial one.

CHAPTER FOUR

The Sabbath Precept in the Divine Pedagogy

The Decalogue is the cornerstone of Western civilization. Its pride of place in Judaism is beyond question, and from her earliest days the Catholic Church received it with reverence among the constitutive elements of her life and doctrine.[1] The Lord Jesus deepened our understanding of the Ten Commandments in his teaching, fulfilled them in the manner of his life, death, and resurrection, and through the gift of the Holy Spirit bestowed upon us the grace to keep them. He did not abrogate them. Already in the second century, Irenaeus of Lyons identified the Decalogue as a set of "natural precepts," a revealed distillation of the immutable moral law.[2] In accord with the Lord's own words, the Church Fathers teach us that if we would "enter into life," we are bound to "keep" the Ten Commandments according to their literal signification.[3]

Or rather, we are bound to keep *nine* of the Ten Commandments. Somehow, one rogue ceremonial precept has insinuated itself into this venerable

1 Geoffrey Wigoder, ed., *The Encyclopedia of Judaism* (New York: MacMillan, 1989), 697; P. G. Kuntz, "Decalogue," *DBI* 1:256–62; Childs, *Book of Exodus*, 428–32. See especially Irenaeus, *Adversus haereses* 4.16.4 (*decalogi verba . . . permanent apud nos*).

2 *Adversus haereses* 4.15.1; cf. 4.13.4.

3 *Adversus haereses* 4.15.1; cf. Matt 19:17–19.

4 According to Augustine's division and enumeration of Exod 20:2–17, which is followed by the Catholic Church and some Lutheran bodies, the Sabbath precept is the *third* commandment, while "You shall not covet your neighbor's wife" and "You shall not covet your neighbor's [possessions]" are treated as two distinct commandments. *Quaestiones in Heptateuchum* 2.71; cf. Deut 5:18. For purposes of the present study, however, it will be more convenient to follow the system used by Jews, Orthodox Christians, and most Protestants, according to which the Sabbath precept is reckoned the *fourth* commandment (with Exod 20:3–6 comprising two

summary of the moral law. This anomaly is the fourth commandment,[4] known as the Sabbath precept—"Remember the Sabbath day, to keep it holy" (Exod 20:8)—which the Church Fathers treat as strictly ceremonial and thus without literal moral signification.[5] Furthermore, the Sabbath precept, according to its literal-ceremonial sense, is understood to have applied only to the people of Israel and only for so long as the Mosaic covenant remained in force.[6] As with the other ceremonies of the old law, the Lord Jesus "cancelled" the Sabbath rest by inaugurating the new covenant.[7] Naturally, the fourth commandment, like "all Scripture," is "divinely inspired and useful for teaching" (2 Tim 3:16), but in the opinion of the Fathers the Sabbath law, like the other ceremonial precepts, instructs those living under the new covenant only by way of its mystical signification or spiritual sense. Unlike the other nine commandments, it is not a universally binding moral precept.[8]

This chapter is concerned with two closely related questions: Why is the Sabbath precept in the Decalogue? And what role did Sabbath observance play in the divine pedagogy of the old covenant? As in previous chapters, I shall pursue the answers to these questions via an ecclesial approach to biblical exegesis. Because the patristic interpretation of the Sabbath precept is complex and problematic, and therefore open to misinterpretation or oversimplification, and because scholastic exegesis significantly modified the patristic interpretation, the ecclesial approach in this case will require an intensive *ressourcement* of the Tradition before we can turn our attention to the biblical texts themselves. First, I shall examine the emergence of the standard patristic interpretation in the first and second centuries, focusing mostly on the contributions of Ignatius of Antioch, Justin Martyr, and

---

commandments and v. 17 counting as only one). This system is much older and was assumed to be correct by first-century Jewish authors such as Philo of Alexandria (*Quis rerum divinarum heres sit* 169–73) and Josephus (*Antiquities* 3.5). Not surprisingly, then, what evidence we have suggests that first-century Christian authors thought of "You shall not covet (your neighbor's possessions)" as a single commandment (Rom 7:7; 13:9; *Did.* 2.2) and of the second table of the Decalogue as therefore comprising six, not seven, commandments (Matt 19:18–19; Mark 10:19).

5 E.g., Augustine, *Epistola* 55.22.

6 Justin Martyr, *Dialogue* 11.2.

7 Irenaeus, *Adversus haereses* 4.16.5. The verb περιέγραψε (which presumably underlies Latin *circumscripsit*) means "cancelled" here. Irenaeus of Lyons, *Saint Irenaeus Bishop of Lyons' Five Books Against Heresies*, ed. W. Wigan Harvey (Rochester, N.Y.: St. Irenaeus Press, 2013; reprint of 1857 edition), 2:40–41, n. 8; 2:192, n. 5; cf. LSJ, 1371a.

8 Augustine states this explicitly in *De Spiritu et littera* 23 and in *Epistola* 55.22.

Irenaeus of Lyons. Second, I shall offer a constructive critique of this interpretation, allowing Justin to display its deficiencies and Irenaeus its promise. Third, I shall consider the contributions of Augustine of Hippo and Thomas Aquinas. With the former, the patristic interpretation attains its classic form, but its central problematic remains unsolved. The latter achieves a major breakthrough, making it possible to view the biblical texts from a fruitful new vantage point. Fourth, I shall sketch out the role of Sabbath observance in the divine pedagogy by commenting on selected passages from the Old Testament. Finally, I shall offer a few concluding remarks.

EMERGENCE OF THE PATRISTIC INTERPRETATION

The seeds of the patristic view of the Decalogue are found in the New Testament and the *Didache*. While the first four commandments (including the Sabbath precept) are never cited in these early Christian texts, various selections of the remaining six commandments are cited frequently, and in such a way as to indicate that their literal moral content is binding on Christians.[9] This so-called second table of the Decalogue is often accompanied by Leviticus 19:18—"You shall love your neighbor as yourself"—which serves as its summary and indicates its mode of fulfillment.[10] The nascent distinction between moral law and ceremonial law is fairly clear in the Epistles of Paul. He anchors his Christian moral paraenesis in the second table of the Decalogue, as fulfilled by ἀγάπη, "love" (Rom 13:8–10), whereas he associates Sabbath observance with the new moon celebration and the annual festivals of the old covenant, all of which constitute "a shadow of the things to come" in Christ (Col 2:16–17).

Meanwhile, in the Gospels, the Lord Jesus in his controversies with the Pharisees makes an explicit claim to supreme authority over the Sabbath and appears to relax the requirement of Sabbath observance for his followers to some extent (Matt 12:1–14), something he by no means does in the case of the second table of the Decalogue (5:17–30; 19:17–19). Most importantly,

9 Matt 5:21, 27; 15:4; 19:17–19; Mark 7:10; 10:19; Luke 18:20; Rom 7:7; 13:8–10; Eph 6:1–3; Jas 2:10–11; *Did.* 2.2–3. The Sabbath precept makes its first appearance in Christian literature a full century after the resurrection, in *Barn.* 15.1–9, where it is cited in two freely adapted forms (vv. 1–2) and given a nonliteral interpretation (vv. 3–9).

10 Matt 5:43; 19:19; 22:39–40; Mark 12:31, 33; Luke 10:27; Rom 13:9–10 (cf. Gal 5:14); Jas 2:8; *Did.* 1.2.

he invites all who are weary and burdened to come to him to find "rest" for their souls and to exchange the yoke of the Mosaic-Pharisaic Torah for *his* yoke—that is, the yoke of the new law (11:28–30). Not coincidentally, Matthew places this great invitation immediately prior to his narration of the Sabbath controversies. The implication, as Epiphanius of Salamis notes, is that Jesus himself is "our rest and our Sabbath observance."[11]

Writing in the mid-second century, Justin Martyr raises the issue of Sabbath observance repeatedly throughout his lengthy *Dialogue with Trypho the Jew*.[12] Justin consistently associates the Sabbath law with Mosaic ceremonies such as circumcision, sacrifices, and festivals,[13] all of which have been abrogated by the new covenant.[14] At the same time, he sharply distinguishes it from certain other precepts found in the Mosaic law—namely, those which enjoin deeds that are "by nature good, pious, and just."[15] By these latter he presumably means the other nine commandments of the Decalogue, though he never mentions the Decalogue by name.[16] An implicit notion of natural law undergirds Justin's thinking in this regard: "God shows to every race of human beings that which is always and everywhere just and all righteousness, and every race knows that adultery, fornication, murder, and all such things are evil."[17] This does not apply to literal Sabbath observance, however, which was imposed exclusively upon Israel because of their peculiar "hard-heartedness" and proclivity to religious infidelity.[18] The day of rest, Justin explains, compelled Israel to remember God at least once a week and was

11 Epiphanius, *Panarion* (aka *Haereses*) 8.6.8, as cited in Willy Rordorf, *Sunday: The History of the Day of Rest and Worship in the Earliest Centuries of the Christian Church*, trans. A. A. K. Graham (London: SCM, 1968), 113n1, where Rordorf also cites Gregory the Great, *Epistola* 13.1, to similar effect.

12 My citations and translations of passages from the *Dialogue* are based on the Greek text presented in Philippe Bobichon, *Justin Martyr, Dialogue avec Tryphon, édition critique, traduction, commentaire,* 2 vols., Paradosis 47 (Fribourg: Academic Press, 2003).

13 Justin, *Dialogue* 8.4, 10.1, 10.3, 18.2, 19.5–6, 23.1–3, 26.1, 27.5, 29.3, 46.2, 47.2, 92.2–5.

14 *Dialogue* 11.2.

15 *Dialogue* 45.3; cf. 44.2 and 47.2, where the distinction between moral law and ceremonial law is especially clear.

16 That Justin has in mind here both tables of the Decalogue (excepting only the Sabbath precept) is indicated by his assertion that these universal commandments were given "for the worship of God [i.e., the first table] and the practice of justice [i.e., the second table]." *Dialogue* 44.2.

17 *Dialogue* 93.1.

18 *Dialogue* 18.2, 23.1–2, 27.2, 43.1, 44.2, 45.3, 46.7, 47.2, 92.4–5; cf. 67.8.

19 *Dialogue* 19.6, 92.4–5.

thus intended to deter them from committing idolatry.[19] At the same time, the Sabbath precept held a deeper meaning that the Jews, being a carnal people, had never grasped but that they could now learn from Christians, who are "the true spiritual Israel."[20] As Justin explains for Trypho's benefit, "the new law wills that you keep the Sabbath perpetually, but you Jews think that you are being devout by remaining idle for one day, because you do not understand why it was enjoined upon you."[21]

Justin's somewhat vague notion of a "perpetual Sabbath" received a variety of refinements from later Church Fathers and became a staple of patristic interpretation.[22] According to Tertullian and many other patristic authors, when the law commands us to abstain from "servile work" on the Sabbath, it is not talking about physical labor but *evil works*, from which we should abstain not just one day each week but every day.[23] Keeping this perpetual Sabbath is not, however, merely a matter of avoiding sin. It is the lifelong moral and spiritual quest to enter into "God's repose" (*requietio Dei*), which Irenaeus of Lyons identifies with the eschatological kingdom.[24] For Clement of Alexandria and Origen, spiritual Sabbath observance is not to be identified with idleness or inactivity of any sort but with the "contemplation" (θεωρία) of heavenly things even in this life, which prepares us for the participation in divine repose that we shall enjoy hereafter.[25] Augustine characteristically modulates this concept to give it a moral and soteriological focus. We "observe a perpetual Sabbath" when we have ceased from our own works, by which we once thought to justify ourselves, and perform the good works that God accomplishes in us.[26] The Christian is called, moreover, to observe a continuous "Sabbath of the heart" in the tranquility and serenity of an undisturbed conscience.[27] The heavenly repose into which we may enter at

20 *Dialogue* 29.2, 11.5.

21 *Dialogue* 12.3.

22 In addition to the texts cited below, see Irenaeus, *Demonstration of the Apostolic Preaching* 96; Clement of Alexandria, *Stromata* 7.7; Augustine, *Epistola* 55.17.

23 Tertullian, *Adversus Iudaeos* 4.2–3; Clement of Alexandria, *Stromata* 6.16; Augustine, *De Spiritu et littera* 27.

24 Irenaeus, *Adversus haereses* 4.16.1.

25 Clement, *Stromata* 6.14; Origen, *Contra Celsum* 6.61. See R. J. Bauckham, "Sabbath and Sunday in the Post-Apostolic Church," in *From Sabbath to Lord's Day: A Biblical, Historical, and Theological Investigation*, ed. D. A. Carson (Eugene, Ore.: Wipf & Stock, 1982), 275–80.

26 Augustine, *De Genesi ad litteram* 4.13; cf. Heb 4:10; Eph 2:10.

27 Augustine, *Enarratio in Psalmos* 91.2.

the conclusion of this wearisome life is "not an indolent sluggishness, but a kind of ineffable tranquility of leisurely action."[28]

As important as these later enhancements are, the truly formative period for patristic interpretation of the Sabbath precept was the second century, when the Church had to steer a careful course between the Scylla of Judaizing tendencies and the Charybdis of Marcionism.[29] The former treated Christianity as a mere upgrade of Judaism, while the latter severed it from its Old Testament roots. How the barque of Peter was to negotiate this treacherous strait would depend in large part on its interpretation of the Pauline Epistles. The times called for the Church not only to distinguish herself from the synagogue in a sociological sense but also to recognize the definitive "newness" (καινότης) of what she had been given and on that basis to experience authentic freedom from the Mosaic law.[30] "The law was our pedagogue unto Christ," Paul had written, "but now that faith has come, we are no longer under a pedagogue" (Gal 2:24–25). When he chided the Galatians for observing "days and months and seasons and years" (4:10), however, he was not declaring that the new covenant would lack external rites altogether. As the parallel passage in Colossians makes clear, it was the liturgical rites of the Mosaic law that he was proscribing (Col 2:16–17). The Church had received her own liturgy in seminal form from the Lord Jesus. It consisted of the Lord's Day (κυριακὴ ἡμέρα) and the Lord's Supper (κυριακὸν δεῖπνον).[31] But for that seed to grow within the soil of the Church, it was necessary to weed out the old observances.

One early reader of the Pauline Epistles who grasped this point was Ignatius of Antioch. Passing through Asia Minor half a century after Paul's death, on the way to his own Roman martyrdom, Ignatius encountered a new strain of the Judaizing heresy in the churches of Philadelphia and Magnesia. In each of these communities, it seems, a faction of Christians had withdrawn from the Sunday eucharistic assembly convened by their bishop, in order to meet separately for Eucharist on Saturday and to observe the Sabbath rest.[32] They

28 Augustine, *Epistola* 55.17; cf. *De civitate Dei* 22.30.

29 Bauckham, "Sabbath and Sunday," 251–69.

30 Note Ignatius of Antioch's pointed use of the term καινότης in *Eph.* 19.3 and especially *Magn.* 9.1, following the example of Paul (Rom 6:4; 7:6).

31 Lord's Day: Rev 1:10; *Did.* 14.1; *Magn.* 9.1. Lord's Supper or Eucharist: 1 Cor 11:20, 23–26; *Did.* 9.1–10.7; *Eph.* 13.1; 20.2; *Rom.* 7.3; *Phld.* 4.1; *Smyr.* 7.1; 8.1. The two are more or less explicitly combined in *Did.* 14.1 and Acts 20:7.

32 Ignatius, *Magn.* 3.2–4.1; 6.2–8:1; *Phld.* 2.1; 3.2–4.1; 6.1; 7.2–8.1.

also considered "the archives" (i.e., the Law and the Prophets) to be more authoritative than the gospel (*Phld.* 8.2). What is more, the instigators of this factionalism, and probably most of their followers, appear to have been gentile Christians rather than Jewish Christians (6.1).

If it strikes us as odd that gentile Christians would be so attracted to Jewish practices, we must take cognizance of non-Jewish attitudes toward Sabbath observance in the early Roman Empire.[33] Since the practice of Judaism enjoyed legal protection and Jewish congregations were sprinkled throughout the Roman world, the most public and frequent of their religious observances could hardly have escaped notice or have failed to influence the ambient culture. While prominent Greek and Latin authors caricatured the Jewish Sabbath as so much laziness and luxury, commoners who labored seven days a week without respite were more likely to admire and envy the Jews for such a humane institution.[34] Those who were able to imitate the practice did so, and some who longed for intellectual and spiritual refreshment even joined the Jews in their synagogues on Saturdays for prayer and to listen to readings from the Septuagint.[35] Since Christians and Jews studied the same Scriptures and served the same God, it is hardly surprising that some Christians, whether of Jewish or gentile background, incorporated elements of Judaism into their religious practice and belief. In Philadelphia, at least one uncircumcised man was arguing from the Jewish Scriptures for such a move and had gained a following by the time Ignatius arrived there (*Phld.* 6.1; 8.2). To Christians who lacked a robustly Pauline sense of the historical economy of redemption, giving precedent to the Sabbath over the Lord's Day may have seemed like a good idea.

In these developments Ignatius recognized a grave spiritual threat to the Church, one that had to be met with a carefully nuanced theological clarification. Two comparable but distinct realities needed to be placed in their proper interrelation within the divine economy. "Judaism" was a well-established religion, and the term Ἰουδαϊσμός had been in use for centuries, but no comparable term existed to designate the religion of the Church. To fill this linguistic and conceptual gap, Ignatius—who was, it should be remembered, the bishop of that local church where the disciples of Jesus had

33 See Thomas A. Robinson, *Ignatius of Antioch and the Parting of the Ways: Early Jewish-Christian Relations* (Peabody, Mass.: Hendrickson, 2009), 65–69.

34 Rordorf, *Sunday*, 31–33; *TDNT* 7:17–18.

35 Acts 13:16, 26, 43; 17:4, 17; 18:7.

first been called "Christians" (Acts 11:26)—coined the term Χριστιανισμός ("Christianism" or "Christianity").[36] The formal similarity between the two words—"Judaism" and "Christianism"—facilitated the juxtaposition of the two religions for sake of comparison, even as the latter term pointed directly to that which makes Christianity new, definitive, and superior to Judaism—namely, the person and mystery of Jesus Christ (*Phld.* 6.1; 9.2). Properly understood, Judaism and Christianity are not merely two contemporary religions but two major historical stages of the one divine economy, with Judaism leading up to the Christ event and Christianity following from it (*Magn.* 10.3). As Ignatius viewed the matter, Judaism had played its role and run its course, and its ceremonies had "grown old and sour" (10.2; cf. Heb 8:13). To practice Judaism, now that Christ had come and had made the grace of the new covenant available, was "incongruous" (*Magn.* 10.3). To observe the Sabbath was tantamount to a public confession that one had not yet received grace and was still living under the Mosaic law (8.1).[37]

In *Magnesians*, Ignatius employs fairly sharp rhetoric in characterizing the practices of Judaism as antiquated and obsolete but, unlike the second-century author of the *Epistle to Diognetus*, he does not ridicule Sabbath observance itself as "superstition," as if God never intended the Israelites to take the Sabbath precept literally (cf. *Diog.* 4.1–3). Writing *Philadelphians* a week or two later, Ignatius nuances his position even more carefully. The relationship between Judaism and Christianity is not bad to good, but "good" to "better" (*Phld.* 9.1) and imperfect to "perfect" (9.2; cf. *Smyr.* 7.2). As we shall see, this perspective anticipates the approach to the old law found in Thomas Aquinas's *Summa Theologiae.*

Ignatius of Antioch is the earliest author on record to draw a direct correlation between the Jewish Sabbath and the Christian Lord's Day and one of the very few Christian writers to do so prior to the fourth century.[38] He writes: "Those who once conducted their lives in accord with ancient practices have come to newness of hope, no longer keeping the Sabbath but

36 Although the fact is often overlooked, the evidence that Ignatius coined the word Χριστιανισμός is quite strong. The term occurs only five times in the first 120 years of Christianity, all in Ignatius's letters (*Magn.* 10.1, 3 bis; *Rom.* 3.3; *Phld.* 6.1). It next appears in the *Martyrdom of Polycarp* (10.1), a text composed circa AD 155 by the church at Smyrna, which seems to have been the first custodian of the Ignatian correspondence (Polycarp, *Phil.* 13.2). See further Robinson, *Ignatius of Antioch*, 203n1.

37 On Ignatius's understanding of the relationship between Judaism and Christianity, see Vall, *Learning Christ*, 200–55.

38 Exceptions include *Barn.* 15.1–9.

living according to the Lord's Day, on which our life dawned through him and his death" (*Magn.* 9.1). Ignatius recognizes that Sabbath observance is the heart and soul of Judaism, while worship on the Lord's Day is the sum and substance of Christianity. But whereas Sabbath observance and the other "ancient practices" of Judaism "have grown old and sour" (10.2), worship on the Lord's Day celebrates the "newness of hope" that has come into the world in Jesus Christ (9.1). The Sabbath therefore has in some sense given way to the Lord's Day, just as Judaism has given way to Christianity. Note, however, that Ignatius does not present the Lord's Day as a "Christian Sabbath," a day on which to abstain from physical labor. Nor does he simply juxtapose "keeping the Sabbath" to "keeping the Lord's Day," which might have suggested that the latter had simply replaced the former, one ceremonial observance replacing another. Instead, Ignatius juxtaposes "keeping the Sabbath" (σαββατίζοντες) with "living according to the Lord's Day" (κατὰ κυριακὴν ζῶντες). Sabbath observance has not been replaced by Sunday observance as such but by a whole new mode of existence. The Christian lives all seven days of the week according to the new life of grace and hope that has come about through the Lord's death and resurrection.[39] Here, Ignatius anticipates Justin Martyr's notion of a "perpetual Sabbath."

The significance of the Lord's Day is that it is the day on which this new life "dawned" (ἀνέτειλεν). The reference is of course to Christ's resurrection, but by deftly employing the verb ἀνατέλλειν ("to spring up, to dawn") Ignatius evokes the sun symbolism that had recently come to be associated with the first day of the Jewish week in the Greco-Roman world.[40] By means of the same word, moreover, he echoes a series of messianic prophecies from the Old Testament, and thus presents the Lord's Day as the great eschatological sign.[41] Indeed, Ignatius frames the correlation between Sabbath

39 A few lines later, Ignatius similarly writes that disciples of Jesus must "learn to live according to Christianity," which involves, among other things, putting away the old and sour "yeast" of Judaism and being transformed into "the new yeast, which is Jesus Christ" (*Magn.* 10.1–2).

40 Rordorf, *Sunday*, 35–38.

41 In biblical Greek (LXX and NT) the verb ἀνατέλλειν is used both astronomically ("to rise") and botanically ("to sprout"). Likewise, the cognate noun ἀνατολή can refer to the "rising" of a star or planet, or to a "shoot" or "sprout" from a plant. These terms are found in several messianic prophecies in the LXX: Num 24:17 ("a star will rise [ἀνατελεῖ] from Jacob"); Mal 3:20; RSV 4:2 ("the sun of righteousness will rise [ἀνατελεῖ] for you who fear my name"); Isa 45:8 ("let the earth sprout forth [ἀνατειλάτω] mercy, and let righteousness sprout forth [ἀνατειλάτω] too"); and Zech 3:8 ("behold, I bring my servant Shoot [ἀνατολήν]"). Cf. Heb 7:14 ("our Lord has risen/sprouted [ἀνατέταλκεν] from Judah").

and Lord's Day in a kind of eschatological parallelism. Just as the Israelite prophets, who were Christ's disciples "by the Spirit," awaited his first advent, so Christians must persevere in discipleship until his second coming (*Magn.* 9.1–2). Implicitly, the Lord's Day commemorates the paschal mystery even as it anticipates the "Day of the Lord" that is still to come. All of this serves Ignatius's basic purpose of viewing the relationship between Judaism and Christianity in terms of the one divine economy. He correlates Sabbath and Lord's Day in order to contrast them, but his correlation presupposes a fundamental continuity between Judaism and Christianity that is grounded in the historical economy of redemption.

Nevertheless, most other Christian writers of the second and third centuries avoided Ignatius's correlation between Sabbath and Lord's Day, presumably because it could lead to viewing the Lord's Day reductively as a kind of Christian Sabbath and thus involve compromising the authentic biblical understanding of the relationship between the old and new covenants. As Paul had explicitly taught, the Sabbath is "a shadow of the things to come, whereas the substance belongs to Christ" (Col 2:16–17). Nor did the Church Fathers see the human need for physical relaxation as any part of what that shadow mystically prefigured.[42] At most, they granted the practical necessity of putting aside profane labor and other worldly activities for a few hours on Sunday to give time to the things of God.[43] They were much more concerned about the spiritual dangers of idleness and sloth than about the harmful effects of what we call workaholism.[44] As for our modern conflation of Sabbath and Lord's Day into a two-day debauch of football and feasting, they could only have viewed it as an appalling profanation of both covenants at once.[45]

42 See Bauckham, "Sabbath and Sunday," 280–87 and 297n204.

43 Tertullian, *De oratione* 23; *Didascalia* 13; Origen, *In Numeris homiliae* 23.4; John Chrysostom, *De eleemosyna homilia* 3.

44 *Didascalia* 13; Augustine, *Ennaratio in Psalmos* 91.2; *Epistola* 55.17.

45 Cf. Gregory the Great, *Epistola* 13.1: "It has come to my ears that certain men of perverse spirit have sown among you some things that are wrong and opposed to the holy faith, so as to forbid any work being done on the Sabbath day. What else can I call these but preachers of Antichrist, who, when he comes, will cause the Sabbath day as well as the Lord's day to be kept free from all work." Translation: *NPNF*[2] 13:92.

CRITIQUE OF THE PATRISTIC INTERPRETATION

The merit in the Church Fathers' interpretation of the Decalogue and the Sabbath precept is that they developed it in fidelity to the New Testament. Following such texts as Matthew 19:16–22 and Romans 13:8–10, they viewed the second table of the Decalogue as a summary of the immutable moral law, the fulfillment of which is necessary for salvation, and they taught that this could only be accomplished by means of the divine charity (ἀγάπη) that has been poured into our hearts under the new covenant (Rom 5:5). In light of Colossians 2:16–17, however, the Fathers understood the Sabbath commandment to belong to the ceremonial precepts of the Mosaic law, the literal observance of which had been abrogated with the promulgation of the new law. Since Paul had identified the Sabbath as a foreshadowing (σκιά) of the new covenant, the Fathers developed a spiritual interpretation according to which the Sabbath precept commands us to keep a "perpetual Sabbath" by abstaining from evil works seven days a week. This interpretation reaches its classic form with Augustine, for whom the Sabbath rest prefigures the life of grace as such. It teaches us to abstain not only from evil works but also from those works of the law ("servile works") by which we thought to justify ourselves.

In the process of hammering out this interpretation of the Sabbath precept, the Fathers made a significant contribution to the broader theological effort to flesh out some of the most basic distinctions in Christian theology—namely, between natural law and revealed law, old law and new law, and moral law and ceremonial law. It is less clear whether their treatment of the fourth commandment made a positive contribution to the concomitant hermeneutical effort to elaborate a theory of the senses of Scripture. The patristic interpretation of the fourth commandment is of the sort that would later be termed tropological, since it makes reference to morals and the life of grace. It is also anagogical inasmuch as the "perpetual Sabbath" that is lived by grace was understood to prepare for and culminate in the repose of heavenly glory. The Fathers did not, however, properly ground this tropological-anagogical sense in the most basic level of spiritual exegesis—namely, the allegorical sense. With rare exceptions prior to the fourth century, they made no attempt to indicate how Christ himself had fulfilled the Sabbath precept. Only with Augustine's *De Genesi ad litteram*, as we shall see, were all the pieces in place for a complete threefold spiritual sense—allegorical, tropological, and anagogical—though not even Augustine connected the dots.

At an even more fundamental level, the Fathers make almost no attempt to found their spiritual interpretation of the Sabbath precept upon the literal sense of the Old Testament. Indeed, they appear to try to avoid anything of the sort. With few exceptions, they show little or no interest in what the Law and the Prophets might have to teach us about the very nature of the Sabbath or the positive, pedagogical role that literal Sabbath observance played in Israel's theological and spiritual development as the Holy Spirit prepared them for the advent of the Messiah. They are content to cite a few passages that portray Jewish Sabbath observance in a negative light. For example, the Fathers frequently cite Isaiah 1:13–14 ("your new moons and Sabbaths I cannot endure")—which they take out of context and tendentiously interpret to mean that Israel's literal Sabbath observance was *never* acceptable to God[46]—whereas they choose to ignore Isaiah 58:13–14 ("then you will find your delight in Yahweh"), from which they might have learned what God was positively trying to accomplish by having his people rest from labor every seventh day. When Trypho the Jew astutely asks Justin Martyr why he never cites this passage, the latter smugly dismisses the question as impertinent and launches into still another ugly tirade about Jewish incorrigibility.[47]

Nor do the Fathers show much interest in the remarkable prominence that the Sabbath precept has throughout the Pentateuch. While the Priestly authors go out of their way to link the fourth commandment to God's own rest on the seventh day of creation,[48] the Fathers mostly ignore this link and are at pains to dissociate the Sabbath commandment from the order of creation and the natural law, even if this means resorting to flimsy arguments. Justin, for example, thinks it probative that the cosmic elements (στοιχεῖα) do not stop for a rest every seventh day.[49] The primordial nature of the Sabbath rest is also evident in the fact that God reveals it to the Israelites in conjunction with the heavenly gift of manna, even before they reach Mount Sinai or receive the Decalogue.[50] The Sabbath precept is promulgated no less than ten times in the Torah, far more often than any other single commandment, and in every case it occupies a position of prominence within the literary structure

46 *Barn.* 15.8; Tertullian, *Adversus Iudaeos* 4.2; Victorinus of Pettau, *De fabrica mundi* 5; Eusebius, *In Psalmo 91 commentarium*. On this last, see Bauckham, "Sabbath and Sunday," 283.

47 Justin, *Dialogue* 27.1–4.

48 Exod 20:8–11; 31:16–17; cf. Gen 2:2–3.

49 *Dialogue* 23.3; cf. 29.3.

50 Exod 16:22–30; cf. Neh 9:14, "your holy Sabbath you made known to them."

of the biblical text.[51] It stands at the head of Israel's liturgical calendar. Yom Kippur, the most solemn day of the Jewish year, is designated a special Sabbath of penitential self-discipline.[52] The narrative about the judicial execution of the Israelite man who was found gathering wood on the Sabbath suggests that willful desecration of this holy day is a sin against God, comparable to idolatry.[53] None of this seems to have left a mark on the standard patristic interpretation of the fourth commandment. Prior to Augustine, the Fathers are remarkably incurious even when it comes to the most obvious question of all: Why is the Sabbath precept included in the Decalogue?

Egregious in this regard is Justin Martyr, whose *Dialogue* supposedly demonstrates the superiority of Christianity to Judaism *on the basis of the Old Testament*. Near the outset of his conversation with Trypho and his friends, Justin declares the Mosaic law null and void, but later he must admit that it does contain some universal and immutable moral laws, which he sharply distinguishes from those temporary precepts enjoined exclusively on Israel due to their singular depravity and hardness of heart.[54] He treats the former class of laws as extrinsic to the Mosaic covenant, as if they just happened to be found in the Pentateuch, and he studiously avoids all reference to the Decalogue as such. Any serious consideration of the Decalogue would call attention to the inconvenient fact that the Pentateuch presents a list of universal moral laws as the very heart of the Mosaic legislation and that, for some untold reason, the Sabbath precept is found near the center of this list.

Justin's difficulty is not with the universal moral law as such, of course, but with the Mosaic covenant and its ceremonial precepts. Why would God give a set of commandments to one people at one time in history that he has not given to all peoples of all times? Justin considers it "absurd" to think that God "does not want every race of human beings always to perform the same just deeds."[55] Therefore, he must not simply distinguish between moral law and ceremonial law but treat the two as extrinsic to each other as far as possible, though they happen to be found together in the law of Moses. The ceremonial precepts cannot make any positive contribution to justice and piety, Justin reasons. Otherwise, they would have been given to all peoples

51 Exod 20:8–11; 23:12; 31:12–17; 34:21; 35:1–3; Lev 19:3; 19:30; 23:3; 26:2; Deut 5:12–15.

52 Lev 23:3; 16:30–31; 23:30–32.

53 Num 15:32–36. See Milgrom, *Numbers*, 408–10.

54 *Dialogue* 11.2; 45.3; cf. 44.2 and 47.2.

55 *Dialogue* 23.1.

of all times. Still, Justin believes these precepts to have been divinely instituted. He is too deeply committed to the apostolic tradition, and too much an opponent of Marcion, to hold any other view.[56] He believes that the ceremonies of Judaism were instituted to prefigure the mystery of Christ,[57] but he also recognizes that their literal observance must have served some purpose during the period when the Mosaic covenant was in force. What then is this purpose?

In answering this question Justin does make a handful of statements that bear a certain resemblance to the idea of a divine pedagogy. After Israel's apostasy with the golden calf, God "adapted" his laws to their sinfulness and commanded them to offer sacrifices to his name, so that they might be less inclined to offer them to idols. Likewise, he enjoined Sabbath observance so that they would hold him in remembrance. Later, he permitted the building of a temple in Jerusalem so that the Israelites would render service to the true God rather than to idols.[58] In sum, the ceremonies of the Mosaic covenant were intended to remind the Jews "to keep God always before [their] eyes," so that they "might someday repent and please him."[59]

Was any of this effective in curbing Israel's sinful propensities? No, it would seem not. Instead, according to Justin, the vicious habits of the Jews only underwent "an increase of intensity" (ἐπίτασις), and they remained "a hardhearted, stupid, blind, and lame people, sons in whom there is no faithfulness."[60] Justin is convinced that the ceremonial rites of Judaism "contributed nothing to righteous action or piety."[61] Insofar as God had a pedagogical purpose in promulgating the ceremonial laws, that purpose was frustrated by Israel's incorrigible sinfulness. Justin does not, of course, think that every last Israelite or Jew who lived under the Mosaic law will be eternally condemned. He readily grants that any individual Israelites "who did what is universally and naturally and eternally good" must have been pleasing to God and will be saved through Jesus Christ at the resurrection, just as will their righteous pre-Mosaic ancestors.[62] But this is entirely a matter of the

56 Justin wrote a book against Marcion that is no longer extant. See Irenaeus, *Adversus haereses* 4.6.2; Eusebius of Caesarea, *Ecclesiastical History* 4.18.

57 *Dialogue* 44.2.

58 *Dialogue* 19.6; 22.11.

59 *Dialogue* 46.5; 27.2.

60 *Dialogue* 27.4; cf. Deut 32:20.

61 *Dialogue* 46.7.

62 *Dialogue* 45.4.

universal moral law and has nothing to do with the ceremonial precepts or the Mosaic covenant as such.

The upshot of all this is that Justin leaves us with a somewhat disjointed picture of the Mosaic law, in which moral law and ceremonial law do not seem to work together toward a common goal, at least not effectively. To some extent this may reflect Justin's selective use of apostolic tradition and the nascent New Testament canon. The *Dialogue* is sprinkled with quotations from the Synoptic Gospels, but nothing explicit from Paul's Epistles; and Justin's laissez-faire attitude toward Christians who attempt to keep the ceremonial precepts of the Mosaic law is certainly at odds with the Epistle to the Galatians.[63] Still, the memory of Paul does "shimmer in the background" of one important passage, where Justin notes that Abraham was still uncircumcised when he was justified by faith, and on that basis concludes that circumcision was later given to Israel "as a sign, but not as a work of righteousness."[64] Although Justin may at times sound more Pelagian than Pauline when it comes to what does justify a man, he is at least consistently clear that works of the ceremonial law do not.

Even if Justin had possessed a superb grasp of the Pauline Epistles, he would have had to deal with the fact that Paul did not write anything like a complete treatise on the law. Having rejected Marcionism, the second-century Church had no other choice but to interpret Paul in conjunction with Matthew, James, and the rest of the emergent Christian canon. Paul makes only one brief statement about the Sabbath (Col 2:16–17), in which he discusses neither why the Sabbath precept is included in the Decalogue nor what role literal Sabbath observance played within the framework of the Mosaic covenant and God's overarching plan of salvation. Both testaments suggest, however, that God gradually but successfully formed, purified, and prepared a remnant of his people Israel for the coming of the Messiah. As we shall see, moreover, many passages of the Old Testament indicate that the ceremonies of the Mosaic covenant, not least literal Sabbath observance, played a significant, positive role in this process and that they played this role in close conjunction with the universal moral law enjoined upon Israel in the Decalogue.

When Justin explains the divine purpose in instituting the Sabbath and the other ceremonial laws, he gets good mileage out of the idea that God did

63 *Dialogue* 47.2–4; cf. Gal 5:2–4.

64 *Dialogue* 23.4–5; Hans Conzelmann, *Gentiles—Jews—Christians: Polemics and Apologetics in the Greco-Roman Era*, trans. M. Eugene Boring (Minneapolis: Fortress, 1992), 296.

this on account of Israel's "hardheartedness" (σκληροκαρδία). He employs this leitmotif at least nine times and in doing so seems to have influenced the later exegetical tradition significantly.[65] A critique of this idea may therefore be in order.

In insisting that the ceremonial precepts were instituted on account of Israel's hardness of heart, Justin is of course extrapolating from the Lord Jesus's statement about the Deuteronomic divorce law: "It was for your hardheartedness that [Moses] wrote you this commandment."[66] Leaving aside the other ceremonial precepts, Justin's implied analogy between the Sabbath precept and the divorce law does not bear scrutiny. In fact, the analogy breaks down immediately. First, the divorce law is a judicial precept, whereas the Sabbath commandment is ceremonial. Second, our Lord's statement that "Moses permitted" divorce accurately reflects Deuteronomy's own programmatic distinction between what God himself spoke to Israel on Mount Horeb (the Decalogue) and the laws that he communicated to Israel through Moses forty years later (the Deuteronomic Code).[67] But the Sabbath precept clearly belongs to the former category, whereas the divorce law belongs to the latter. Where, then, is the analogy?

Third and most decisively, the Lord's refutation of the Pharisees' position concerning divorce rests on an even more basic contrast, namely, between what "Moses permitted" (divorce) and what God instituted "from the beginning of creation" (marriage). To uphold the primordial nature of marriage, therefore, Christ cites a composite quotation from the twofold creation narrative: "male and female he made them" and "the two will become one flesh."[68] Now, if we similarly view the Sabbath precept within its canonical context, we find that—like the institution of marriage but unlike the divorce law—Scripture presents the Sabbath as primordial and of divine origin. It is rooted in God's rest on the seventh day of creation. It is revealed to the Israelites even before they reach Sinai. It is promulgated as part and parcel of the Decalogue. It is reiterated throughout the Pentateuch. And it is enforced with the severest of penalties. Arguably, there is no single precept in the entire Pentateuch that makes for a weaker analogy with the Deuteronomic

65 *Dialogue* 18.2, 27.2, 43.1, 44.3, 45.3, 46.5, 47.2, 67.8, 10.

66 Mark 10:5; cf. Matt 19:8; Deut 24:1–4.

67 See Deut 5:22–6:3. The Deuteronomic redaction of the Decalogue is given in Deut 5:6–21, and the Deuteronomic Code is found in chapters 12–26.

68 Mark 10:4–5; cf. Gen 1:27; 2:24.

divorce law. Scripture does not in any way present the Sabbath precept as an afterthought or a concession to Israel's hardheartedness.

One Church Father who does glimpse the positive role that literal Sabbath observance played in the divine pedagogy of the Mosaic covenant—the exception who proves the rule—is Irenaeus of Lyons. In *Against Heresies* book 4, in the course of defending the unity of the old and new covenants against the Marcionites, he writes: "The law ordered them [i.e., the Israelites] to refrain [on the Sabbath] from all servile work, that is, from all avarice, which is stimulated by conducting business and other earthly pursuits. Instead, it encouraged works of the soul, which are accomplished through thinking, as well as wholesome discourses for the benefit of their neighbors."[69] In connection with the Sabbath legislation, it is the standard procedure of the Fathers to take the phrase "servile work" to signify sin generally,[70] but in this passage Irenaeus gives the phrase a more precise interpretation, specifying the sin of avarice. Although this is not quite an *ad litteram* interpretation, it does reflect Irenaeus's careful attention to the full range of Old Testament passages dealing with the Sabbath, which has brought the bishop of Lyons considerably closer to the pedagogical intention that lies behind Yahweh's promulgation of the Sabbath precept. Avarice is precisely the sort of sin that the institution of the Sabbath brought to the surface (Amos 8:4–6), and excessive concern with one's own "business" is precisely that which devout Sabbath observance was meant to temper (Isa 58:13–14). Irenaeus's interpretation of the phrase "servile work" is thus less arbitrary than the standard patristic interpretation. Irenaeus does not view the Sabbath merely as a curb on vices and inordinate desires, however. His reference to "works of the soul" and "wholesome discourses" suggests something more positive in the way of virtue formation.

In the same context Irenaeus makes an attempt, rare among the Fathers, to explain how the Lord Jesus fulfilled the Sabbath. He writes: "The Lord rebuked those who unjustly reproved him for healing on the Sabbaths. He did not abolish the law but fulfilled it, performing the works of a high priest: propitiating God for men, cleansing lepers, healing the infirm, and himself

69 Irenaeus, *Adversus haereses* 4.8.2.

70 Tertullian, *Adversus Iudaeos* 4.2; Augustine, *De Spiritu et littera* 27. "Servile work" (ἔργον λατρευτόν, *opus servile*) is a traditional translation of Hebrew *məlě'ket ăbôdâ* in Lev 23:7, 8, 21, 25, 35, 36, where it designates the sort of work that may not be done on certain days of rest in Israel's liturgical calendar. The phrase does not occur in the verse that refers to the Sabbath itself (23:3), but ancient exegetes understood it to apply to the Sabbath nonetheless.

dying so that exiled man might go forth from condemnation and return without fear to his inheritance."[71] Apart from the fact that Christ performed some of his healings on the Sabbath, it is not immediately clear how most of the actions mentioned here by Irenaeus would fulfill the Sabbath precept in particular. In framing the Lord's ministry and death as "the works of a high priest," Irenaeus may have in mind the fact that under the Mosaic law the priests were required to make a special battery of offerings at the temple every Sabbath (Num 28:9–10). Alternatively, Irenaeus may simply mean that the Lord's high-priestly ministry, culminating in his paschal self-oblation, fulfilled the Mosaic law as a whole. Either way, the law that the Lord Jesus "did not abolish but fulfilled" includes the Sabbath and the other ceremonial precepts. Since Irenaeus also says a few chapters later that the Lord "cancelled" the ceremonial precepts, either he understands there to be a clear distinction between "abolish" (καταλύειν) and "cancel" (περιγράφειν), or he simply preserves an unresolved tension from the New Testament. Toward the end of this chapter, we shall see that Augustine provides a more cogent and satisfying explanation of how the Lord Jesus fulfilled the Sabbath precept.

Later in book 4 of *Against Heresies* (chapters 12–16), Irenaeus returns to the topic of the Sabbath precept, this time in the context of an impressive attempt to present a unified view of the Mosaic law under the aspect of divine pedagogy and within the framework of the divine economy as a whole. Since this passage represents arguably the single greatest patristic contribution to the whole question of how to understand the Sabbath precept, and because it anticipates Thomas Aquinas's treatment of the old law and the Sabbath precept, we shall examine it in some detail.

In approaching the Mosaic law, Irenaeus works with the same basic distinction between natural precepts and ceremonial precepts that we encountered in Justin's *Dialogue*, but unlike Justin, Irenaeus does not shy away from the problem of how immutable moral laws and temporary ceremonial observances fit together within a historical economy in which God makes a covenant with a particular people. For the philosopher Justin, universal and immutable moral truth seems to float free within the Mosaic law, presumably because he does not know how to ground it in a text that is so particularistic in its concerns, so awash in the flux of history.[72] This is less a problem for Irenaeus, who has more

71 Irenaeus, *Adversus haereses* 4.8.2.

72 This is one aspect of a larger problematic that lies near the center of Justin's thought and perhaps of patristic theology generally—namely, the relationship between the philosophical view of reality and the biblical economic-historical view. See Conzelmann, *Gentiles—Jews—Christians*, 292–303.

fully assimilated Scripture's sacramental-historical view of reality, according to which God summons his people "to definitive realities by means of figures, to eternal things by means of the temporal, to spiritual things by means of the fleshly, to heavenly things by means of the earthly."[73]

According to Irenaeus, the natural precepts are present at all three major stages of the economy of redemption—from Adam to Moses, from Moses to Christ, and from Christ to the eschaton—and they contribute to its unity. "The righteous ancestors" who lived before Moses did not have the Decalogue itself, but they did have "the virtue of the Decalogue written on their hearts and souls, which is to say, they loved the God who made them and abstained from injustice toward their neighbor."[74] Under the old covenant the natural precepts had "a beginning and a springing up" through the Decalogue in the lives of faithful Jews, while under the new covenant "they received growth and fulfillment" through the teaching of Jesus in the lives of Christians.[75] By means of a careful examination of Matthew 5:21–30, Irenaeus explains how Christ, far from abrogating the natural precepts, "extended and fulfilled" them.[76] Irenaeus does not, however, simply identify the natural precepts with a text of Scripture, be it the Decalogue or the Sermon on the Mount. At all three stages of the economy the natural precepts are present first and foremost in the minds and actions of those who live by them. The scriptural words of the Decalogue and the Sermon on the Mount are the quasi-sacramental means by which the natural precepts are promulgated and made historically and salvifically present to Israel and the Church.

As for the ceremonial precepts, they are "particular precepts" adapted to Israel's condition of "bondage."[77] This does not simply refer to their slavery at the hands of the Egyptians, but to the moral and spiritual degradation into which they (and apparently all of humanity) lapsed "when justice and love for God passed into oblivion and became extinct" during their sojourn in Egypt, compounded by the idolatry into which they later fell when they "turned back to Egypt in their hearts" and worshiped the golden calf.[78] Following Justin's lead, Irenaeus holds that the ceremonial precepts were

73 Irenaeus, *Adversus haereses* 4.14.3.

74 *Adversus haereses* 4.16.3.

75 *Adversus haereses* 4.13.4

76 *Adversus haereses* 4.13.1.

77 *Adversus haereses* 4.12.3; 4.15.1.

78 *Adversus haereses* 4.16.3; 4.15.1.

enjoined upon the Israelites "on account of their hardness." He employs this idea with greater reserve, however, and draws a plausible analogy between Moses's permitting of divorce due to Israel's hardness of heart, on the one hand, and the concessions that the apostle Paul made for the Corinthians due to their lack of self-control, on the other.[79] In both testaments the same God, who is just and merciful, acts to educate and save his people.

To accomplish this in Israel's case, God used the ceremonial precepts in close coordination with the Decalogue. He promulgated the Mosaic law "for the benefit of the people, enticing them by means of the aforementioned observances, so that they, while heeding the salvation of the Decalogue, might render him gifts by means of these rites and, restrained by him, might not revert to idolatry, nor become apostates from God, but might learn to love him with their whole heart."[80] Irenaeus is clear that the ceremonial observances cannot justify sinners, whereas fulfillment of the natural precepts is necessary for salvation.[81] Nonetheless, he sees the two working together to lead Israel from hardheartedness to wholehearted love of God and neighbor. This is a much more positive view of the ceremonial precepts and a more unified view of the Mosaic law than we found in Justin's *Dialogue*.

In what appears to be a programmatic statement, Irenaeus writes that the law of Moses was given to Israel "both as education and as a prophecy of future things."[82] "Prophecy" in this context must refer both to literal prophecies of the Messiah, such as Balaam's "star" oracle,[83] and to mystical prefigurations of Christ and the Church. These latter are to be found in the Pentateuchal narratives and in the ceremonial precepts, but presumably not in the natural precepts. What unifies all these elements in Irenaeus's understanding of the law, in any case, is the concept of "education" (παιδεία).[84] The Mosaic law represents one major stage in the divine pedagogy. In the days of the patriarchs God "formed a people in advance, teaching those who were indocile to follow God." Later he raised up prophets, "accustoming man to

79 *Adversus haereses* 4.15.2; cf. 1 Cor 7:5–6, 12, 25.

80 *Adversus haereses* 4.16.2; 4.15.1.

81 *Adversus haereses* 4.15.1.

82 *Adversus haereses* 4.15.1.

83 Num 24:17, which is cited by Irenaeus in *Demonstration of the Apostolic Preaching* 58.

84 The Latin text has *disciplina*, which almost certainly reflects παιδεία in the original Greek. Robert M. Grant's translation, "a demand upon them," in *Irenaeus of Lyons*, The Early Church Fathers (London: Routledge, 1997), 148, thus misses the point.

bear his Spirit within and to have communion with God."[85] Through Moses he promulgated "laws of bondage" that were "suitable for their instruction or chastisement."[86] The tabernacle too, with its many offerings, was a means of instruction.[87] Thus, "by many means he worked to restore the human race to the harmony of salvation."[88] Finally, in what appears to be an intentional allusion to Galatians 3:24, Irenaeus indicates that pedagogy and prophecy converged and formed an integral whole insofar as they together prepared Israel for the coming of the Messiah: "The law of God educated them for the advent of Christ."[89]

How, then, does the Sabbath fit into this divine pedagogy? Irenaeus observes that, according to the prophet Ezekiel (20:12) and the book of Exodus (31:13), the Sabbath, like circumcision, was instituted as a "sign" (σημεῖον) of the covenant between God and Israel. Then he adds this important comment: "But the signs were not without symbolism—that is, not without meaning—nor were they to no purpose, inasmuch as they were given by a wise artificer."[90] One of Irenaeus's most basic theological convictions—namely, that the one true God is a wise artificer who has designed and implemented a single, unified "plan" (οἰκονομία) of creation and redemption[91]—assures him that a divinely instituted ceremonial observance such as the Sabbath must have an inherent significance and purpose. His long experience refuting Gnostic exegesis, moreover, tells him that this significance must be neither arbitrary in itself nor discovered by means of an arbitrary interpretation of Scripture. It must be in accord with divine wisdom and the rule of faith, and it must cohere with the overall plan of Scripture.

Earlier in book 4, as we have seen, Irenaeus briefly discussed the pedagogical purpose that the Sabbath had for Israel under the old covenant—namely, to discourage "avarice" and excessive concern with one's own "business," while providing the opportunity for "works of the soul" and "wholesome discourses." In the present context he gives an overlapping but fuller interpretation:

85 *Adversus haereses* 4.14.2.

86 *Adversus haereses* 4.16.5.

87 *Adversus haereses* 4.14.3.

88 *Adversus haereses* 4.14.2.

89 *Adversus haereses* 4.12.1. The Latin text has *instituenti*, which Harvey takes to reflect παιδαγωγοῦντι in the original Greek. *Saint Irenaeus* 2:177n6.

90 *Adversus haereses* 4.15.2.

91 See Eric Osborn, *Irenaeus of Lyons* (Cambridge: Cambridge University Press, 2001), 74–94.

> The Sabbaths were teaching perseverance in daily devotion to God. For "we have been reckoned," the apostle Paul says, "all the day as sheep for slaughter," that is, consecrated, and attending at all times to our faith and persevering in it, and abstaining from all avarice, neither acquiring nor possessing treasures on earth. Moreover, the repose of God—that is, the kingdom—was being manifested, as it were, from those things that have been made. And that man who, by reposing in it, will have persevered in the service of God will partake at the table of God.[92]

The main idea of this passage should be familiar by now. It is a fine example of the patristic "perpetual Sabbath" interpretation of the fourth commandment. It begins with tropology and ends with anagogy, and the link between the two is perseverance in the faith. The curious quotation of a quotation (Irenaeus quotes Paul quoting the Psalter) suggests that daily "consecration" to Christ involves suffering with him. The Sabbath rhythm, be it the weekly rhythm of the old covenant or the daily rhythm of the new, purifies man from avarice, detaches him from storing up "treasures on earth," and thus prepares him for the life of heaven.

The most significant and evocative phrase in this passage is "the repose of God" (ἡ κατάπαυσις τοῦ θεοῦ).[93] It recalls God's rest on the seventh day of creation (κατέπαυσεν [ὁ θεός], LXX Gen 2:2), but Irenaeus also identifies it with God's eschatological kingdom.[94] The person who would attain that eternal repose must *repose in the repose of God* already in this life. Irenaeus does not explain exactly what that means, but this intriguing affirmation adumbrates both the Alexandrian notion of "contemplation" (θεωρία) and the Augustinian notion of "repose of the mind in God," which Thomas Aquinas will make the centerpiece of his interpretation of the Sabbath precept, as we shall see below.

92 *Adversus haereses* 4.16.1.

93 This is my retroversion of the Latin *requietio Dei*. Harvey suggests that Irenaeus used "the Valentinian term ἀνάπαυσις" (*Saint Irenaeus* 2:190n1). Both terms have significant background in LXX, but κατάπαυσις seems the more likely choice for Irenaeus because of Gen 2:2; Exod 35:2; 2 Chron 6:41; 2 Macc 15:1; Ps 94:11; 131:14; and Isa 66:1.

94 Since for Irenaeus the kingdom is the millennial age, he may be thinking here of the scheme according to which the seventh day of the week prefigures the seventh age of one thousand years. Justin Martyr resists this idea in favor of a scheme according to which the eighth day, rather than the seventh, holds "some mystery" (*Dialogue* 24.1). The two ideas are combined in *Barn.* 15.3–9.

Before leaving this intriguing text and completing our critique of the patristic interpretation of the Sabbath precept, a hermeneutical observation is in order. Within the larger context of this passage, Irenaeus's use of the imperfect tense ("were teaching ... was being manifested") suggests that he is primarily concerned here with what weekly Sabbath observance was intended to inculcate over time in the lives of those who were under the Mosaic law.[95] He is indicating the pedagogical significance that this covenantal sign had during a particular stage in the historical economy. At the same time, however, his summary of the Sabbath's pedagogical content is imbued with New Testament concepts and language. After quoting Paul, Irenaeus echoes a dominical logion from the Gospels ("treasures on earth") and concludes with a distinctively Christian image for the eschatological kingdom, complete with eucharistic overtones ("partake at the table of God").[96] In other words, he makes no clear distinction between what weekly Sabbath observance taught Israel during the Old Testament period and what the Sabbath precept now teaches the Church.

This is hardly surprising. When Irenaeus wrote *Against Heresies* in the 180s (just about the time Origen was born in Alexandria), the patristic theory of the senses of Scripture was in an early stage of its development. Beginning with Paul's Epistles, all Christian interpretation of the Old Testament had been spiritual exegesis of one sort or another, whether typological (Melito of Sardis's *Peri Pascha*), or tropological (Clement of Rome's *Epistle to the Corinthians*), or prophetic proof-texting (Justin's *Dialogue*). It is doubtful whether any second-century Christian spoke of or even practiced what Jerome or Augustine would consider *ad litteram* exegesis. The very idea that a Christian might actually *want* to explicate the sense of the "letter" would take some getting used to. Had not Paul taught that "the letter kills, but the Spirit gives life" (2 Cor 3:6)? Still less should we expect a second-century author to approach the interpretation of the Sabbath precept with modern historical consciousness, searching for the commandment's "originally intended meaning." In any case, Irenaeus's whole project was aimed at indicating the harmony between the testaments. He would hardly have wished to drive a wedge between what the Sabbath precept *meant* and what it *means*, as a modern exegete might.

95 The Latin text has *edocebant* and *manifestabatur*, which probably reflect the Greek imperfect forms ἐδίδασκον and ἐφανεροῦτο respectively.

96 Cf. Matt 6:19; Luke 13:29; 14:15; 1 Cor 10:21.

Nonetheless, any number of considerations might have suggested to Irenaeus that some distinction could be made and ought to be made between what God "was teaching" Israel during the centuries leading up to the advent of Christ and what he now teaches Christians when they read the Old Testament in light of the New. There was, for example, the opening sentence of the Epistle to the Hebrews, which distinguishes between God's speaking "in many partial and varied ways to our ancestors by the prophets" and his definitive self-revelation in Jesus Christ "in these last days." Under such circumstances, even the most faithful of the ancestors, even the prophets themselves, must have learned gradually and only in part. The very notion that Israel had received the law as "education" implies as much. Furthermore, an implicit distinction between literal sense and spiritual sense is already present in Irenaeus's reflection on circumcision and the Sabbath as two "signs" of Israel's covenant with God. Since he could affirm that "circumcision in the flesh presignified the circumcision that is spiritual,"[97] he presumably also understood that God really did intend Israel under the Mosaic law to observe the Sabbath *once a week*, but that this weekly observance "presignified" a greater reality: the new covenant and its perpetual Sabbath.

Irenaeus's treatment of the Sabbath precept anticipates that of Thomas Aquinas in three important respects. First, his clear affirmation that a covenantal "sign" such as the Sabbath must have its own purpose and symbolism anticipates Aquinas's conviction that every precept in the old law, including the ceremonial precepts, must have a rational "cause" (*causa*) or literal "reason" (*ratio*). Second, Irenaeus's serious attempt to articulate a more or less comprehensive theory of the Mosaic law, its inner unity, and its relationship to the new covenant anticipates Aquinas's treatise on law, which includes a systematic exposition of the old law. Third, Irenaeus, like Aquinas, appreciates the heuristic value of Paul's statement that "the law was our pedagogue unto Christ" for viewing the Mosaic law as both pedagogy and prophecy. Taken together, these shared insights of the bishop of Lyons and the Angelic Doctor provide a locus within Sacred Tradition where the modern study of the Old Testament and of Israel's religious development can be brought into a purifying light and bear fruit for the life of the Church.

97 *Adversus haereses* 4.16.1.

AUGUSTINE AND AQUINAS

If even Irenaeus, despite these real gains, seems to have come up short, and the patristic "perpetual Sabbath" interpretation is in the last analysis found to be less than fully satisfying, it is perhaps due to the fact that the early Fathers left one very basic question unanswered—rather, unasked: *Why is the Sabbath precept found in the Decalogue?* This question could not be deferred interminably, however. By the early fifth century, when the Decalogue was becoming more important than ever to Christian moral theology and catechesis, the presence of a lone ceremonial precept among the nine moral precepts—the former imposed on a single nation and only for a time, the latter binding for the entire human race and for all time—had become the elephant in the room. And what an elephant! In the biblical text of Exodus 20, the fourth commandment is considerably longer than all six commandments of the second table combined. Its presence cried out for an explanation.

Because the early Fathers had done such a good job of ignoring the problem and had bequeathed no solution to their successors, later authors were left to their own devices. Hesychius of Jerusalem, a prolific exegete and younger contemporary of Augustine, resorted to a desperate tactic curiously akin to modern redaction criticism. Taking advantage of the notorious uncertainty surrounding the Decalogue's division into individual commandments and their proper enumeration, Hesychius creatively redivided the text of Exodus 20:2–17 into *eleven* commandments. Ten of these he identified as the true moral Decalogue, while he dismissed the Sabbath precept as an interpolation.[98] This was an ingenious solution but of the sort that tends to breed a certain lack of confidence in Scripture itself. Eight centuries later, Thomas Aquinas would gently dismiss it as "unfitting."[99] One might in any case have expected someone named Ἡσύχιος ("quiet, restful") to hold the Sabbath in higher regard.

The problem of the Sabbath precept's place in the Decalogue was also keenly felt by Augustine, who was not one to sidestep an exegetical difficulty. His solution was to observe that the Sabbath's spiritual significance was "concealed within a prefigurative precept" and placed among the other nine commandments in order to signify that the era of the Mosaic covenant

98 Hesychius, *In Leviticum* 7, *super* 26:26 (PG 93:1150). On the attribution of this commentary to Hesychius, see Johannes Quasten, *Patrology*, vol. 3 (Utrecht: Spectrum, 1960), 490.

99 *STh* I-II, q. 100, a. 4, corp.

was "the time for concealing that grace which was to be revealed in the New Testament through Christ's passion, as if through the rending of a veil."[100] In other words, the Decalogue, though it is the epitome of immutable moral truth, bears within itself the mark of its having been given to humanity at a particular moment in history—namely, at the very inauguration of the Mosaic covenant. The Sabbath itself, according to Augustine, as we shall see further on, is a kind of mystical sign pointing to the paschal mystery of Christ, to our sacramental insertion into that mystery in baptism, and to our eschatological entrance into the divine repose. But because the time had not yet come for these things to be revealed, they were hidden "within a prefigurative precept."

According to Augustine, what was concealed during the time when the Mosaic law was in force was grace itself, the grace without which even the nine moral precepts of the Decalogue remain a dead letter, a law that is "holy and just and good" but that nevertheless cannot of itself "impart life."[101] When Christ and the grace of the new covenant finally arrived, the Mosaic ceremony, like the temple veil, was rent asunder so that the Sabbath precept might now point with prophetic clarity to the realities of the new covenant. In this way, the law itself was transformed. "Indeed, the same law that was given through Moses has become grace and truth through Jesus Christ, for the Spirit has come to the letter, so that the justice of the law might begin to be fulfilled."[102]

This solution to the problem of the Sabbath precept's presence in the Decalogue is theologically impressive, especially within the context of Augustine's *De Spiritu et littera*, where it helps clarify the place and status of the Decalogue within both the old and new covenants. It reflects the serious thought that Augustine had given over the course of many years to the role of the immutable moral law within the plan of salvation unfolding in history.[103] Above all, it reinforces Augustine's careful reading of Paul's doctrine of law and grace. The presence of one ceremonial precept within the Decalogue moors the natural precepts to the whole historical economy. As a prefigurative precept, the Sabbath commandment indicates that the nine

100 Augustine, *De Spiritu et littera* 27.

101 *De Spiritu et littera* 24; cf. Rom 7:12; Gal 3:21.

102 Augustine, *Contra Faustum* 15.8.

103 *De Spiritu et littera* is a relatively late work, written in AD 412. Peter Brown, *Augustine of Hippo: A Biography*, 2nd ed. (London: Faber & Faber, 2000), 280.

moral precepts of the Decalogue can only be lived in their fullness by the grace of the new covenant. At the same time, it shows, at least to those who have the benefit of hindsight, that the period of the Mosaic covenant was the time of concealment, during which the grace that was to come lay hidden within such ceremonial precepts.

The shortcoming of this solution, however, is that it does nothing to illuminate the role of literal weekly Sabbath observance under the Mosaic covenant itself. According to Augustine, the Sabbath served *only* to prefigure the mystery of Christ and the life of grace, and it did so in a *concealing* manner. Presumably Moses and a few other prophets and saints understood its spiritual meaning, but for the vast majority of the many thousands of Israelites and Jews who kept the Sabbath week after week, year after year, generation after generation for over a millennium prior to the coming of Christ, it was all pointless "carnality." Is this even plausible? Yahweh had told the Israelites after the exodus that the Sabbath is "a sign between me and you for all your generations, so that you may know that it is I, Yahweh, who sanctify you" (Exod 31:13). Certainly this sign pertains in the first instance to the old covenant itself and to the sort of imperfect but very real sanctification available under that covenant. Certainly the dozens of Old Testament passages dealing with the Sabbath are primarily concerned to instruct Israelites and Jews living under that covenant. But Augustine sweeps away the modest gains of Irenaeus and once again renders the Sabbath precept all prophecy and no pedagogy.

Why was even Augustine of Hippo unable to supply a truly satisfying explanation for the Sabbath precept's place in the Decalogue? Could it be that something very basic had been overlooked for centuries and could only be rediscovered from a fresh point of view? Perhaps some significant dimension of the Sabbath had been theologically eclipsed in the second century, when the Church, while endeavoring (of necessity) to distinguish herself from the synagogue, was infected by a viral strain of anti-Judaism, according to which Jewish Sabbath observance ought to be ridiculed as idleness and wanton luxury. Further, could it be that literal Sabbath rest, a ceremonial observance "particular" to the Mosaic covenant, also embodied a timeless moral and spiritual value that long lay dormant in Christianity and only slowly reemerged in late antiquity and the Middle Ages with the practice of observing *the Lord's Day* as a day of rest from labor? If so, Catholic theology would need to recover and articulate this value in such a way as to indicate its basis in the natural law and its relation to the twofold law of charity. It would also need to clarify what exactly the Sabbath precept enjoined upon Israel and to determine which aspects remain binding under the gospel.

The opportunity for such a recovery and clarification came in the thirteenth century, when Albert the Great and Thomas Aquinas, with the help of Moses Maimonides's *Guide for the Perplexed*, applied Aristotelian principles to biblical exegesis and hermeneutics. This brought new clarity to the question of what exactly constituted the *sensus litteralis* and how it was related to the *sensus spiritualis*.[104] With respect to the Pentateuch in particular, "Rabbi Moses" taught the two great Dominicans that every law, including each ceremonial precept, had not simply a literal sense but a rational "cause" or "reason" (*causa* or *ratio*) that pertains to the literal sense.[105] As their main conduit for Jewish exegetical tradition, Maimonides also encouraged them to think of divine revelation under the aspect of law, and of Moses the lawgiver as something like a philosopher-king whose role was to teach and govern his people.[106] The results of this movement included a new impetus for the scholarly study of the human author's words in order to grasp his communicative intention, and a renewed appreciation for divine pedagogy in the Old Testament à la Irenaeus of Lyons.[107]

In his *Commentary on the Sentences* of Peter Lombard, Albert the Great argues that the Sabbath precept is not only ceremonial but also moral. Among Albert's proofs, two are notable for the way they reflect his careful attention to the Old Testament passages that deal with the Sabbath. First, he observes that God spoke the Ten Commandments "in the hearing of the people," whereas the other precepts were delivered to the people through Moses. This was fitting, he says, since the Ten Commandments belong to the natural law, "which agrees with the common knowledge of all people." But since the Sabbath precept was among those spoken in the presence of the people, it too must belong to the natural law.[108] Second, Albert astutely notes that Isaiah 58 deals exclusively with a series of moral matters, "to which, at the end, the Sabbath is subjoined." This suggests that Sabbath observance is likewise a moral matter.[109] He concludes that the Sabbath precept is "moral

104 For this development and its context, see Smalley, *Study of the Bible*, 292–308.

105 Smalley, 305–6; Aquinas, *STh* I-II, q. 102, aa. 1–2.

106 Smalley, *Study of the Bible*, 294–95.

107 Smalley, 306.

108 Albert the Great, *Super IV libros Sententiarum* III, dist. 37, a. 7, sc. 2. Cf. Deut 5:22–31; Exod 20:18–22.

109 *Super IV libros Sententiarum* III, dist. 37, a. 7, sc. 3; cf. Isa 58:13–14.

with respect to sanctification, and ceremonial with respect to the mode of observance."[110] Albert's discussion would benefit from a further explication of what the phrase "moral with respect to sanctification" means and a more explicit affirmation that this moral significance pertains to the *literal* sense of the Sabbath precept. He is nonetheless on the verge of a major breakthrough here.

Thomas Aquinas takes up the interpretation of the Sabbath precept in his treatise on law in the *Summa Theologiae*. Building on his mentor's insight, Thomas rejects outright the patristic premise that the fourth commandment has no moral content according to its literal sense. He affirms, rather, that it is both moral and ceremonial. It is moral insofar as it commands man to "make some time for divine things" and requires "repose of the heart in God," but it is ceremonial insofar as it designates the seventh day of the week as the proper time to do this.[111] Its moral principle is universal and unchangeable, but its ceremonial dimension is a determination of the moral principle specifically for the people of Israel during the period of the Mosaic covenant. Under the new covenant this moral principle receives a new determination, whereby "the Sabbath ... is changed into the Lord's Day" (*sabbatum ... mutatur in diem dominicum*).[112] With these few statements Thomas Aquinas has cut the Gordian knot.

The merit in Thomas's interpretation of the Sabbath precept derives from its inclusion in a comprehensive and unified vision of law. The treatise on law in the Prima Secundae (qq. 90–108) deals with eternal law, natural law, human law, and divine law. This last division is further subdivided into old law and new law, and the section on the old law treats of moral, ceremonial, and judicial precepts in that order. Thomas defines law as "an ordinance of reason for the common good" and teaches that every type of law participates in the unchangeable and eternal law that is "the Supreme Reason"—that is, God himself.[113] This analogical use of the term *lex* also indicates that the various types of law *are related to each other* by virtue of their various modes of participation in the prime analogate, eternal law.

Thomas's treatment of the old law is long and detailed, comprising well over half the treatise. This length and complexity reflect the extraordinary

110 *Super IV libros Sententiarum* III, dist. 37, a. 7, solutio.

111 Aquinas, *STh* I-II, q. 100, a. 3 ad 2; a. 5, corp.

112 *STh* I-II, q. 103, a. 3, ad 4.

113 *STh* I-II, q. 90, a. 4, corp.; q. 91, a. 1, sc.

effort that Thomas makes to identify the literal *ratio* for each of the various laws or types of law found in the Pentateuch. By so doing, he is able to show how they participate in eternal law, presuppose natural law, together constitute a coherent dispensation called the old law, and prepare for and prefigure the new law of the gospel. Attention to the *ratio* of each law also enables Thomas to ground the allegorical interpretation of the old law in its literal sense. This last point is especially pertinent to the ceremonial precepts, which depend partly on their literal sense and partly on their spiritual sense for their relation to the new law.

Here we should note an important difference between the respective approaches of Augustine and Aquinas. The bishop of Hippo does not so much as hint at the notion that Jewish Sabbath observance has been transferred to (much less transformed into) Christian observance of the *dies Dominica*, an idea that was just beginning to gain currency in his day.[114] On the contrary, with the arrival of the new covenant literal Sabbath observance "has been done away with" (*ablata est*). For Augustine, therefore, only the spiritual sense of the Sabbath precept is worth expounding. Its literal sense is of no interest to him. Insofar as he alludes to Jewish Sabbath observance at all, it is to note that the Jews kept this commandment "in a carnal fashion" (*carnaliter*).[115] Nor does Augustine give any scope to the idea that literal observance of the Sabbath precept played a salutary role in Israel's religious development or their being prepared for the advent of the Messiah. He is not averse to the notion that God "trained" the "few faithful ones" who were among the Israelites by means of temporal punishments,[116] but he never ascribes this sort of educative function to the Sabbath precept taken literally. Instead he heaps opprobrium upon the Jews for the dancing and trifles that he imagines must have characterized their hebdomadal abstention from labor.[117] No, according to Augustine, literal Sabbath observance was imposed on the Jews for one reason only: to prefigure the spiritual repose that was to be made available by grace.[118] This way of looking at things reflects Augustine's distinctive take on the intertwining Pauline polarities of old and new, law and gospel, grace and works, spirit and letter.

114 Bauckham finds the earliest clear instances of this idea in the writings of Eusebius of Caesarea and Ephrem of Syria. See "Sabbath and Sunday," 282–87.

115 Augustine, *De Genesi ad litteram* 4.13.

116 *De civitate Dei* 17.2.

117 *Ennaratio in Psalmos* 91.2.

118 *De Genesi ad litteram* 4.11; *Epistola* 55.18, 22.

For Thomas, by contrast, the literal *ratio* of the old law, including its ceremonial precepts, is of real interest because it is understood to have played a positive, formative role in Israel's historical life leading up to the advent of the Messiah. The intention of the ceremonial precepts was not merely to restrain Israel from idolatry but "to induce reverence for the divine cultus."[119] This is a positive pedagogical purpose. It is not simply a matter of regulating behavior but of forming Israel to be a certain sort of people. Naturally, Thomas is just as eager to conform to Paul's doctrine as Augustine was, but he emphasizes different aspects of that doctrine. Rather than stress the polarity of letter and spirit, Thomas makes much of Paul's reference to the Torah as "our pedagogue to Christ" (Gal 3:24–25).[120] This concept helps him establish deep organic connections between literal sense and spiritual sense, between ceremonial precepts and moral precepts, and between old law and new law without in any way compromising the superiority and definitiveness of the new.

The old law and the new law are distinct, Thomas teaches us, not as two species of divine law, but "as perfect and imperfect in the same species." In other words, they differ from each other not as horse differs from ox but as boy differs from man.[121] Thomas uses this image of boy and man to relate the distinction between imperfect and perfect to the understanding of Mosaic law as pedagogue. The old law was imperfect because it "brought nothing to perfection,"[122] but it did "dispose" Israel to the advent of Christ and the giving of the perfect law. "The old law disposed unto Christ, as the imperfect to the perfect" (*lex vetus disponebat ad Christum sicut imperfectum ad perfectum*).[123] Even the ceremonial precepts, according to their literal sense, "disposed human beings to the justifying grace of Christ, which they also signified" without actually imparting this grace.[124] Without relativizing the distinction between old and new, this crucial distinction between disposing to perfection and actually bringing to perfection enables Thomas to view the letter of the old law, including its ceremonial precepts, as positively contributing to the divine pedagogy.

119 Aquinas, *STh* I-II, q. 102, a. 5, ad 10.

120 *STh* I-II, q. 91, a. 5, corp.; q. 98, a. 2, ad 1; q. 99, a. 6, corp.; q. 104, a. 3, corp.

121 *STh* I-II, q. 91, a. 5, corp.

122 *STh* I-II, q. 98, a. 1, corp.; cf. Heb 7:19.

123 *STh* I-II, q. 99, a. 6., corp.

124 *STh* I-II, q. 100, a. 12, corp.

Unlike modern thinkers, Thomas does not restrict the realm of morality to the horizontal dimension—that is, to relationships between human beings. Morality also includes the vertical dimension of man's relationship with God. "You shall love your neighbor as yourself" does not summarize the entire moral law by itself, but only together with "You shall love the Lord your God with your whole heart and your whole soul and your whole mind" (Matt 22:34–40). Or as Thomas puts it, "to worship God, since it is an act of virtue, pertains to a moral precept."[125]

But what exactly does the Sabbath precept command? Unlike the first three commandments, it does not simply prohibit an irreligious species of act, such as worshiping other gods, making idols, or taking the divine name in vain. Rather, it commands something positive, the hallowing of the seventh day. But what does that involve? According to Thomas, "the sanctification of the Sabbath, in so far as it is a moral precept, commands repose of the heart in God."[126] Because this comment has an Augustinian ring, one can easily overlook the departure from Augustine that it represents. If the fourth commandment *qua moral precept* (and therefore as belonging to the immutable natural law) requires repose of the heart in God, it must have required this of ancient Israelites just as much as it does of later Christians. And this observation raises an important question: How exactly did Sabbath observance under the old covenant help pious Israelites cultivate repose of the heart in God and thus dispose them to the advent of grace? To sketch out an answer to this question, we now turn to the Old Testament.

THE SABBATH PRECEPT IN THE OLD TESTAMENT

Scripture and Tradition use the word οἰκονομία ("arrangement, plan, economy") to refer to God's master plan for the universe, comprising the orders of creation and redemption. By this divine "economy" God acts to reveal himself and to bring his creation to its appointed end. The term "divine pedagogy" refers to the specifically educative and remedial dimension of the divine economy. In the Old Testament we see God reveal himself gradually, teaching and forming the people of Israel step by step, preparing them for the advent of Jesus Christ, in whom he will reveal himself definitively.[127] Within

125 *STh* I-II, q. 99, a. 3, ad 2.

126 *STh* I-II, q. 100, a. 5, corp.

127 *CCC* 53; cf. *Dei Verbum* 15, where the term is likewise applied to the Old Testament but without the same emphasis on gradualness.

this divine pedagogy the Sabbath precept has played a vital role. Throughout the entire period of the Mosaic covenant, up to and including the public ministry of Christ, God used weekly Sabbath observance to instruct and form his people. Christ then fulfilled and transformed the Sabbath through his death, burial, and resurrection. The remainder of this chapter will sketch out the role of the Sabbath in the divine pedagogy under the Mosaic covenant by considering a selection of Old Testament passages.

To get a running start, we shall recall a few salient aspects of man's primordial vocation and of the way original sin would prevent us from living it out. Made to the image and likeness of God, man is uniquely endowed to receive creation from the hand of God, to subdue and make use of it, and to offer it back to him.[128] Man utilizes his intelligence and ingenuity to transform natural resources into manmade goods that enhance human life and further release his artistic, intellectual, and spiritual potencies. The development of human culture as we know it was triggered by the Neolithic Revolution some 10,000 years ago. This great transition from hunting and gathering to agriculture and settlement, or to nomadic pastoralism, opened spaces of leisure in human life and thus made possible all the works of culture.[129] Following a religious instinct to honor the Source of all blessings, man offered some of the first fruits of the earth and of the products of culture back to him who gave them. Agriculture begets culture, and culture in turn finds its highest expression and proper end in cultus—that is, ritual worship of the Creator. Due to original sin, however, man's natural knowledge of the Creator was imperfect at best, and often so badly confused (as in the case of polytheism) that the honor due to the Creator was often diverted to the creature, especially to other human beings or even to oneself. This is the first deadly sin: κενοδοξία ("vainglory"). In his every accomplishment, man faces the most fundamental decision of his existence—namely, whether he works for his own glory or for the glory of his Maker.

In the Priestly creation narrative the famous passage about the *imago Dei* and man's vocation to "fill the earth and subdue it" is immediately followed by the account of the seventh day, on which God "rested from all his work" (Gen 1:26–2:3). Although the noun "Sabbath" (*šabbāt*) does not occur

128 *CCC* 358; Pope John Paul II, Apostolic Letter *Dies Domini* 10.

129 On the importance of nomadic pastoral tribes (alongside sedentary agriculturalists) for the early development of human culture, see Christopher Dawson, *The Age of the Gods: A Study in the Origins of Culture in Prehistoric Europe and the Ancient East* (Washington, D.C.: The Catholic University of America Press, 2012), 177–80.

there, the text implies that man's vocation as created in the divine image involves imitating God not only in creative work but in rest from work. This point is made expressly in the book of Exodus, where the Sabbath precept is twice explicitly grounded in God's rest on the seventh day of creation (Exod 20:8–11; 31:16–17). By obeying the Sabbath precept, Israel will discover the true rhythm of human temporality and the proper proportion of work to rest, and they will come to the conviction that the order of creation is oriented to a telos that transcends God's work of creation itself. Ceaseless labor, labor without a clear telos, is selfish, futile, and enslaving. But work that is ordered to an end that transcends work itself is in accord with man's dignity and vocation.

After struggling for decades to discover the literal sense of the words *et requievit Deus die septimo ab omnibus operibus suis* ("and God rested on the seventh day from all his works"), Augustine finally arrived at a satisfying exegesis of this passage.[130] Noting that the sacred text says that the Lord rested "from" (*ab*) his works, not "in" (*in*) his works, Augustine says that Scripture thus represents God as pleased with his creation, but "not as delighting in his work in such a way as to indicate that he needed to make it . . . or that he was happier having made it."[131] God's repose consists in his finding perfect happiness in himself alone. We human beings, therefore, imitate our Creator and partake in his eternal repose when "we are made happy in the good that he is" rather than attempting to find rest in ourselves or in any other creature.[132]

Due to certain hermeneutical blind spots, however, Augustine did not see how literal observance of the Sabbath precept could ever move Israel in the direction of this true repose and happiness. He could only view literal Sabbath

130 Gen 2:2, according to the Old Latin. The Manichees used this passage both to mock the Old Testament's depiction of the Creator as apparently needing rest due to fatigue, and to demonstrate that the Old Testament is contradicted by the New Testament, where the Lord Jesus says, "My Father is working even until now, and I am working" (John 5:17). Augustine responded (circa 388) that God is said to "rest" only in the sense that "he will furnish us with rest" after our good works (*De Genesi contra Manichaeos* 1.25), an interpretation with which he himself was never satisfied. In *De Genesi ad litteram imperfectus liber* (circa 393) he did not comment on the seventh day. In *Confessions* 13.35–38 (circa 401) he insisted that God's repose is strictly eternal and immanent, not in any sense temporal (he rests in himself, not in any creature), but he offered no new interpretation of Gen 2:2. Finally, he devoted fourteen chapters of *De Genesi ad litteram* (circa 410) to the exegesis of the seventh day and at last achieved his mature interpretation (4.8–21). For the dates of these works of Augustine, see Brown, *Augustine of Hippo*, 64, 178.

131 *De Genesi ad litteram* 4.15.

132 *De Genesi ad litteram* 4.16.

observance as carnal self-indulgence and idleness, and therefore found it "laughable."[133] He did not perceive that the literal *ratio* of the Sabbath precept within the Mosaic law, along with the whole thrust of the interpretation it received from the prophets, was instructing Israel to find happiness in Yahweh their God as it gradually prepared them for the grace of the new covenant.

Of course, the Sabbath precept is not merely educative but also remedial. It addresses the specific wound of nature that is the result of original sin. In Genesis 3, the serpent tempts the woman in these words: "You will not die. For God knows that on the day you eat of it your eyes will be opened, and you will be like gods, knowing good and evil" (Gen 3:4b–5). The diabolic insinuation here is that God is not to be trusted, that he does not will our happiness. He is selfishly reserving godlikeness to himself. This allegation is profoundly ironic. There is nothing God wants more than to make us partakers of his divine nature, to make us godlike (2 Pet 1:4). That is why he made human nature in his image and created our first parents in the state of original justice.

Nevertheless, our first parents accepted the dark insinuation of the evil one and allowed their trust in their Creator to die in their hearts. "All subsequent sin" involves this "lack of trust" in God. Fallen man wants to be "like God," but on his own terms and independently.[134] Equality with God is henceforth viewed as something to be grasped at. And if this be so, every good thing that comes from the hand of the Creator is also something to be grasped at. Insofar as we doubt that God truly wills our happiness and are suspicious of his motives, we feel that we must seize what we want for ourselves before God or someone else deprives us. We do not trust in his providential care. Indeed, we refuse to accept our status as created beings defined by a specific nature, and we resent God's claim over us and his very offer to make us supremely happy in himself. In a word, we refuse to receive ourselves from the hand of God and to offer ourselves back to him.

To trust or not to trust is not a matter of sheer will, however. It is the act of a rational being, either in accord with reason or not. Inseparable from the death of trust is the fact that our first parents "conceived a distorted image" of God and thus became irrationally fearful of the intimate presence of the one who is Goodness itself.[135] They forfeited what the prophet Hosea calls

133 *Epistola* 55.22.

134 *CCC* 397–98.

135 *CCC* 399.

dáʿat ʾĕlōhîm, "the knowledge of God" (Hos 4:1; 6:6). And we their children have likewise "exchanged the truth of God for a lie" and have "worshiped and served the creature rather than the Creator" (Rom 1:25). This tragic choice of self over God, creature over Creator, results in concupiscence, the disorder of human desires. Due to concupiscence, we love created things for their own sake, and our immortal souls desperately try to find repose in that which can never bring us true and lasting joy.

This condition is what the theological tradition refers to as the "infirmity of nature" (*languor naturae*), in accord with the many passages of Scripture that compare sin to bodily illness.[136] Within the divine pedagogy of the Old Testament period, the precepts and institutions of the Mosaic law accomplished at least three things. First, they brought humanity's sinful condition to the surface. As the apostle Paul puts it, "through the law comes knowledge of sin" (Rom 3:20). Second, they disposed those who allowed themselves to be trained by them to the remedy of grace that was to come in Christ. Third, they prophetically signified various aspects of the new covenant. All this is true of Sabbath observance, which is "at the heart of Israel's law."[137]

We turn now to the book of Exodus to see how this begins to play out. As the book opens, the sacred author describes the desperate plight of the Israelites by means of the emphatic use of words from the Hebrew semantic root *ʿbd*, the basic meaning of which is "to work, to serve."

> And Egypt made the children of Israel serve [*wayyaʿăbídû*] with rigor. And they made their lives bitter with harsh servitude [*ʿăbôdâ*] in mortar and bricks and in all manner of servitude [*ʿăbôdâ*] in the field, all their servitude [*ʿăbôdātām*] by which they made them serve [*ʿābədû*] with rigor. (Exod 1:13–14)

Yahweh hears the groaning of the Israelites and delivers them "from the house of bondage" (*mibbêt ʿăbādîm*), still another term from the root *ʿbd*. Having delivered the Israelites from harsh servitude, however, Yahweh does not simply set them at large. No, his act of deliverance has a specific telos. He bestows upon Israel a new status and vocation, instructing Moses to make this declaration before Pharaoh: "Thus says Yahweh: Israel is my son, my firstborn. And I say to you: Release my son, so that he may serve me [*wəyaʿabdēnî*]" (4:22–23a).

136 Aquinas, *STh* I-II, q. 82, a. 1, corp.; cf., Isa 1:5–6; Jer 8:22; 17:14; Hos 5:13; 11:3; 14:5.

137 *CCC* 348.

The Israelites are delivered from "servitude" (*ʿăbôdâ*) in order to "serve" (*ʿābad*). How is that a change for the better? The difference is, of course, that they are moving from falsehood to truth, from servitude within a polytheistic system and under an oppressive regime to service of the one true God. And to serve the truth is authentic freedom. Israel is both servant and son. Yahweh has adopted the people of Israel (understood as *one corporate person*, comprising many individuals) as his son in order to lead him from *ʿăbôdâ* to *ʿăbôdâ*, from one type of servitude to another. These paradoxical statements sum up the whole spiritual dynamic of the divine pedagogy.

We get a first glimpse of this dynamic and of the pedagogical role of Sabbath observance in Exodus 16, even before Israel has reached Mount Sinai. Consider these words of the people as they complain to Moses and Aaron in the wilderness, and note how they reflect concupiscence, a distorted image of God, and a lack of trust in his goodness: "Would that we had died by the hand of Yahweh in the land of Egypt while we sat by the fleshpots, eating our fill of food. For you have brought us forth into this wilderness to starve this entire assembly to death" (v. 3). In response, Yahweh puts Israel on a strict diet of manna in order to teach them trust in his daily providence and to purify their desires. The unique properties of this "bread from heaven" make it impossible to stockpile, so as to discourage avarice and self-reliance (vv. 4, 19–20).

On the sixth day a double portion of manna is provided, so that Israel can keep the seventh day as "a holy Sabbath rest" consecrated "to Yahweh" (v. 23). The noun *šabbāt* appears here for the first time in the canon of Scripture. Thus, even before the Decalogue has been promulgated, Israel begins to learn the proper proportion of work to rest, and the temporal rhythm of a life ordered to grateful acknowledgment of the Creator. In this way, Sabbath observance appears not as an arbitrary or merely symbolic ceremony but as one rooted in the order of creation.[138] Before the Sabbath is imposed as a precept, it is revealed to be a providential blessing and Yahweh's special gift to Israel (v. 29). The Sabbath precept belongs to the natural law, but it is revealed first to Israel as a sign of the covenant and a component of the divine pedagogy. But Israel can only learn the inner meaning of the Sabbath and experience its blessing by submitting to its discipline, which requires trustful obedience. The fact that some Israelites go out on the seventh day

138 "The Manna cycle reestablishes the seven-day week, built into Creation but never before enjoined upon humanity." William H. C. Propp, *Exodus 1–18: A New Translation with Introduction and Commentary*, AB 2 (New York: Doubleday, 1999), 597.

to look for manna, after being explicitly told that none will be given on that day, suggests that this will be a long process (vv. 26–27).

In Exodus 19 the people arrive at Mount Sinai, where Yahweh formally announces his intention to make Israel his "special possession" among all the nations (v. 5). In chapter 20 he promulgates the Decalogue. The Decalogue is a revelation of God's moral will and thus a revelation of God himself, but Yahweh speaks to Israel out of the midst of a terrifying theophany. His power and majesty are manifest in meteorological and perhaps volcanic phenomena on the holy mountain, striking fear into the Israelites (19:16–18). They cry out to Moses, "Do thou speak with us that we may hear, but let not God speak with us, lest we die" (20:19). This request reveals the people's objective condition before their Creator. They are not ready for face-to-face intimacy with God. But it also reflects their subjective lack of hope, their inability to imagine that for Yahweh to speak with them directly can have any other purpose or result than their demise. Through the exodus event they have come to believe in Yahweh and in his servant Moses (14:31), but they still lack any clear sense of what a covenant relationship with the living God entails. Yahweh wishes to be their "healer"[139] and to draw them up into a life-giving dynamic, but they can only see death on the horizon.

Moses responds with the paradox of the two fears: "*Fear not!* For it is in order to test you that God has come, and in order that the *fear* of him may be before your faces, so that you may not sin" (Exod 20:20). To paraphrase: "Do not fear. God just wants to instill fear in you." This is much like the paradox of the two servitudes. Insofar as Israel's fear is based on a distorted image of God and lack of trust in his goodness, it must be banished. This irrational and paralyzing fear of God is to be replaced by a servile but nonetheless salutary "fear of Yahweh" that will raise them above the idea that God is out to kill them. Through a long historical process of testing, chastising, cajoling, and wooing, this servile fear will dispose the faithful remnant of Israel to a third fear, the filial fear that will become possible with the gift of divine charity. Servile but salutary fear is the dynamic exterior motive of the Mosaic law, just as filial fear, which is really "the love of God poured into our hearts" (Rom 5:5), is the dynamic interior motive of the gospel. Thomas Aquinas approves Augustine's paronomastic axiom according to which the difference between the old law and the new law is but slight, inasmuch as it is the difference between *timor* and *amor* ("fear" and "love").[140]

139 Exod 15:26; 23:25; cf. Hos 6:1; 7:1; 11:3; 14:5 (RSV 14:4).

140 Aquinas, *STh* I-II, q. 107, a. 1, obj. 2 and ad 2.

The Sabbath precept is promulgated no less than ten times in the Pentateuch, far more often than any other precept. We find it in the Priestly redaction of the Decalogue (Exod 20:8–11), in the Covenant Code (23:12), in the so-called Ritual Decalogue (34:21), twice in the sanctuary instructions (31:12–17 and 35:1–3, framing the pivotal chapters 32–34),[141] four times in the Holiness Code (Lev 19:3; 19:30; 23:3; 26:2), and finally in the Deuteronomic redaction of the Decalogue (Deut 5:12–15).[142] This is quite extraordinary. Clearly, the authors and compilers of the Pentateuch considered the Sabbath precept to be at the very core of the Mosaic covenant. We must make an effort to understand why. We should notice, first of all, that in the various law codes of the Pentateuch the Sabbath precept is repeatedly associated with three things: agriculture, the liturgical calendar (which is itself rooted in the annual agricultural cycle), and the sanctuary with its various ceremonies. Put simply, the Sabbath is closely linked to agriculture and cultus.

This leads us back to the verb *ʿābad*, which we have heretofore translated as "to serve." The root meaning of *ʿābad* is "to work," but it also has a range of more specific senses. Sometimes *ʿābad* means to "work" the earth and cultivate crops. Indeed, it is the verb used in some versions of the Sabbath precept: "Six days you shall *work*" (Exod 20:9; 34:21; Deut 5:13). This could refer to almost any sort of labor, but for most Israelites it would be six days of agriculture. This is clearly implied in Exod 34:21: "Six days you shall work, but on the seventh day you shall rest. Even during the time of plowing and the time of harvesting you shall rest."

But *ʿābad* can also mean to offer liturgical service, to worship God in ritual. This sense of *ʿābad* is certainly intended when Yahweh tells Moses at the burning bush, "When you bring forth the people from Egypt, you will *serve* God on this mountain" (3:12), and also when Yahweh commands Pharaoh: "Release my son [Israel], so that he may *serve* me" (4:23). Indeed, the cultic aspect of the "service" Israel must render Yahweh is prominent throughout the book of Exodus, which is concerned above all with the telos

141 On the exegesis and theological significance of this framing device, see Daniel C. Timmer, *Creation, Tabernacle, and Sabbath: The Sabbath Frame of Exodus 31:12–17; 35:1–3 in Exegetical and Theological Perspective*, Forschungen zur Religion und Literatur des Alten und Neuen Testaments 227 (Göttingen: Vandenhoeck & Ruprecht, 2009).

142 In addition, three Pentateuchal narratives presuppose the reader's knowledge of the Sabbath precept (Gen 2:1–3; Exod 16:1–36; Num 15:32–36). Of these thirteen texts, ten are found in passages composed or redacted by the Priestly School, suggesting the Sabbath precept's special importance in their theology.

of the exodus event. The proximate goal of the exodus is for Israel to "serve" God on Mount Sinai (3:12), but the long-term plan is for Yahweh to bring Israel into the land of Canaan and "plant" them on his holy mountain, where he will establish his sanctuary forever (15:17). As we learned in chapter 2 of this volume, the construction of the portable wilderness sanctuary, which dominates the second half of the book of Exodus (chapters 25–40), is proposed as the means by which Yahweh will dwell in Israel's midst and travel with them from Mount Sinai to Mount Zion.

This long-term plan is placed in jeopardy by Israel's apostasy with the golden calf but is salvaged through Moses's intercession. At the book's dramatic climax Yahweh reaffirms his commitment to this plan: "My presence will go along, and I will give you rest" (33:14), which is to say, "I will bring you to the place of rest, to the goal of your journey, to the telos of my covenant with you." Throughout the Old Testament the holy land is spoken of as the place where Yahweh "gives rest" (the Hiphil stem of the verb *nûaḥ*) to Israel, and Jerusalem is described as Yahweh's own "resting place" (*mənûḥâ*).[143] The divine economy will come to its fruition when Israel worships the true God in his permanent sanctuary forever. Already in the Old Testament, interpreted *ad litteram*, the goal of God's plan is revealed to be participation in divine rest.

The various senses of *ʿābad* are closely interrelated, and this interrelation is a key to grasping the role of the Sabbath precept within the Mosaic covenant and the divine pedagogy. We must be careful, however, to understand this interrelationship correctly. According to Scott Hahn and Curtis Mitch, the early chapters of Exodus utilize the verb *ʿābad* to build thematic tension between "work" and "worship." Pharaoh demands "work," but Yahweh wants "worship." In the end, Yahweh wins out and decides the matter in favor of "liturgy" over "labor."[144] By reducing a complex matter to alliterative slogans, Hahn and Mitch have introduced a false dichotomy. The authors of Exodus do not present profane work as the exclusive purview of Pharaoh; conversely, they frequently use the verb *ʿābad* to refer to the worship of false gods, from which Yahweh is anxious to deliver Israel. Yahweh wants *both* work and worship from Israel, but both must be in service of the truth.

143 Deut 3:20; 12:9–10; 25:19; Josh 1:13; 21:44; 22:4; 2 Sam 7:1; 1 Kgs 5:18 (RSV 5:4); 8:56; Isa 14:1–3; 63:14; 1 Chron 22:9; 23:25; 28:2; 2 Chron 15:15; 20:30; 32:22; Ps 95:11; 132:8, 14.

144 Scott Hahn and Curtis Mitch, *Exodus: Commentary, Notes, & Study Questions*, Ignatius Catholic Study Bible (San Francisco: Ignatius, 2012), 22.

The book of Exodus views human labor quite positively, as an integral element of the "service" to which Yahweh calls Israel. Under the Mosaic covenant and in accord with the moral law, six sevenths of Israel's life will be given over to profane labor. But the sanctification of the seventh day transforms profane work by ordering *the whole of human life* to the public worship of the Creator. The Sabbath precept indicates the unity of work and worship. There is no inherent tension or opposition between them.[145]

Human work involves tapping natural resources, recombining them in novel ways, and adapting them to human use and enjoyment. But in what spirit does a man do his work? Does he receive natural resources with gratitude, trust, and praise of the Creator, or does he seize and horde them out of fear and avarice? Is he looking to gain power over others, or to participate in a common good? Does he produce and create for his own glory, or for the glory of God? The institution of the Sabbath is intended to order human work and the whole of human life to a single telos, the glory of God, in which man discovers his own telos, repose of the mind in God.

Within the dispensation of the Mosaic covenant, the weekly Sabbath anchored the entire liturgical calendar with its cycle of feasts and observances.[146] At their root, Israel's religious festivals were agricultural, but they gradually became commemorations of God's saving deeds in Israel's history as well. The Sabbath itself commemorated both the creation of the world (Exod 20:11) and the exodus from Egyptian bondage (Deut 5:15)—in other words, the order of creation and the order of redemption. The ceremonies of Israel's liturgy were fundamentally a matter of taking the blessings of the land and offering a first portion of them back to Yahweh. Thomas Aquinas explains the significance of such rites: "In the oblation of sacrifices man bore witness that God is the first principle of the creation of things and the last end to which all things are to be rendered back." In this connection Thomas aptly cites a prayer of King David: "For everything comes from you, and what we have received from your hand we give back to you."[147]

145 Elsewhere, Hahn formulates his slogan more felicitously: "The Sabbath orders work to worship, labor to liturgy." Scott W. Hahn, "Canon, Cult and Covenant: The Promise of Liturgical Hermeneutics," in *Canon and Biblical Interpretation*, Scripture and Hermeneutics 7, ed. Craig G. Bartholomew et al. (Grand Rapids: Zondervan, 2006), 216.

146 Note how the Sabbath precept stands at the head of the liturgical calendar in Lev 23:1–3.

147 *STh* I-II, q. 102, a. 3; 1 Chron 29:14; cf. Deut 26:10.

There was also a social and humanitarian dimension integral to Sabbath observance. In both versions of the Decalogue the Israelite landowner is commanded to give his son, daughter, manservant, maidservant, migrant worker (*gēr*), and even his draught animals the seventh day off of work (Exod 20:10; Deut 5:14a). The Sabbath rest is not a special privilege tied to age, sex, wealth, social status, or ethnicity. The Deuteronomic version further accents this leveling function of the Sabbath by adding, "so that your servant and maidservant may take a rest *just as you do*," and then it immediately links this humanitarian dimension to the memory of Yahweh's saving action on Israel's behalf: "And you must remember that you were a slave [*'ébed*] in the land of Egypt and that Yahweh your God brought you forth from there" (vv. 14b–15a). The moral-humanitarian dimension is thus inseparable from the salvation-historical and cultic dimensions, for "the seventh day is a Sabbath *to Yahweh your God*" (v. 14a).

During the monarchic period, Sabbath observance was a mainstay of Israelite life and piety. The Old Testament frequently mentions the Sabbath in conjunction with the new moon festival and other liturgical feast days. Israelite attitudes toward the Sabbath varied widely. On the one hand, we learn of a devout woman of Shunem who apparently looked forward to the next Sabbath or new moon as an opportunity to make a pilgrimage to Mount Carmel, where she might visit Elisha, the holy man of God (2 Kgs 4:23). On the other hand, the prophet Amos tells us of certain unscrupulous grain merchants who found the Sabbath rest an annoyance because it forced them to put away their rigged scales and false-bottomed bushel baskets for a whole day (Amos 8:4–6). Even for less ethically challenged Israelites, the temptation to carry on a little business on the Sabbath often proved irresistible. Jeremiah identifies economically motivated Sabbath profanation as one of the main sins that led to the destruction of Jerusalem and the Babylonian captivity (Jer 17:19–27), and after the return from exile Nehemiah had to deal with the same problem (Neh 13:15–22). Within the precarious economy of the ancient Near East, the Sabbath precept called upon Israel to make a weekly act of trust in divine providence.

For many pious Israelites the Sabbath day was an occasion of religious joy and a welcome reprieve from otherwise ceaseless labor. The prophets, however, had their doubts about the spiritual quality of such sentiments, since the multiplication of holy days, sacred assemblies, and animal sacrifices had apparently done nothing to lower the crime rate. Isaiah warned that the endless overlapping cycles of weekly Sabbath, monthly new moon celebration, and annual harvest festivals had become an intolerable "burden" to Yahweh (Isa 1:13–14), and Hosea used a wordplay to threaten Israel that Yahweh would bring all this rejoicing to an end. He would *šābat* the *šabbāt* (Hos 2:13; RSV 2:11). In other words, he would "give it a rest"!

What sort of joy *was* the Sabbath meant to instill in the human heart and mind? This question, which really is the core issue, comes into clear focus in the last eleven chapters of the book of Isaiah. This series of prophetic oracles was delivered in Jerusalem shortly after the return from the Babylonian captivity, when a first attempt was made to rebuild the temple in the 530s BC. They were delivered by an unnamed prophet of the Isaian school, who is conventionally referred to as Trito-Isaiah.

According to Trito-Isaiah, the essence of the covenant is to keep the Sabbath from profanation and to choose that which is pleasing to Yahweh (Isa 56:4). In this way, even non-Israelites can "join themselves" to the true God, become his "servants," and come to "love the name of Yahweh." Yahweh, for his part, promises to bring these foreigners to his holy mountain and to make them joyful in his house of prayer (56:6–7). In other words, a covenant bond is created between God and man when the human will is conformed to the divine will, not under duress but in human freedom and by the divinely conferred restoration of what Aquinas calls "the due order of the affections."[148] Through literal Sabbath observance and prayer at the temple, the Holy Spirit bestowed a gift of authentic religious joy and filial affection for the God of Abraham.

Two chapters later, we come to the Old Testament's quintessential statement on the spiritual dynamic of the Sabbath. Yahweh addresses his people through Trito-Isaiah:

> If you hold back your foot on the Sabbath,
> so as not to do your own desire [*ḥēpeṣ*] on my holy day;
> and you call the Sabbath a delight,
> Yahweh's holy day honorable;
> and you honor it by not going your own way,
> nor pursuing your own business [*ḥēpeṣ*] or negotiating a deal;[149]
> then you will find your delight in Yahweh,

148 Aquinas, *In Rom.*, c. 5, lect. 2; cf. *STh* I-II, q. 82, a. 1, corp.

149 On the idiom *dabbēr dābār*, "negotiating a deal" (not "talking idly," as in RSV), see Shalom M. Paul, *Isaiah 40–66: Translation and Commentary*, Eerdmans Critical Commentary (Grand Rapids: Eerdmans, 2012), 494–95.

and he will make you ride on the heights of the land,
and feed you with the inheritance of Jacob your father;
for the mouth of Yahweh has spoken. (Isa 58:13–14)

The prophet uses the Hebrew word *ḥēpeṣ* twice in this passage, with two distinct shades of meaning—"desire" and "business"—in order to highlight the close connection between these two realities. The Sabbath was not only for the benefit of day laborers, who would not need prophetic encouragement to view a weekly day of rest as a delight. It was also for the spiritual benefit of merchants, craftsmen, and landowners, who might otherwise become completely absorbed in their business pursuits.

The Sabbath provided all observant Israelites with a weekly opportunity to turn away from their own interests and pursuits, from doing their own will. It was not a question of attempting to deny one's own desire or will absolutely but rather of recognizing the superficial and self-centered character of the desires that tend to dominate one's life. Yahweh's holy day was a tangible object to which one might choose to turn one's attention and desire. The Sabbath played a mediating role inasmuch as it drew one's affections outward and upward, away from self and toward God. If the ancient Israelite gave the Sabbath a real chance—treated it as a delight and honored it—his affections were gradually purified and elevated, and he soon found himself taking delight in God.

The extent to which some postexilic Jews actually experienced such a transformation of affections and learned how to practice repose of the mind in God is not to be underestimated. Consider for example the *ḥāsîd* ("devout one") who speaks in Psalm 116. He begins by confessing his "love" for Yahweh, who delivered him when the "cords of death" surrounded him (vv. 1–6). Then he exhorts himself, "Return, O my soul, to your resting place [*mənûḥâ*]" (v. 7). The soul's "resting place" is Yahweh himself, and its "return" to Yahweh is realized in acts of prayer, especially at the Jerusalem temple, where Yahweh is present in a unique manner.[150] The *ḥāsîd* next asks himself what "return" he can make to Yahweh for all the benefits he has received, and he instinctively thinks first of the temple liturgy—taking up the cup of salvation, calling upon the name of Yahweh, and paying his vows in the presence of God's people (vv. 12–14). Then, recognizing that these rites are all ordered

150 Mays, *Psalms*, 369.

to a self-oblation, he says, "Precious in the eyes of Yahweh is the death of his devout ones [*ḥăsîdîm*]" (v. 15).

Here we glimpse the deep organic connection between the literal *ratio* of the Mosaic ceremonies and their mystical fulfillment in Christ. Israel's prophets, psalmists, and martyrs gradually came to realize that the *ratio* of sacrifice required man to receive *himself* from the hand of God and to render *himself* back to God through filial obedience (Mic 6:6–8; Ps 40:7–9). The Epistle to the Hebrews teaches us that this was realized in a unique and definitive manner in the self-offering of Jesus Christ "once and for all" (Heb 10:10). By assuming a created body-soul humanity in the Virgin's womb and offering himself on the cross, he offered all of creation back to the Father on our behalf.[151]

To see how this relates to Sabbath observance, I shall piece together a threefold spiritual exegesis of the fourth commandment from a series of remarks found in Augustine's *De Genesi ad litteram*, book 4. Though Augustine does not use the words allegorical, tropological, or anagogical in this context, these terms may be suitably applied to his interpretation. Allegorically, Sabbath observance was imposed on the Jews to foreshadow the way Jesus Christ would "finish" his "work" of redemption on the cross on the sixth day of the week (Good Friday), "rest" in the tomb on the Sabbath (Holy Saturday), and institute the Lord's Day through his glorious resurrection on Easter Sunday.[152] Tropologically, the Jewish Sabbath prefigures the sacrament of baptism, by which we are joined to Christ in his death and burial and receive the grace to "walk in newness of life." When we live by this grace, we "observe a perpetual Sabbath," because we have ceased from our own works, by which we once thought to justify ourselves, and perform the good works that God accomplishes in us.[153] Anagogically, the Sabbath signifies "the future rest," which we now await in the hope of glory. This "supreme" state of rest will be entirely free of pride, since we shall rest even from the good works that God has accomplished in us in this life and find perfect repose of mind and body in his immutable goodness.[154]

151 See chapter 8 below.

152 *De Genesi ad litteram* 4.11; cf. John 4:34 ("my food is to do the will of him who sent me and *to finish his work*"); 17:4; 19:30–31, 41–42.

153 *De Genesi ad litteram* 4.13; cf. Rom 6:3–4; Heb 4:10; Eph 2:10.

154 *De Genesi ad litteram* 4.13; 4.17.

CONCLUSION

We return one last time to a question that we have posed repeatedly: Why is the Sabbath precept in the Decalogue? If we accept the view of Albert the Great and Thomas Aquinas, the Sabbath precept belongs in the Decalogue because it is a moral precept after all. Like the other nine commandments, it is an unchanging precept of the natural law. According to the *Catechism of the Catholic Church*, the immutable moral requirement of the Sabbath precept (fulfilled by Christians in their observance of the Lord's Day) is "to render to God an outward, visible, public, and regular worship" (*CCC* 2176). But that is only half an answer. Albert and Thomas agree with the entire exegetical tradition that the Sabbath commandment is (also) a ceremonial precept. As such, it is unique within the Decalogue, and its presence there still calls for an explanation. Is there some special reason why the Decalogue should contain a precept that is *both* moral and ceremonial?

To answer this question we must view the Decalogue as part and parcel of the historical economy of redemption. Justin Martyr was wrong to try to keep the natural precepts of the Mosaic law separate from the rest, as if that which is universal, immutable, and moral must hover above that which is particular, historical, and ceremonial. Irenaeus of Lyons was right to view the entire law as "education" and to stress the close working relationship between the moral and the ceremonial in the divine pedagogy by which God leads Israel and humanity from hardheartedness to wholehearted love of God and neighbor. By viewing the Mosaic law in terms of divine pedagogy, Irenaeus glimpsed elements of the Sabbath precept's literal moral sense, but he was not able to grasp them with conceptual clarity, in part because the very distinction between *sensus litteralis* and *sensus spiritualis* had yet to be worked out in theory and practice.

A millennium later, Thomas Aquinas was able to affirm clearly that the Sabbath precept is both moral and ceremonial according to its literal sense. On that basis he could see that the unity of the moral and the ceremonial is realized in a unique manner in this one precept. Its presence in the Decalogue, therefore, indicates that the entire, particularistic law of Moses is joined to the natural moral law within the divine economy. As Thomas puts it, "all the ceremonial precepts are superadded to the third precept [i.e., the Sabbath commandment]."[155] In other words, they belong to the Decalogue

155 *STh* I-II, q. 100, a. 11, corp. Aquinas follows the Augustinian enumeration of the Ten Commandments (n. 4 above).

virtually. Viewing things from a slightly different angle, we might also say that the natural moral law itself is grounded in the concrete, the particular, and the historical by virtue of the Sabbath precept's presence in the Decalogue and the Decalogue's presence in the Mosaic law. This is most fitting in an economy in which God leads his people upward "to eternal things by means of the temporal, to spiritual things by means of the fleshly, to heavenly things by means of the earthly."[156]

The Sabbath precept is the hub of the Decalogue. It concludes the first table, which pertains to reverence and worship of the true God, but unlike the first three commandments it is not simply a prohibition. In fact, it may be that the tendency to view the Sabbath precept as essentially a prohibition of work on the seventh day contributed to that legalistic distortion of Sabbath observance that we find among some of the Jewish leaders in the Gospels. Rightly understood, the Sabbath precept is essentially a positive commandment to "sanctify" the seventh day as "a Sabbath *to Yahweh*" (Exod 20:10). Reciprocally, it served as a "sign" to remind Israel that Yahweh is the one who "sanctified" them (31:13). Moreover, insofar as the Sabbath was meant to inculcate "taking delight in Yahweh" (Isa 58:14), it must have moved some faithful Israelites a bit beyond the *timor* of the old covenant, disposing them to the *amor* of the new. At the same time, the social and humanitarian dimension of the Sabbath precept, found in the requirement to release one's children and servants from work on the seventh day, begins the transition to the second table of the Decalogue, which pertains to one's obligations to one's neighbor.

Within the divine pedagogy of the old covenant, the Sabbath taught Israel the proper proportion of work to rest. The six-to-one ratio presumably corresponds to natural human somatic and psychological rhythms and needs, and it is probably ultimately rooted in the solar and lunar cycles that establish the basic patterns of human temporality (Gen 1:14). The Creator's blessing and sanctifying of the seventh day confers a telos on what would have been a mere seven-day cycle, thus encouraging Israel to order their work toward worship and to view time as moving toward a goal. By opening a regular period of nonwork in Israel's societal life, the Sabbath challenged the chosen people to trust in divine providence rather than in their own industriousness and ingenuity. Above all, it taught Israel to view their work as a way of receiving creation from the hands of the Creator, and their worship as a way of offering it back to him.

156 Irenaeus, *Adversus haereses* 4.14.3.

CHAPTER FIVE

The Knowledge of God in Israel's Prophetic Literature

The topic of "knowledge" (*dáʿat*) is prominent in Israel's prophetic literature, which comprises prose narratives and poetic oracles. Sometimes it is a question of God's own knowledge (1 Sam 2:3; Amos 3:2), but more often the concern of these texts is with the knowledge that human beings, Israel and the nations, may come to possess by way of divine revelation. These sacred texts do not pose epistemological questions in an abstract philosophical manner (What is knowledge? Is certitude possible?). They are concerned, rather, with the concrete possibility of knowing Yahweh the God of Israel and his "counsel"—that is, his wise plan for humanity. But insofar as they demonstrate how such knowledge is mediated through the prophetic ministry and may be appropriated through a multifaceted response of faith, we may speak of a nascent epistemology of faith. The Old Testament prophetic literature testifies to and invites the reader to partake in a mode of knowledge that is *wholehearted*, involving intellect, memory, and will in a concrete, personal, and communal response to God's historical revelation. My hope is that a fresh examination of selected texts and a brief epistemological reflection will deepen our appreciation of this mode of knowledge.

Accordingly, this chapter will consist of three sections. The first will consider a selection of five prose narratives involving three preclassical prophets: Samuel (in 1 Samuel 3), Elijah (in 1 Kings 17 and 18), and Elisha (in 2 Kings 4 and 5). In these narratives, each of which involves a conversion of one sort or another, the Hebrew verb *yādaʿ* ("to know") has programmatic significance. It is found especially in confessions of faith and refers either to the recognition of a true prophet or to the knowledge of the true God that comes through the prophetic word. The second section will examine the leitmotif of "knowledge of God" (*dáʿat ʾĕlōhîm*) in the poetic oracles of the classical prophet Hosea. Rather than attempt a general survey of the classical prophets, I have chosen to focus on Hosea because of the significant attention that he gives to this theme and because of the influence he seems to have had on later prophets, especially Jeremiah. The third section will employ philosophical categories drawn from the work of Terry J. Tekippe in order to flesh out the epistemology that is operative in Hosea's oracles and in the narratives from Samuel and Kings. In particular, I will develop the thesis that the prophetic "knowledge of God" is a primordial or protological mode of knowledge.

FAITH-KNOWLEDGE IN PROPHETIC NARRATIVES FROM SAMUEL AND KINGS

The books of Samuel and Kings together narrate half a millennium of Israelite history, from the rise of the monarchy to its fall and the immediate aftermath (roughly 1060–560 BC). The first sixteen chapters of this long narrative focus on the figure of Samuel and present his multifaceted ministry not only as the inauguration of the monarchy but as the dawning of a new age of prophecy in Israel.[1] In 1 Samuel 1–4, Eli the priest and his sons Hophni and Phineas serve as foils for Samuel. Eli's advanced age (2:22), diminished eyesight (3:2; 4:15), and obesity (4:18) symbolize the lassitude and spiritual obtuseness of Israel's leadership as the age of the judges draws to a close. He takes Hannah's fervent prayer to be the babbling of a drunkard (1:12–16) and is slow to discern that it is Yahweh who is summoning the young Samuel (3:4–8). The narrator explains that "the word of Yahweh was rare in those days, there being no frequent vision" (3:1). The narrative of Samuel's prophetic call (3:1–21) represents a dramatic development for Israel collectively (vv. 11, 20) and for Samuel personally. He goes to bed as a "lad" who "did not yet know Yahweh" (vv. 1, 7) and rises the next morning as a prophet. But whereas Samuel's initial lack of knowledge of Yahweh is due to the fact that "the word of Yahweh had not yet been revealed to him" (v. 7), the statement that Eli's sons "did not know Yahweh" (2:12) is expounded in terms of their venality and sexual immorality (vv. 13–17, 22). Thus, at the outset we encounter two complementary dimensions of the knowledge of God that are found throughout the prophetic literature: the intellectual-spiritual understanding

1 Augustine of Hippo, *De civitate Dei* 17.1.

of God that comes through the reception of divine revelation, and the practical knowledge of God constituted by righteous moral conduct.[2] The latter dimension, like the former, is present in Samuel, whose conduct is above reproach (12:3–5).

Significantly, the oracle that inaugurates the age of prophecy is one of judgment (3:11–14), and the events that it foretells—the defeat at Aphek-Ebenezer and the Philistine captivity of the ark (circa 1050 BC)—foreshadow the catastrophe toward which the entire narrative of 1–2 Samuel and 1–2 Kings inexorably moves: the destruction of Jerusalem in 586 BC and the Babylonian Captivity. The prophetic word will come to Israel within a specific series of historical events, and, broadly speaking, it is through exile and restoration from exile that Israel will come to "know" Yahweh (Ezek 39:28). That is, Israel will come to a new depth of theological understanding and a new epistemic assurance of faith when God deals decisively with their sin.

The narrative of Samuel's call concludes on an epistemological note. The text itself embodies a prophetic judgment, narrating the consistent fulfillment of Samuel's oracles as the historical action of Yahweh, who "did not allow any of [Samuel's] words to fall to the ground" (1 Sam 3:19). By further reporting that, in view of this prophetic success, "all Israel from Dan to Beer-sheba *knew* [*wayyēdaʿ*] that Samuel had been confirmed as a prophet of Yahweh" (v. 20), the author calls upon the reader to receive the authoritative witness of the inspired text in a corresponding act of epistemic faith—that is, faith as a mode of acquiring knowledge. In 1–2 Samuel and 1–2 Kings, the recognition of the true prophet and the knowledge that Yahweh the God of Israel is the true God constitute, implicitly or explicitly, two halves of a single confession of faith (e.g., 1 Kgs 18:36). This confession is made by believers within the narrative, but it is proper to faithful Israelites of all ages, to whom the deeds and words of Yahweh are available through the witness of the inspired text. Biblical Israel did not cultivate the memory of such past events in oral tradition and written texts merely for the sake of antiquarian interest but precisely as a living witness and with an eye to the situation and needs of the people of God, present and future.

2 As will become clear in my treatment of the book of Hosea, these two aspects are not extrinsic to each other, so it would be wrong to say that righteous conduct merely "evidences" the knowledge of God. Faith and charity are both integral to what Scripture calls knowledge of God, such that *fides informis*, which is not enlivened by charity and does not "work through love" (Gal 5:6), does not constitute knowledge of God in the full biblical sense of the term (1 John 2:3–6). On charity as the form of faith, see Aquinas, *STh* II-II, q. 4, a. 3.

We turn now to the two narrative cycles that deal with the great preclassical prophets Elijah and Elisha respectively. In these cycles, texts that narrate (and invite) confessions of knowledge-imparting faith in Yahweh and his prophets have a special prominence.[3] The chapter in which Elijah first appears (1 Kings 17) has as its punch line the widow of Zarephath's confession of faith-knowledge: "Now I know [*yādáʿtî*] that you are a man of God and that the word of Yahweh is truly in your mouth!" (v. 24). Though the form-critical classification of this passage as a "prophetic legitimation narrative" discloses one dimension of the text, by itself such a classification yields a truncated exegesis.[4] A narrative-critical analysis discloses other dimensions, such as characterization, and enables us to read the passage also as a conversion story and to ask what sort of "knowledge" the non-Israelite widow attains.

Her first words (v. 12) reveal that she is near despair. Elijah offers encouragement—"Do not fear" (v. 13a)—and the divine promise of miraculous sustenance for the duration of the drought (v. 14). But to receive this blessing she must first pass a test of faith. Before caring for herself and her son, she must take what little food and water she has left and use it to feed the Israelite prophet (v. 13b), who ironically is the cause of her distress, inasmuch as it was he who called for the drought (v. 1). She passes the test and presumably gains some sense that the God of Israel cares for her and has chosen to provide for her through the man of God (vv. 15–16). But when a sterner test follows, it is precisely this truth that she begins to doubt. The death of her son brings to the surface her sense of guilt and a growing suspicion that Yahweh and his prophet must be out to punish her after all (vv. 17–18). The raising of her son is a sign aimed at healing her of this suspicion and convincing her that God has brought the prophet into her life with good intent. The confession of verse 24 thus expresses more than mere recognition or even acceptance of

3 We are concerned here with "divine faith," so called, first, because it is the acceptance of divine revelation; and second, because it is a divinely infused supernatural virtue. Such faith "gives" knowledge not of itself but in conjunction with divine revelation. Unless revelation is met by faith, no knowledge is imparted. Thus faith can properly be said to produce knowledge.

4 See Simon J. DeVries, *1 Kings*, WBC 12 (Waco, Tex.: Word Books, 1985), 221; similarly, Richard Nelson, *First and Second Kings*, Interpretation (Louisville: John Knox, 1987), 108. Even less satisfying is the bland "sociocultural" description of 1 Kings 17 as "a kind of advertisement for belief in the prophet's ability to provide solutions to problems." Tamis Hoover Rentería, "The Elijah/Elisha Stories: A Socio-cultural Analysis of Prophets and People in Ninth-Century B.C.E. Israel," in *Elijah and Elisha in Socioliterary Perspective*, ed. Robert B. Coote (Atlanta: Scholars Press, 1992), 101.

Elijah's prophetic authority.[5] Prior to the second miracle, the woman already believed Elijah to be a "man of God" with real spiritual influence (v. 18). The "knowledge" that she possesses at the conclusion of the narrative is the sort that is acquired only when one's heart has been transformed by a personal experience of the prophetic word.

The docility and faith-knowledge of the non-Israelite widow of Zarephath stand in contrast to the willful ignorance of Israel in the adjacent narrative of the contest on Mount Carmel (1 Kings 18). Here, Elijah accuses the people of "limping on two crutches"—that is, wavering between two opinions—noting that they must decide the question of whether it is Yahweh or Baal who is the true God and commit themselves wholeheartedly to the one truth (v. 21a). Implicitly, this requires them to exercise reason together with faith in order to come to knowledge of the truth. In other words, they must consider what has been proposed for faith about Yahweh's saving deeds and moral character as well as the counterclaim made for Baal,[6] and "through an act of choice" they must "turn voluntarily to one side rather than the other" and "cleave firmly" to that side.[7] Their silent refusal to respond to this challenge ("but the people did not answer him even a word," v. 21b) indicates their unwillingness to come to knowledge of God in this way.[8] But when Elijah proposes a contest that will virtually prove who the true God is (thus minimizing the role of faith), they are all in favor (vv. 22–24). Elijah then prays that they would come to knowledge nolens volens: "Yahweh, God of Abraham, Isaac, and Israel, let it be known today that you are God in Israel and that I am your servant" (v. 36). Through the miracle of the fire from

5 *Pace* Judith A. Todd, "The Pre-Deuteronomistic Elijah Cycle," in *Elijah and Elisha*, ed. Coote, 15.

6 What is proposed for faith is precisely that "Yahweh is God" and that Baal is not (v. 21). Yahweh's unique identity as the transcendent God and his deeds and moral character are elaborated in many texts in the Deuteronomistic History (e.g., 1 Kgs 8:23–24, 27). The implicit claim for Baal is that he sends lightning and rain, and it is just this claim that Elijah's announcement of the drought (17:1) and the contest on Mount Carmel disprove. The theological difference between Yahweh and Baal is especially clarified by Hosea.

7 This is how Thomas Aquinas describes the act of faith in *STh* II-II, q. 1, a. 4 and q. 2, a. 1. Translation: Anton C. Pegis, ed., *Basic Writings of Saint Thomas Aquinas*, vol. 2 (New York: Random House, 1945), 1060 and 1075.

8 To this exchange one might compare the Lord Jesus's interaction with the synagogue elders in the story of the man with a withered hand, as narrated by Mark (3:4–5a): "And he said to them, 'Is it lawful on the sabbath to do good or to do harm, to save life or to kill?' But they were silent. And he looked around at them with anger, grieved at their hardness of heart."

heaven their dramatic confession—"Yahweh is God! Yahweh is God!" (v. 39)—is all but coerced. Their fault lies not in needing a sign but in requiring one up front. The widow of Zarephath (like the two figures that we shall consider below) acts in faith on the prophetic word prior to receiving a confirmatory sign of God's love and power.

Turning from the Elijah cycle to the Elisha cycle, we find two more conversion stories, both masterpieces of literary technique. Superficially, the narrative of the woman of Shunem (2 Kgs 4:8–37) parallels the story of the widow of Zarephath. But in its exploration of the spiritual dynamics of conversion and its epistemology of faith, it picks up where the earlier story left off. The woman of Shunem makes her confession of faith-knowledge not at the end but at the beginning of the story. "I know that this is a holy man of God who passes our way continually," she tells her husband (v. 9). Whereas the impoverished non-Israelite widow of Zarephath becomes involved with Elijah due to the exigencies of the drought, the woman of Shunem is married and well-to-do and thus has no need of material assistance from Elisha. She is an Israelite of mature faith who eagerly seeks out the spiritual companionship of this "man of God," apparently making regular pilgrimages to Mount Carmel on holy days (v. 23). The narrator labels her a "great woman" (*'iššâ gədôlâ*, v. 8), which on one level refers to her wealth and social influence, but on another level to her forceful personality and the spiritual desire that leads her to a deeper conversion.

If the woman of Shunem has a character flaw, it is that she is too self-sufficient and does not allow others to repay her kindnesses (v. 13). To this extent her worldly "greatness" may even be an obstacle to personal growth. The underlying spiritual defect seems to be a certain imperfection of hope, akin to that of the widow of Zarephath but perhaps more deeply submerged in her personality. She has long since given up on ever bearing a child—convinced, no doubt, that God simply does not want her to experience that joy[9]—and she is very reluctant to have her hopes raised in this regard, wishing to avoid any further disappointment (vv. 16, 28).[10] In the meantime, her

9 Scripture frequently speaks of God's direct involvement both in the conception of a child and in the failure to conceive (Gen 4:1; 16:2, 10–11; 18:14; 20:17–18; 25:21; 29:31–33; 30:1–2; 41:51–52; Judg 13:3; 1 Sam 1:5, 11, 19–20).

10 The Hebrew verb *šālâ* in the Hiphil stem (v. 28) means "to set at ease, lead to a false hope" (*HALOT* 4:1504). Although it obviously corresponds to the verb *kāzab* in the Piel stem ("to deceive") in v. 16, the two words are not mere synonyms. The woman's restatement in v. 28—which we should translate, "Did I not say, 'Do not get my hopes up'?"—adds an important

sublimated desire for motherhood has been transferred to her relationship with the prophet, for whom she cooks meals and prepares a bedroom (vv. 8, 10). In accord with the "double portion" of Elijah's spirit given to Elisha (2:9), the woman of Shunem is given a twofold sign that God indeed wills her full happiness: the child's miraculous birth (to which there is no parallel in the story of the widow of Zarephath) as well as his revivification. To the latter event she responds, not with a verbal confession of faith (which she has made already at the outset of the story), but with a silent gesture of profound gratitude (v. 37). With this the narrative ends, leaving the reader to ponder the transformation that has taken place in the heart of the "great woman."

Forming something of a diptych with the story of the Israelite woman of Shunem is the narrative of the conversion of the non-Israelite Naaman (2 Kings 5), who is described as a "great man" (*ʾîš gādôl*, v. 1). Once again, the adjective "great" cuts in two directions. In order to receive a cure for his leprosy and attain spiritual greatness, Naaman must overcome the obstacle of his own worldly status and pride. In this narrative the great ones of the earth (kings and generals) harbor mistaken notions about where God's power lies and how it may be accessed. Naaman is led to conversion by those who are lowly—a captive slave girl, his own servants, and the self-effacing prophet Elisha—who through their humility possess a proper understanding of the ways of God. Naaman, for his part, needs to learn to approach Elisha in humility so that, like the Hebrew slave girl, "he may come to know [*wəyēdaʿ*] that there is a prophet in Israel" (v. 8; cf. v. 3). Instead, he arrives at Elisha's house with a large retinue and expects the prophet to join him in this ostentation by coming forth from the house to greet him. When Elisha refuses to play the game but instead sends out a page to tell Naaman to bathe in the Jordan seven times, pride and anger nearly get the best of Naaman, who is ready to storm off without having received his cure (vv. 9–12). But at the narrative's climax his servants convince him with simple wisdom to perform the humble gesture called for by the prophet (v. 13).

When Naaman's newly cleansed flesh is described as like that of "a young lad" (*náʿar qāṭōn*, v. 14), we recognize that the leprosy had symbolized his pride and that he has now become humble like the Israelite captive, who earlier had been described as "a young lass" (*naʿărâ qəṭannâ*, v. 2). His newfound humility is evident in the deference with which he now speaks to

nuance to the gradual disclosure of her motives as the narrative unfolds. This sort of subtle variation is typical of the narrative artistry of the Old Testament authors.

Elisha, and even more so in the cordial generosity he shows to Gehazi, the prophet's servant (vv. 17–18, 21–23).[11] Most importantly, Naaman's conversion from pride to humility is also a conversion from ignorance to knowledge of the true God (v. 15).

This chapter's oft-noted universalism—that is, its portrayal of Yahweh as the one true God, whose influence extends beyond Israel (v. 1)—is combined with an equally striking (and for moderns, more difficult to comprehend) accent on particularism. Yahweh is the God of Israel, and Israel is the people of Yahweh. Rather than presuppose an intrinsic opposition between universalism and particularism, however, we should recognize that Scripture (here and elsewhere) presents us with what might be call "mediated universalism." Yahweh reveals himself to the nations *through* his unique relationship with Israel.

However, it is not only the *people* of Israel (i.e., the slave girl and the prophet) who mediate healing and faith-knowledge to the gentile Naaman. Mysteriously, the *land* of Israel itself plays a quasi-sacramental role. The slave girl is twice said to be "from the land of Israel," and Elisha is identified as a prophet "in Samaria" (vv. 2–4). In order to receive his healing, Naaman must go to the land of Israel and plunge himself in "the waters of Israel"—that is, the river Jordan—for which the more beautiful rivers of Damascus are no substitute (v. 12). In this way Naaman not only comes to "know that there is a prophet *in Israel*" (v. 8) but to "know that there is no God in all the earth, *except in Israel*" (v. 15). Accordingly, Naaman's request for two mule loads of Israelite soil (v. 17) reflects his new understanding that, by choosing to reveal himself in a particular place, God has consecrated the land of Israel to his own worship.[12] The land itself is thus a tangible sign of the grace of the knowledge of the true God that makes authentic worship possible.

At this point we can take stock of what we have learned from the conversion narratives of 1–2 Samuel and 1–2 Kings. Knowledge of the true God entails a life-transforming encounter and comes to those who welcome a true prophet of Yahweh in humility and faith. Miraculous signs are given

11 Nelson, *First and Second Kings*, 179–80.

12 Commentators who do not hold a sacramental view of reality are puzzled by this request. John Gray finds it "naïvely inconsistent" with the monotheistic confession of v. 15, overlooking the fact that the confession itself contains the same particularism, insisting as it does that the true God is "in Israel." *I & II Kings: A Commentary*, OTL (Philadelphia: Westminster, 1963), 455. T. R. Hobbs implausibly suggests that Naaman is motivated by "sentiment" and is asking for "a souvenir of Israel." He nevertheless finds Naaman's request "strange" and in "conflict" with the author's universalism (expressed in v. 1). *2 Kings*, WBC 13 (Waco, Tex.: Word Books, 1985), 60, 66.

to the docile, enabling them to overcome spiritual impediments such as discouragement (the widow of Zarephath), self-sufficiency (the woman of Shunem), and pride (Naaman), but the Israelites present on Mount Carmel in 1 Kings 18 appear to be obstinate and weak in faith by comparison. They witness a great sign and confess Yahweh to be the true God but do not seem to undergo a profound spiritual transformation. Baalism will continue to be a rampant problem in Israel through the remainder of the monarchic period. Finally, these narratives are not mere timeless tales but integral parts of sacred history. Knowledge of the true God comes into the world through the mystery of Israel—people and land—and can never be abstracted from this divinely chosen mediation.

KNOWLEDGE OF GOD IN THE BOOK OF HOSEA

Hosea was among the earliest of the classical or "literary" prophets—that is, those whose collected oracles are preserved mostly in poetic form in the books of Isaiah, Jeremiah, Ezekiel, and the Twelve (Hosea through Malachi).[13] He lived about a century after Elisha (a preclassical prophet) and prophesied in the Northern Kingdom during the tumultuous quarter century that culminated in its collapse before the advancing Assyrian Empire (746–722 BC). Like his older contemporary Amos, Hosea understands this political catastrophe to be divine chastisement for Israel's sins, both cultic and social. Reflecting on a long history of covenantal infidelity, he provides a penetrating theological and spiritual diagnosis of Israel's chronic malady—namely, their persistent apostasy—and concludes that his people is "perishing for lack of knowledge" (Hos 4:6).

There is a consensus among scholars that the concept of *dáʿat ʾĕlōhîm* or "knowledge of God" (4:1; 6:6) lies near the center of Hosea's thought, but there is less agreement regarding precisely what Hosea means by this expression. According to Bruce Vawter, it denotes "a practical knowledge of Yahweh's moral will,"[14] and Joseph Blenkinsopp similarly finds evidence of "an

13 Israel's prophetic age extends from Samuel to Malachi (c. 1060–460 BC). The distinction between "preclassical" and "classical" is a convenient way to divide the prophetic age into two periods of about 300 years each. This distinction might be qualified and nuanced in any number of ways, but who can deny that when we come to the oracles of Amos (c. 760 BC) we have turned a decisive corner in terms of literary expression and theological acumen?

14 Bruce Vawter, CM, *The Conscience of Israel: Pre-Exilic Prophets and Prophecy* (New York: Sheed & Ward, 1961), 115.

emerging consensual ethic" in Hosea 4:1–2.[15] While granting this practical-moral dimension, G. J. Botterweck takes a more romantic view, stressing that for Israel's prophets "knowledge of God" has to do with "true religious feeling," a "subjective attitude," and a "spontaneous preoccupation with the interests of Yahweh."[16] Abraham Heschel moves even farther in this direction, defining Hosea's *dáʿat ʾĕlōhîm* as "sympathy for God" and laying heavy emphasis on its "emotional component." What Hosea finds lacking in Israel is "inwardness."[17] Steering away from this stress on the subjective and emotional dimension, Gerhard von Rad characteristically identifies "knowledge of God" as "familiarity with the historical acts" of Yahweh.[18] Each of these views contains at least a grain of truth.

Many interpreters seem eager to downplay, if not to deny outright, any "theoretical" or "propositional" dimension in Hosea's use of the phrase "knowledge of God."[19] As Heschel sees the matter, *dáʿat ʾĕlōhîm* "does not connote a knowledge *about* God, but an awareness *of* God."[20] Occasionally such judgments are explicitly based on the well-worn dichotomy between "Hebraic" and "Hellenic" conceptions of knowledge, the former taken to be "practical" and the latter "purely speculative."[21] One senses here that certain modern views may be imposing themselves too forcefully on the biblical text. Whether it is a question of the Enlightenment view of "true religion" as concerned with morals rather than rituals, or Romanticism's emphasis on religious feeling and subjective experience, the potential for distortion of Hosea's theology is quite real. While it is true that the book of Hosea contains few propositional statements of a strictly theological nature (but see 11:9), at the very heart of the prophet's concern is the contention that the Israelites have a deficient *understanding* of who Yahweh is, rendering themselves thus incapable of authentic worship.

15 Joseph Blenkinsopp, *A History of Prophecy in Israel*, 2nd ed. (Louisville: Westminster John Knox, 1996), 90.

16 G. Johannes Botterweck, "Knowledge of God," in *Encyclopedia of Biblical Theology*, ed. Johannes B. Bauer (London: Sheed & Ward, 1970), 2:473.

17 Abraham J. Heschel, *The Prophets* (New York: Harper & Row, 1962), 59–60.

18 Gerhard von Rad, *Old Testament Theology*, vol. 2, *The Theology of Israel's Prophetic Traditions* (London: SCM, 1965), 143; similarly, Hans Walter Wolff, *Hosea: A Commentary on the Book of the Prophet Hosea*, trans. Gary Stansell, Hermeneia (Philadelphia: Fortress, 1974), 79.

19 E.g., Botterweck, "Knowledge of God," 473.

20 Heschel, *Prophets*, 60.

21 E.g., O. A. Piper, "Knowledge," *IDB* 3:44; and with more nuance, Vawter, *Conscience of Israel*, 120.

One exegete who grasps this point and bucks the scholarly trend is Robert C. Dentan, who holds that Hosea favors the term "knowledge of God" (rather than, say, "the fear of Yahweh") precisely to give priority to "the act of understanding." Without sacrificing the practical-moral and emotional-subjective dimensions, Dentan takes the phrase (*dáʿat ʾĕlōhîm*) to mean "knowing who God is and what he expects" and thus to be roughly equivalent to our word "theology."[22] While there is some risk of anachronism and overstatement here as well, two considerations especially support Dentan's interpretation. First, alongside his frequent use of the words "know" (*yādaʿ*) and "knowledge" (*dáʿat*), Hosea employs other terms that accent the noetic dimension of what Israel lacks. Israel is "a people that does not *understand* [*bîn*]" (4:14). They are "like a dove, silly and without *sense* [*lēb*]" (7:11) or "a son who is not *wise* [*ḥākām*]" (13:13). Significantly, the book's final verse is loaded with such terms, maintaining as it does that only the reader who is "wise" (*ḥākām*) and "discerning" (*nābôn*) will be able to "understand" (*bîn*) and "know" (*yādaʿ*) the realities dealt with in Hosea's oracles.[23]

Second and even more decisive in this regard is Hosea's properly theological concern to differentiate clearly between Yahweh and "the Baals" (the fertility deities of Canaan). An explication of this crucial point will help us grasp not only what he means by "knowledge of God" but also how the various key elements in his theology cohere within a broad prophetic vision of reality. These elements include (1) frequent allusions to Israel's historical traditions, (2) the presentation of Yahweh as Israel's "husband" and of Israel's covenant infidelity as "harlotry," (3) a concern with cultic matters and idolatry, (4) a nascent moral theology, and (5) poetic imagery dominated by references to land, weather, agriculture, and human fertility.

The storm god Baal and the other Canaanite fertility deities are mythological personifications of meteorological phenomena and cyclic forces of nature. As such, they are incapable of historical activity, self-revelation, or entrance into a covenant relationship. Yahweh, by contrast, is "the living God" (2:1), who has acted in sovereign freedom within the course of history to claim Israel for himself and who holds them accountable to his moral will. The "knowledge" to which Israel is called is an interpersonal relationship between a free and righteous God and free human moral agents. Since the exodus from Egypt, Yahweh has "known" Israel, and Israel is to "know" Yahweh (5:3; 13:4–5).

22 Robert C. Dentan, *The Knowledge of God in Ancient Israel* (New York: Seabury, 1968), 36.

23 Hos 14:10 (RSV 14:9).

Hosea identifies the wilderness as the locus of Yahweh's first espousal of Israel and of Israel's initially faithful response to Yahweh.[24] Israel's infidelity began when they entered the fertile land of Canaan. Already in the Transjordan they "consecrated themselves" to the Baal of Peor (9:10), and after crossing the Jordan they committed similar acts of apostasy at Adam (6:7), Gilgal (9:15), and Gibeah (10:9).[25] In the poetic symbolism of Hosea these incidents all represent the same primal defection, and the rest of Israel's history in the land up to the prophet's own day has been merely a further living out of that original sin. Having experienced the fruitfulness of the land—that is, vegetative, animal, and human fertility—Israel's heart was enticed and led astray to worship the gods who had been associated from time immemorial with that fertility (10:1–2a). Perhaps because Yahweh for his part was associated with the exodus from Egypt and his original home was understood to be the Sinai wilderness, there were—in addition to simple apostasy to "other gods" (3:1)—syncretistic attempts to assimilate Yahweh to Canaanite fertility religion.[26]

In his attempt to untangle this web of theological confusion, Hosea does not buy into the notion that Yahweh is properly the god of the wilderness, whereas the land of Canaan belongs to "the Baals." In fact, he calls Canaan "the land of Yahweh" (9:3). Still less does the prophet accept a division of labor whereby Yahweh is the god of history while the Canaanite deities supply the goods of creation. Israel needs to come to "know" that it is emphatically Yahweh, not Baal, who gives them "the grain, the wine, and the oil."[27] And while Hosea speaks nostalgically of Israel's time in the wilderness, he does not accord the wilderness some absolute advantage over the arable land. Although agricultural blessings provide the occasion for Israel's apostasy, this does not mean that there is anything inherently wrong with them.

On the contrary, much as we saw in the narrative of Naaman's conversion (2 Kings 5), Hosea presents the holy land as a sort of sacrament of the knowledge of God. But his teaching in this regard can only be understood within the context of his view of salvation history. Yahweh delivers Israel from servitude in Egypt so that they will know him and be free to worship him in truth. Israel's taking up residence in the land of Canaan is the goal of

24 Hos 9:10; 13:5; 2:16–17 (RSV 2:14–15).

25 On the city of Adam and its significance, see *ABD* 1:64.

26 Hos 2:18 (RSV 2:16); 4:15; 8:5–6; 10:5.

27 Hos 2:10 (RSV 2:8).

this self-revelatory act of God. Upon arrival, they are to enjoy the fruits of the earth as signs of Yahweh's special love for them, and they are to render these blessings back to him via the cultus as an expression of their commitment to him and of their clear conviction that it is he who provides for them. In other words, the blessings of the land are intended to promote authentic worship of the true God, not sinful idolatry.

Israel's national sin, which Hosea ascribes in the first place to the priests and prophets, is fundamentally their willful "rejection" of this revealed "knowledge" of the true God (4:4–6). Israel has become "as stubborn as a stubborn heifer" (4:16). They have chosen to regard the blessings of the fruitful land as "a prostitute's pay" from their "lovers," the gods of Canaan.[28] The Israelites celebrate many religious festivals,[29] but their syncretism and outright idolatry indicate that these cultic acts are devoid of any true understanding of who God is (13:2). In the exuberance of worship they may cry out, "We know you [*yəda'ănûkā*], O God of Israel!" (8:2), but in fact they do not. Meanwhile, the injustice and decadence of Israelite society reflect the people's failure to appropriate Yahweh's own righteous character:

> There is no truth, no steadfast love, no knowledge of God in the land;
> rather cursing, lying, killing, stealing, and adultery abound. (4:1b–2)

That Hosea both condemns literal adultery and speaks figuratively of Israel's idolatry as "adultery" or "harlotry" is significant.[30] It suggests that Israel's moral and cultic failures are symptoms of a single defect of the heart—namely, infidelity. When they "consecrated themselves" to Baal (a god known to have multiple consorts), they became, by a sort of connaturality with the object known, "as detestable as that which they loved" (9:10). This was a travesty of what ought to have taken place. Had they drawn close to Yahweh, Israel would have appropriated something of his characteristic fidelity. To imitate his "steadfast love" (*ḥésed*) would have been to possess the "knowledge of God" that Yahweh desires more than any mere sacrifice or offering (6:6).

Deeply troubled by Israel's apostasy, Hosea offers a penetrating diagnosis of Israel's defect of the heart that touches on the mystery of human freedom and its abuse. In classical Hebrew thought there is no heart-versus-head

28 Hos 2:7, 14 (RSV 2:5, 12); 9:1.

29 Hos 2:13 (RSV 2:11); 5:6; 6:6; 8:11–13; 10:1.

30 Hos 2:4–15 (RSV 2:2–13); 4:10–19.

dichotomy. The "heart" (*lēb*) is the seat of intellect, will, conscience, and emotion. When Yahweh "fed" Israel with the good things of the land, "they were sated, and their heart was lifted up; therefore they forgot [him]" (13:6). To have a heart that is "lifted up" is to be self-sufficient and willful and to rely on one's own understanding. To "forget" God is not merely to experience a memory lapse but to choose to ignore him, to relinquish the knowledge of God.[31] In sum, Israel's heart was drawn to the creature for its own sake and away from the Creator. In this regard, syncretism represents an attempt to have one's cake and eat it too. Israel was fatally attracted to a hybrid of Yahweh worship and Canaanite fertility worship because, on the one hand, it provided the exhilaration of orgiastic rites (4:14; 13:2), the promise of agricultural bounty (2:7), and a sense of devotion to Yahweh (8:2), but on the other hand, it left them free to ignore Yahweh's moral requirements (4:1–2) and to construct objects of worship "according to their own understanding" (13:2).

Like the other classical prophets, Hosea describes Yahweh's jealous love for Israel in rather intense terms.[32] To empathize with Israel just a bit, we may suppose that the encounter with Yahweh was simply too much for them. Their infidelity might then be viewed as an effort to temper Yahweh's absolute claim over them with an admixture of Baal worship:

> When Israel was a lad, I loved him; and out of Egypt I called my son.
> The more I summoned them, the farther they went from my presence;
> they sacrificed to the Baals, burnt incense to idols. (11:1–2)

Such behavior will be intelligible to anyone who, in attempting to draw near to the Other, whose absolute freedom qualifies human autonomy, has reached the point where the experience becomes terrifying. In such a case there is an ever-present temptation to attach oneself to almost any created thing rather than abandon oneself into the hands of the Creator. And those created realities that can provide an ersatz elevation of the human spirit—such as music, art, sexuality, or the intellectual life—may hold the most powerful allurement.

Hosea speaks in this connection of a "spirit of harlotry" that has led to Israel's apostasy (4:12). By this striking expression he seems to mean a strong inner susceptibility to any creaturely enticement that may divert one from wholehearted union with God. The same phrase figures into a succinct articulation of Hosea's diagnosis of Israel's chronic malady:

31 Hos 2:15 (RSV 2:13); 4:6; 8:14.

32 E.g., Hos 2:4–8 (RSV 2:2–6); 13:7–8.

> Their misdeeds do not allow them to return to their God,
> for a spirit of harlotry is within them, and they do not know Yahweh. (5:4)

To paraphrase, sin has become so deeply habitual for Israel that repentance is not within their power. Their fatal attraction to fertility worship has become an interior spiritual principle that holds them in bondage, with the result that they lack the theological understanding, the moral rectitude, and the wholehearted personal devotion to Yahweh that together constitute the knowledge of God. Implicitly, only a divine act of spiritual deliverance can save Israel.

The initial step in Yahweh's therapy for Israel's defect of the heart is withdrawal. He will take the blessings of the land away from them for a time, first through drought and famine, and then by means of foreign invasion followed by exile to pagan lands such as Assyria and Egypt. There, God's people will eat food that is "unclean . . . like mourners' bread" (mourners were defiled by contact with the dead), fit only to satisfy one's hunger and by no means to be offered in sacrifice to the holy God.[33] The bounty of "Yahweh's land" was meant to be a sign of the covenant and of the spiritual "fruitfulness" that the true God alone can give to his people.[34] The sacrificial offering of abundant crops and livestock was to be a sign that the true God was known and worshipped in the land. Instead, the land "withers" and "mourns" as a sign that there is "no knowledge of God in the land."[35] The land itself bears witness to Israel's idolatry when "thorns and thistles . . . grow up around their altars" at the outdoor shrines, and the land is poetically depicted as the agent of Yahweh's eschatological wrath when Israel is imagined to cry out to the mountains, "Cover us!" and to the hills, "Fall upon us!" (10:8). Through the desolation of the land and Israel's exile from it, Yahweh himself "withdraws" from Israel until such time as they "realize their guilt and seek [his] face," saying, "Come, let us return to Yahweh! . . . Let us know, let us strive to know Yahweh!"[36]

After this repentance, Israel will be ready for the eschatological "covenant."[37] In a remarkable passage that anticipates and closely parallels the famous "new covenant" oracle of Jeremiah 31:31–34, Hosea poetically describes Yahweh's eschatological "espousal" of his people in such a way as

33 Hos 2:11 (RSV 2:9); 9:2–5.

34 Hos 9:3; 14:9 (RSV 14:8).

35 Hos 4:1–3. The Hebrew verb *'ābal* in 4:3 denotes both "to wither" and "to mourn."

36 Hos 5:6, 15; 6:1, 3; cf. 2:9 (RSV 2:7); 3:1–5.

37 Hos 2:20 (RSV 2:18).

to suggest the mysterious role that the physical creation will have in mediating the knowledge of God to Israel.[38] First, Yahweh will "allure" Israel and "lead her" once again "into the wilderness," where he will "speak to her heart" (2:16). This Hebrew idiom ("speak to her heart") suggests that Yahweh will reveal himself—indeed, *offer* himself—to Israel in a highly personal and intimate manner. Removed temporarily from the distractions and temptations of the fertile land of Canaan, Israel will be able to "respond" to these overtures, much as she did "in the days of her youth" following the exodus (2:17b). Yahweh will espouse Israel to himself "in righteousness and justice, in steadfast love and compassion"—in a word, "in faithfulness"—with the result that they will "know Yahweh" (2:21–22). That is, he will communicate something of his own character to his people, so that they will know him through experiencing and imitating his love.[39]

At this point, Yahweh will bestow the gift of the land upon Israel a second time (2:17a). But this time Israel will receive the concomitant grace to call upon Yahweh as "my husband" with clarity of understanding and purity of devotion, no longer calling him "my Baal" in syncretistic confusion, nor invoking many "Baals" in polytheistic idolatry (2:18–19). Yahweh will banish warfare from the land and even draw the land's wild denizens into his covenant with Israel, so that the land may be a place of security and peace (2:20). Yahweh's loving "response" to Israel's prayer will flow from the heavens to the earth, from the earth to "the grain, the wine, and the oil," and through these blessings to Israel (2:23–24). Prosaically rendered, this means that Israel will pray for rain and get it. But Hosea's point is that the blessing of rain and the resultant agricultural bounty will now be correctly received by Israel as a word of love from her covenant partner, who is the true master of heaven and earth, not as "harlot's pay" for services rendered to the fertility deities.

Israel is referred to in this passage as "Jezreel," which means "God sows," and in a striking modulation of the oracle's guiding metaphor we find that it is not simply "the grain, the wine, and the oil," but Israel herself that Yahweh will "sow" for himself "in the land" (2:25a). The imagery of Israel as Yahweh's special agricultural project is of course an important theological symbol elsewhere in Hosea and throughout Scripture.[40] Here it embodies a poetic

38 Hos 2:16–25 (RSV 2:14–23).

39 Cf. Vawter, *Conscience of Israel*, 120–21.

40 Hos 10:1; 14:6–9 (RSV 14:5–8); Exod 15:17; Isa 5:1–7; Ps 80:9–17; Mark 12:1–12; Luke 13:6–9; John 15:1–10; Rom 11:16–24; 1 Cor 3:6–9.

insight into the way God's mysterious purpose for Israel will be realized in and through a particular piece of land. I shall return to this important biblical theme in chapter 7.

THE KNOWLEDGE OF GOD AS PRIMORDIAL KNOWLEDGE

To this point my analysis has been largely exegetical and theological. In this final section I shall employ epistemological categories in order to consider from a more philosophical angle what sort of knowledge of God is spoken of in the narratives of 1–2 Samuel and 1–2 Kings and in the poetic oracles of the book of Hosea. My thesis is that the knowledge referred to in these texts has several features in common with what Terry J. Tekippe calls "primordial knowledge." This term refers to "a family of kinds of knowledge" that have in common that they communicate their insights without the aid of discursive reasoning or rigorous conceptual logic.[41] My analysis will be organized by discussing five types of primordial knowledge that often overlap and in fact converge in the knowledge of God spoken of in the Old Testament prophetic literature. These are: (1) knowledge of (and through) concrete particulars, including the contingencies of history; (2) knowledge communicated through a literary work of art; (3) practical knowledge or "doing-knowing," including the knowledge present in and witnessed to by moral acts; (4) personal and interpersonal knowledge, including the mystical knowledge of God; and (5) knowledge attained through faith—that is, through the willing and rational acceptance of testimony.

With respect to the first of these types, it is clear that the biblical texts we have been examining are concerned first and foremost with concrete particulars and the contingencies of history. Universal truth—above all, the reality of the one true God and of his steadfast love and mercy—is revealed through these texts, but this revelation takes place in and through particulars of geography, ethnicity, and temporal sequence. We saw this emerge as a theological theme in our narrative analysis of the healing and conversion of Naaman (2 Kings 5). It is also present in the oracles of Hosea, whose overriding concern is with the historical Israel and their encounter with the "living God" in the wilderness and in the holy land. Prior to the early twentieth century, the

41 Terry J. Tekippe, *Scientific and Primordial Knowing* (Lanham, Md.: University Press of America, 1996), 451–62, at 458.

Western philosophical tradition was largely concerned with the deductive, conceptual knowledge of universals, so that knowledge of concrete particulars—and inductive knowledge of universals *through* the contingencies of history—presented something of a problem. Is such knowledge possible? If so, is it genuinely intellectual? That is, does it qualify as "knowledge" in the true sense? The now well-known turn toward the subjective-personal, the inductive-experiential, and the linguistic-contextual in late modernity and postmodernity suggests that more recent philosophies may supply tools for elucidating this dimension of biblical knowledge. Ultimately, however, such contemporary insights will be of little avail in this endeavor unless they are combined with a recovery of the traditional theological notion of *mystery* as the remedy to modernity's truncated understanding of event. I shall touch upon these matters in chapter 6.

The second type of primordial knowledge is present in Old Testament prophetic literature insofar as these texts present the knowledge of God to the reader by way of literary art—namely, historical narratives and poetic oracles—rather than through the sort of discursive argumentation and rigorous deductive reasoning prized by the Western philosophical tradition. To forestall any misunderstanding in this regard, three caveats are in order. First, it is necessary to avoid the common mistake of pitting literature against historicity. Though they may not supply the empirically verifiable data that modern historians value, the narratives of 1–2 Samuel and 1–2 Kings do embody a historiographical intentionality that must be respected. And however creative and imaginative Hosea's poetry may be, he is concerned all the same with social, political, and religious realities present in the Fertile Crescent in the eighth century BC. We can best discern the sacred author's communicative intention if we attempt to view all such realities referred to in Scripture according to their proper relationship to the one divine economy of revelation and redemption. The events that are integral to this economy do not merely recede into the past, such that they may or may not be retrievable in terms of empirically verifiable data. Rather, they live on via Scripture in the tradition and liturgy of Israel and the Church. In this way, the people of God in every age experiences something of the efficacy of these events through the witness of the sacred text.

The second caveat is that nothing in these texts suggests that the authors employed literary artifice in order to dress up a preconceived theological "message." It is simplistic, for example, to read the narratives of 1–2 Samuel and 1–2 Kings looking for "the moral of the story," as if a universally applicable meaning could be extracted so easily. The Old Testament is not *The Book of Virtues*, and it is doubtful in any case whether the question "What would Elisha do?" could provide one with a clear moral compass. Likewise, if Hosea presents his privileged prophetic understanding of Yahweh's dealings with Israel by way of poetry and symbol, it is presumably because this understanding came to him in the form and modality of a poetic insight. The interpretive act by which one comes to share in this understanding cannot, therefore, be merely a matter of textual decoding, whether simple or complex, but must more nearly involve the whole person and the whole of one's life. If, moreover, as Michael Polanyi maintains, it is generally the case that, "in order to describe experiences more fully, language must be less precise,"[42] this would be a fortiori true of Israel's encounter with God and should caution us not to disparage the Bible's protological literary presentation of that encounter.[43]

The third caveat regarding the second type of primordial knowledge is that Romanticism's claim that the meaning of a poem or narrative is untranslatable into an abstract and discursive statement is but a half-truth. Such an assertion represents an overreaction to the simplistic idea that I have just rejected—namely, that the meaning of a literary text is reducible to its "message." It is an overreaction because poetry and narrative rarely dispense with abstract concepts altogether and because Israel's prophetic literature, like the rest of Scripture, has proven amenable to the sort of discursive commentary that sends one back to the biblical text for an enhanced rereading. The via media here may be found in Kant's felicitous formulation by which the "aesthetic idea" embodied in a work of art "induces much thought," but in such a way that no conceptual articulation "can be wholly adequate" to it.[44] Biblical exegesis thus has a legitimate and necessary role at the various levels of the Church's appropriation of the inspired text's witness (dogmatic, exegetical, liturgical, homiletic, and devotional), but it never renders the text obsolete.

42 Michael Polanyi, *Personal Knowledge: Towards a Post-Critical Philosophy* (Chicago: University of Chicago Press, 1962), 86.

43 Biblical thought is "protological" insofar as it does not conform to Western canons of logical argumentation or consistency and precision of expression but relates to reality via more or less undifferentiated symbols.

44 Immanuel Kant, *The Critique of Judgment*, trans. James C. Meredith (Oxford: Clarendon Press, 1952), 175–76; cited in Tekippe, *Scientific and Primordial Knowing*, 293. My aim here is to disengage this element from Kant's idealist epistemology and transpose it into a realist key.

We turn now to the third type of primordial knowledge. Hosea may refer to a sort of practical knowledge or "doing-knowing" when he seems to imply that moral action itself constitutes the "knowledge of God" (Hos 4:1–2; 6:6). But here we must avoid three reductionist pitfalls. First, we must not suppose that Hosea has in mind a knowledge that is *merely* practical and thus without any real theological content. As we have already seen, the *dáʿat ʾĕlōhîm* that he wishes Israel to possess has a noetic dimension. Second, only a highly selective reading of Hosea would restrict his notion of "knowledge of God" to the moral realm. Hosea (in contrast to Amos) refers far more often to Israel's cultic aberrations than to their moral shortcomings, and the former reflect Israel's deficient understanding of who God is at least as much as the latter (13:2). At the same time—and this signals the third pitfall to avoid—Hosea's moral doctrine is more profound and more integral to his covenant theology than is generally recognized. To act in justice and steadfast love constitutes "knowledge of God" not simply because it reflects an accurate knowledge of what God requires, but because such human virtues constitute a true participation in Yahweh's own character and thus actually put one in touch with the living God. The moral demands that Yahweh places on Israel are part and parcel of his plan to bind Israel to himself in a covenant relationship.

The fourth type of primordial knowledge is the personal involvement of the knower with the known, especially the interpersonal knowledge of committed love. The widow of Zarephath, the Shunemite woman, and Naaman the Syrian all come to the knowledge of Yahweh through a life-changing encounter with a "man of God" and a personal experience of conversion. The personal dimension of Hosea's own prophetic knowledge of God is hinted at in the enigmatic passages concerning his marriage to Gomer and the symbolic naming of their children (1:2–9; 3:1–5), but this dimension of the prophetic vocation is far more obvious in the lives of Samuel, Elijah, and later prophets such as Jeremiah and Ezekiel. As for Israel's covenant with Yahweh, Hosea presents it in the most personal of terms. Yahweh is portrayed as a jilted lover or an offended father, and Israel's sin is described as infidelity, rebellion, betrayal, and deceit. In the end, when Yahweh "heals their defection" and "loves them freely," their knowledge of him will have the intimacy of a spousal union.[45]

The fifth type of primordial knowledge is faith-knowledge. Where it is not an explicit theme, the role of faith as a means of attaining knowledge

45 Hos 14:5 (RSV 14:4); 2:21–22 (RSV 2:19–20).

of God pervades Scripture as an epistemological and hermeneutical presupposition. It is hermeneutical in the sense that the Scriptures themselves constitute a testimony to be received by faith. This testimony is offered in a variety of modes, in accordance with the Bible's many genres. For example, a conversion narrative such as 2 Kings 5 calls upon the reader to make an act of humility and faith that is analogous to that made by Naaman and thus to enter into an experiential faith-knowledge of the realities to which the sacred text bears witness. Something similar is operative in the book of Hosea, the final verse of which challenges the reader to put forth the considerable effort necessary to understand "these things." The reference is of course to Hosea's words, but not merely so. Through understanding the words and accepting their testimony the reader comes to know the corresponding realities. The same verse thus points to the practical and personal dimensions of the life of faith that attains the knowledge of God via connaturality: "The ways of Yahweh are upright, and the righteous walk in them, but transgressors stumble in them."[46]

One begins to sense how closely intertwined these five types of primordial knowledge are in the case of the *dáʿat ʾĕlōhîm* spoken of by Hosea. Indeed, they represent five aspects of a single, unified mode of knowledge. The convergence of these aspects will come into still sharper focus if we consider a leitmotif in Hosea's prophecy that was touched on briefly above—namely, Israel's "return" (*šûb*) to Yahweh.[47] Long before the divine call to repentance was addressed to all peoples of all times in the gospel, repentance was Yahweh's particular requirement for Israel at a decisive moment in her history. We can hardly expect, then, to understand this theme if we attempt to abstract it from the classical prophets' schema of salvation history and turn it into a mere timeless ideal. The political catastrophe that overtook Israel and Judah, beginning with the Assyrian advance in Hosea's day and culminating in the Babylonian exile, was the revelation of Israel's sin and thus of her need for repentance. This "moment" comprised events stretching over two centuries, and it was precisely the role of the classical prophets to discern the providential trajectory and significance of this succession of events.

At the same time, a flat, linear view of history will hardly suffice either. Hosea presents Israel's "return" to Yahweh first as an event in the eschatological future. However, after indicating how Israel's sin and pride presently hold

46 Hos 14:10 (RSV 14:9).

47 Hos 2:9 (RSV 2:7); 3:5; 5:4; 6:1; 7:10; 12:7; 14:2–3 (RSV 14:1–2).

them in spiritual bondage, making repentance humanly impossible, Hosea concludes—incongruously, to modern ears—by summoning contemporary Israel to their eschatological repentance and salvation.[48] While remaining truly in the future, the eschatological call to repentance is a grace in which Old Testament Israel may somehow participate in advance. For our purposes, it is especially important to note that, just as the failure to repent keeps one ignorant of God, so acceptance of the eschatological grace of repentance is precisely the entryway into Israel's eschatological knowledge of God.[49] This knowledge, though it certainly arrives at that which is noncontingent and universal—namely, God himself—is primordial insofar as it is attained through the prophetic vision of God's mysterious plan unfolding in the concrete particulars and contingencies of history, and insofar as this prophetic vision of history is communicated through a poetic mode of thought that defies strict logic.

Knowledge of God by way of repentance is also primordial knowledge in the sense that it is an instance of "doing-knowing" and is profoundly interpersonal and mystical. However much Israel's "return" is possible only "by the help of [their] God"—that is, by grace—it also necessarily entails a free movement of the will expressed in concrete action, and this action involves both the horizontal-moral dimension of "maintaining steadfast love and justice" and the vertical-spiritual dimension of "hoping in your God continually" (12:7). Hosea closely associates Israel's repentance with "seeking" Yahweh and "striving to know" him.[50] He also subtly accents the interpersonal and mystical dimension of the knowledge of God by several references to the words of prayer by which Israel directly addresses Yahweh. In their present ignorance they confusedly call Yahweh "my Baal" and say "our God" to the work of their hands; they falsely swear, "As Yahweh lives..." and falsely confess, "We know you, O God of Israel!"[51] But "words" of prayer will also play an essential role in Israel's "return" to Yahweh, and through the eschatological grace of repentance they will be enabled to say, "My husband!" in the authentic intimacy that is possible only through true knowledge. The new covenant

48 Israel's eschatological "return": Hos 2:9 (RSV 2:7); 3:5; 5:15–6:3. Repentance humanly impossible: 5:4; 7:10. Israel summoned to eschatological repentance: 12:7; 14:2–9 (RSV 14:1–8).

49 Hos 5:4; 2:16–22 (RSV 2:14–20); 6:1–3.

50 Hos 3:5; 5:15; 6:3.

51 Hos 2:18 (RSV 2:16); 14:4 (RSV 14:3); 4:15; 8:2.

thus takes the form of a dialogue of interpersonal communion: Yahweh will say, "You are my people," and Israel will reply, "My God!"[52]

Finally, when we consider how the *dá'at 'ĕlōhîm* comes to eighth-century Israel and to the contemporary reader only through the faith-acceptance of prophetic testimony, we see just how epistemologically decisive repentance is. Why, after all, should Israel accept Hosea's witness over that of the contemporary prophets whom he condemns? And how is Israel really to know that Yahweh is the "living God" but Baal a mere idol if Hosea offers no miracle of the sort performed by Elijah and Elisha?[53] The confirmatory sign offered by Hosea and the other classical prophets lies, I suggest, in the entire historical process by which Israel comes to recognize their guilt and their bondage to sin, experiences deliverance and authentic freedom in repentance and righteous conduct, and comes to know the true God as one who first wounds and then heals (Hos 6:1). Yahweh shows himself to be "God and not man, the Holy One in [Israel's] midst," first in the jealous love that leads him to punish and then even more so in the mercy by which he relents and restores (11:9). Baal never required Israel to face her sin, never called Israel to rise above the selfish and degrading passions of the fertility cult, and never provided the grace that would enable her to go out from herself to a spousal union with God through participation in God's own righteous character.[54] In sum, the true God reveals himself to us as the one who cares enough to deal with our sin and is able to do so.

52 Hos 14:3; 2:18, 25 (RSV 14:2; 2:16, 23).

53 Hos 4:5; 2:1 (RSV 1:10).

54 Hos 2:21–22 (RSV 2:19–20).

CHAPTER SIX

Word and Event: A Reappraisal

For those who recognize much of real worth in modern biblical scholarship but at the same time find deeply problematic presuppositions at work within it, Joseph Cardinal Ratzinger's Erasmus Lecture of 1988 has been a guiding light for over thirty years. At the heart of the Erasmus Lecture, as we have seen, is the call for a new hermeneutical synthesis. The future pontiff describes this as a project in two stages. First, there must be a self-critique of the historical-critical method and its philosophical foundations, and then there comes "the positive task" of joining the tools of the historical-critical method to "a better philosophy," one that "contains fewer *a prioris* foreign to the [biblical] text" and "offers more resources for a real listening to the text."[1] Ratzinger, moreover, closely correlates the "exegetical problem" to modernity's broader "dispute over foundations." The search for a new synthesis, as Ratzinger conceives it, must take modernity and modern questions as starting points but must not confine itself to the philosophically "restricted horizon" of modern thought. Patristic exegesis and medieval philosophy in particular will play important roles in broadening our horizon beyond that of the positivistic worldview of modernity.[2] That is why Ratzinger also envisions the new synthesis as a sort of rapprochement between the patristic-medieval approach to Scripture and modern approaches.[3]

1 Joseph Ratzinger, "Biblical Interpretation in Conflict: On the Foundations and the Itinerary of Exegesis Today," in *Opening Up the Scriptures*, ed. Granados, Granados, and Sánchez-Navarro, 20.

2 Ratzinger, 19.

3 See Stallsworth, "Story of an Encounter," 107–8.

The last portion of the Erasmus Lecture is devoted to "Basic Elements of a New Synthesis." Ratzinger offers nothing systematic or comprehensive here but attempts "merely to cut a few initial openings in the thicket."[4] Among these basic elements he gives considerable attention to the need for a fresh appraisal of "the relationship between event and word." Ratzinger maintains that "the mainstream of modern exegesis" operates with a badly truncated notion of event, according to which "the event represents irrationality; it belongs to the domain of pure facticity, which is composed of chance and necessity. For this reason, fact as such cannot be the bearer of meaning. The meaning lies only in the word."[5] This "dualism between word and event" not only "banishes the event into the realm of the word-less" and the meaningless; it "actually robs the word itself of its capacity to mediate sense, because the word then stands in a world from which all sense has been stripped." Ultimately this dualism "cuts the biblical Word off from creation and undoes the coherence of sense between the Old and New Testaments in favor of a principle of discontinuity."[6]

According to Ratzinger, this problem is at root philosophical, and its solution must be both philosophical and theological. Modern exegesis regards events as *bruta facta* because it holds as an unquestioned presupposition "the methodological principle used in natural science, that everything that occurs can be explained causally, on the basis of purely immanent functional connections."[7] Over against this view, which reduces intelligibility to the realm of efficient causality, Ratzinger recommends the teleological philosophy of Thomas Aquinas, according to which all things in creation "follow a certain course, that is, a movement toward a goal." Only teleology can safeguard the biblical notion of the unity of creation and history under the aegis of a divine economy. In Scripture "God's action thus appears as the principle of the intelligibility of history," and all of history—past, present, and future—finds its unity in the person and event of Jesus Christ. In Christ, the Word incarnate, we see the most profound and perfect unity of word and event, and we come to recognize that "the event itself can be a 'word.'"[8]

Ratzinger's observations on word and event are profound and of great importance, but they need to be spelled out in a more systematic and

4 Ratzinger, "Biblical Interpretation in Conflict," 20.

5 Ratzinger, 23.

6 Ratzinger, 25.

7 Ratzinger, *God's Word*, 119.

8 Ratzinger, "Biblical Interpretation in Conflict," 24.

thorough manner. Anyone who has made a serious attempt to bring modern biblical scholarship to the service of theological work carried out under the authority of the rule of faith will already have some awareness of the problem to which Ratzinger refers here and will appreciate what is at stake. For the sake of clarity, however, I shall begin with an example of how the dualism of word and event manifests itself in modern biblical scholarship. The remainder of the essay will then attempt to sketch out, rather more fully than the Erasmus Lecture does, Scripture's own theological vision of the unity of word and event. I shall consider in turn: creation and the *imago Dei*; language and truth; God's word in human events; time, narrative, and history; and the Christ event and the Gospels.

THE DUALISM OF WORD AND EVENT: AN EXAMPLE

After a brief preface, Vatican II's 1965 Dogmatic Constitution on Divine Revelation *Dei Verbum* turns almost immediately to the unity of word and event in the divine economy. The text affirms, "this economy of revelation is realized in deeds and words intrinsically interconnected [*gestis verbisque intrinsece inter se connexis*], such that the works accomplished by God in the history of salvation manifest and corroborate the teaching and realities signified by the words, while, conversely, the words proclaim the deeds and illuminate the mystery contained in them."[9]

The complementarity between deeds and words of which this text speaks is evident throughout Scripture. For example, the wonders by which Yahweh wrought Israel's deliverance from bondage in Egypt lead directly to and are completed by the revelation of the law at Sinai. Again, the great chastisement of the exile both fulfills and is explained by the words of the prophets. Employing poetic parallelism, the psalmist confesses: "Yahweh is faithful in all his words, and loyal in all his deeds" (Ps 145:13). In the New Testament, similarly, Jesus's public ministry is comprised of mutually illuminating works of power and words of instruction, and each of the evangelists draws attention to this fact in his own way. Matthew, for example, dovetails narrative units with large blocks of the Lord's teaching in an architectonic fashion.[10] John, for his part, presents Jesus's miracles as "signs"—that is, inherently

9 *Dei Verbum* 2.

10 See John P. Meier, "Matthew, Gospel of," *ABD* 4:628–29; and the chart in Raymond E. Brown, *An Introduction to the New Testament*, ABRL (New York: Doubleday, 1997), 172.

significant deeds—and typically couples a sign-narrative with a discourse or dialogue that draws out the given sign's significance.[11]

In his 1967 commentary on *Dei Verbum*, Ratzinger suggests that in drafting the passage quoted above the fathers of Vatican II "were merely concerned with overcoming neo-scholastic intellectualism, for which revelation chiefly meant a store of mysterious supernatural teaching . . . in order to express again the character of revelation as a totality, in which word and event make up one whole."[12] Whether it was intentional or not, however, the conciliar statement also guards against the opposite error—namely, that which would privilege events over words in the economy of redemption in order to play down the propositional content of revelation and the intellectual dimension of the act of faith, perhaps also in order to pit the intuitive, imagistic, and poetic elements in Hebraic thought against Greek rationality to the detriment of the latter.

In February of 1964, while the antepenultimate draft ("Form E") of what was to be called *Dei Verbum* was being prepared in Rome for consideration at the third session of the council later that year, the Scottish biblical scholar James Barr was delivering his Currie Lectures at Austin Presbyterian Theological Seminary in Texas. With characteristic "prosecutorial zeal" Barr undertook to dismantle the allegedly biblical concept of "revelation through God's acts in history," complaining that it had gained a status of unquestioned normativity in the "biblical theology" movement, which was then at the zenith of its popularity.[13] Barr rightly points out that any attempt to locate revelation in God's historical acts while dissociating it from verbal communication flies in the face of the biblical evidence. Referencing the many Old Testament passages in which Yahweh is said to have spoken to Moses

11 As Robert Kysar notes, John combines narrative and discourse in a variety of ways, and he sometimes allows a sign to stand on its own and speak for itself. "John, The Gospel of," *ABD* 3:916. For an in-depth discussion of the concept of "sign" in Johannine theology, see Rudolf Schnackenburg, *The Gospel According to John*, vol. 1, *Introduction and Commentary on Chapters 1–4*, trans. Kevin Smyth (New York: Herder & Herder, 1968), 515–28.

12 Ratzinger, Grillmeier, and Rigaux, "Dogmatic Constitution on Divine Revelation," in Vorgrimler, *Commentary*, 172. Ratzinger is responsible for the passage in question.

13 James Barr, *Old and New in Interpretation: A Study of the Two Testaments* (New York: Harper & Row, 1966), especially 65–102 ("The Concepts of History and Revelation"). Cf. David Penchansky, "Barr, James," in *Historical Handbook*, ed. McKim, 423–27. Penchansky's admiring reference to Barr's "prosecutorial zeal" is on p. 423. Barr had already presented a devastating critique of the exaggerated contrast between "Hebrew thought" and "Greek thought" in his first major work, *The Semantics of Biblical Language* (London: SCM, 1983; first published 1961).

and the prophets, as well as the words by which Israelite tradition itself was transmitted, Barr observes that "it is entirely as true to say that in the Old Testament revelation is by verbal communication as to say that it is by acts in history."[14] Thus on a certain level, the level of the content of Scripture itself, Barr too seems to affirm the inseparability of word and event.

To this point we have dealt with the relationship between word and event as these are found *within* Scripture. In specifying the locus and content of revelation, the Neoscholastics, whom Ratzinger identifies as the primary targets of *Dei Verbum*'s formulation about "deeds and words intrinsically interconnected," give the words of the prophets and the teaching of Jesus and the apostles a certain priority over the events of the historical economy as such.[15] But this is, at least in principle, a matter of privileging one part of the biblical record over another. Even if Neoscholasticism expresses the content of revelation in the postbiblical language of dogmatic propositions, these propositions are assumed to be accurate "translations" of what Scripture itself teaches. Conversely, the proponents of "biblical theology," against whom Barr polemicizes, privilege the narrated events of redemptive history over biblical words of law, prophecy, and instruction. In either case, then, the alleged dualism of word and event is largely reducible to what we might call the intrabiblical level. The discursive teaching of the prophets, the Lord, and the apostles is given priority over Scripture's narrative of events, or vice versa.

Indeed, whether this prioritization amounts to a real dualism or merely an exegetical and theological imbalance depends to a significant degree on how a given version of Neoscholasticism or of biblical theology views the nature of events in general and of the biblical events in particular. Provided that the neoscholastic theologian and the biblical theologian could agree that events are not merely brute facts, and provided they could also come to a basic agreement about the sort of reference that Scripture makes to the events of redemptive history, they might be able to work toward a resolution of their differences by way of careful exegesis of the biblical text.

But this strictly exegetical and intrabiblical level, however important it may be, is not where the major difficulty lies. All parties should be able to agree that Scripture accords vital significance to words and events alike, that it presents these as inextricably bound together within the economy of

14 Barr, *Old and New*, 77.

15 René Latourelle, SJ, *Theology of Revelation: Including a Commentary on the Constitution "Dei Verbum" of Vatican II* (Staten Island, N.Y.: Alba House, 1966), 210–12.

revelation and redemption, and that any attempt to pit one against the other must therefore be misguided. As long as we remain on the merely exegetical level, therefore, the council fathers and James Barr both appear to be doing little more than stating the obvious. The real difficulties emerge when we press the philosophical question about the nature of words and events and their interrelation and the theological question about the nature of revelation and redemption and their interrelation.

Furthermore, we have yet to consider a second and potentially much more problematic dimension of the whole matter—namely, the relationship between Scripture itself as "word" (comprising both narrative and discourse) and redemptive history as "event" (an event that involves many words). The very strong tendency of modern biblical scholarship, as we shall see presently, is to view the history of Israel, the life of the historical Jesus, and the first two generations of Church history as lying somewhere "behind" the texts of the Old and New Testaments, at best faintly discernible in the mists of the ancient world. While this problematizing of the relationship between Scripture (word) and history (event) was to some extent inevitable, given the archeological discoveries and philological progress of recent centuries, one would not be mistaken to detect the modern dichotomy between fact and value at work here as well.

To gain a concrete sense of how these tendencies manifest themselves in the deliberations of modern biblical scholars, we may return to the Currie Lectures. Here it is interesting to note that while Barr, ever the master debunker, is able to identify a host of "contradictions and antinomies" involved in the way his contemporaries bandy about the idea of "revelational history," he offers precious little in the way of a positive counterproposal.[16] He chides the leaders of the biblical theology movement for "treating so grossly uncertain a concept as *Heilsgeschichte* [salvation history] as if it was some kind of firm ground," but the very real theological insight that this term crystalizes seems to escape him almost entirely.[17] While not explicitly embracing the dichotomy between fact and value, he opines that "the acts of God [recounted in the Old Testament] are not really and strictly 'revelatory,' except in the trivial sense in which any act done, or any thing said, may be considered to 'reveal' something of the doer."[18]

16 Barr, *Old and New*, 66–67.

17 Barr, 86.

18 Barr, 82. Punctuation added for clarity.

With unintended irony, Barr here puts his finger on a phenomenon that many twentieth-century Catholic philosophers, from Blondel to Wojtyła to Sokolowski, have considered anything but trivial—namely, the self-disclosure of the human person through action.[19] It is even less trivial to consider the possibility that the eternal and transcendent God might indeed act within space and time in a manner that is analogous to human action and that can thus be narrated as something like a matter of historical record. The cumulative claim of Israel's Scriptures—namely, that the one true God, creator of heaven and earth, not only can act within human history but in fact has acted in very particular ways on behalf of a particular people, thus revealing himself to be a personal God, a knowable Who rather than an unknowable What—is of the greatest theological import. It is quite impossible to imagine Judaism or Christianity apart from this claim. Barr's attempt to relegate the notion of God's self-revelatory action within history to the margins of the biblical view of reality must in the last analysis be judged unconvincing.

Still, Barr's broader project of discrediting the biblical theology movement has been largely successful, at least among biblical scholars. The "contradictions and antinomies" to which he draws attention appear insoluble indeed, particularly to those who, like Barr, rule out of court any appeal to metaphysics or "mysticism" where the interpretation of the Bible is concerned. One problem, which is the direct result of what Hans Frei famously tagged "the eclipse of biblical narrative," seems especially intractable. Modern biblical scholars have become acutely conscious of two distinct and often quite divergent accounts of Israel's history: the Old Testament's own account, and the account that has emerged from historical-critical investigation.[20] According to Barr, the proponents of *Heilsgeschichte* disagree among themselves, if they do not simply equivocate, about which of these two accounts gives us access to God's alleged self-revelation in history.[21]

19 Maurice Blondel, *Action (1893): Essay on a Critique of Life and a Science of Practice*, trans. Oliva Blanchette (Notre Dame, Ind.: University of Notre Dame Press, 2004); Karol Wojtyła, *The Acting Person: A Contribution to Phenomenological Anthropology*, trans. Andrzej Potocki, Analecta Husserliana 10 (Boston: D. Reidel, 1979); Robert Sokolowski, *Phenomenology of the Human Person* (Cambridge: Cambridge University Press, 2008).

20 Hans W. Frei, *The Eclipse of Biblical Narrative: A Study in Eighteenth and Nineteenth Century Hermeneutics* (New Haven: Yale University Press, 1974). For a helpful account of how this problem resurfaced in the context of twentieth-century Old Testament theology, see Henning Graf Reventlow, *Problems of Old Testament Theology in the Twentieth Century* (Philadelphia: Fortress, 1985), 59–124.

21 Barr, *Old and New*, 66–67.

Barr apparently views the very attempt to resolve this problem as misguided. Responding to those who argue that the solution lies in approaching the whole question with an authentically "biblical view of history"—that is, one obtained from Scripture itself—Barr notes that they have reached no consensus regarding what this "biblical view of history" in fact is. He is confident, in any case, that the Old Testament's narrative of events is quite incommensurable with what we moderns mean by "history." This does not trouble Barr, however, since he contends that history is "not a biblical category" to begin with.[22] The biblical theology movement's tragic flaw, in his estimation, has been to read the modern understanding and valuation of history back into the Bible. Barr is much more sanguine when it comes to the capacity of archeology and historical-critical research to give us a certain kind of reliable access to the "real history" of the ancient Near East. But this sort of investigation yields only "plain history," which "cannot honestly be called 'revelatory' in any sense relatable to the actual intentions of the Old Testament texts." Further, Barr scoffs at those who, unable to bridge the gap between Scripture and "real history," take it upon themselves to invest the latter "with a kind of religious mysticism" and thus provide themselves with "a kind of theology-substitute."[23]

At this point in Barr's discussion, the dualism of word and event has unmistakably reared its head, not at the exegetical or intrabiblical level but precisely at the level of the relationship between biblical word and historical event. It is tolerably clear that Barr has no expectation of finding any profound theological significance, much less God's self-disclosure, in "real" or "plain" history. Aside from the "trivial" case of persons revealing something of themselves in their deeds, the human actions and other events of ancient Israel's actual history appear to be essentially mute.

It should perhaps come as no surprise that the chasm which opens here between the Old Testament text and Israel's "real" history is accompanied by other, similar dichotomies and leads to a significantly diminished sense of the Bible's divine origin and authority. "Scripture," Barr matter-of-factly informs us, "does not come into existence by direct action of God, but by a human action which is a reflex of contact with God." The logical corollary to this position is that the human action that produced the Bible "shares in the distortion and inadequacy which applies to other human acts, and

22 Barr, 69.

23 Barr, 68.

especially to those human acts which claim to relate themselves to the will of God."[24] Ever the uncompromising opponent of "fundamentalism," Barr does not evince so much as a hint of nostalgia for the traditional doctrines of inspiration and inerrancy, which in any case can only be sustained "by recourse to the sheer supernaturalism of miraculous divine intervention." As Barr views the matter, one must choose between an utterly infallible Bible that is the product of "sheer supernaturalism" and a radically human Bible that "meets the needs of sinful men just because it is itself not free from its sinful element."[25] The irony in all this is that, having excoriated the biblical theology movement for locating God's self-revelation in the nonverbal realm, Barr now reduces Scripture to a merely human "reflex," a partly sinful, subjective response to something he vaguely terms the human authors' "contact with God."

Barr's assault on "biblical theology," in several major works throughout his career, has contributed not a little to the movement's long, slow decline. Writing a generation after the Currie Lectures, Thomas L. Thompson treats the dichotomy between Old Testament narrative and ancient Israel's actual history as self-evident and Barr's diagnosis of the biblical theology movement as beyond cavil. According to Thompson, the proponents of biblical theology have introduced "considerable confusion" by using the word *Heilsgeschichte* to refer both to the biblical narrative's presentation of Israel's past, which is neither more nor less than "a form of theologically motivated *Tendenz*," and to Israel's actual history as (supposedly) revelatory and salvific. In Thompson's opinion, the latter use has been "largely discredited," for it locates revelation in a realm that is "open in every way to historical-critical research," and such a realm almost by definition cannot be viewed as "an object of faith alone."[26] History and faith must be kept neatly separate. (This is the legacy of Rudolf Bultmann.)

Still, Thompson holds that the *Tendenz* of Old Testament narrative can be viewed positively as a locus of theology and faith—paradoxically, it can even be called "salvation history"—provided we ascribe no significant historicity or historiographical intentionality to it.[27] Elsewhere, Thompson explains that Israel's faith "is not an historical faith." It "has its justification,

24 Barr, 163.

25 Barr, 163.

26 Thomas L. Thompson, "Historiography (Israelite)," *ABD* 3:209.

27 Thompson, 210.

not in the evidence of past events, for the traditions of the past serve only as the occasion of the expression of faith, but in the assertion of a future promise."[28] Indeed, he asserts, "Salvation history is not an historical account of saving events open to the study of the historian. Salvation history did not happen; it is a literary form which has its own historical context."[29] Following the trajectory of Barr's thought well beyond Barr's own conclusions, Thompson affirms a "biblical faith" that is invulnerable to historical-critical investigation because it is not really concerned with past events but only with present experience and future hope. It is Israel's "experience" that is (to some extent) "communicated," and Israel's "faith" that is "revealed" in the Old Testament. This nonhistorical faith-experience can become "our faith," too, through an existential reading of the Old Testament.[30] The Christian is thus able to maintain a "theology of the word" and of "existential experience," while he or she is freed from the burdensome and ultimately untenable notion that revelation and salvation consist in a series of divine interventions in history culminating in Jesus's resurrection.[31] Thompson's radical transformation of biblical theology, building on Barr's critique, thus furnishes a consummate example of the dualism of word and event.

CREATION AND THE *IMAGO DEI*

If the modern dualism of word and event "cuts the biblical Word off from creation,"[32] the place to begin our attempt to recover the true unity of word and event is with the biblical doctrine of creation. Scripture's opening sentence shows us that the unity of word and event is rooted in God's primordial act of creation (Gen 1:1–3).[33] The inspired narrative displays a perfect correspondence between God's creative word—*yəhî 'ôr* ("let there be light")—and its immediate result—*wayhî 'ôr* ("and there was light"). What God says happens, with no remainder and no surprises. We do not read, "God

28 Thomas L. Thompson, *The Historicity of the Patriarchal Narratives: The Quest for the Historical Abraham* (Harrisburg, Pa.: Trinity Press International, 2002), 329.

29 Thompson, 328.

30 Thompson, 330.

31 Thompson, 329.

32 Ratzinger, "Biblical Interpretation in Conflict," 25.

33 The first three verses of Genesis constitute a single sentence in Hebrew, though English translations usually break it into two or three sentences for the sake of readability.

said, 'Let there be light,' and there was a chicken," but "God said, 'Let there be light,' and there was light." His word of creation is perfectly efficacious. Moreover, God is neither compelled to create nor hindered from creating. The world is not the result of some combination of chance and necessity, nor is it the product of a battle among the gods.

Genesis presents God's act of creation as a speaking-into-being and thus traces the unity of word and event back to a primordial act of divine performative speech. The phrase *yəhî 'ôr* is a volitive speech act. As such, it is an expression of both knowledge and will. As rational discourse, *yəhî 'ôr* has intelligible content. And because the verbal form *yəhî* is grammatically a jussive, or third-person volitive, it is also a sort of command.[34] One speaks what one knows, and one commands what one wills.[35] Furthermore, when one wills what is good, the volitional word is an expression of love. And the Priestly narrative of creation emphatically asserts that everything God created is "very good" (1:31).

Creation flows forth from an eternal act of knowledge and love, or what Augustine calls God's "eternal counsel and will."[36] If the intrinsic unity of word and event that pervades the economy of revelation and redemption is rooted in God's act of creation, this act, the word of love by which God speaks the world into being, is rooted in his inner life. The οἰκονομία flows forth from the realm of θεολογία.[37] The unity of word and event, then, ultimately traces back to the eternal processions of knowledge and love within the Holy Trinity. Perhaps we should not then dismiss too hastily the Church

34 Biblical Hebrew employs three classes of volitive verb forms: the cohortative (first-person volitive), the imperative (second-person volitive), and the jussive (third-person volitive). See Joüon, *Grammar of Biblical Hebrew*, 125 (§40b).

35 In commenting on "the idea of creation by the word" in Gen 1:3, Gerhard von Rad places all the emphasis on God's "personal will," at the expense of any notion of the word as possessing intelligible content or as divine self-communication. He is right to insist that the Priestly author affirms a "radical essential distinction between Creator and creature" and that creation "cannot be even remotely considered an emanation from God," but he goes much too far in concluding that the created world is therefore in no sense a "reflection of his being." *Genesis*, 51–52. In order to uphold a biblical view of reality, one must distinguish between emanation and reflection in this regard.

36 *Aeternum consilium voluntatemque*. Augustine, *De civitate Dei* 11.4.

37 In this context, the term θεολογία refers to God's inner life and eternal being, which is the realm of the absolutely necessary and immutable. It is a question of who God is in himself, who he would be even if he had never created a world. The term οἰκονομία refers to God's master plan of creation and redemption, which is the realm of the contingent and mutable. It is a question of what God freely does, going, as it were, beyond himself.

Fathers' tendency to discover all three persons of the Trinity in the opening lines of Genesis.[38] In support of this reading, they like to cite Psalm 33:6: "By the word [*dābār*] of Yahweh the heavens were made, by the breath [*rûaḥ*] of his mouth all their host."[39] Both texts present creation as a perfectly unified action of God, his *dābār*, and his *rûaḥ*.[40]

The biblical doctrine of God's creation by his word is developed in the Old Testament wisdom literature. In Proverbs 3:19, for example, we read: "By his wisdom [*ḥokmâ*] Yahweh founded the earth; he established the heavens by his understanding." The category of *ḥokmâ* further discloses the unity of knowledge and love in God's act of creation. Human "wisdom" includes both the theoretical and the practical among its essential aspects. It is the virtue by which one does the truth for the sake of the good. To say, analogically, that God created the world by his wisdom is to say that he has acted in intelligence and love. He orders everything toward an end that is good. This is what sets the authentically biblical notion of divine power apart from every defective notion of omnipotence. As Augustine puts it, "God is omnipotent, not by reckless power, but by the strength of wisdom."[41]

The world created by "the only wise God" (Rom 16:27) is itself intelligible and good, an expression of divine truth and love. Each creature, and creation as a whole, is ordered toward an end that is good. The physical universe is an event and a thing, but it is not irrational or mute. It is a word of truth and love rather than a brute fact. But for creation to speak its word of truth and love there needs to be a creature who possesses the capacity to hear and understand this word, a creature who is able to "interpret" the world.

38 Ephrem of Syria, e.g., comments on Gen 1:2: "It was appropriate to reveal here that the Spirit hovered in order for us to learn that the work of creation was held in common by the Spirit with the Father and the Son. The Father spoke. The Son created. And so it was also right that the Spirit offer its work, clearly shown through its hovering, in order to demonstrate its unity with the other persons. Thus we learn that all was brought to perfection and accomplished by the Trinity." Andrew Louth, ed., *Genesis 1–11*, Ancient Christian Commentary on Scripture, Old Testament 1 (Downers Grove, Ill.: InterVarsity Press, 2001), 6.

39 E.g., Ambrose, *In hexaemeron* 1.8.

40 We need not suppose that the Hebrew authors possessed anything like an explicit conceptual knowledge of the doctrine of the Trinity. Since the God whom they knew by revelation was in fact the true God—who is, was, and always will be three divine persons—it should not surprise us if the Old Testament contains here and there intimations of God's inner life, intimations which come into a new light when read from the perspective of the fullness of revelation in Jesus Christ.

41 *Neque enim potentia temeraria, sed sapientiae virtute omnipotens est.* Augustine, *De Genesi ad litteram* 9.17.

Man, created in the image of God, is endowed with precisely this capacity, and the created universe is "a gift addressed to man" (*CCC* 299).

According to the theological tradition that comes to us through Augustine and Aquinas, "all things which occur in time are certain similitudes of those things which have been from eternity."[42] In this sense, every creature is made to the likeness of God. Man, however, is made "in the image and likeness of God" in a unique sense. This same theological tradition locates the *imago Dei* in man's rational soul with its faculties of intellect and will. For present purposes, it may be helpful to restate this interpretation of Genesis 1:26–27 in terms of the *analogia verbi*. God, creation, and man are all λογικός ("rational"), but each in its own way. God is supremely and properly speaking λογικός. In eternally generating his Logos and breathing forth his Spirit, he eternally knows and loves all things. Creatures too are λογικός, analogously speaking—in a finite and somewhat passive sense, as the products and expressions of God's knowledge and love. They are intelligible and good, knowable and lovable. As a creature, man too is λογικός in this sense. At the same time, however, he participates in God's rationality in a manner that is more active and more perfect than that enjoyed by other creatures in the physical realm. He is not only intelligible and good but intelligent and capable of choosing and doing the good. He is not only knowable and lovable but capable of knowing and loving.

Early in the history of Christian theology there emerged a strong and enduring tendency to identify the *imago Dei* in man with the faculty of reason (λόγος) and with the mind (νοῦς), but this did not always involve dissociating it completely from man's bodily form. The second-century *Epistle to Diognetus*, in presenting the biblical teaching on the *imago Dei*, emphasizes man's intellectual endowment but immediately complements this emphasis with the idea that man's upright posture also distinguishes him from other bodily creatures and reflects his special orientation to God and heaven (*Diog.* 10.2).

In his *De hominis opificio*, Gregory of Nyssa develops the notion that it is the whole human person in the unity of body and soul that is made to the image of God, and not the mind alone. According to Gregory, we see in man's rational soul a kind of participation in God's incorporeal nature that we do not find in the body. Nevertheless, man is a single "compound nature" (σύγκριμα) and must be viewed as such.[43] The mind "would have been

42 Aquinas, *STh* III, q. 23, a. 2, ad 3.

43 Gregory of Nyssa, *De hominis opificio* 16.9 (PG 44:181). Translation: *NPNF*^{2} 5:405.

incommunicable and isolated if its motion were not manifested by some contrivance," and so the Creator prepared the human body as the appropriate "instrument" (ὄργανον) for the exercise of reason. For example, the mouths of beasts are designed primarily for feeding and so produce only inarticulate sounds such as bleats or barks, but the human mouth is configured to produce the much more varied sounds that are necessary for intelligible speech.[44] Similarly, the suppleness and dexterity of human hands make them apt for every art of human ingenuity and to do the bidding of reason.[45] In a word, the Creator endowed human nature with superior intelligence and a refined body "fit for the exercise of royalty," so that human beings might be the "living image" of his kingship over all creatures.[46]

The retrieval of an authentically biblical anthropology and somatology is of the utmost importance for our fresh appraisal of the relationship between word and event. Genesis places before our eyes God's creation of a world that is ordered toward human life and human action. The body gives man a place within this world of space and time. Man exercises his intelligence and realizes his freedom in and through the body. Actions performed in the body, and thus in the world of time and space, have real consequences. In fact, strictly speaking, they are irreversible. If I become intoxicated, get behind the wheel of a car, and kill someone, many lives, including my own, have been altered forever. I cannot press Ctrl+Z and reverse the course of events. Real life has no "undo" function. This is true, of course, not only in the case of vicious or irresponsible acts. It applies equally to acts of wisdom and virtue.

Because the physical universe has been created by a wise and loving God and thus bears the imprint of divine wisdom and love, there is no such thing as a brute fact, an event utterly devoid of rationality. Even events in which human beings are completely uninvolved, such as a volcanic eruption on a distant planet, must have some inherent significance. But our special concern, and certainly that of the biblical authors, is with events in which human beings *are* involved, events that engage the human intellect and freedom, events with ramifications for human beings. In such events, human souls acting through bodies that have been created for the exercise of reason and the disclosure of personhood leave, as it were, an indelible mark on the physical universe.

44 *De hominis opificio* 8.8–9.1 (PG 44:148–49). Translation: *NPNF*[2] 5:394–95.

45 *De hominis opificio* 8.2; 8.8 (PG 44:144, 148).

46 *De hominis opificio* 4.1 (PG 44:136). Translation: *NPNF*[2] 5:390–91.

Though we cannot devote space to the topic here, it would be helpful in this regard to reflect on the myriad ways we take up the subhuman world into the fabric of human life and culture and in so doing humanize and spiritualize the world.[47] In any case, this must not be viewed as an imposition of the sheer will to dominate. Even where the impulse to make the subhuman world serve anthropic ends is deeply tainted by sin, there takes place some authentic disclosure of the truth of things and a discovery of their true ends. Here, in the consideration of the relationship between spirit and matter, we approach the very heart of the problem, and here our modern minds stand most in need of the healing light of Scripture's own sacramental view of reality.

LANGUAGE AND TRUTH

Our reappraisal of the relationship between word and event also requires careful and extensive consideration of language itself and its place in human life. We tend to dive into questions about the nature of revelation and the inspiration of Scripture under the assumption that we already pretty much know what language is and how it functions. It is premature, however, to attempt to describe the nature of divinely inspired words when we have not yet devoted serious thought to the mystery of language as such. As Ratzinger notes in the Erasmus Lecture, the modern dualism of word and event is the result not simply of a deficient understanding of event but also of a truncated notion of word.[48] Modern biblical scholars and theologians tend to operate with an instrumentalist or merely functional view of language. Language for them is essentially a tool of the isolated, autonomous thinker who asserts his will over external reality and then utilizes knowledge as a means of power over against his environment (including other autonomous individuals). This view of things can never appreciate the true genius of language, which is fundamentally a mystery of truth and love, not of "knowledge as power."

Among material beings, man is uniquely endowed with the capacity to "hear" the voice of creation and to "translate" it into rational discourse. Creation's relation to the divine Logos is reflected in its intelligibility and goodness, while man's unique relation to the same Logos is reflected in his intelligence and will, including his linguistic endowment. Jacques Maritain

47 For some initial thoughts, see chapter 7 in this volume, especially the section entitled "Agricultural Symbolism."

48 Ratzinger, "Biblical Interpretation in Conflict," 25.

refers to this complementarity as the "nuptial relationship between mind and being."[49] Man's vocation is to speak on behalf of the rest of creation, and in so doing to ascribe glory to the Creator. As Norris Clarke puts it, the human person is called to listen to the voice of being "with reverence" and to speak out "its meaning in a recreative human *logos*."[50]

Human language is closely bound up with man's bodily nature and embeddedness in the physical universe. The brain and the organs of speech and hearing are physical. Spoken communication depends on sound waves moving through the air. Written communication depends on physical implements such as ink and paper or computers. Yet language mediates intellectual and spiritual realities. Human language is thus an externalization of interior life, while at the same time it involves a spiritualization of material things. A book is at once a materialized idea and a spiritualized tree. Speaking, listening, writing, and reading are activities proper to man as a unity of physical body and spiritual soul. Human language can even be called "sacramental," in the sense that it gives invisible realities a presence in the world of space and time.[51]

Language is a function of man's freedom and of his vocation to "subdue the earth" (Gen 1:28). According to the Genesis narrative, God brought the animals to man "to see what he would name them," and "whatever the man called" each animal, "that was its name" (2:19). The seeming quaintness of this story should not lead us to overlook its profundity. Assigning names to the beings that surround him gives man real leverage to explore, organize, and master his environment. At the same time, Genesis does not suggest that human acts of linguistic denomination and predication constitute an *imposition* upon external reality. At the narrative's culmination, the man's naming of "woman" is presented rather as a response of wonderment upon his joyful *discovery* of her true identity and relation to himself (2:23). Language can be a way of receiving creation from the hand of God in gratitude and praise.

All man's subsequent words, however, will be spoken under the shadow of temptation and sin. They will be liable to duplicity and to various distortions

49 As quoted (without exact citation of the source) in W. Norris Clarke, *The One and the Many: A Contemporary Thomistic Metaphysics* (Notre Dame, Ind.: University of Notre Dame Press, 2001), 18.

50 Clarke, 29.

51 Pope John Paul II describes the human body as "a primordial sacrament . . . a sign that efficaciously transmits in the visible world the invisible mystery hidden in God from eternity." *Man and Woman He Created Them: A Theology of the Body*, trans. Michael Waldstein (Boston: Pauline Books & Media, 2006), 203 (*TOB* 19.4).

of the truth of being. An adequate reappraisal of the relationship between word and event must therefore also consider the effect of sin on language as well as the manner in which human speech, marred by sin, is progressively purified and "redeemed" precisely by being taken up into the economy of revelation. Beginning with Genesis, the Bible presents human language as deeply involved in the drama of man's alienation from God and in the divine pedagogy by which God reconciles human beings to himself. This important topic has been given surprisingly little attention in fundamental theology and biblical hermeneutics.

If we wish to appreciate how biblical words communicate the truth of events (which really is the heart of the matter), we would do well to attend to what Scripture itself teaches us about the act of narration. This is a vast topic, and here we shall have to content ourselves with an observation or two. The truth of an event, the truth that really matters, runs much deeper than the mere facts of the case, for what we take to be "fact" is often only the most superficial dimension of an event or action. Therefore, to judge the truth or falsehood of a speech or narration on the basis of how accurately it represents this superficial level of the event will yield a deficient notion of truth and falsehood.

Let us take an example. Under interrogation by Yahweh, Adam says, "The woman whom you gave to be with me gave me from the tree, and I ate" (3:12). In terms of its accuracy of representation of the facts (of the narrated story), this statement is absolutely inerrant. It is true that God gave the woman to the man to be with him, and it is true that the woman gave the fruit of the tree to the man. And yet, Adam's speech-act is profoundly sinful. Rather than accept responsibility for his actions, he manages to point blame at both God and his wife in the same breath. He speaks with ingratitude and attempts to deflect attention away from his own culpability.[52] A speech-act may accurately narrate the facts of the case and still fail to lead us closer to the truth of the event. Conversely, a fictional narrative can communicate real truth—not only a general moral truth, but even the truth of a specific event. For example, Nathan's parable enables David to face the sinfulness of his own actions involving Bathsheba and her husband Uriah (2 Sam 12:1–15).

Language pertains to man's personhood and his call to interpersonal communion. It enables a person to reach outside his own solitude, to share something of his interiority with others, and to receive what they choose to share of themselves in return. Language enables us to make promises, ask

52 Von Rad, *Genesis*, 91.

favors, give commands, share knowledge, articulate feelings, or construct an argument. It permits human beings to share a common life and common projects. It makes possible both a personal and a communal sense of past, present, and future—a shared history. It enables "I"-subjects to belong to "we"-subjects and to participate in various human institutions.

Language comes to each of us as the heritage of the human community and it keeps us connected to that community throughout our lives. The individual realizes his or her freedom through language and action, but only within the realm of community, tradition, custom, and law. Indeed, it is by virtue of its communal dimension that language serves man in his ongoing discovery of the truth of things. Understanding comes via conversation. Hans-Georg Gadamer describes how an authentic dialogue is more than the sum of its parts and can take on a life of its own, leading its participants together toward a deeper understanding of the topic under discussion. Thus "the sphere of the 'We'"—where language lives—mediates between the "I"-subject and the objective reality that would disclose its truth.[53] As Augustine says, "Reasoning does not make things but discovers them. Before they are discovered, therefore, they abide in themselves; and when they are discovered, they renew us."[54] This principle applies not only to the reasoning of the individual but also to that of a community of persons in dialogue.

Ultimately, language is able to mediate between man and the truth of the created universe (including the reflexive truth of man himself) because each of these realities—man, language, and the universe—participates in its own way in the divine Logos and thus in the mystery of Trinitarian knowledge and love. This *analogia verbi* forms the basis for the very possibility of divine revelation and thus of our capacity for saying anything true about God in human language.

GOD'S WORD IN HUMAN EVENTS

As we ponder the mystery of human language and action in general terms, we must also begin to consider the specific ways God has revealed himself "in deeds and words intrinsically interconnected" within the divine

53 Hans-Georg Gadamer, *Philosophical Hermeneutics*, ed. and trans. David E. Linge (Berkeley: University of California Press, 1976), 65–66.

54 *Non enim ratiocinatio talia facit, sed invenit. Ergo antequam inveniantur, in se manent, et cum inveniuntur, nos innovant.* Augustine, *De vera religione* 39.73.

economy. The Epistle to the Hebrews tells us that during the Old Testament period God spoke to Israel "in many partial and varied ways" (1:1). Broadly speaking, these are reducible to law, prophecy, psalmody, and wisdom, but under each of these headings one might identify numerous more specific modes by which God's word came to Israel. For present purposes it may prove helpful to focus our attention on the way Israel sometimes discerned God's will in the unfolding of an event per se, without any of the usual intermediaries, and then gave this revelatory event a new verbal mode of existence through narrative artistry, so that a word-event became an event-word.

As an example of this, let us briefly consider the betrothal of Rebekah in Genesis 24, aided by Meir Sternberg's masterful analysis of this Hebrew narrative.[55] At the outset of the story, Abraham commissions a trusted servant to return to his homeland in northern Mesopotamia in order to fetch a suitable bride for his son Isaac. He promises the servant that Yahweh "will send his angel before" him (v. 7), but as things turn out no angel appears in the story. Nor does the servant have a revelatory dream at a holy place en route. No prophet approaches him with an oracle. He meets no seer along the way. In order to discern God's will in the affair, the servant is "thrown on his own devices" and "takes a twofold initiative that weds good sense to piety."[56]

In other words, he employs faith and reason together. Rather than contrive a designedly arbitrary test of God's will, such as Gideon does with the fleece (Judg 6:36–40), Abraham's servant devises a rational test for finding a friendly, strong, and hospitable woman. A maiden who would grant his request for a drink of water and then go the extra mile by drawing water for his ten thirsty camels would be just the sort of woman he is looking for. Parking his camels near the well in the late afternoon, when he knows women will be coming forth to draw water, he prays, "Yahweh, God of my master Abraham, make things come together before me today, and keep steadfast love with my master Abraham" (Gen 24:12).[57]

At this point the narrator duly notes that before the servant even finishes this prayer, Rebekah makes her appearance at the well, suggesting that

55 Meir Sternberg, *The Poetics of Biblical Narrative: Ideological Literature and the Drama of Reading* (Bloomington, Ind.: Indiana University Press, 1985), 131–52.

56 Sternberg, 137.

57 The Hiphil stem of *qrh* means "to cause to converge," sometimes with connotations of divine providence working through apparent coincidence (cf. Gen 27:20, and other forms of the same root in Ruth 2:3 and 2 Sam 1:6).

things are in fact already "coming together" (v. 15). Rebekah's great physical beauty makes her an especially attractive candidate for the test, which she passes with flying colors (vv. 16–20). But for the servant the clincher comes when he learns that Rebekah is Isaac's second cousin. Surely, he reasons, it was Yahweh who "guided" him directly to Abraham's family (vv. 24–27). This could be no mere coincidence. As Sternberg puts it, Rebekah "is, literally, God's answer (in the medium of plot) to the servant's prayer."[58] Her timely arrival is a word from Yahweh.

Now the servant's job is to convince Rebekah's family, specifically her older brother Laban, that this is indeed a match made in heaven. He makes his pitch by way of a lengthy renarration of the sequence of events that led him to this juncture, in the course of which he takes quite a few liberties with the details (vv. 34–49). He tactfully omits anything that may have given offense to the Mesopotamian family, rearranges the order of events slightly, and even modifies Abraham's instructions in such a way as to give the impression that it was the patriarch's intention all along for Isaac to marry a close relative. Sternberg illuminates the way each of these changes serves a precise rhetorical end.[59]

His point, however, is emphatically not that the servant is a spin doctor who sacrifices truth on the altar of persuasion. Rather, taking into consideration the lower theological proficiency of his polytheistic audience, the servant tempers his narrative to meet them at their level of understanding and leads them to recognize that Yahweh, the god of Abraham, has manifested his will for Isaac and Rebekah in a remarkable confluence of events. As Sternberg phrases it, "the servant, like many novelists after him, resorts to invention in order to give the truth a more truthlike appearance," for "the unvarnished truth would not [have carried] enough weight to induce [the family] to part with Rebekah."[60]

The servant has employed *mythos*, or "emplotment," which always includes a fictive dimension, in order give the providential and revelatory event a new verbal mode of existence. The word-event has become an event-word. When narrative artistry is used in this way by someone whose mind has been illumined by the Spirit of Truth to judge concerning the action of God in history, narration is a prophetic act.

58 Sternberg, *Poetics of Biblical Narrative*, 137.

59 Sternberg, 145–51.

60 Sternberg, 149–50.

Of particular interest for present purposes is Laban's response (v. 50), which indicates that he has been led by the servant's narrative to draw precisely the correct conclusion about the event that has transpired. "The thing [*dābār*] has come forth from Yahweh," he declares. "We cannot speak to you bad or good. Behold, Rebekah is before you. Take her and go, that she may become the wife of your master's son, just as Yahweh has spoken [*dibber*]." The Hebrew noun *dābār* means "thing, event, or word." The verb *dibber*, "to speak," is its cognate. No angel, prophet, seer, diviner, or dream-interpreter appears anywhere in the story—and yet, Yahweh has spoken! He has revealed his will in the course of events. He has *dibber*-ed through a *dābār*. The event-*dābār* is in itself already a word-*dābār* inasmuch as Yahweh has truly guided the course of events, but it takes on a new verbal mode of existence when the servant narrates it for Rebekah's family and again, of course, when the inspired author of Genesis 24 narrates it for us.

TIME, NARRATIVE, AND HISTORY

A serious reappraisal of word and event within the economy of redemption must also take stock of the biblical view of time and human temporality as well as the biblical narrative's relation to history. In the present context we can merely touch on these complex matters.

The Priestly Heptaemeron, or first creation account (Gen 1:1–2:3), shows us that as soon as God speaks light into being and separates it from darkness, "the march and rhythm of time" is set in motion.[61] The "days" of Genesis 1, each with its evening and morning, represent real time, a temporality regulated by cosmic cycles and thus rooted in the created order. This temporality is comprised of the days and months and years with which Israelite readers were familiar and within which they lived their lives. It is not, however, a mere succession of moments. The unique character of the seventh day (2:2–3) gives creation's divinely instituted temporality a teleological dimension and indicates that it is ordered to man's vocation to work and rest in imitation of the Creator.

The seven-day sequence of Genesis 1:1–2:3 is the anchor for an elaborate Priestly chronology that includes the genealogies of Genesis 5 and 11 and extends throughout the first four books of the Bible. This chronological

61 Westermann, *Genesis 1–11*, 112.

framework removes the primeval stories of fall, fratricide, and flood from the mythical realm of a time-before-time and places every event, from creation to the death of Moses and beyond, within a single historical sequence. This Priestly chronology does not, of course, supply us with anything like accurate historical information regarding the age of the cosmos, the lifespans of the patriarchs, or even the date of the exodus. It accomplishes something much more important. It teaches us that there is one seamless economy comprising creation and redemptive history. Israelite readers of Genesis, living during the crisis of the exile or the early postexilic period, would recognize that the events of their own lives fall within a single divine master plan. The story that Genesis narrates from its opening chapter is the story within which they live. In a homily given many years ago, Ratzinger aptly sums up the teaching of the first creation narrative this way: "God created the universe in order to enter into a history of love with humankind."[62]

As noted in the previous section, the act of emplotment or narration—the act by which an event is given a new verbal mode of existence—necessarily contains a fictive dimension. At a minimum, the author's selection, arrangement, and choice of words embody an interpretive judgment. But this fictive dimension does not necessarily compromise the truth of a real event. Even if it involves a significant element of literary license, the art of emplotment, with its fictive dimension, can serve the truth of an historical event. In a moment of "invention," the author draws forth and displays the inherent λόγος-dimension of the event. As the term's etymology suggests, to "invent" is simultaneously to discover and to contrive.

What we have just said about the Priestly chronology, however, requires us to push the envelope a bit in this regard. Can a narrative that is not historical in anything like the usual sense of the term provide authentic revelation concerning a fundamentally historical economy? The short answer to this question is yes, at least when that narrative is part of a larger historical tradition and a unified, incipiently canonical testimony to history.

The Old Testament contains a remarkable variety of narrative genres and subgenres, each bearing its own sort of witness to historical events and to the historical economy. The book of Jeremiah, for example, contains a great deal of reliable historical information about the final years of the kingdom of Judah, information drawn from contemporary sources and verified in many

62 Joseph Ratzinger, *'In the Beginning...': A Catholic Understanding of Creation and the Fall*, trans. Boniface Ramsey, Ressourcement (Grand Rapids: Eerdmans, 1995), 30.

cases by extrabiblical accounts. By contrast, the book of Daniel, which was written centuries after the events it purports to recount, intentionally flouts the historical record (beginning with its opening verse) and weaves a variety of legends into a highly artificial schema of political events.[63] Still, it would be quite mistaken to conclude that the authors of Daniel are unconcerned with history. Properly understood, this unusual book of Scripture bears a profound prophetic witness to the establishment of the kingdom of God within the real history of the ancient Near East.

The basic theological impulse behind the composition, compilation, and canonical shaping of the Hebrew Scriptures is historiographical. From the late preexilic period to the early postexilic period, the Holy Spirit prompted Israelite authors and redactors to gather the traditions of their people into a single, coherent macronarrative. The result is the so-called Primary Narrative, which stretches from Genesis through 2 Kings—that is, from the creation of the world to Israel's great political and spiritual crisis, the exile. The redactors of the Primary Narrative joined the Priestly Tetrateuch (Genesis, Exodus, Leviticus, and Numbers) to the Deuteronomistic History (Joshua, Judges, Samuel, and Kings), with the book of Deuteronomy as the keystone of the arch.[64] Each of the remaining books in the biblical canon bears its witness to the divine economy by an explicit or implicit orientation to this macronarrative. For example, 1–2 Chronicles, together with the books of Ezra and Nehemiah, constitute the Secondary Narrative, a highly interpretive *relecture* of the Primary Narrative that carries the story forward into the postexilic period.

Neither the Holy Spirit nor the human authors and redactors seem to have been greatly troubled by the fact that the Primary Narrative is a hybrid with respect to the historiographical character of its sources. In composing their account of Israel's political history in the monarchic period, the inspired authors drew heavily upon the royal archives of Israel and Judah, but they also wove into their framework narrative cycles about Elijah and Elisha that must have originated in the circle of those prophets' disciples. For earlier periods, such as that of the judges, they had recourse to at least some legendary material, as is patently the case in the narratives about Samson

63 See John J. Collins, "Daniel, Book of," *ABD* 2:29–37.

64 In other words, the Primary Narrative comprises those books which in the Jewish canon belong to the Torah and the Former Prophets. The book of Ruth, which was composed somewhat later, belongs to the Writings.

(Judges 13–16). For still earlier periods, such as that of the patriarchs (Genesis 12–36), the sacred authors seem to have worked with material that has a certain affinity to folklore.

Throughout the age of the monarchy, the exile, and the postexilic period, Israel continued to look back to the exodus and wilderness wandering as their historical point of reference and theological touchstone. Nothing that had happened in their history, whether prior to or since the Mosaic age, made much sense if viewed apart from those founding events. But the exile did make sense as chastisement for sins against the Mosaic covenant, and the return from exile made sense as a new exodus and the promise of a new covenant.

Remarkably, however, at least to our way of thinking, the Israelites never seem to have asked themselves such questions as: "Did the exodus really happen? How do we know whether or not it happened? Which of the many versions of the exodus story preserved in our tradition is the most factual?" They did not view past events as irretrievably past and as leaving behind only traces in the archeological strata and literary record. Nor did they suppose that the only valid access to the past is by way of historical-critical research. The redemptive and revelatory events of the past were present to them in and through sacred tradition, by which we mean the whole authentic life of the people of Yahweh as it was handed down from generation to generation and constantly enriched and deepened by new encounters with the word of God. For faithful Israelites, there was no need to question the reality of the exodus. Their very existence and communal life as the people of Yahweh were the vital unfolding and trajectory of the founding events. If there had been no exodus, there would be no Israel.

In further exploring the way the truth of Israel's past was carried over into their present and future by a living tradition, Gadamer's notion of *Wirkungsgeschichte*, or "history of effects," may prove helpful. As Francis Watson points out, *Wirkungsgeschichte* is not merely a matter of texts generating more texts. The "historic" event—that is, "the event that marks an enduring turning point in a historical process"—"generates its own *Wirkungsgeschichte* out of which it is constantly interpreted and reinterpreted."[65] Textual traditions and other elements of tradition play their role within this larger historical process, which in the case of biblical Israel is the

65 Watson, *Text and Truth*, 51. On this point, see also Brice Wachterhauser, "Getting it Right: Relativism, Realism, and Truth," in *The Cambridge Companion to Gadamer*, ed. Robert J. Dostal (New York: Cambridge University Press, 2002), 65.

very life of the people, lived in the presence of God. As Andrew Hayes has expressed it, the *Wirkungsgeschichte* of an historic event is "the temporally distended impression" which that event leaves on the flow of history.[66]

Maintaining a teleological view of salvation-historical events is crucial here. Israel's many interpretations and reinterpretations of the exodus must not be viewed as so many layers of ideology superimposed upon the brute facts. The exodus event is from the beginning dense with inherent significance, but this significance only gradually unfolds and discloses itself within the subsequent history of Israel. The exodus, like every other event in Israel's history, manifests its inner truth more and more fully as that history approaches its telos. The Christ event is, as it were, the final cause of the exodus, for "Christ is the end [τέλος] of the law" (Rom 10:4).

THE CHRIST EVENT AND THE GOSPELS

In the life, death, and resurrection of Jesus of Nazareth we see the most perfect unity of word and event. Here, the eternal Logos makes his definitive entrance into the realm of time and space, rendering that moment "the fullness of time" (Gal 4:4). It is important to note that all the lower levels of the unity of word and event discussed above are taken up into this fullest manifestation of unity. Through the incarnation the eternal Logos takes to himself a created humanity of physical body and rational soul, made to the image of God, and makes it the "sacrament"—that is, the "sign and instrument"—of his divine personhood (*CCC* 515). In this way, the Son of God "communicates to his humanity his own personal mode of existence in the Trinity" (*CCC* 470). The eternal Word has spoken in human language and revealed the Father in historical deeds. Though the incarnation is a truly marvelous condescension, it is nevertheless true that the λογικός ("rational") humanity of Christ was an apt instrument for the divine Logos to employ in this manner, since the Logos could not have been hypostatically united to some lower, irrational nature. Furthermore, the "many partial and varied ways" by which God spoke to Israel in the Old Testament (Heb 1:1) have been taken up into this definitive personal entry of the Logos into creation and history and, having reached their telos, have been transformed.

66 Written assignment for my master's level course on the Old Testament, Ave Maria University, October 29, 2004.

Through the glorification of his humanity in the resurrection and ascension, all that Jesus Christ accomplished for our salvation in the days of his flesh has been given a suprahistorical presence and, through the mission of the Holy Spirit, has been made available to believers in all times and places through the Church's sacramental life and in a special way through the Gospels. We do not access the saving words and deeds of our Lord's life by stripping away the layers of interpretation in order to get down to some supposed historical bedrock. Any attempt to do so gives a priori assent to the dualism of word and event. Rather, we must allow the four Gospels to lead us into the mystery of Christ on their own terms.

In recent years small but important steps have been taken, both by theologians and by the Magisterium of the Catholic Church, to retrieve the biblical and patristic notion of the *mysteria vitae Iesu* ("mysteries of the life of Jesus").[67] It is vital that this work be carried forward, for in the last analysis only a robust and well-articulated understanding of "mystery" (μυστήριον or *mysterium*) can strike at the heart of the dualism of word and event. A mystery is an event in which God has acted manifestly in order to reveal himself and to redeem humanity. It is a moment of divine disclosure, but it always retains an unfathomable plenitude. It is a moment of knowledge, but it is accessible only to one who loves.

The term *mystery* is best understood in correlation with the term *economy*, for a mystery is essentially an "economic" event. Because each mystery participates in the economy, it must be viewed in light of the economy as a whole, even as it also illuminates that economy.[68] The ultimate mystery is the "theological" mystery of God's inner life and his eternal counsel and will, and the divine economy may be defined as his master plan for "dispensing" a certain participation in this mystery to us in time and space. It is "the economy of the mystery hidden from eternity in God, who created all things" (Eph 3:9). The centerpiece of this master plan, the definitive economic mystery, is the person and event of Jesus Christ. He contains the whole economy within himself, for he recapitulates creation, humanity, and Israel, while he

67 See, for example: *CCC* 512–667; Pope John Paul II, Apostolic Letter *Rosarium Virginis Mariae* (October 16, 2002), 18–25; Christoph Schütz, "The Mysteries of the Life of Jesus as a Prism of Faith," *Communio* 29 (Spring 2002): 28–38; Martin Bieler, "The Mysteries of Jesus' Public Life: Stages on the Way to the Cross," *Communio* 29 (Spring 2002): 47–61; and G. K. Beale and Benjamin L. Gladd, *Hidden But Now Revealed: A Biblical Theology of Mystery* (Downers Grove, Ill.: InterVarsity Press, 2014).

68 The Lord's baptism in the Jordan is a good example of this. See Gregory Vall, "*Lucis Mysterium*: Ignatius of Antioch on the Lord's Baptism," *Nova et Vetera* 8, no. 1 (2010): 143–60.

"precapitulates," so to speak, the life of the Church and the eschaton. The divine plan is therefore "the economy of the fullness of times, to sum up all things in Christ" (1:10).

Gospel is a literary genre developed to present the mystery of Christ, and the mysteries of the life of Christ, precisely as economic realities. It is axiomatic in New Testament scholarship to note that the evangelists relate the story of Jesus to the Old Testament story by way of allusion and quotation while they simultaneously have the Church in mind as they narrate the events of Christ's life. But their real reasons for doing this can only be grasped from within a theology of mystery and economy. In each discrete mystery of the life of Jesus the whole person and saving reality of Christ is truly present, and so the evangelists narrate the individual events of Christ's life in light of the Christ event as a whole. At the same time, because creation, man, and Israel are summed up in the person of Christ, the evangelists present the Christ event and the discrete moments within that event as the telos and fullness of the Old Testament economy. Finally, because the Church's whole life of grace and glory is already present in Jesus of Nazareth—"he who is your life" (Col 3:4)—the evangelists narrate the past words and deeds of Jesus in light of his glorious presence at the Father's right hand and his future coming.

As a convenient example of this manner of narrating, let us consider John 6:1–71. Structurally, this passage consists of four panels. First, there is the miracle of the loaves and fishes, which John narrates with considerable detail and characteristically presents as a "sign" performed for the benefit of "the people" (6:1–15). Second, there is the much shorter narrative of Christ's walking on the sea, which John presents as a private theophany to the disciples rather than as a public sign (6:16–21). In composing these first two panels, John seems to have relied heavily on a Synoptic-like (perhaps pre-Synoptic) source, since his account agrees with Mark 6:30–52 in many particulars but does not appear to be directly dependent on it.[69] Third, there is a long dialogue between Jesus and "the people" (also called "the Jews," especially when they begin to demonstrate doubt and hostility), which evolves into a synagogue discourse given at Capernaum (John 6:22–59). Fourth, there is a shorter dialogue between Jesus and his own disciples concerning their response to his teaching (6:60–71). While these last two panels do contain a few echoes of Synoptic tradition, they appear more heavily dependent on distinctively Johannine tradition than the first two panels.

69 Craig S. Keener, *The Gospel of John: A Commentary* (Peabody, Mass.: Hendrickson, 2003), 663–64, 671–72.

John has combined all of this with literary skill. On the one hand, the chapter moves back and forth between Jesus's interaction with the people and his interaction with his disciples, while, on the other hand, it moves from action to dialogue—in other words, from event to word.

vv. 1–15	action on behalf of the people
vv. 16–21	action on behalf of the disciples
vv. 22–59	dialogue with the people
vv. 60–71	dialogue with the disciples

Since the first and third panels are by far the longest, and both dialogues serve to unfold the significance of the miracle of the loaves and fishes, the chapter is reducible to a Synoptic-like sign followed by a characteristically Johannine discourse, much as the previous chapter is. In fact, chapter 5 has prepared us for chapter 6 by thematizing the importance of Jesus's "works" and "words" (5:36, 47).

What, then, is the significance of the multiplication of loaves and fishes? In the first place, the miraculous gift of superabundant food, specifically "bread," signifies Jesus's teaching itself. A close association between Jesus's teaching ministry and the miracle of the loaves is already hinted at in the Markan account (Mark 6:34), and John develops this link in dependence on the way bread sometimes symbolizes divine revelation in the Old Testament.[70] On one level, then, John 6 is a teaching about Jesus the Teacher. The people call him "Rabbi" (v. 25) and even acclaim him the long anticipated Moses-like "Prophet" (v. 14), but neither of these titles rises to a true understanding of the qualitative difference between the Mosaic law and Jesus's doctrine.[71] During the synagogue discourse, the Lord hints at the true nature of what is taking place in his teaching ministry by quoting a line from the prophets—"And they will all be taught by God" (v. 45; cf. Isa 54:13)—and later he tells his disciples, "The words that I have spoken to you are spirit and life" (John 6:63). Finally, Simon Peter confesses that Jesus is "the Holy One of God," who alone offers "words of eternal life" (vv. 68–69).

70 In the Old Testament, bread signifies divine revelation in three modalities: law (Deut 8:3; Neh 9:13–15), prophecy (Amos 8:11–12; Isa 55:1–3, 10–11), and wisdom (Prov 9:5; Sir 15:3).

71 The Torah portrays Moses as enjoying "face to face" intimacy with Yahweh (Exod 33:11; Deut 34:10; cf. Num 12:8) but also qualifies this claim by noting that, strictly speaking, neither Moses nor any human being can see God's face and live (Exod 33:20). The Bread of Life Discourse locates Jesus's superiority to Moses and his uniqueness as God's definitive self-revelation precisely in the fact that he alone "has seen the Father" (John 6:46; cf. 1:17–18).

Of course, John has already informed his readers that Jesus not only speaks the word of God but is himself the eternal Word made flesh (1:1–2, 14). That is why Jesus is less concerned to refer the sign of the loaves to his teaching as such than he is to identify *himself* as "the bread of God, who comes down from heaven and gives life to the world" (6:33). The sign of the loaves quite naturally reminds Jesus's Jewish interlocutors of the miracle of the manna in the wilderness, but when they mention this Old Testament event in an effort to get another free meal from Jesus, they unwittingly provide him with an opportunity to compare and contrast himself to the Mosaic law. John has them quote a line from Scripture that actually combines elements of several Old Testament passages without reproducing any one of them verbatim: "Bread from heaven he gave them to eat" (v. 31).[72] At least some of these texts associate the miracle of the manna with the law of Moses, which was likewise "heavenly bread"—that is, divine revelation—given to Israel in the wilderness. The "bread" by which man truly "lives" is the word of God (Deut 8:3). This Old Testament symbolism is presupposed when Jesus responds to their quotation by identifying himself as "the *true* bread from heaven"—that is, the definitive self-revelation of God, far superior to the Mosaic law (v. 32).[73] Starting with this exchange, the bulk of the Bread of Life Discourse develops the idea that the sign of the loaves points to the incarnation of the Logos, with the Old Testament manna-law symbolism as background (vv. 31–51). Jesus himself is "the bread that has come down from heaven" (v. 41).

The manna-law connection is, however, only one element in a rich texture of Old Testament echoes in John 6. The basic plot of the miracle of the loaves and fishes, as found in all four Gospels, recalls a similar miracle worked by the prophet Elisha (2 Kgs 4:42–44). John strengthens this reminiscence by specifying that the loaves multiplied by Jesus were made of barley, as was also the case in the Elisha story (John 6:9, 13). John's concise narrative of the walking on the sea, like its Synoptic parallels, echoes theophanic imagery from the Old Testament,[74] and Jesus's exclamation to the disciples in the boat—"I am he! Fear not!" (John 6:20)—recalls similar expressions of divine reassurance in the oracles of Deutero-Isaiah.[75] In the book of Sirach, Lady Wisdom promises her devotees that the acquisition of wisdom engenders a desire for still more wisdom: "Those who eat of me will hunger for more,

72 Cf. Exod 16:4, 15; Ps 78:24; Ps 105:40; Neh 9:15; and Wis 16:20.

73 Keener, *Gospel of John*, 679–81.

74 John 6:19; cf. Job 9:8; Ps 77:19.

75 Isa 41:10; 43:5, 10.

and those who drink of me will thirst for more" (Sir 24:21). Immediately following this statement, Ben Sira informs his readers that this wisdom is found especially in the law of Moses (v. 23). In the Bread of Life Discourse, however, the Johannine Jesus turns Lady Wisdom's statement on its head in order to indicate that he is the definitive Wisdom, who gives perfect satisfaction: "The one who comes to me will hunger no more, and the one who believes in me will never again thirst" (John 6:35). Jesus is superior to the law of Moses (cf. 1:17).

Though all the action in John 6 takes place in Galilee, the evangelist makes a special point of noting that these things occurred when "Passover, the feast of the Jews, was near" (v. 4).[76] This statement hearkens back to the cleansing of the Jerusalem temple, which according to John's chronology took place at a previous Passover at the beginning of Jesus's ministry (2:13), while it simultaneously anticipates the later Passover in Jerusalem that is the setting of Jesus's passion.[77] This two-way linkage contributes to the sense that the miracle of the loaves and fishes is a pivotal event in Jesus's ministry—the fourth of seven "signs"—while it relates the events and words of chapter 6 to John's overarching presentation of Jesus as the "Lamb of God."[78] The "flesh" that the Word takes to himself in the incarnation is the very flesh that he gives as "bread for the life of the world" on the cross (John 1:14; 6:51). As a Christological sign, therefore, the miracle of the loaves and fishes simultaneously points back to the incarnation and ahead to the paschal mystery. In this way, John relates the sign of the loaves to the entire career of the Son of Man, who "came down from heaven, not to do [his] own will but the will of the one who sent [him]" (v. 38), and who is "ascending to where he was previously" in order to make available the "life-giving" Spirit (vv. 62–63; cf. 7:39).

John 6 relates the sign of the loaves and fishes not only to the story of Israel and to the Christ event as a whole but also to the life of the Church. "The twelve," including four named members of the group, play a prominent role in this chapter, which can be read almost as a kind of treatise on faith and discipleship. Jesus involves Philip and Andrew in the miracle itself, not because he needs their help but in order to "test" them (vv. 5–13). Then, in the synagogue discourse he explains at some length that only those who are

76 The availability of barley loaves and the abundance of green grass may also suggest a setting in early spring (John 6:9–10; cf. Mark 6:39).

77 John 11:55; 12:1; 13:1; 18:28, 39; 19:14.

78 John 1:29, 36; cf. 19:36 (a citation of Exod 12:46, pertaining to the Passover lamb).

drawn by the Father can come to the Son, and only those who believe in the Son have eternal life (vv. 37–40, 44–47). When "many of his disciples" are scandalized by his teaching and fall away, Jesus directly challenges the twelve concerning their commitment to him (vv. 60–67). Speaking on behalf of the group, Peter makes an astute confession of faith, but Jesus ominously points out that even within his specially chosen group of twelve there is "a devil" who will betray him (vv. 68–71).

Moreover, by placing subtle emphasis on the Lord's having "given thanks" (εὐχαριστήσας), John drops an initial hint that the multiplication of loaves and fishes is a type of the Eucharist (vv. 11, 23) and thus prepares us for the explicit teaching on the Eucharist with which the synagogue discourse culminates (vv. 52–58). The connection between miracle and sacrament lies not so much in the simple fact that both involve bread as it does in the fact that the former signifies the revelation and "life" that come into the world in the person and event of Jesus Christ, while the latter is the mode by which that life will be available to the Church in all places and times. The crucial link between the two is the paschal mystery: Jesus gives his "flesh" as "bread for the life of the world" upon the cross, so that his disciples may receive this same flesh in the Eucharist (vv. 51–53).[79]

In the last analysis, "life" is the unifying theme of John 6. In its mundane dimension, the meal of loaves and fishes is merely "the food that perishes," but for those with faith it signifies "the food that remains for eternal life" (v. 27). In the Fourth Gospel "life" designates the true and definitive revelation of the Father, which is uniquely present in and through the person and event of the incarnate Son. Revelation is "life" because it brings one into knowledge of "the only true God and Jesus Christ, whom [he has] sent," and this knowledge is the very essence of eternal life (17:3). As Word made flesh, Jesus is "the bread of God that comes down from heaven and gives life to the world" (6:33). This life or revelation is present in his teaching, which, because it consists in "words of eternal life" (v. 68), is qualitatively superior to the Mosaic law. The latter had its own sign in the gift of the manna, which the ancestors "ate in the wilderness and yet died" (v. 49). The life or revelation that is present in Jesus's words is present also in the deeds, or "signs," by which he does "the will" of the one who sent him (vv. 38–40), above all in the great sign of the Son of Man's being "lifted up" on the cross.[80] Finally, it

79 Cf. Ignatius of Antioch, *Smyr.* 7.1.

80 John 3:14–15; 8:28; 12:32, 34.

is sacramentally available to those who "eat the flesh of the Son of Man and drink his blood" in the Eucharist (6:53).

The gift of life or revelation that is definitive within the historical economy is by definition also eschatological, and so it should come as no surprise that eschatology is woven throughout John 6. The particular accent that John places on the superabundance of loaves and fishes may hearken back to those prophetic oracles that present the eschatological blessing as a meal of great abundance.[81] Jesus himself is this meal, "the bread of life" (John 6:35, 48). As is well known, Johannine eschatology combines a realized dimension with a future dimension. The one who believes in Jesus already "has eternal life" (v. 47), and Jesus himself "will raise him up on the last day" (v. 40). These two complementary dimensions are frequently mentioned throughout the main part of the synagogue discourse, which presents Jesus himself as the bread of life, and faith as the mode of access to that life (vv. 32–51), but the same two dimensions of eschatology are, if anything, even more emphatically present in the Eucharistic portion of the discourse, and in the very same terms (vv. 53–58):[82] "The one who feeds on my flesh and drinks my blood *has* eternal life, and I *shall* raise him up on the last day" (v. 54). The Eucharist is, then, a foretaste of the heavenly banquet (v. 58).

In sum, the narrative of John 6 presents the multiplication of the loaves as a "sign" (vv. 14, 26), a term that is for all intents and purposes the Johannine equivalent of *mysterium*. John illuminates this event's place within a complex web of economically interrelated events and in the process spreads before our eyes almost the whole economy of redemption: from Mosaic law, to prophecy and wisdom, to the Christ event, to the life of the Church, to the parousia. The foregoing analysis is meant to provide an example of how the evangelists bring literary artistry to the service of the *mysteria vitae Iesu*, viewed precisely as "economic" realities.

According to *Dei Verbum*, "the Church unhesitatingly asserts" the "historical character" (*historicitatem*) of the four Gospels. At the same time, she recognizes quite clearly their literary character, noting that the evangelists "selected some things from the many which had been handed on by word of

81 John 6:11–13; cf. Isa 25:6; 55:1–3; Keener, *Gospel of John*, 668.

82 This suggests that faith in the historical Jesus and reception of the Eucharist are two equally essential, fully integral, and entirely compatible aspects of the disciple's adherence to Christ. The particularly solemn negative formulation of verse 53—"Amen, amen, I say to you, unless you eat the flesh of the Son of Man and drink his blood, you have no life within you"—may well warn against treating the Eucharist as somehow secondary or unessential.

mouth or in writing, reduced some of them to a synthesis, explained some things in view of the situation of their churches, and preserved the form of proclamation" (no. 19). A careful comparison of the four Gospels leads to the unavoidable conclusion that the evangelists exercised a considerable degree of literary license. For example, they could insert a saying of Jesus into an entirely new context, conflate two or more events into a single account, or even change one demoniac into two demoniacs.[83] To be sure, the evangelists "faithfully hand on what Jesus Christ . . . really did and taught" (no. 19), but the Gospels are for all that very far from supplying us with raw video of Jesus's ministry.

It is quite understandable that faithful Christians would be put on the defensive by the shenanigans of the Jesus Seminar, but any attempt to "defend" the Gospels by means of the implausible harmonization of surface details is entirely wrongheaded, for such a procedure buys into the truncated notion of event that is the root of our problem.[84] The evangelists employ literary artistry, with its fictive dimension, in order to draw out and display something of the event's economic significance.

In order to draw these reflections to a conclusion, I shall attempt to sum up what is going on in John 6 in terms of the unity of word and event. In the incarnation, the eternal Logos entered the world of space and time, the inherently λογικός ("rational") world that he himself had created. In order to act personally within this world, he assumed a λογικός humanity, which was created in the image of God, and he made it the apt instrument of his divine personhood. In this concrete humanity—Israelite "flesh" drawn from a daughter of Israel—he entered the current of Israelite history and human history at a particular point in space and time. That current carried

83 For example, Matthew reworks the logion about sitting with Abraham, Isaac, and Jacob in the kingdom of God and inserts it into his account of the healing of the centurion's servant in order to sharpen the contrast between gentile faith and Jewish unbelief (Matt 8:11–12; cf. Luke 7:1–10; 13:28–29). John's account of the anointing at Bethany (John 12:1–8) combines elements from two rather different anointing stories from the Synoptic tradition (cf. Mark 14:3–9 and Luke 7:36–50). Matthew changes Mark's one demoniac into two (Matt 8:28–34; cf. Mark 5:1–20), just as he also turns blind Bartimaeus into two blind men (Matt 20:29–34; cf. Mark 10:46–52) and has Jesus enter Jerusalem on two donkeys rather than one (Matt 21:1–11; cf. Mark 11:1–11)!

84 For a brief account of the work of the Jesus Seminar, see H. K. McArthur and R. F. Berkey, "Jesus, Quest of the Historical," *DBI* 1:583–84. For an attempt to defend the inerrancy of the Gospels by means of an implausible harmonization of surface details, see Karl Keating, *What Catholics Really Believe—Setting the Record Straight: 52 Answers to Common Misconceptions about the Catholic Faith* (San Francisco: Ignatius, 1992), 34–36.

within it all that made Israel Israel: the cultural influences of Mesopotamia, Egypt, Canaan, and Greece; the virtues and vices of patriarchs, prophets, and kings; exodus, independence, and exile; the exultant canticle of Hannah and the wordless martyrdom of Naboth; "many partial and varied" words of Yahweh, intrinsically interconnected with his marvelous deeds; a liturgical calendar replete with ancient rites and inspired psalms; and so forth. He walked among a people who were the product of this powerful current of history and culture, and he took upon himself their sins. Meanwhile, every authentic trajectory of prophecy and piety from Israel's past found its telos in his ministry.

On the mountain in Galilee Jesus served this people a miraculously abundant meal, and in the synagogue at Capernaum he taught them the significance of the sign. Here we see a case of revelation given in words and deeds intrinsically interconnected. In fact, the barley loaves signify his teaching itself, "words of everlasting life" that are more truly manna from heaven than was even the Mosaic law. The loaves signify the Logos himself, come down from heaven in the incarnation. They signify his flesh, which he gives as bread for the life of the world—historically in his passion, sacramentally in the Eucharist, eschatologically in the resurrection on the last day.

Decades after the multiplication of the loaves and fishes, an event that by that time had already found its way into three Gospels, John the evangelist, under the inspiration of the Holy Spirit, composed his own unique account, combining pre-Markan, Synoptic-like tradition with the unique perspective of the beloved disciple. John's concern was not to represent the event "as it actually happened" (*wie es eigentlich geschehen war*) but to disclose and make available its vertical dimension and its economic character, and to this end he exercised literary license. But John's narrative itself also has an economic character, for inspired Scripture plays its own proper role within the economy of redemption. In it, the word-event of the multiplication of loaves and fishes is present in a new modality. It has become an event-word. The holy Gospels are themselves living bread, the Church's daily bread, because they put us in touch with the person and event of Jesus Christ.

CHAPTER SEVEN

Man Is the Land: The Sacramentality of the Land of Israel

JOHN PAUL II'S THEOLOGY OF THE HOLY LAND

In a January 1992 address, Pope John Paul II expressed his profound hope that the Holy Land, which has seen so much violence down through the centuries and in recent decades, might soon become "a special place of encounter and prayer for peoples," and that Jerusalem, which has become a veritable symbol of religious division, might soon serve as "a sign and instrument of peace and reconciliation." Eugene Fisher suggests that the pontiff's choice of words here may reflect a "sacramental" understanding of the Holy Land.[1] However, the phrase "sign and instrument of peace and reconciliation" contains only a faint echo of the classic definition of a sacrament as an "efficacious sign of grace" (*signum efficax gratiae*), and it seems unlikely that John Paul wished to compare the land of Israel directly to the seven sacraments. A more striking and significant parallel to the pope's words is found in the description of the Church as "like a sacrament, that is, a sign and instrument of profound union with God and of the unity of the whole human race" in *Lumen Gentium*, a document that also refers to the Church as "the universal sacrament of salvation."[2] It may be, then, that John Paul's choice of words is aimed at directing our attention to one facet of the relationship between Israel and the Church.

1 Eugene J. Fisher, "A Commentary on the Texts: Pope John Paul II's Pilgrimage of Reconciliation," in Pope John Paul II, *Spiritual Pilgrimage: Texts on Jews and Judaism 1979–1995*, ed. Eugene J. Fisher and Leon Klenicki (New York: Crossroad, 1995), xxxiv.

2 *Lumen Gentium* 1 and 48 (cf. *CCC* 775–76).

At the heart of John Paul's understanding of the Holy Land lies the conviction that the land of Israel, and Jerusalem in particular, is a "meeting place" and the locus of historical revelation. In the 1984 Apostolic Letter *Redemptionis Anno*, John Paul refers these terms not only to Christ's incarnate presence in the land but to the Old Testament revelation to Israel as well. He writes, "before it was the city of Jesus the Redeemer, Jerusalem was the historic site of the biblical revelation of God, the meeting place, as it were, of heaven and earth, in which more than in any other place the word of God was brought to men."[3] Because it is "the place where, according to faith, the created things of earth encounter the infinite transcendence of God," the Holy Land, and Jerusalem in particular, can function as "a symbol of coming together, of union, and of universal peace for the human family."[4] The logic here is important. Because the Holy Land is a meeting place along the vertical axis—that is, between Creator and creation—it can serve as a symbol of union along the horizontal axis—that is, among human beings. The seriousness with which John Paul takes the Judeo-Christian belief in divine revelation also suggests that by "symbol" he does not have in mind a merely cultural or literary convention.

In connection with his 1965 pilgrimage to Israel, then-Cardinal Karol Wojtyła composed a series of poems dealing with the Holy Land. Not surprisingly, in these very personal meditations, Wojtyła allows his spiritual insight and poetic imagination to roam free and expresses himself rather more daringly than he does later in his official statements as pontiff. In this "pilgrimage to identity . . . the identity of finding one's own self in landscape," he pursues a series of mystical connections—for example, between the land of Israel and the whole earth, between Christ's presence in the land and Wojtyła's own presence there two thousand years later, between Mary's womb as Christ's "inner place" and the land as his "outer place," and between Christ's body as the "outward place" he had on earth and the Eucharist as his "place" within us.[5] Most hauntingly and elusively, Wojtyła searches for the true relation between man and land, at one point baldly asserting that "man is the land," but elsewhere developing the biblical images of the cross as the tree of life and of man himself as a plant. "Man is born to blossom like a

3 John Paul II, *Spiritual Pilgrimage*, 34.

4 John Paul II, 34–35.

5 Karol Wojtyła, *The Place Within: The Poetry of Pope John Paul II*, trans. Jerzy Peterkiewicz (New York: Random House, 1982), 109–18, at 115, 114, 118.

flower," and the Holy Land is the "place of the blossoming of man."[6] Several of these connections converge in one particularly luminous composition titled, "Space Which Remains in You," in which the poet adopts the persona of John the Beloved Disciple (many years after the resurrection) and imagines what the latter might have thought and felt when he confected the Eucharist and gave it to the Mother of God.[7] These poems suggest that years of prayer and profound reflection lie beneath the surface of John Paul's comparatively straightforward official statements concerning the Holy Land. Moreover, since the leitmotif of the Holy Land as a "meeting place" runs through the poems, the mystical connections explored in the poems give us some idea what John Paul means by this phrase in his official statements.

My immediate purpose in the following pages is neither to exegete the poems of Cardinal Wojtyła nor to attempt an in-depth analysis of Pope John Paul II's statements about the people and land of Israel, nor yet again to discuss the implications of these texts for Jewish-Christian relations. Instead, I wish to offer a biblical essay on the Holy Land as "sacrament" of God's covenant with Israel and on the organic manner by which this Old Testament reality spiritually signifies a New Testament reality—namely, the sacred humanity of Christ, which he received from the Blessed Virgin Mary. My reflection thus to some extent runs parallel to, and contains points of contact with, the poems of Cardinal Wojtyła and his later teaching as Pope John Paul II, but I do not claim that it is an exposition of either.

At the same time, I do wish to place my ecclesial exegesis at the service of Jewish-Catholic relations and to situate it within the context of that vitally important endeavor. During his famous 1986 visit to the Great Synagogue of Rome, Pope John Paul II, drawing on *Nostra Aetate* 4, noted that the relationship between the Jewish and Christian religions is an "intrinsic" rather than an "extrinsic" one, and that the Church thus "discovers her 'bond' with Judaism by 'searching into her own mystery.'"[8] Four years later, in another address in Rome, he noted that the converse is also true—to understand her own mission and nature, the Church must reflect on the "mystery" of the people of Israel, especially as that mystery is disclosed in Sacred Scripture—and that biblical scholars thus play a particular role in this continued reflection.[9] The

6 Wojtyła, 115, 117, 116.

7 Wojtyła, 46–47. This poem seems to have been composed prior to the pilgrimage.

8 John Paul II, *Spiritual Pilgrimage*, 63.

9 John Paul II, 141–42.

way the pontiff in this address repeatedly applies the theologically charged word "mystery" to both biblical and contemporary Israel is quite striking and suggests that a reflection on the land of Israel under the closely related category of "sacrament" may prove a fruitful avenue of approach.[10]

The teaching of *Nostra Aetate* also informs John Paul's articulation of the biblical hermeneutic that should guide Catholic reflection on the mystery of Israel and its land. In an address in West Germany in 1980, the pope made the fascinating observation that Jewish-Christian dialogue is "at the same time a dialogue within our Church, that is to say, between the first and the second part of her Bible." He then proceeded to quote from official Church directives for the implementation of *Nostra Aetate*: "The effort must be made to understand better everything in the Old Testament that has its own permanent value . . . since this value is not wiped out by the later interpretation of the New Testament, which, on the contrary, gave the Old Testament its full meaning, so that it is a question rather of reciprocal enlightenment and explanation."[11] The effort to listen more attentively and empathetically to our Jewish brethren calls for and is in turn enhanced by a correlative effort to listen afresh to the first part of the Christian canon of Scripture and to allow it to speak in its *vox Israelitica*. At the same time, it would be foreign to the Christian spirit to attempt to read Israel's Scriptures in complete isolation from the New Testament. Therefore, in the following pages I attempt to approach the theological question of the land of Israel in the manner of a dialogue between the testaments, aiming at "reciprocal enlightenment and explanation."

SPIRITUALIZATION AND SACRAMENTALIZATION

Much valuable exegetical and historical work has been devoted to the "theology of the land" in Judaism and Christianity.[12] W. D. Davies, Waldemar Janzen, and Robert L. Wilken have focused in large measure on the

10 In the Latin Bible and the Western theological tradition the terms *mysterium* and *sacramentum* are closely associated, serving as alternative renderings of the Greek word μυστήριον. See *CCC* 774 and Avery Dulles, SJ, "Mystery (In Theology)," in *New Catholic Encyclopedia*, ed. William J. McDonald (New York: McGraw-Hill, 1967), 10:151–53.

11 John Paul II, *Spiritual Pilgrimage*, 15. Similar statements about the Old Testament's "permanent value" or "intrinsic value" can be found in *CCC* 121 and 129.

12 Important recent contributions in English include: W. D. Davies, *The Gospel and the Land: Early Christianity and Jewish Territorial Doctrine* (Berkeley: University of California Press, 1974) and *The Territorial Dimension of Judaism, With a Symposium and Further Reflections* (Minneapolis: Fortress, 1991); Lawrence A. Hoffman, ed., *The Land of Israel: Jewish Perspectives* (Notre Dame, Ind.: University of Notre Dame Press, 1986); Robert L. Wilken, *The Land Called*

important issue of spiritualization, and these three scholars are in broad agreement on two points. First, they hold that the Hebrew Bible is marked by a sense of "territorial realism." However much the Torah, Prophets, and Psalms ascribe holiness and theological significance to the land of Israel and the city of Jerusalem, these texts, properly understood, refer to geographical, this-worldly realities. As Wilken puts it, "for the ancient Israelites *land* always referred to an actual land. Eretz Israel was not a symbol of a higher reality."[13] Second, Davies, Janzen, and Wilken agree that this theology of geographic realism has been spiritualized in Christianity and in some forms of postbiblical Judaism. Prophecies of Israel's restoration to the land and of the glorification of Jerusalem have come to be interpreted as references to a transcendent or heavenly order.

There is, however, some disagreement with regard to when exactly this occurred in Christianity. For Davies and Janzen, the process is already well under way in the New Testament (especially in the Epistle to the Hebrews), but Wilken offers a very different view of the matter. According to him, the second-century chiliasts, including Justin Martyr, Tertullian, and Irenaeus, interpreted the New Testament correctly when they understood it to promise that "God would establish a future kingdom *on earth* centered in Jerusalem."[14] Wilken even suggests that references to "the Jerusalem above" (Gal 4:26) and "the heavenly Jerusalem" (Heb 12:22) can be understood in this way. As he sees it, there is a fundamental continuity of eschatological outlook between the two testaments of the Christian Bible, and this continuity extends through the first two centuries of orthodox Christianity. According to Wilken, then, the culprit responsible for spiritualizing the territorial realism of the Bible and for laying to rest "the dreams of an earthly kingdom" is Origen.[15]

Holy: Palestine in Christian History and Thought (New Haven: Yale University Press, 1992); Waldemar Janzen, "Land," *ABD* 4:143–54; Norman C. Habel, *The Land is Mine: Six Biblical Land Ideologies* (Minneapolis: Fortress, 1995); Walter Brueggemann, *The Land: Place as Gift, Promise, and Challenge in Biblical Faith*, 2nd ed. (Minneapolis: Fortress, 2002); and Gary M. Burge, *Jesus and the Land: The New Testament Challenge to "Holy Land" Theology* (Grand Rapids: Baker Academic, 2010).

13 Wilken, *Land Called Holy*, 8. The phrase "territorial realism" is found on the same page.

14 Wilken, 56; emphasis added. Wilken holds that the term "chiliasm" is a "misnomer" (62), since the specific expectation of a *thousand-year* reign is not essential to the basic eschatological tradition shared by the various New Testament writers. It comes from the book of Revelation, which represents an "idiosyncratic" form of the shared tradition (56). The New Testament tradition (according to Wilken) is, then, broadly "chiliastic" or "millenarian" in the sense of holding that upon his second coming Christ will establish his kingdom *on earth*.

15 Wilken, 65.

This hypothesis (in either form) calls for a clarification of what is meant by "spiritualization," and it is this that I wish to supply by viewing the land of Israel as a "sacrament." By spiritualization Davies and Wilken seem to mean that biblical words and images that originally referred to geophysical and geopolitical realities were later taken to refer to something that exists only in the realm of ideas.[16] Davies finds a pervasive "danger of unrealism" in Christian history,[17] and both he and Janzen (but not Wilken) find portions of the New Testament itself to represent a complete "abrogation" of the Old Testament's realistic promise of land. The Epistle to the Hebrews, they allege, replaces Israel's territorial realism with a heavenly homeland and sanctuary that are entirely "nonphysical."[18]

This view is mistaken, in my opinion, insofar as it overlooks the decisive element in New Testament eschatology. At the heart of the New Testament is the belief that the humanity of Jesus Christ has been glorified and is now in the presence of the Father. To speak of Christ's resurrected humanity as a "spiritual body," as Paul does (1 Cor 15:44–45), is to indicate a transformation and glorification of the physical. It most certainly does not mean that the physical has been left behind.[19] This fundamental conviction is found throughout the New Testament, not least in the Epistle to the Hebrews.

At the same time, Davies, Janzen, and Wilken tend to overlook important elements of spiritualization already present in the Old Testament. It is true that the ancient Israelites never ceased to be concerned with questions of literal possession of the land—that is, with matters of real estate and politics. At the same time, the land was never *merely* a matter of these things. It had from the beginning a profoundly spiritual meaning for Israel, inasmuch as it was a tangible sign and instrument of their covenant with God. That this meaning was not divorced from mundane realities such as agriculture or politics is quite to the point. In its historical concreteness the land mediated spiritual realities. In a word, it was sacramental.

Scripture does indeed reflect a process by which the land is spiritualized, but it is not a question of replacing physical realities with mere ideas. The process of spiritualization begins with creation itself and continues

16 The charge may not stick to Janzen, who understands the Epistle to the Hebrews to speak of "nonphysical eternal *realities*." "Land," 152; emphasis added.

17 Davies, *Territorial Dimension*, 93.

18 Janzen, "Land," 151–52; Davies, *Gospel and Land*, 366.

19 Aquinas, *In I Cor.* c. 15, lect. 6, no. 984.

throughout Israel's history. Properly understood, the spiritualization of the land of Israel is a matter of sacramentalization, and it is based on the sacramental role that the material universe plays in God's plan from the beginning. In other words, there is an incarnational or sacramental principle at work throughout the drama of creation and redemption.

Since it does no good to clarify one concept while introducing another that is unclear, I shall at this point indicate more precisely how I am using the term "sacrament." For this I turn to John Paul II's general audience of February 20, 1980, in which the pope discussed the "sacramentality of creation." He describes a "sacrament," in the broadest sense, as "a sign that efficaciously transmits in the visible world the invisible mystery hidden in God from eternity," or more simply, as that which is "capable of making visible what is invisible"—namely, "the spiritual and the divine." According to John Paul, the body is a "primordial sacrament," and the world itself and "man in the world" are "sacraments," insofar as they are "instituted for holiness."[20] His point in using such language is not to blur the distinction between nature and grace but to point to the way in which nature is the substratum for grace and the order of creation is "instituted for" and taken up into the order of redemption.[21] Ultimately, to call something a "sacrament" is to specify its relation to Christ, the incarnate Logos, who is the definitive sacrament of God's presence to the world.

THE ECONOMY OF CREATION AND REDEMPTION

In light of this teaching, the "dust of the earth" as presented in Genesis 2:7 can be viewed as a primordial sacrament. It represents physical matter as that which makes visible what is invisible. It is "fashioned" by God into a creature who is apt to receive the "breath of life" directly from God and thus to become a body-soul unity. Man's body makes visible his own spiritual interiority and, as created in the image of God, man is designed to make visible the mystery of God himself. Drawing on the richness of this text from Genesis, the book of Wisdom indicates that because the first man was "earth-born"

20 John Paul II, *Man and Woman*, 203 (*TOB* 19.4).

21 John Paul's broadened use of the term "sacrament" is characteristic of much twentieth-century theology. For a sense of this context, see Raphael Schulte, "Sacraments," in *Encyclopedia of Theology: The Concise Sacramentum Mundi*, ed. Karl Rahner (New York: Seabury, 1975), 1477–85.

(γηγενῆς), the earth remains "sympathetic" (ὁμοιοπαθῆς) to man through all generations (Wis 7:1–3). Man's affinity to the earth is hinted at already in the famous Hebrew wordplay of Genesis 2:7—"man" (*'ādām*) is formed from the "earth" (*'ădāmâ*)—and the earth's sympathy with man is suggested in Genesis 3:17–19, where the ground bears a curse "on account of" man and brings forth the thorns and thistles that symbolize the multidimensional rupture caused by sin. This understanding of the earth as a primordial sacrament in the order of creation is foundational for appreciating how the particular land of Israel might have a sacramental role in the economy of Israel's covenant with Yahweh, and how the close affinity between man and earth in the order of creation is taken up into the peculiar bond that is established between the people of Israel and the land of Israel within the dynamics of the covenant.

It should be noted in passing that if I speak of the symbols of Israel's covenant with God—the land, the temple, the Davidic dynasty, circumcision, and Sabbath—as "sacraments," I view them from a Christian perspective as mediating between the primordial sacrament of creation and the definitive sacrament of Christ. These interrelations are perhaps best viewed in terms of participation. The land of Israel, as a "sacrament" of the old covenant, participates in the order of creation insofar as it is a created reality that serves as a visible sign of this covenant, while it also participates in the mystery of Christ by anticipation and preparation insofar as the Spirit of the preincarnate Christ is present to Israel and educates Israel precisely by means of such "sacraments."

It is both curious and significant that the first occurrence of the phrase "holy land" (*'admat qódeš*) in the Bible refers not to the land of Canaan but to the "mountain of God," called Horeb or Sinai, specifically as the site of the theophany of the burning bush (Exod 3:5). Sinai is holy because it is the primordial locus of revelation (3:2) and worship (3:12). There, Moses will hear God's Name (3:14–15; 34:5–7), receive the Torah (31:18), and view the heavenly pattern of the sanctuary (25:8–9; 26:30). By means of the wilderness tabernacle the glory of Yahweh and the primordial holiness of Sinai are transported, as it were, to the land of Canaan, where Yahweh's command to Moses—"Remove your sandals from your feet, for the place where you stand is holy ground" (3:5)—is repeated nearly verbatim to Joshua upon Israel's arrival in the land (Josh 5:15). The land of Canaan becomes "Yahweh's land" by a sort of adoption and is then given to Israel as their inheritance.[22] In

22 Hos 9:3; cf. Lev 25:23; Ps 85:2. Strictly speaking, of course, "all the earth" belongs to Yahweh (Exod 19:5). The land of Canaan becomes the special locus of his presence through the establishment of his covenant with Israel, which is inaugurated in his dealings with the patriarchs.

other words, holiness is conferred upon the land of Israel through the act of salvation. From his home base at Sinai Yahweh delivers Israel from Egypt and draws them to his holy mountain; from there he travels with them through the wilderness and leads them to Canaan. As the telos of this act of salvation and the "place of rest" (*mənûḥâ*), the land of Israel is from the start an eschatological symbol of sorts.[23] Its particular holiness and sacramentality cannot be understood in abstraction from the drama of salvation history.

To stress that the land becomes holy through an act of salvation is not, however, to deny that it already possesses in the order of creation a certain aptness to receive this status. On the contrary, to adopt John Paul II's phrase, the land of Canaan was "instituted for holiness."[24] The book of Deuteronomy extols the natural bounty of the "good land" (8:7–9) and in a particularly beautiful passage explains that whereas the flat and rainless land of Egypt is irrigated from the Nile, Canaan is "a land of hills and valleys, which drinks in water by the rain from heaven, a land which Yahweh your God looks after; the eyes of Yahweh your God are continually upon it, from the beginning of the year to the end of the year" (11:10–12). Therefore, one who would practice agriculture in Canaan is directly dependent on the rain, and since in any given year, "the early rain and the later rain" may or may not come according to the predominant pattern, there is a constant need to trust and to please the deity responsible for the rain (11:13–14). Put another way, the precipitation patterns of Canaan are regular enough to indicate God's special providence for the land and its people but just irregular enough also to indicate his pleasure or displeasure on a given occasion.[25]

The land's distinctive topography and climate had a decisive influence both on the myths and rituals of Canaanite fertility religion and on the tenets and symbols of biblical monotheism. In a sense, these two religions represent two overlapping but ultimately incompatible interpretations of the land. The Canaanites served a pantheon of deities who gave mythological personification to the immanent forces of nature and to the cyclic meteorological phenomena characteristic of their land. As such, these deities were incapable of historical agency or self-revelation and thus could not enter into a moral covenant with their devotees. Despite containing elements of truth tending toward a sense of justice and knowledge of the true God, some of which

23 Deut 12:9–10; Ps 95:11; cf. Exod 33:14; Deut 26:19.

24 John Paul II, *Man and Woman*, 204 (*TOB* 19.5).

25 This is implicit throughout Deuteronomy 28, for example. Note especially the reference to Yahweh's giving "your land's rain in its time" (v. 12).

were appropriated and "baptized" by the Israelites, Canaanite religion never escaped this immanence, except perhaps in the case of rare individuals such as Melchizedek, who came to worship the Canaanite high god El as the "maker of heaven and earth" (Gen 14:18–20). On the whole, Canaanite fertility worship was marred by cult prostitution, sympathetic magic, and child sacrifice.[26]

The prophet Hosea recognized the moral degradation that this involved and observed that those who ascribed the land's bounty to Baal received it from him as "a prostitute's wages."[27] Moreover, he discerned clearly that both the worship of Canaanite deities and the syncretistic rites by which many Israelites attempted to worship Yahweh reflected a lack of "knowledge of God."[28] In truth, Yahweh is "the living God" (Hos 2:1; RSV 1:10), who has acted in sovereign freedom, though not arbitrarily, within the course of history to claim Israel for himself, and who holds them accountable to his moral will. As transcendent Creator, he bestows "the grain, the wine, and the oil" on his people not as compensation for services rendered but in freedom and as a sign of his gracious love for them.[29] The Israelite worshipper who understood this was able to offer back to Yahweh a "first portion of the fruit of the soil," not only as an acknowledgement that the land is a gift from Yahweh (Deut 26:10) but as a way of confessing the whole series of saving historical acts by which Yahweh had kept his promises to the patriarchs by delivering their descendants from bondage and bringing them to "this place" (vv. 3–9). As Janzen phrases it, the land is "the tangible token of God's faithfulness" and "the concrete expression of the covenant relationship."[30] Or, as John Paul II might say, the land "makes visible what is invisible."[31]

John Paul II's strong assertion that before the time of Christ Jerusalem was already the "historic site" of revelation and the place "in which more than

26 See John Day, "Canaan, Religion of," *ABD* 1:831–37. Quoting a Ugaritic votive prayer in which Baal is petitioned to drive an enemy from the city walls, Day concludes: "Clearly this prayer, disregarding Baal's importance as a nature god, sees him as an agent in history" (834). To be sure, the prayer embodies elements of genuine piety and indicates that the Baal cult rose somewhat above sheer nature worship. Nevertheless, the phrase "agent in history" in Day's statement must be taken in a very loose sense. Nothing in the corpus of Ugaritic texts is analogous to the sort of prophetic judgments about Yahweh's action in history that permeate the Old Testament, not even in the limited way that the Moabite inscription on the Mesha Stela can be said to be analogous to Hebrew prophetic narrative.

27 Hos 2:7, 14 (RSV 2:5, 12); 9:1.

28 Hos 4:1, 6; 5:4; 6:6.

29 Hos 2:10, 23–25 (RSV 2:8, 21–23).

30 Janzen, "Land," 147.

31 John Paul II, *Man and Woman*, 203 (*TOB* 19.4).

in any other place the word of God was brought to men"[32] seems to ignore the fact that the Torah was given to Israel at Mount Sinai, not in Jerusalem. Indeed, our Jewish friends are probably not mistaken if they detect here a typically Christian tendency to privilege the Prophets and Psalms over the Torah. Nevertheless, it is important to note that even in the case of the Pentateuch, Scripture indicates an extremely close relationship between the gift of revelation and the gift of the land. The book of Deuteronomy depicts Moses, on the last day of his life, giving the commandments to Israel for the first time, as it were, just across the Jordan from Jericho, and it relentlessly drives home the point that these statutes and ordinances are given precisely to be observed "in the midst of the land" that Israel is crossing the Jordan to inherit.[33] In fact, the vast majority of the laws found in Deuteronomy have some more or less direct pertinence to Israel's life in the Holy Land.

The blessings that accompany obedience to God's commands are blessings of the land, and the curses that follow upon disobedience are curses of the land.[34] "Life" means to prolong one's days "on the land," and "death" means to be "uprooted from the land."[35] To do what is abominable to Yahweh in the land is to "cause the land to sin," and after Israel goes into exile the land itself will bear the scars of Yahweh's wrath for all to see.[36] Loving obedience to Yahweh will enable Israel to "rejoice in all the goodness" of the land and to find rest from their enemies in the safety of the land, but in exile among the nations Israel will experience perpetual restlessness, anxiety, sickness, blindness, and even madness.[37]

AGRICULTURAL SYMBOLISM

We have been considering certain basic features of the Old Testament's theology of the land that are pertinent to our topic, drawing especially on the books of Deuteronomy and Hosea. At this point I would like to turn from

32 John Paul II, *Spiritual Pilgrimage*, 34.

33 Deut 4:5, 14; 5:31; 6:1; 12:1. "According to Deuteronomy, Moses received the law at Sinai (5:28) but delivered it to the people only in the plains of Moab before their entrance into the promised land." Moshe Weinfeld, *Deuteronomy 1–11: A New Translation with Introduction and Commentary*, AB 5 (New York: Doubleday, 1991), 202.

34 Deut 26:15; 28:1–69.

35 Deut 4:40; 5:30; 11:9; 25:15; 28:63; 29:27 (RSV 29:28).

36 Deut 24:4; 29:21–26 (RSV 29:22–27).

37 Deut 26:11; 12:9–10; 28:27–29, 65–67.

what the Old Testament says more or less discursively about the land to a consideration of how the sacramentality of the land of Israel is also disclosed through symbolization.

Above I alluded to the very close bond that is established between the people of Israel and the land of Israel through the covenant. Note, for example, how people and land constitute the twofold object of God's heavenly regard and blessing in the following prayer.

> Look down from heaven, your holy habitation,
> and bless your *people* Israel and the *land* you have given to us,
> just as you swore to our fathers: a land flowing with milk and honey. (Deut 26:15)

In similar fashion, the psalmist links land and people via poetic parallelism.

> Yahweh, you have shown favor to your *land*;
> you have brought *Jacob* back from captivity. (Ps 85:2)

But a still more powerful way of disclosing the relationship between Israel and its land is through agricultural symbolism. According to the ancient Song of the Sea, after the exodus Yahweh "planted" Israel in the Holy Land (Exod 15:17). The same metaphor, with the same referent, is found in several others texts[38] and is extended into parables about Yahweh's vine or vineyard as a way of recounting Israel's story from exodus to exile, or beyond.[39] As we have already seen, the book of Deuteronomy speaks of the punishment of exile as an "uprooting" from the land, and several prophecies of restoration speak of Yahweh's "sowing" or "replanting" Israel in the land after the exile.[40] While the dominant image is that of vine or vineyard, Israel can also be represented as an olive tree or fig tree.[41] Indeed, the imagery of Israel as Yahweh's special agricultural project—whether vine, vineyard, olive tree, or fig tree—becomes a conventional way of telling and prophetically

38 Ps 44:3; Jer 2:21; 2 Sam 7:10; 1 Chron 17:9.

39 Ps 80:9–17; Isa 5:1–7; Ezek 19:10–14; Isa 27:2–6.

40 Deut 28:63; 29:27; Hos 2:25; Amos 9:15; Isa 60:21; 61:3; Jer 24:6; 32:41; 42:10; 2 Macc 1:29.

41 Jer 11:16; Hos 14:6. The image of Israel as a fig tree per se is not found in the Old Testament, but it is suggested by several texts (Jer 8:13; 24:1–10; Hos 9:10; Mic 7:1) and finds expression in the New Testament in Christ's prophetic cursing of the fig tree (Mark 11:12–14; Matt 21:18–19) and in his parable of the fig tree (Luke 13:6–9).

interpreting Israel's story.[42] It appears in all of these varieties in the New Testament as well.[43]

Agricultural imagery is versatile and rich in significance. It can suggest the great care and patience God shows in his dealings with his people, the moral and spiritual "fruit" that he expects to receive from them, and so forth. It is also worth noting that the specific application of agricultural imagery to Israel belongs to a broader domain of metaphors by which human beings generally may be compared to various types of vegetation. "All flesh is grass, and its glory is like the blossoms of the field."[44] The proud exalt themselves like cedars of Lebanon and oaks of Bashan (Isa 2:13). The wife of the man who fears Yahweh will be like "a fruitful vine" in his house, his children like "olive shoots" around his table (Ps 128:3). The degree to which such images penetrated Hebrew thought and language is evident in the lexicalized metaphors by which human offspring are spoken of as one's "seed"[45] or as "the fruit of the womb."[46] Especially important for our topic, as will become clear further on, is the way the metaphor of vegetation can be joined to the symbolism by which water represents divine revelation. For example, the man who meditates on Torah is "like a tree planted by streams of water, that yields its fruit in season," but the wicked are "like chaff which the wind drives away" (Ps 1:1–6).

At the most basic level, the domain of agricultural images and symbols reflects and expresses the close existential bond to the soil experienced by peoples in nonindustrialized societies. Put simply, agriculture is one of the principal ways in which a people becomes, quite literally, one with its land. In the industrialized West we eat mostly processed foods, and even much of

42 The story of Naboth's vineyard (1 Kings 21) is probably to be read, on one level, as a parable. Note that it is set in Jezreel, which means "God sows." Cf. Hos 2:24–25 (RSV 2:22–23). Other pertinent texts include Isa 3:14; 17:6; Jer 12:10; Ezek 15:1–8; 17:1–24; Hos 9:10; Mic 7:1; Hab 3:17; and Zech 4:1–14.

43 John 15:1–10 (vine); Mark 12:1–12; Matt 20:1–16; 21:28–46 (vineyard); Rom 11:16–24 (olive tree); and Luke 13:6–9 (fig tree).

44 Isa 40:6, reading *kəbōdô* ("its glory") for MT *ḥasdô* ("its love"); cf. LXX, Syriac, Vulgate, and 1 Pet 1:24.

45 The word *zéraʿ* ("seed") can refer to semen (Lev 15:16) or offspring (Gen 13:15). It refers very often to human offspring but only rarely to animal offspring (Gen 7:3). The term *ṣeʾĕṣāʾîm* ("issue") can refer to the produce of the earth (Isa 42:5) or to human offspring (48:19). Note how the dead metaphor can be revived by being combined with a fresh simile: "And you will know that your seed (*zarʿékā*) will be many, and your issue (*ṣeʾĕṣāʾéykā*) like the grass of the earth" (Job 5:25).

46 Gen 30:2; Ps 127:3; Isa 13:18.

the nonprocessed food we buy is shipped in from other agricultural regions. We wear clothing produced in far-off countries, much of which is made of synthetic fabrics in any case. Many household items that even sixty years ago were made of wood, metal, or glass are now made of plastics. Combined with the fact that we spend most of our lives in air-conditioned buildings and vehicles, all of this contributes to our axiomatic loss of contact with the land. By contrast, most members of a traditional society such as ancient Israel were directly involved in some capacity in raising or processing goods. And while some goods (mostly luxury items) were imported, the Israelites depended in the main on the produce of their own land. They wore clothing made from sheep wool and locally grown flax. They burned olive oil in their lamps, and local timber was used in the production of furniture, tools, window frames, and roof beams. It is hardly surprising, then, that some of the agricultural staples of ancient Canaan—grain, wine, olive oil, figs, and sheep—should serve as literary and theological symbols in Sacred Scripture. Moreover, the earth was literally taken up into the daily life of the people in even more direct ways. In ancient Israel houses were made largely of stone and adobe, and most household vessels were made of clay. Metals were used in the production of weapons, tools, and jewelry, though in many cases they were imported.[47]

The use and manipulation of the earth's resources is essential to human culture and represents a spiritualization of the material world. This is not merely a matter of using metaphorical language to represent ideas. Rather, it is a question of transforming material blessings so that they serve as bearers of spiritual realities even while they remain material. Instances of this include the writing of texts on stone monuments, clay tablets, or parchment; the production of musical instruments out of a ram's horn, beaten metal, wood, reeds, or animal gut; and, of course, the offering of grain, wine, and livestock in cultic acts of worship. In each of these cases invisible realities are made visible through the mediation of the bounty of the land. In this sense, too, the land is sacramental.

Eating and drinking the produce of the land is the most striking way in which the earth is taken up into man. The land is literally spiritualized when its fruits are assumed into the body-soul unity of the human person. Through

47 For metals the Israelites seem to have been largely dependent on imports, though there is evidence of some local mining and smelting of copper and iron at various periods. See B. S. J. Isserlin, *The Israelites* (Minneapolis: Fortress, 2001), 160–65.

man the earth contributes to a new sort of fruitfulness: intellectual, artistic, and spiritual. Israel understood and expressed this through poetic symbols, such as speaking of a human person as a fruit tree or of the whole people as a vine. John Paul II's jarring metaphor—"man is the land"—might have been more readily intelligible to them than it is to us.

The spiritualization of the land through eating and drinking its produce is probably also related to the traditional symbolism by which food and drink can represent wisdom. Thus, Jesus ben Sira speaks of "the bread of understanding" and "the water of wisdom," and Lady Wisdom invites those who lack understanding to come to the banquet of meat, bread, and wine that she has prepared.[48] In the Hebrew Scriptures this symbolism is applied to divine revelation, especially to the prophetic word as that which is to be internalized. Thus, Jeremiah confesses, "Your words were found, and I ate them" (Jer 15:16), and Ezekiel is instructed to eat a scroll on which the prophetic word is written (Ezek 3:1–3). Amos announces that there will be "a famine in the land—not a hunger for [literal] bread or a thirst for [literal] water, but rather for hearing the word of Yahweh" (Amos 8:11).

An important modulation of this symbolism occurs in a series of passages in which the manna provided in the wilderness is closely associated with the Torah given at Mount Sinai. Since manna was not ordinary bread and appeared in a wondrous manner, it is a particularly apt symbol for divine revelation. It was given to Israel that they might "know that man does not live on bread alone, but on every word that issues from the mouth of Yahweh."[49] No less than four Old Testament passages refer to manna as "bread from heaven."[50] The point of this expression is that true wisdom, the wisdom given uniquely to Israel, does not have its origins in the earth or in man but comes through divine revelation.

The same truth is expressed under a slightly different figure in Isaiah 55, where God's word is symbolized by "the rain and snow [that] come down from heaven" (v. 10). This passage has a particular importance for our topic since it employs the metaphor of agriculture to stress that while God's word comes from heaven, it has a real effect on earth. It is like the rain that "causes [the land] to give birth and makes it sprout, providing seed for the sower

48 Sir 15:3; Prov 9:1–5; cf. Sir 24:19–21.

49 Deut 8:3; cf. Wis 16:26.

50 Neh 9:15; Pss 78:24–25; 105:40; Wis 16:20.

and bread for the eater" (v. 11).[51] True wisdom does not originate in man, but when he accepts it, it transforms him and makes him fruitful.

ISRAEL'S IDENTITY AND VOCATION

The land of Canaan also plays a sacramental role in Israel's history by serving as an efficacious sign of Israel's identity as a people. A group's geographical continuity over many generations contributes to the establishment and maintenance of its ethnicity by facilitating marriage within the group and the development of a distinctive culture. In Israel's case, God calls Abram and Sarai to leave Mesopotamia so that their descendants will become a new people, distinct from the clan of Abram's father Terah. In the promised land they live on the fringe of Canaanite society, avoiding assimilation. When it comes time for Isaac to be married, Abraham insists on two things: first, that he not marry any of the Canaanite women; and second, that he not return to Mesopotamia. Abraham's steward is thus instructed to fetch a wife for Isaac from Abraham's homeland and to bring her back to Canaan (Gen 24:1–9). In this way, both assimilation with the Canaanites and reassimilation with the Mesopotamians are avoided, and the family of Abraham can emerge as a distinct people in the world.

Although Abraham's descendants will move away from and back into the land more than once in their history, the promise of the land as the goal of their covenant with Yahweh provides a point of reference and a principle of historical continuity. The sequence of books from Joshua to Kings recounts a crucial period of six centuries in the land, from entry to exile (roughly 1200–560 BC), in which Israel is given a concrete opportunity to love Yahweh and obey his commandments "in the midst of the land" (Deut 4:5). The history of Israel in this period, with its successes and failures, virtues and vices, is written not only in the books of Joshua to Kings but in the land itself. From the fortified cities built by Solomon to the water tunnel dug by Hezekiah, from the high place discovered on a ridge in northern Samaria to the siege ramp thrown up by the Assyrians at Lachish in Judah, the story of Iron Age Israel can be read in the archeological record.[52] Israel's art and architecture,

51 The image of the land "giving birth" (τίκτουσα) is also found in Heb 6:7–8, a passage that likewise employs "rain" as a symbol of the word of God and agriculture as an image for the appropriation of revelation.

52 See Yohanan Aharoni, *The Land of the Bible: A Historical Geography*, trans. A. F. Rainey, 2nd ed. (Philadelphia: Westminster, 1979).

religion and literacy, urban planning and agriculture, and pottery styles and burial practices all left traces in the sacred dust.

Much as the human body gives an individual a locus in the world, a basis for meaningful action, and thus a personal history, so the land of Canaan gave Israel the opportunity to develop a distinctive culture and identity among the nations of the ancient Near East and to play a role in the history of the world. Consider, for example, how settlement in the land made possible Israel's literary development. Had the descendants of Abraham remained slaves in Egypt or seminomads in the southern wilderness, literacy would hardly have developed to any significant degree among them. But over the centuries, and especially during the period of the monarchy, they developed a diversified society consisting of agriculturalists, artisans, merchants, professional soldiers, and bureaucrats, a society that needed and could sustain a literate class. Jesus ben Sira observes that "the wisdom of the scribe depends on the opportunity for leisure," and he goes on to explain that whereas agriculture and crafts are necessary to an advanced society, the sage himself must be free of such occupations in order to "devote himself to the study of the law of the Most High" and to "seek out the wisdom of all the ancients" (Sir 38:24–39:11). Although the ancient Israelites could not compare to the Babylonians in astronomy or to the Egyptians in art and architecture, their literary accomplishment is astounding. Had they left us only the books of Genesis, Job, and Psalms, we should have had to rank them among the most literarily gifted of ancient peoples.[53]

Of course, Israel achieved this not because they aspired to literary merit but because they responded to divine revelation. And this is the heart of the matter. Living in the land of Canaan and developing a fairly advanced culture enabled Israel to assist in the "incarnation" of God's word in the "flesh" of human words. Under the impulse and guidance of the Holy Spirit Israel drew upon the ancient Near East's already rich cultural heritage—its politics, religion, jurisprudence, wisdom, poetry, mythology, and folklore—and transformed all of these into vectors of divine revelation. On one level, the Hebrew Scriptures frequently testify to Israel's stubborn refusal to heed God's word, but on another, these same texts by their very existence bear witness to a fruitful reception of revelation among faithful Israelites. To a significant degree, Israel lived out its vocation to be a "light to the nations" (Isa 42:6;

53 This is not to suggest that literacy was especially widespread, much less universal, in Israel, but simply to point out that some Israelites who did write wrote extremely well. For literacy in ancient Israel, see A. R. Millard, "Literacy (Israel)," in *ABD* 4:337–40.

49:6) by composing and preserving the sacred texts. The book of Wisdom refers to Israel as God's "sons, through whom the imperishable light of the law was to be given to the world" (Wis 18:4).

Already in the preexilic kingdom of Judah, and especially during and after the exile, the sacramental significance of the Holy Land came to be focused upon Jerusalem and its temple. Ezekiel, Deutero-Isaiah, Trito-Isaiah, Haggai, Zechariah, Ezra, and Nehemiah all realized how crucial it was for at least some of the exiles to return to the land, to rebuild and repopulate the holy city, and to reinstitute the worship of the God of Israel there. Although a vibrant and important Jewish community would remain in Babylon for well over a millennium after the time of Cyrus the Great—and large Jewish communities were established before the time of Christ in major cities such as Alexandria, Antioch, Damascus, and Rome—Judaism could never have become a world religion apart from the postexilic restoration of Jerusalem. The Jewish diaspora derived its identity and enduring significance in the world from Zion as a common focal point and symbolic center. In the postexilic period Jerusalem became, more than ever, a sacrament of unity and identity for Israel. Her very stones and dust engendered a sense of devotion in pious Israelites (Ps 102:15).

At the same time, Jerusalem came to symbolize Israel's unique vocation to mediate knowledge of the true God to the gentiles. Micah envisions the nations streaming to Jerusalem to be instructed in Yahweh's ways, while he conversely speaks of divine revelation going forth from Zion (Mic 4:1–5). Trito-Isaiah speaks of foreigners "joining themselves to Yahweh" and worshipping at his "holy mountain," and he famously refers to the temple as "a house of prayer for all peoples" (Isa 56:6–8). Another early postexilic prophet, Zechariah, speaks in similar terms of "many nations joining themselves to Yahweh" and becoming his "people," and he links this closely to Israel's return from Babylon and Yahweh's own coming to dwell in Zion.[54] Significantly, it is precisely in this context that Zechariah becomes the first to refer explicitly to the land of Israel as "the holy land" (*'admat qódeš*).[55]

It is true, of course, that not all postexilic texts have quite so congenial a regard for the gentiles,[56] and one might even suppose that the walls of Jerusalem rebuilt by Nehemiah symbolized isolationism, if not xenophobia. The

54 Zech 2:10–17 (RSV 2:6–13).

55 Zech 2:16 (RSV 2:12).

56 E.g., Psalm 137; Isaiah 34; Obadiah.

matter is complex,[57] but our attempt to understand it is not well served by positing a simplistic thematic opposition between inclusivity and separatism, or still less between universalism and particularism. Indeed, the crux of the matter lies in the recognition that the Bible's version of universalism is not only *not* in conflict with its particularism but depends upon it and is mediated by it. Put simply, God's plan of salvation for the whole world is to come about in and through his election of Israel. This principle applies, I suggest, not only to the people of Israel but to the land as well.

This point can be illuminated by a brief look at 2 Kings 5, where the Aramean general Naaman is healed of "leprosy" by the prophet Elisha. (The reader will pardon the overlap with chapter 5 above.) This skillfully crafted narrative presents physical healing as a sign and symbol of spiritual conversion. The ignorant and somewhat arrogant gentile protagonist must humble himself in order to receive not only the physical cure that he seeks but also knowledge of the true God. Most commentators find a theme of theological universalism in this story, which reaches its climax with Naaman's unqualified confession that the God of Israel is the only true God (v. 15). On the other hand, the narrative's equally striking accent on particularism is usually either overlooked or misconstrued. Naaman is led to healing and conversion by a humble but knowledgeable Israelite slave girl and by the prophet Elisha. Yet it is not only the *people* of Israel that mediates healing and knowledge of God to this gentile. Mysteriously, the *land* of Israel itself seems to play a sacramental role.

The narrative presents the land of Israel as the locus of prophetic knowledge, healing power, and true worship. The slave girl is twice said to be "from the land of Israel" (vv. 2, 4), and Naaman's healing hinges on his coming to realize that "there is a [true] prophet *in Israel*" (v. 8). Moreover, to obtain his healing, Naaman must dip himself seven times into "the waters of Israel"—that is, the River Jordan—for which the more beautiful rivers of Damascus are no substitute (v. 12). After confessing that "there is no God in all the earth, except *in Israel*" (v. 15), Naaman asks to take home two mule loads of Israelite earth (*'ădāmâ*), that he might offer sacrifice to Yahweh in Syria (v. 17).

Commentators who lack a sacramental view of reality are puzzled by this request. For example, John Gray finds it "naïvely inconsistent" with Naaman's monotheistic confession.[58] In doing so, he overlooks the fact that the

57 For an overview of Israel's relationship to the nations as presented in the Old Testament, see Preuss, *Old Testament Theology*, 2:284–307.

58 Gray, *I & II Kings*, 455.

confession itself contains the very same particularism, insisting as it does that the true God is "in Israel" (v. 15). Properly interpreted, Naaman's request reflects his new understanding that, by choosing to reveal himself in a particular place, God has consecrated the very soil of Israel to his worship. Far from being a superstitious vestige of Naaman's former belief system, this conviction about the particular holiness and sacramentality of the land is *that to which* he is converted.

EARTHLY AND HEAVENLY REALITIES

Returning now to the specific symbolism of Jerusalem and its temple, I would like to consider whether and in what way the Old Testament might prepare for the New Testament proclamation of a heavenly Jerusalem and heavenly temple. I have already cited Robert Wilken's opinion: "For the ancient Israelites *land* always referred to an actual land. Eretz Israel was not a symbol of a higher reality."[59] Clearly, however, Wilken does not mean to exclude all symbolism from the Old Testament's presentation of the land. He readily grants that "the land was never simply territory" or "a piece of real estate," and he explains that after the exile the traditions concerning the promise of the land were "reinterpreted" and "taken to refer to the restoration of Jerusalem." In this way, "Jerusalem came to symbolize the hope of redemption."[60] But Wilken's overriding concern is to stress that throughout this process of symbolization the prophets continued "to refer to restoration of the actual city."[61] Jerusalem never ceased to be Jerusalem, even when it symbolized something more. On this point, I agree. In fact, that is close to what I have in mind by speaking of land and city as "sacramental."

Ultimately, however, I find that neither Wilken's categories nor the scope of his discussion does justice to Old Testament thought in this regard. When he insists that the prophets spoke of "a real city, not a celestial haven," he seems to imply a semantic opposition between "real" and "celestial."[62] Does "celestial" then mean unreal? Is talk of a heavenly Jerusalem merely pie in the sky? The authors of the Hebrew Bible certainly distinguish between Yahweh's

59 Wilken, *Land Called Holy*, 8.

60 Wilken, 9–11.

61 Wilken, 15.

62 Wilken, 14.

earthly dwelling place in Jerusalem and his abode in heaven, but they view these two as intimately linked entities and by no means oppose them as real to unreal. Both are real, but the earthly temple derives its reality from the heavenly dwelling.

We may consider a few examples. The Priestly authors of Exodus stress that Moses must build the wilderness tabernacle according to the "pattern" shown him on the mountain of God, so that Yahweh can "dwell" in Israel's midst.[63] The book of Deuteronomy uses more cautious language, avoiding the notion that God himself "dwells" with Israel and speaking instead of his plan to "make his name dwell" in the place that he will choose for an earthly sanctuary.[64] In the Deuteronomistic History, Solomon explicitly denies that Yahweh could dwell in an earthly temple and speaks of God's "dwelling place" in "heaven" (1 Kgs 8:30). Psalm 48, by contrast, speaks of Jerusalem in more daring terms, nearly assimilating Mount Zion to God's heavenly dwelling through the mediating symbolism of Zaphon, the erstwhile mountain of the gods in Canaanite mythology. For over three centuries the city of David, graced by Solomon's temple, stood firm as a tangible sign of Yahweh's commitment to Israel and his presence among them, but when this "sacrament" was destroyed in 586 BC, at least some Israelites instinctively turned their gaze heavenward to the unchangeable reality to which the temple had always pointed. Trito-Isaiah laments the burning of "our *holy and beautiful* temple, where our ancestors praised you" but calls upon God to "look down from heaven and see, from your *holy and beautiful* throne," and he even prays that God would "rend the heavens and come down."[65] Zechariah encourages the returnees from exile to rebuild the earthly temple by proclaiming that Yahweh "has roused himself from his holy habitation" in heaven and will "dwell in [Israel's] midst" once again.[66] Finally, the Hellenistic book of Wisdom sums up the whole tradition by portraying Solomon as praying in the following manner:

> You have said to build a temple on your holy mountain,
> and an altar in the city where you dwell,
> a copy of the holy tent that you prepared from the beginning. (Wis 9:8)

63 Exod 25:8–9, 40; 26:30; 27:8; 29:45–46.

64 Deut 12:11; 14:23; 16:2, 6, 11; 26:2.

65 Isa 64:10 (RSV 64:11); 63:15; 63:19b (RSV 64:1).

66 Zech 2:15–17 (RSV 2:11–13).

As so many variations on a theme, all of these texts view the temple as an earthly counterpart to God's heavenly dwelling. The Old Testament is shot through with this sort of thinking, but Wilken ignores it almost entirely.[67]

But this hardly scratches the surface of the Old Testament's spiritualization of land and temple. Before moving on, I shall touch on just a few more aspects of this vast topic, beginning with Ezekiel's restoration oracles. Ezekiel associates Israel's return from exile with a whole series of glorious promises, at least some of which must be termed spiritual, including the forgiveness of Israel's sins and the gift of the Spirit, which will transform Israel's heart of stone into a "new heart" and a "new spirit" (Ezek 36:26–27). Clearly, Ezekiel envisioned a real restoration of Israel to the land, but equally clearly, the reality of which he speaks cannot be reduced to its geopolitical dimension. Just as his way of speaking of God's "servant David" shepherding Israel "forever" (37:24–25) suggests something that will far transcend the glory of the tenth-century BC Davidic Empire, so the emphatic promise that Yahweh will place his own "sanctuary" or "dwelling" in Israel's midst forever (37:26–28) points to something far more glorious than a mere rebuilding of Solomon's temple. The impression of transcendence is only strengthened by the highly symbolic vision of the temple that occupies the book's final nine chapters, throughout which Jerusalem is never mentioned by name.

Nowhere is the restoration of Zion spoken of in more glorious terms than in the final chapters of the book of Isaiah, and nowhere else is the destiny of Jerusalem so closely linked to that of its people. Here the glorification of Zion is virtually identified with the temporal and spiritual blessings to be bestowed upon her repentant children, and this all amounts to a renewal of creation. Yahweh's promise to "create new heavens and a new earth" is identified as a plan to "create Jerusalem a rejoicing and her people a joy" (Isa 65:17–18), and the returned exiles' efforts to rebuild the Jerusalem temple must be viewed from this transcendent perspective:

> Thus says Yahweh:
> Heaven is my throne, and the earth is my footstool.
> What is this house that you will build for me, and where is my place of rest?
> All these my hand has made, and all these have come to be—oracle of Yahweh.
> But to this one I look: to the humble one,
> to the one who is contrite of spirit and trembles at my word. (66:1–2a)

67 By way of exception, he acknowledges that "Ezekiel portrays Jerusalem as a cosmic mountain, a meeting place of heaven and earth." Wilken, *Land Called Holy*, 11; cf. 262–63n26.

The implication of this oracle is reasonably clear. Yahweh will dwell on earth through the spiritual transformation of humble and repentant Israel. God's dwelling will truly be with man, for man himself will be that dwelling.

It is quite true that in the prophets' understanding none of this is divorced from geopolitical reality, but neither can it be reduced to that dimension. The sacred authors are not concerned with what exists merely in the realm of ideas, but they are concerned with realities that are properly called spiritual and heavenly. These realities will come about only by God's power, and they will bring Israel into real communion with God. In this process the created realm is not left behind but is transformed. For the prophets the Holy Land is "the place where . . . the created things of earth encounter the infinite transcendence of God."[68] Finally, we must bear in mind that this encounter takes place within time and specifically within the drama of salvation history. The glorification of Zion, the restoration of Israel, and the conversion of "many nations" are eschatological in the sense that they represent the culmination of this drama, which from the perspective of Israel's prophets was still to come and not yet fully revealed.

This last consideration leads us to the decisive difference between the two testaments of the Christian canon with regard to their respective views of the Holy Land. The common premise behind all twenty-seven books of the New Testament is their authors' unanimous conviction that the eschatological and heavenly realities foretold by Israel's prophets have arrived and are truly present in Jesus Christ, who has been raised from the dead. But lest we fail to appreciate the continuity within which that decisive difference exists, we must recall that hope for the resurrection of the dead had emerged among some Israelites already toward the end of the pre-Christian period. I can hardly do justice to this topic in the present essay but would like to offer a few comments about one of the pertinent texts.[69]

The Isaian Apocalypse (Isaiah 24–27) is concerned from beginning to end with land.[70] On the one hand, there is the earth and its inhabitants and the "city of chaos" (24:10) that they have built for themselves. On the other hand, there is the Holy Land, the people of Israel, and the "holy mountain"

68 John Paul II, *Spiritual Pilgrimage*, 34.

69 For an overview, see the twin articles on "Resurrection" by Robert Martin-Achard and George W. E. Nickelsburg in *ABD* 5:680–91.

70 For two different views of the original historical context of these chapters, see J. J. M. Roberts, *First Isaiah: A Commentary*, Hermeneia (Minneapolis: Fortress, 2015), 306–7, and Joseph Blenkinsopp, *Isaiah 1–39: A New Translation with Introduction and Commentary*, AB 19 (New York: Doubleday, 2000), 346–48.

of Jerusalem. Not surprisingly, much of the imagery in these chapters is agricultural, and especially viticultural. The apocalyptic vision begins with the devastation of the earth, which "mourns and languishes" because it "lies desecrated under its inhabitants," who have "broken the everlasting covenant" (24:4–6). As was the case before the flood, the earth is under a curse, and because "the vine withers," there is no wine to bring men joy (24:6–11).[71] But in the next scene Yahweh himself promises to provide "on this mountain" (i.e., Jerusalem) a banquet of "wine on the lees," and immediately we are told that this banquet will mark Yahweh's definitive victory over death (25:6–8).

This promise is emphatically universal. The banquet is prepared "for all the peoples" (25:6), and death is described as "the web that has been woven over all nations" (25:7). In accord with earlier prophecies, it is the revelation of Yahweh's righteous ways that will make all the difference for mankind: "When your judgments are in the earth, the world's inhabitants learn righteousness" (26:9). A little further on, the promise of God's victory over death is expressed in terms of bodily resurrection. The "residents of the dust" will "wake up and sing for joy" (26:17–19). Toward the end of the Isaian Apocalypse, Israel comes back into view, as the prophet breaks into a new "song of the vineyard" and promises that in days to come "Jacob will take root, Israel will blossom and sprout; and they will fill the face of the earth with fruit" (27:2–6). And in the final scene, Yahweh himself harvests the Holy Land, beating out the grain and gathering up the people of Israel "one by one," like so many grapes fallen from the vine (27:12).

What are we to make of all this? Using traditional imagery, the Isaian Apocalypse provides a comprehensive view of Yahweh's plan for Israel and for the world. God's wrath has come upon the physical world because of man's sin, and the universal curse of biological death is symbolized by worldwide agricultural devastation. But Yahweh has chosen a special piece of real estate, "from the river Euphrates to the wadi of Egypt" (27:12), and there he has undertaken his special agricultural project. By means of Israel, his "desirable vineyard" (27:2), he will provide a banquet of revelation on his holy mountain and thereby "destroy death forever" (25:8). The rebirth and renewal of creation will culminate with bodily resurrection. If we bear in mind that this Old Testament passage locates the telos of the people and land of Israel, and indeed of the whole created order, in the resurrection of the dead, we

71 Cf. Gen 5:29; 9:20. On the intertextual connections between Isa 24:1–13 and Gen 5–11, see Blenkinsopp, *Isaiah 1–39*, 351–52.

will avoid the mistake of viewing the New Testament's handling of the Old Testament's theology of the land as an abrupt and arbitrary reinterpretation.

INCARNATION AND GLORIFICATION

Turning now to the New Testament, I shall begin by summarizing the view of W. D. Davies. Near the end of his impeccably researched volume, *The Gospel and the Land*, Davies concludes that the New Testament contains two "apparently contradictory attitudes": (1) a transcendence of land, Jerusalem, and temple, and (2) a residual concern with these same *realia*.[72] Although he finds a "reconciling principle" in the way the New Testament "personalizes 'holy space' in Christ, who, as a figure of History, is rooted in the land," Davies nonetheless continues to speak here, as he has throughout his treatment, in terms of replacement or substitution: "In sum, for the holiness of place, Christianity has fundamentally, though not consistently, substituted the holiness of the Person: it has Christified holy space."[73]

While Davies is careful to note lines of continuity between the testaments and anticipations of the New within the Old, the language of replacement suggests that the Christian "deterritorialization" of the promise of the land contains a significant measure of arbitrariness. According to Davies, the apostle Paul, for example, does not simply downplay or ignore the territorial aspect of the promise to Abraham; he deliberately rejects it.[74] A gap opens between the testaments, and Davies does not seem especially concerned to close it. Ultimately, the problem here is hermeneutical. Davies treats the meanings that the New Testament authors assign to the traditional symbols of Judaism as extrinsic to those symbols and thus arbitrary. In taking up the topic of Paul's "substitution" of the Jerusalem temple with the body of the individual Christian or the "living community in Christ," Davies refuses to be "detained" by the question of how the human body came to be symbolically related to the temple in the first place.[75] Similarly, he contrasts the natural symbolism by which the vine in the Old Testament is "the symbol of what attaches a man to the land"—and thus an apt figure for Israel as a people

72 Davies, *Gospel and Land*, 367.

73 Davies, 367–68.

74 Davies, 179.

75 Davies, 188–90.

with an indissoluble connection to the land—to the Johannine parable of Jesus as the "true vine," which "takes up this metaphor" and "personalizes it completely," so that "geographical considerations are simply otiose."[76]

At times, Davies comes tantalizingly close to identifying the true organic connection between the Old Testament symbols and the interpretation they receive in the New Testament. He observes that in John's Gospel "the idea of the humanity of Christ as the dwelling place of God with men and as the new temple" is rooted in "the concept of the Logos becoming flesh," and that the authors of the Fourth Gospel and the Epistle to the Hebrews "believed in a sacramental process," such that "physical phenomena for them are the means whereby the infinite God and spiritual realities are made imaginable."[77] This is close to the mark, except that it is debatable whether the word "imaginable" does justice to the sacramentalism of John and Hebrews. Does it not reflect rather a typically modern incapacity to come to terms with sacramental thinking? In any case, Davies does not care to pursue this line of inquiry much further. Similarly, he chooses to "pass by" the "transference of Christian hope from the earthly Jerusalem, the quintessence of the land in Judaism, to the heavenly."[78] And when he does touch on this issue later in the volume, he makes a fatal error. According to Davies, in certain "strata" of the New Testament (implicitly including the Epistle to the Hebrews) "physical entities" such as the land, Jerusalem, and the temple have been "taken up into a non-geographic, spiritual, transcendent dimension" so that they "cease to be significant, except as types of realities which are not in essence physical." In such cases at least, it is "justifiable to speak of the *realia* of Judaism as being 'spiritualized' in the Christian dispensation."[79] Presently, I shall attempt to show that this interpretation—which understands the New Testament to speak of a completely "nonphysical" realm whenever it refers to something "heavenly"—is fundamentally mistaken because it overlooks the decisive element in Christian eschatology: the glorified humanity of Jesus Christ.

Janzen, while recognizing that the Epistle to the Hebrews cannot be passed over so easily, makes the same mistake in its interpretation. In Hebrews, as Janzen reads it, the "land realism" of the Old Testament is "totally dissolved" and its *realia* are "bracketed out as ephemeral shadows

76 Davies, 333.

77 Davies, 298, 367.

78 Davies, 162.

79 Davies, 366.

of nongeographical, nonphysical eternal realities."[80] Janzen is more positive about Paul's theology in this regard. He correctly notes that "the incarnate Christ himself represents a certain realism of geographical presence associated with the places of his ministry and the memories that attach to them. This realism of the incarnation then continues in the presence of the resurrected Christ in his body, the church, and its members, repeatedly referred to as 'temple' by Paul."[81] This statement would be even more helpful if it spelled out clearly *how* the resurrection extends the realism of the incarnation to the Church. Paul's images of the Church as body of Christ and temple of God are empty metaphors unless a real connection has been established between heaven and earth. The resurrected Christ can be present to his body on earth only because he is present in his glorified humanity at God's right hand and has poured out the Holy Spirit. This is the conviction that unites Paul, Luke, John, the author of Hebrews, and every other New Testament author.[82]

1 Corinthians 15 is especially instructive in this regard. According to Paul, the difference between an earthly body and a heavenly body is that each has its proper "glory," not that one is material and the other immaterial (v. 40). The resurrected body is a "spiritual body." This is no oxymoron, for "spiritual" (πνευματικός) here is not the semantic opposite of "physical," or even of "carnal," but of "natural" or "soulish" (ψυχικός, v. 44). Similarly, to say that through the resurrection "the last Adam became a life-giving spirit [πνεῦμα]" is not to say that he dematerialized. Rather, it is to differentiate him from the first man, who "became a living soul [ψυχή]" (v. 45), and to indicate that through his glorified humanity Christ has become the source of imperishable life. The semantic opposition between ψυχή or ψυχικός on the one hand and πνεῦμα or πνευματικός on the other hand corresponds to the very basic biblical distinction between creation and *new creation*, not to a static dichotomy between the material and the ideal. According to Paul, the corruptible body is "sown" in the earth in weakness and dishonor, but *it* (the same body!) is raised incorruptible in power and glory (vv. 42–43). That agriculture provides Paul with his guiding metaphor here (vv. 35–38) is hardly surprising and suggests that the physical creation is by no means left behind in his eschatology (cf. Rom 8:21). Indeed, the exalted Christ is "the first fruits of those who have fallen asleep" (1 Cor 15:20).

80 Janzen, "Land," 151–52.

81 Janzen, 152.

82 E.g., Acts 2:33; John 7:39; 16:7.

A strikingly similar image is found in a dominical logion in the Gospel of John. Speaking of his own death and resurrection, Jesus says: "Amen, amen, I say to you, unless a grain of wheat falls into the ground and dies, it remains alone; but if it dies, it bears much fruit" (John 12:24). Read within the context of John's theology of the incarnation, this agricultural image is no mere metaphor. In the "flesh" of Christ, the Word has "tabernacled among us" (1:14), and in his death he has given this same "flesh" as "bread" to the world (6:51). Through his death and resurrection his humanity has been "glorified" (12:16)—that is, it has been introduced into the heavenly glory that he had with the Father before the world came into being (17:5)—and the "temple of his body" (2:21) has become, like Bethel of old, the meeting place of heaven and earth (1:51; cf. Gen 28:12). This glorification of Christ's humanity also makes possible the sacramental life, by which those who "eat [his] flesh and drink [his] blood" possess eternal life even now and thus have hope of their own bodily resurrection (John 6:54; cf. 5:25–29). When it is a question of the fruit of the ascension of the Son of Man, to say that "the Spirit is the life-giver [but] the flesh avails nothing" (6:62–63) must not be taken to signify that created realities cannot mediate God's life. On the contrary, "flesh" here refers to humanity in its state of weakness and mortality, just as it does in 1:14. The Word indeed assumed humanity in this "fleshly" condition but "glorified" it through the paschal mystery so that the life-giving Spirit might be made available to the world (7:39).

This same theology of incarnation and glorification is the proper context for understanding the parable of the true vine (15:1–6). The Old Testament background makes our starting point for interpretation inescapable. To say "I am the true vine" (v. 1) is to say "I am the true Israel." For Christ to call his disciples "branches" is to say that they are incorporated into Israel through their union with him. But to appreciate the force of these statements, we must have a correct hermeneutic. The evangelist is not simply adapting or reusing Old Testament symbols. He has not merely transferred the symbolism of the vine from Israel to Christ. Rather, this parable is better read as giving the *sensus spiritualis* of the Old Testament. That is, it is not so much the literary image itself but the *res* ("thing, reality") to which that image refers that "signifies" Christ. Christ recapitulates the living mystery of his people and their land. If the parable is read in this manner, Israel (people and land) is not left behind but is taken up into the mystery of Christ and glorified in him. The image of the vine expresses a similar sense of real continuity between the mystery of Israel and the mystery of Christ in an early Christian eucharistic prayer: "We thank you, our Father, for the holy vine of David your servant, which you made known to us through Jesus your servant" (*Did.* 9.2).

THE VIRGIN MARY AND THE LAND

The organic image of the vine may also lead us to reflect on the fact that the Word assumed a specifically Israelite humanity. Since many generations of Abraham's descendants had eaten the produce of the land and thus taken it up into their persons, the flesh he received from the Virgin Mary was literally drawn from the Holy Land. And of course, it continued to be nourished by the produce of that land throughout his life. Admittedly, John the evangelist regards concern with the specifics of Christ's terrestrial origins as a distraction from what really matters—namely, knowledge of his heavenly origin.[83] At the same time, Christ's flesh-and-blood humanity has a special prominence in the Fourth Gospel,[84] in which Mary also plays an important role as mother of the Messiah, representative member of the renewed Israel, and mother of the Church.[85]

As early as the second century, we find Irenaeus of Lyons drawing an explicit connection between the "virgin" earth from which Adam was formed and the Virgin Mary from whom Christ received his "enfleshment" (σάρκωσις).[86] Jerome's free rendering of Isaiah 45:8 clearly indicates that this passage is fulfilled in the incarnation:

> *Rorate caeli desuper et nubes pluant iustum,*
> *aperiatur terra et germinet salvatorem.*
>
> Drop down dew, O heavens, and let the clouds rain down the just one;
> let the earth be opened and bud forth the savior.[87]

83 John 1:46; 6:41–42; 7:25–29, 40–43.

84 John 1:14; 2:18–22; 4:6–7; 6:51–58; 11:35; 12:3, 7; 19:28, 34; 20:20, 22, 25–27.

85 John 2:1–11; 19:25–27. See Raymond E. Brown, SS, *The Gospel According to John (i–xii)*, AB 29 (Garden City, N.Y.: Doubleday, 1966), 107–9; and *The Gospel According to John (xiii–xxi)*, AB 29A (Garden City, N.Y.: Doubleday, 1970), 922–27.

86 Irenaeus, *Demonstration of the Apostolic Preaching* 32. Translation: St. Irenaeus of Lyons, *On the Apostolic Preaching*, trans. John Behr (Crestwood, N.Y.: St. Vladimir's Seminary Press, 1997), 61. When Adam was formed, the earth was still "virgin" because "God had not caused it to rain, and there was no man to till the soil" (Gen 2:5).

87 The Hebrew text speaks of "justice" (rather than "the just one") and of "salvation" (rather than "the savior").

Consistent with imagery found a few chapters later in Isaiah (55:10–11), the rain and dew are understood here to refer to the eternal Word descending from heaven, while the earth presumably refers to Mary and her virginal womb. This verse provides the opening lines for the famous *Rorate caeli* antiphon, which was more readily appreciated in the Middle Ages, when "the notion that a woman's body is like a field or a piece of earth" in which a man sows his "seed" was a commonplace.[88] A similar interpretation is sometimes given to Psalm 85 (84):11–13, which I translate from Jerome's *Psalterium iuxta Hebraeos*:

> Mercy and truth have met, justice and peace have kissed;
> truth has sprung from the earth, and justice has looked down from heaven.
> Moreover, the Lord will give the good, and our land will give its produce.

Here "our land" refers specifically to the land of Israel, which can spiritually signify the Virgin Mary.[89] The fact that the phrase that is translated "its produce" (*germen suum*) can also mean "her embryo" makes this interpretation even more attractive.

But does the New Testament itself ever hint at a significant connection between Mary and the Holy Land? Perhaps it does, in the words of Elizabeth: "Blessed are you among women, and blessed is the fruit of your womb!" (Luke 1:42). The second part of this macarism alludes to the blessings that Israel will receive if they hearken to the voice of Yahweh: "Blessed will be the fruit of your womb and the fruit of your land."[90] Human reproduction and agricultural fertility are closely linked here (cf. Deut 28:11, 18). The

88 John F. A. Sawyer, *The Fifth Gospel: Isaiah in the History of Christianity* (Cambridge: Cambridge University Press, 1996), 69. According to Sawyer, this unscientific image promotes a degrading view of women, and he rejoices that the "image of the Virgin, and of women in general, as parcels of land . . . has mercifully little or no appeal today" (71).

89 Prosper Guéranger, OSB, connects this passage to Isa 45:8 and understands *terra* in both passages to refer to "the blessed Virgin Mary made fruitful by the dew of heaven." *The Liturgical Year: Advent*, trans. Laurence Shepherd (Westminster, Md.: Newman, 1948), 133.

90 Deut 28:4; cf. 7:13. I have translated the Hebrew phrase *pərî biṭnəkā* literally ("the fruit of your womb," as in the NABRE), in order to make the verbal echo apparent. Because this promise is addressed to the *male* Israelite (the pronoun "your" is grammatically masculine in the Hebrew text), the phrase is often translated "the fruit of your body" (so RSV). Indeed, the word *béṭen* does sometimes clearly refer to the "abdomen" or "body" of a male (e.g., Judg 3:21; Ps 31:10; Job 19:17), and the phrase *pərî biṭnəkā* does seem to mean "the fruit of your (masc.) loins" in Ps 132:11 (cf. Mic 6:7). Alternatively, however, it is possible to understand the stock phrase *pərî béṭen* as functioning here somewhat in the manner of a compound noun ("womb-fruit"; cf. Gen 30:2), in which case "your womb-fruit" might mean roughly, "the womb-fruit that you have through your wife."

first part of Elizabeth's macarism makes a double allusion. First, it contains strong verbal echoes of blessings pronounced over two Old Testament heroines: Jael wife of Heber the Kenite (Judg 5:24) and the widow Judith (Jdt 13:18), each of whom courageously dispatched an enemy of Israel. Second, it alludes to the long series of formerly barren Old Testament women of faith who were enabled to conceive by a special blessing from Yahweh: Sarah, Rebekah, Rachel, the wife of Manoah, Hannah, and the Shunemite woman.[91] This allusion is strengthened by the fact that the words "blessed are you among women" are spoken by Elizabeth, who was barren herself and was miraculously enabled to conceive (Luke 1:36–37).

Luke's infancy narrative is filled with such allusions to the Old Testament, and clearly he wishes us to read it as the beginning of the climax of salvation history. The Virgin Mary is "blessed" because the fruit of her womb is precisely the eschatological blessing that has come upon the faithful remnant of Israel.[92] The "great things" done for her (1:49) both recapitulate and transcend the miracles done in and through the daughters of Sarah. Before the hope of resurrection was revealed to Israel, the blessings of agricultural and reproductive fertility were essential to Israel's corporate personhood and identity and constituted a sort of immortality. As Jesus ben Sira aptly puts it: "The days of a man's life are few in number, but the days of Israel are without number" (Sir 37:25). To bear children was to participate in the mystery of Israel and, by anticipation, in the eschatological blessings. It is fitting that the realization of the hope of eternal life should finally come to Israel through the fruit of the womb, which is also the fruit of the land.

91 See Gen 17:16; 18:14; 21:1–2; 24:60; 25:21; 30:22–24; Judg 13:2–3; 1 Sam 1:19–20; 2:20–21; 2 Kgs 4:14–17. Perhaps the memory of the widows Ruth and Naomi (Ruth 4:13–15) and of Sarah daughter of Raguel (Tob 3:16–17; 6:18; 9:6; 10:11; 11:17; 14:3) is also evoked.

92 In Luke's infancy narrative the Messiah and his herald come from the midst of the faithful remnant of Israel—namely, those who are "awaiting the consolation of Israel" and "the redemption of Jerusalem" (Luke 2:25, 38; a double allusion to Isa 52:9). This remnant is embodied by three pairs of faithful Israelites, who together represent the *munus triplex* of Israel and its messiah—Zechariah and Elizabeth (priestly), Joseph and Mary (royal), and Simeon and Anna (prophetic)—and in a particular way by Mary, who identifies herself as "the servant of the Lord" (1:38, 48), which is a prophetic title that expresses Israel's true identity and vocation (Isa 41:8–9; 42:1, 19; 43:10; 44:1–2, 21, 26; 45:4; 48:20; 49:3–6; 50:10; 52:13; 53:11).

THE EPISTLE TO THE HEBREWS

Finally, we turn to the Epistle to the Hebrews, which, according to both Davies and Janzen, represents a complete "abrogation" of the Old Testament's realistic promise of land, replacing it with the promise of a heavenly homeland and heavenly sanctuary that are "nonphysical eternal realities."[93] The grain of truth in this assertion is that Hebrews does indeed offer its readers a hope that far transcends the terrestrial land of Canaan or the restoration of the earthly city of Jerusalem. Wilken's attempt to deny this and to offer in its place a chiliastic interpretation, according to which the author of Hebrews allegedly holds forth the hope of an earthly eschatological kingdom, is, in my opinion, entirely unconvincing.[94] Though Wilken's interpretation is in this respect almost diametrically opposed to that of Davies and Janzen, he seems to share with these two scholars the mistaken assumption that any proclamation of an "otherworldly" homeland would of necessity leave far behind the particularism and territorial realism of the Hebrew Scriptures. Apparently, he is drawn to a chiliastic interpretation because he assumes that the only alternative is an interpretation by which Hebrews has transformed the Old Testament promise of land into "a spiritual concept that has no relation to the actual land of Canaan."[95]

All three scholars err in their interpretation of Hebrews because they overlook what the sacred author explicitly identifies as his "main point" (κεφάλαιον)—namely, the session of the high priest Jesus "at the right hand of the throne of majesty in the heavens" (Heb 8:1). The notion that the messiah, as both king and "priest forever," has "taken his seat" at the "right hand" of God is drawn from Psalm 110.[96] This affirmation occupies a central place in the solemn period with which Hebrews opens, and it recurs at key points throughout the epistle.[97] It can be properly understood only in relation to Hebrews' incarnational Christology and soteriology, which I shall summarize in the following paragraphs.

Christ is the preexistent Son of God, the "refulgence" of the Father's glory and "the imprint of his substance" (1:3). When he came into the world, the

93 Janzen, "Land," 151–52.

94 Wilken, *Land Called Holy*, 52–55.

95 Wilken, 53.

96 Cf. Heb 1:13; 5:6; 7:17, 21.

97 Heb 1:1–4; 8:1; 10:12; 12:2.

Son assumed the "body" that was "furnished" for him (10:5). This need not be taken in an adoptionist sense—as if the concrete, individual humanity already existed in the Virgin's womb prior to the Word's descent—but it is worth reflecting on the fact that God in a sense prepared Christ's humanity through the creation of the world, and of man in his own image, and specifically through the election of Israel *and their land*. The provision of a "body"—indeed, of *this* body—for Christ must have been in God's mind eternally.

By taking to himself a concrete humanity, the Son attained what the author of Hebrews discerns to be a fitting solidarity with the human race. As "son of man" he was "for a little while made lesser than the angels," in order that he might "taste death for all" (2:6–9). More specifically, he "partook" (μετέσχεν) in the "blood and flesh" of the "seed of Abraham" so that he might "in all things be made like his brethren" and thus serve as a merciful and compassionate high priest and "atone for the sins of the people" (2:14–17). In this passage, the phrases "seed of Abraham," "his brethren," and "the people" all refer specifically to Israel (cf. 13:12). According to the divine logic of salvation history, the incarnate Son attains solidarity with the whole human race and a universally efficacious high priesthood *through* his union with his own people and his atoning sacrifice on their behalf. The universal is achieved through the particular.[98]

The assumption of a body provides the Son of God with a concrete place and moment in history, and thus he is able to act in human freedom. It was

98 Many commentators have stumbled over the particularism of this passage. Most take "seed of Abraham" (v. 16) and "the people" (v. 17) as figurative ways to refer to Christians. See, for example, F. F. Bruce, *The Epistle to the Hebrews*, NICNT (Grand Rapids: Eerdmans, 1964), 51; Hugh Montefiore, *A Commentary on the Epistle to the Hebrews* (London: Adam & Charles Black, 1964), 66–68; Harold W. Attridge, *The Epistle to the Hebrews*, Hermeneia (Philadelphia: Fortress, 1989), 94; Victor C. Pfitzner, *Hebrews*, Abingdon New Testament Commentaries (Nashville: Abingdon, 1997), 68; and, with some hesitation over the first phrase, Paul Ellingworth, *The Epistle to the Hebrews: A Commentary on the Greek Text*, New International Greek Testament Commentary (Grand Rapids: Eerdmans, 1993), 178, 190. This interpretation fails to appreciate the seriousness with which the New Testament authors take Israel's role in the economy of the new covenant. George Wesley Buchanan, on the other hand, while recognizing that the phrases "seed of Abraham" and "the people" refer to Israel *secundum carnem*, draws from this fact the doubtful conclusion that, because the author of Hebrews addresses a community consisting entirely of Jewish Christians, he is unconcerned with how his teaching might apply to gentile Christians. See *To the Hebrews: Translation, Comment and Conclusions*, AB 36 (Garden City, N.Y.: Doubleday, 1972), 36–38. In either case, the biblical principle of *the universal through the particular* proves to be a scandal for the post-Enlightenment mind. Bruce comes closer to this principle in the second edition of his commentary. F. F. Bruce, *The Epistle to the Hebrews*, 2nd ed., NICNT (Grand Rapids: Eerdmans, 1990), 87.

"in the days of his flesh" that he offered prayers to the Father and "learned obedience" from his sufferings, and it is precisely in his humanity that he has been "perfected" forever.[99] The priestly, sacrificial act by which he obtains our salvation has both an interior dimension and an exterior dimension. In an interior act of obedience he chooses God's "will," but this interior act is realized in time and space through "the offering of [his] body once and for all" (10:10). The body is thus a sacrament of his human will inasmuch as it makes visible his intention to obey the Father and gives it a concrete, historical realization. Meanwhile, at another level, the entire body-soul humanity of Christ serves as the "'sacrament,' that is, the sign and instrument, of his divinity" (*CCC* 515).

Now, in order to demonstrate that the "heavenly calling" in which the addressees of Hebrews are "participants" (μέτοχοι, 3:1) is no mere "spiritual concept that has no relation to the actual land of Canaan"—which is my main purpose here—it will be necessary to consider next how the author views the relationship between Christ's earthly offering and his heavenly priesthood. Since Christ is a high priest, it was "necessary that he have something to offer" (Heb 8:3). The author of Hebrews identifies this something as "himself" (7:27; 9:14) or "his body" (10:10), which he compares to a sacrificial animal that is "without blemish" (ἄμωμος, 9:14). Moreover, Christ makes this offering "by his own blood" (9:12)—that is, by his death. How, then, is this death on earth effective in heaven?

The author of Hebrews generally eschews the traditional language of resurrection (employing it only in 13:20), and his manner of viewing the paschal mystery is unique in the New Testament. In several passages, he speaks of two distinct phases: an earthly offering and a heavenly exaltation, with the latter being variously described in terms of session, perfection, or glorification:

> Having made purification for sins,
> he took his seat at the right hand of the Majesty in the high places. (1:3)
>
> On account of the suffering of death,
> [he was] crowned with glory and honor. (2:9)
>
> He learned obedience from what he suffered
> and [was] made perfect. (5:8–9)

99 Heb 5:7–9; cf. 2:10; 7:28.

> He [offered a sacrifice for sins] once and for all when he offered himself . . .
> [and he was] made perfect forever. (7:27–28)
>
> Having offered one sacrifice for sins,
> he took his seat forever at the right hand of God. (10:12)

But in other passages these two phases seem to merge into one, so that Christ's offering on earth is also an "event" in heaven. For example, as the author looks to the Yom Kippur ritual (Leviticus 16) to illumine its antitype, he claims that Christ "entered" the heavenly sanctuary "once and for all" through his own blood (Heb 9:12). This use of the word ἐφάπαξ ("once and for all") correlates with the frequent use of the same or similar terms elsewhere to insist that Christ's self-offering took place as a singular and definitive event.[100] We should probably not regard Christ's shedding of blood on earth and his entrance into the heavenly sanctuary "by his own blood" as two distinct events but as two dimensions of the same event, or as the same event in two modalities. At the same time, it is hardly necessary or advisable to obliterate the temporal distance between Good Friday and Easter Sunday. We can maintain the proper distinction between Christ's death and his resurrection if we recognize that it is precisely through the glorification of his humanity that the "once and for all" event of his self-offering is transposed to the heavenly realm. Through his exaltation he brings into the Father's presence "all that he lived and suffered for us" (*CCC* 519).

We may say, then, that the glorification of Christ's humanity mediates between his earthly offering and its heavenly efficacy. Because he "lives forever" he possesses a priesthood that "does not pass away," and he is thus able to "intercede for" and "save forever those who approach God through him" (7:24–25). This priestly intercession is not a second act added onto his once-and-for-all self-offering (v. 27). It *is* the latter, transposed to the heavenly realm. But it is especially through the notion of "perfection" that the author of Hebrews expresses the intimate relation between earthly offering and heavenly efficacy. "In the days of his flesh" (i.e., when his humanity was still in its mortal state), Christ "learned obedience from what he suffered," and this act of conforming his human will to the divine will already effected the interior (moral and spiritual) perfection of his humanity (5:7–9; cf. 2:10). This perfection received its somatic counterpart through the resurrection and ascension (7:28), which conferred upon Christ's humanity "the power

100 Heb 7:27; 9:26, 28; 10:10, 12, 14; cf. Rom 6:10; 1 Pet 3:18.

of an indestructible life" (7:16) and established him as "the source of eternal salvation" (5:9). This salvation is appropriated by "all who obey" Christ as he obeyed the Father (5:9), and who thus "advance to the perfection" that was unavailable under the Mosaic law and the Levitical priesthood.[101]

Naturally, we must bear in mind that all of this is entirely dependent on the incarnation of the Word.

> Christ's human nature belongs, as his own, to the divine person of the Son of God, who assumed it. Everything that Christ is and does in this nature derives from "one of the Trinity." The Son of God therefore communicates to his humanity his own personal mode of existence in the Trinity. In his soul as in his body, Christ thus expresses humanly the divine ways of the Trinity.[102]

Christ's self-offering "in the days of his flesh" is therefore already a heavenly act because it is a Trinitarian act. Through it the Son "expresses humanly" his eternal relation to the Father. The author of Hebrews indicates this by means of a terse Trinitarian formula.

> How much more will the blood of *Christ*, who through the eternal *Spirit* offered himself without blemish to *God*, cleanse our consciences from dead works, to worship the living God. (9:14)

Through the incarnation, the eternal Trinitarian act has entered history and is most perfectly expressed in the historical act of obedience and love by which Christ laid down his life. Conversely, through the glorification of Christ's humanity, history has entered heaven. There is thus a mysterious interpenetration between the temporal and the eternal, and between the created and the uncreated.

At this point we must consider an element of Hebrews' theology about which there has been no little confusion and disagreement—namely, the heavenly sanctuary.[103] Our author refers to it as "the true tent, which the Lord has set up, not man" (8:2) and distinguishes it from its "copy and shadow" on earth—that is, Israel's sanctuary (8:5; cf. 9:23). The latter is κοσμικός, which means "of the created order" (9:1), but the former is "not made with

101 Heb 6:1; cf. 5:14; 7:11, 19; 9:9; 10:1, 14; 11:40; 12:23.

102 *CCC* 470.

103 Fortunately, Attridge has clarified a great deal in his fine excursus on this subject (*Epistle to the Hebrews*, 222–24) and throughout his commentary.

hands—that is, not of this creation" (9:11). The earthly sanctuary and its accoutrements are "antitypes of the true things," while the sanctuary that Christ entered is "heaven itself" (9:24).[104] These statements suggest that this heavenly sanctuary is in the first instance an eternal, uncreated reality. It would therefore be incorrect to identify it, without further qualification, as the glorified humanity of Christ.

At the same time, the sacred author's patent use of Platonic terminology (e.g., "copy and shadow") should not lead us to conclude that his metaphysics is thoroughly or merely Platonic, nor should we assume that the heaven-earth polarity stands on its own as the only such differentiation operative in Hebrews. As Harold W. Attridge observes, "the earthly-heavenly dichotomy of the temple imagery intersects with, interprets, and is at the same time transformed by another dichotomy, that of new and old."[105] Thus, immediately after introducing the heavenly sanctuary in Platonic terms in 8:1–5a, the author of Hebrews quotes two Old Testament texts for support. The first of these recalls how Moses was instructed to follow the "pattern" shown him on Mount Sinai in constructing the wilderness tabernacle, and the second is the famous "new covenant" oracle from Jeremiah.[106] Together these two texts place everything that the author of Hebrews will have to say about the earthly and heavenly sanctuaries in chapters 9 and 10 within a framework established by the Law and the Prophets, to which Platonic categories are subservient. Indeed, the Platonic elements in Hebrews stand in the service of a comprehensive biblical view of reality, which includes not only the salvation-historical schema to which Attridge points ("new and old"), but also the biblical view of God and creation. Within this worldview, created realities possess a sacramental dimension. Remarkably, the author of Hebrews teaches us that something has *taken place* in heaven and that this event involves the *entrance* of created realities into the heavenly sanctuary, beginning with the blood and flesh of Jesus Christ.

We saw above that in the Old Testament Israel's sanctuary is viewed as the earthly counterpart to Yahweh's abode in heaven, and that while the former is derivative and mutable, the latter is transcendent and enduring. But the relationship between these two realities is not static, and the historical

104 Here "antitype" (ἀντίτυπος) refers not to the greater reality but to that which is derivative. Ellingworth, *Epistle to the Hebrews*, 480; BDAG, 91a.

105 Attridge, *Epistle to the Hebrews*, 224.

106 Heb 8:5b (Exod 25:40); Heb 8:8–12 (Jer 31:31–34).

vicissitudes of the earthly temple lead up to an eschatological event. Whether this event is described in terms of Yahweh's placing his own sanctuary in Israel's midst (Ezek 37:26–28), or his "rousing himself from his holy habitation" in heaven in order to dwell among Israel (Zech 2:15–17), or in terms of the exaltation and glorification of Jerusalem,[107] it is always a question of a new union between earth and heaven. Yahweh will "create new heavens and a new earth" by "[re]creating Jerusalem" (Isa 65:17–18). Similarly, in Hebrews, the sharp distinctions between created and uncreated realities and between the Mosaic tabernacle and the heavenly sanctuary ultimately serve to indicate how a new union of earth and heaven has been effected through the removal of sins, and that this could never have transpired by means of the Levitical priesthood but only "through the offering of the body of Jesus Christ once and for all" (Heb 10:10).

The passage that is most decisive for Hebrews' understanding of the relationship between the earthly and heavenly realms is one that has received diametrically opposed interpretations.

> Therefore, brethren, since we have confidence of access into the sanctuary by the blood of Jesus, via the fresh and living way, which he has dedicated (ἐνεκαίνισεν) for us, through the curtain, that is, his flesh, and a great priest over the house of God, let us approach with a true heart in full conviction of faith, our hearts having been sprinkled [clean] from an evil conscience and our bodies having been washed with pure water. (10:19–22)

The verb ἐγκαινίζω ("create anew, dedicate") has a two-pronged Septuagint background, evoking here both the decisively "new" (καινός) event by which Yahweh would transform and renew Israel,[108] as well as the "dedication" of the temple.[109] This consideration leads to the central interpretive issue posed by this text. Clearly Christ is presented here as both priest and sacrificial

107 Isa 54:11–12; 60:1–22; 62:1–12; 65:17–25; Bar 5:1–4.

108 Jer 31:31–34 (LXX 38:31–34); Ezek 36:26–28; Isa 43:19; 48:6; 65:17.

109 In LXX ἐγκαινίζω serves as a translation for the Hebrew verbs *ḥdš* in the Piel stem ("to renew, create anew": Lam 5:21; Sir 36:5 [RSV 36:6]; Ps 50:12 [RSV 51:10]) and *ḥnk* in the Qal stem ("to dedicate, rededicate": 1 Kgs 8:63; 2 Chron 7:5; 1 Macc 4:54, 57; 5:1). From the latter is derived the noun *ḥănukkâ* ("dedication"), which as the name of the festival of 25 Chislev (i.e., Hanukkah) is rendered τὰ ἐγκαίνια in Greek (John 10:22). See Ceslas Spicq, OP, *Theological Lexicon of the New Testament*, trans. and ed. James D. Ernest (Peabody, Mass.: Hendrickson, 1994), 1:396–97. Note also that the precise form ἐνεκαίνισεν ("he dedicated") occurs together with the phrase τὸν οἶκον τοῦ θεοῦ ("the house of God") in LXX 2 Chron 7:5, just as in Heb 10:20–21.

victim, as he is elsewhere in Hebrews, but is he in any sense also the new temple? Admittedly, this is far from explicit, but the language of this passage is suggestive. What Christ "dedicates" is a new *via sacra* into God's presence. To say that it is "fresh and living" (or "new and living") would be odd if the reference were simply to heaven as an uncreated, eternal reality. The phrase might, then, quite appropriately be applied to the glorified humanity of Christ, which has acquired "the power of an indestructible life" (7:16).[110] The heavenly "tent" is "not of *this* creation" (9:11), but it is of the *new* creation, which is eternally anticipated, as it were, in heaven.

The identification of the temple curtain with Christ's "flesh" has suggested to some that "the flesh of Jesus constituted an obstacle to God,"[111] but this idea is alien to the Epistle to the Hebrews and ill fits the context.[112] Whether or not we are to think of the "curtain" of Christ's flesh being rent in two to provide access into heaven (cf. Mark 15:38), the term "flesh" connotes mortality, and the conjunction of "blood" and "flesh" certainly evokes Christ's sacrificial death. But this by no means requires the deduction that the author of Hebrews takes a pejorative view of Christ's humanity, even in its preglorified state. As we have seen, the act of reverent obedience by which Christ achieved eternal redemption was made "in the days of his flesh" (Heb 5:7) and consisted in the offering of his "body" as a sacrifice "without blemish" to the Father (9:14; 10:10). We have also noted how closely linked Christ's death and exaltation are in Hebrews. We might even say that Christ's death is the formal cause of his glorification, inasmuch as the former confers upon the latter the character of a priestly offering, even while the latter confers an everlasting efficacy on the former. Christ's body is the sacrament both of his

110 The phrase "fresh and living" might simply contrast the newness and immediacy of access available to the Christian with the impotent symbolic rites of the old covenant, but in 7:16 "the law of fleshly commandment" is contrasted not simply with what is new and immediate but precisely with "the power of an indestructible life"—that is, the power flowing from Christ's glorified humanity (cf. Eph 1:19–21; Phil 3:10, 21). Since the term πρόσφατος (here translated "fresh") can simply mean "new" or "recent" and is "common in Greek literature" (Attridge, *Epistle to the Hebrews*, 285n27), we should not be surprised to find it used by so literate an author as ours and should not press its meaning simply because this is its only occurrence in the New Testament. (The corresponding adverb is found in Acts 18:2 with no other nuance than "recently.") On the other hand, it might have been chosen over καινός ("new") in order to suggest the "powerful effects" and "incorruptible freshness" of this new *via sacra*. Christian Maurer, "πρόσφατος," in *TDNT* 6:767.

111 *The New American Bible*, with Revised New Testament, Saint Joseph Edition (New York: Catholic Book Publishing, 1986), marginal note on Heb 10:20.

112 Maurer, *TDNT* 6:767; Attridge, *Epistle to the Hebrews*, 287.

divinity and of his human perfection, and it has this dual sacramental character both in the "once and for all" history of "the days of his flesh" and in the glory that makes of that history a "once and for all" entrance into heaven of the one who then "lives forever to intercede" for "those who approach God through him" (7:25).

CONCLUSION

Taking my lead from the poems of Karol Wojtyła and his papal teaching as John Paul II, in this chapter I have presented the land of Israel as a "sacrament" and considered how it can be truly said that "man is the land." This mysterious identification is rooted in the order of creation, manifests itself in the bond between the people and land of Israel in the Old Testament, and is truly present in Christianity through the incarnation of the Word and the glorification of Christ's Israelite humanity. I have offered corrective nuances to the thesis that Israel's "territorial realism" has been "spiritualized" in the New Testament. Properly understood, this spiritualization is not a matter of exchanging physical realities for immaterial ideas. In the order of creation and in Israel's covenant with Yahweh, the land itself already serves in a variety of ways as the bearer of spiritual realities. There is a sort of sacramental union between the material and the immaterial, whereby the invisible is made visible. This involves various transformations of the land—such as the manufacture of cultural implements and objects of art, or the nourishing of the body with the bounty of the land—but the material dimension is never left behind. And all of this is ultimately ordered to man's union with God. Thus spiritualization is sacramentalization. This sacramentalization of the land of Israel achieves a new level—indeed, it makes a quantum leap—in the incarnation and through the paschal mystery. Nevertheless, physical reality is not left behind. In a very real and physical sense the land of Israel has been taken up into the Christian mystery, and this spiritualization, while unique and unprecedented, is nevertheless fully in continuity with the Old Testament mystery of Israel's covenant with Yahweh.

CHAPTER EIGHT

Psalms and Christ Event in the Epistle to the Hebrews

The ancient Christian homily known as the Epistle to the Hebrews is principally concerned with a person and an event.[1] In the book's exordium the person is introduced to us as God's own Son, the "reflection of his glory and imprint of his substance," through whom all things were created. The event is tersely summed up by saying that this Son accomplished "the purification of sins" and "took his seat at the right hand of the majesty in the high places" (1:2–3). Over the next ten chapters the sacred author gradually unfolds the soteriological significance of this event as a high-priestly self-offering.

1 Scholarly opinions regarding the authorship, date, place of origin, and destination of the Epistle to the Hebrews vary widely. For a judicious survey and critique, see Ellingworth, *Epistle to the Hebrews*, 3–33. My own working hypothesis, admittedly speculative, is that Hebrews was written by Apollos from Ephesus circa AD 60, to be read to a synagogue of Jewish Christians in Corinth, presumably the "Apollos faction" to which Paul alludes (1 Cor 1:10–12; 3:4). In terms of literary genre, Hebrews is not precisely an epistle but a "word of exhortation" (λόγος παρακλήσεως) or synagogue homily with an epistolary conclusion (Heb 13:22; cf. Acts 13:15). It is aimed at dissuading members of the community from "drifting away" from authentic faith in Christ and into a Judaized distortion of Christianity (Heb 2:1–4; 6:1–12; 10:19–31; 12:14–28) and appears to have been composed in two stages. First, Apollos composed chapters 1–12 (the homily proper, from solemn exordium to dramatic conclusion), intending to visit Corinth soon in order to deliver the homily in person. However, upon hearing that Timothy had been released from imprisonment (probably in the Holy Land), Apollos decided to delay his trip until Timothy should arrive in Ephesus and could accompany him (13:23). But when the situation in Corinth became even more urgent and Timothy had not yet arrived, Apollos appended a final exhortation and epistolary conclusion (chapter 13) and dispatched a trusted coworker whom he had commissioned to read the homily publicly on his behalf. On some points this hypothesis is similar to that of Montefiore (*Commentary on the Epistle to the Hebrews*, 9–31), although I arrived at it independently.

Throughout these chapters the author frequently quotes or alludes to the books of the Old Testament. These quotations and allusions are not window dressing, nor would it be adequate to describe them as proof texts. The author turns to the Scriptures of Israel in order to gain inspired insight into the mystery of Jesus Christ and the new covenant in his blood. He takes it as given that these ancient Jewish texts refer in various ways to the person and event of Christ, and that they speak the "living and effective" word of God to Christians (4:12).

Among the books of the Old Testament the Psalter plays an especially prominent role in the Epistle to the Hebrews. Notably, quotations from and allusions to Psalm 110 are woven through the argument as its central leitmotif.[2] This psalm identifies Israel's messiah as "a priest forever according to the order of Melchizedek," a priest-king who has taken his seat "at the right hand of God" (vv. 1, 4). There is even some justification for viewing Hebrews as an elaborate Christological exegesis of Psalm 110.[3] Nonetheless, citations of several other psalms play a supporting but vital role within the homily's unfolding argument.

The present essay is concerned with a pair of citations from the Psalms that stand like two pillars, one near the beginning and the other near the end of Hebrews' main expository section (chapters 1–10). The first of these is the citation of Psalm 8:5–7 in Hebrews 2:5–9, and the second is the citation of Psalm 40:7–9 in Hebrews 10:5–10. These two passages are of about equal length and have the same structure, comprising an introduction, the citation itself, and an exegetical comment. Most importantly, the two passages have in common that the author of Hebrews has discovered a succinct narration of the Christ event in the given psalm. He comes to a deeper understanding of these psalms in light of the Christ event and simultaneously comes to a deeper understanding of the Christ event in light of the psalms.

2 Heb 1:3, 13; 5:6, 10; 6:20; 7:3, 11, 17, 21; 8:1; 10:12–13; 12:2.

3 Buchanan opens his commentary by declaring Hebrews to be a "homiletic midrash" on Psalm 110 (*To the Hebrews*, xix). Gert J. C. Jordaan and Pieter Nel go much further, attempting to demonstrate that Psalm 110 "controls" the structure of Hebrews and that the author of Hebrews even "used the thought-structure" of Psalm 110 as the "blueprint" for his homily. "From Priest-King to King-Priest: Psalm 110 and the Basic Structure of Hebrews," in *Psalms and Hebrews: Studies in Reception*, ed. Dirk J. Human and Gert J. Steyn, Library of Hebrew Bible/Old Testament Studies 527 (New York: T&T Clark, 2010), 229–40. Their argument fails to carry conviction because they find allusions to Psalm 110 where there are none (e.g., Heb 2:9; 3:1; 7:25; 12:22) and greatly exaggerate the thematic correlations between Psalm 110 and Hebrews (e.g., by identifying the theme of *battle* in the former with the theme of *suffering* in the latter).

For each passage, I shall first consider the psalm according to the original Hebrew and in its Old Testament context. Next, I shall look briefly at how the psalm has been translated into Greek in the Septuagint, for in both cases the Septuagint mediates between the Hebrew psalm and its New Testament interpretation. Finally, I shall examine the exegesis that the psalm receives at the skillful hands of the author of the Epistle to the Hebrews. When we come to the citation of Psalm 40, I shall draw upon the insights of Gregory of Nyssa, Thomas Aquinas, and John Paul II regarding the human body and the humanity of Christ in order to understand more deeply the reality to which Scripture refers in these passages.

Like the other chapters in this volume, the present study is intended to contribute to the development of an ecclesial approach to biblical interpretation. One important component of this endeavor is to gain a full and proper understanding of the relationship between Scripture and Tradition. According to *Dei Verbum* 9, "Sacred Tradition and Sacred Scripture are closely interconnected and even participate in each other."[4] The author of the Epistle to the Hebrews can provide invaluable insights in this regard, inasmuch as he is both an interpreter of Scripture and an author of Scripture. He was keenly aware of the fact that the deposit of faith had its originating principle (ἀρχή) in the preaching of the Lord Jesus and that it was validly transmitted to him and his first readers by those who had heard Christ teach in person (Heb 2:3). He draws upon this apostolic Tradition as he writes his homiletic epistle, which will later be canonized as a book of the New Testament.

From the first sentence of his work, the author of Hebrews is also intensely concerned with the relationship between the old covenant and the new covenant. He unfolds his insight into this relationship largely by interpreting various parts of the Old Testament. In the two passages with which we are especially concerned in this chapter, he does not merely cite passages of Scripture in support of his argument but actually comments on portions of Psalms 8 and 40, arguing from the very wording of the text.[5] This sort of exegetical procedure is relatively rare in the New Testament, and these may be the two best examples of it.[6] They place us close to the source of the Christian exegetical tradition, which will eventually produce full-fledged

4 *Sacra Traditio ergo et Sacra Scriptura arcte inter se connectuntur atque communicant.*

5 For the exegetical technique of the Epistle to the Hebrews, see Hans Hübner, "New Testament Interpretation of the Old Testament," in Sæbø, *Hebrew Bible/Old Testament*, 362–67.

6 Another example is found in Eph 4:7–10.

biblical commentaries. More importantly, the Epistle to the Hebrews bears witness to the deep interpenetration of Sacred Tradition and Sacred Scripture at a point very close to the single "divine wellspring" (*divina scaturigine*) from which they both flow (*Dei Verbum* 9).

PSALM 8 IN THE HEBREW OLD TESTAMENT

In the original Hebrew, Psalm 8 is a tightly structured song of eleven poetic lines.[7]

1 Yahweh, our Lord, how (*mâ*) majestic is your name in all the earth!

2 You have placed[8] your splendor above the heavens.
3 From the mouths of babes and sucklings you have founded strength,
4 because of your foes, to silence the enemy and avenger.

5 When I look upon your heavens, the work of your fingers,
the moon and stars that you have established,
6 what (*mâ*) is man that you remember him,
the son of man that you should look after him?
7 You have made him a little less than the gods;
with glory and honor you have crowned him.

8 You made him rule over the works of your hands,
placed all under his feet:
9 sheep and cattle, all of them; even the beasts of the field;
10 birds of the sky and fish of the sea, whatever passes the lanes of the seas.

11 Yahweh, our Lord, how (*mâ*) majestic is your name in all the earth!

The song begins and ends with an antiphon of praise. This framing device has two functions. First, it gives the psalm a doxological character. The author's meditation on creation and man's place within creation is offered in praise of the God of Israel. Specifically, Psalm 8 praises Yahweh for the majestic way he has made his name known *upon earth*. Second, the antiphonal framing device in lines 1 and 11 lends the psalm a degree of symmetry and draws the reader's attention to line 6, the psalm's structural center, where we

7 To illuminate this structure, I have omitted the superscript and numbered the text according to the scansion of poetic lines, dispensing with the traditional verse numbers.

8 For MT *tənâ* ("place," imperative), read *nātáttâ* ("you have placed"); cf. Syriac, Symmachus, and *Psalterium iuxta Hebraeos*.

find the theological question that is also its thematic center: "What is man that you remember him, / the son of man that you should look after him?"[9]

The structural and thematic correlation between the antiphon of lines 1 and 11 and the question of line 6 is reinforced by the use of the Hebrew word *mâ* in both cases. In lines 1 and 11 *mâ* functions as an exclamatory adverb, translated "how": "How majestic is your name!" (*mâ ʾaddîr šimkā*). In line 6 *mâ* serves as an interrogative pronoun, translated "what": "What is man?" (*mâ ʾĕnôš*). This question is quasi-rhetorical and can be heard as an exclamation of praise. The Hebrew author marvels that God should have given thought to man at all. On another level, however, *mâ ʾĕnôš* is a serious theological question: "What *is* man?" Or rather, it is an anthropological question—the "man question"—placed within a theological and doxological framework.[10]

Thematically, Psalm 8 is concerned with man's ontological place within the big scheme of things. By placing the man question at the structural center of his poem, the inspired author already hints at the answer that he will give to this question. Man stands in the middle, at the juncture of heaven and earth. Above him are the heavens, "the moon and the stars," and God has made him "a little less than the gods"—that is, than the heavenly beings. Below man are sheep and cattle, the beasts of the field and the fish of the sea. Even the birds that fly overhead are ontologically "under his feet." As the question *mâ ʾĕnôš* is the centerpiece of the poet's creation, so man is the centerpiece of Yahweh's creation.

Psalm 8 is concerned with the connection between God's glory and man's glory. The phrase "the work of your fingers" (line 5) suggests the Creator's delicate craftsmanship and attention to intricate detail, such that creation constitutes a revelation of divine wisdom and majesty.[11] This manifestation takes place throughout the cosmos, but the psalmist's particular concern is with the revelation of God's name "in all the earth." This is where man comes in. His unique dignity is not merely to rule over the whole terrestrial creation but to glorify the Creator by doing so.

9 This sense of structural symmetry is further enhanced by a kind of parallelism between lines 5 and 7. The former refers to heavenly bodies ("moon and stars"), the latter to heavenly beings ("gods"). These references immediately surround the centerpiece, line 6.

10 Mays, *Psalms*, 66–68.

11 Avroham Chaim Feuer, *Tehillim: A New Translation with a Commentary Anthologized from Talmudic, Midrashic and Rabbinic Sources* (Brooklyn: Mesorah Publications, 1985), 125. Feuer also notes that references to God's "finger" elsewhere in Scripture indicate the clarity and explicitness of his revelation: Exod 8:15 (RSV 8:19); 31:18; Deut 9:10; Luke 11:20.

The Israelite psalmist, for his part, not only speaks about this special role of man but participates in it. He looks upward at the night sky, at the moon and stars, and marvels at Yahweh's providential concern for man and the authority he has given him. Then he composes a song that praises God for all of this. Even as he meditates on man's unique vocation, the psalmist lives out that vocation.

PSALM 8 IN THE SEPTUAGINT

About two centuries before Christ, the Hebrew Psalter was translated into Greek by Jews living in Alexandria, Egypt.[12] In the case of Psalm 8, this Septuagint rendering is an accurate one that finds the sweet spot between the overly literal and the freely idiomatic. (Not every Septuagint translator was so successful.) For present purposes, we need only examine the translation of the first half of line 7. The Hebrew psalmist has written:

> *wattəḥassərēhû məʿaṭ mēʾĕlōhîm*
> And you made him a little less than the gods.

The Septuagint translator gives us:

> ἠλάττωσας αὐτὸν βραχύ τι παρ' ἀγγέλους
> You made him (for) a little (while) less than angels.

Two features of this rendering are to be noted. First, the translation ἀγγέλους correctly indicates that in this context the Hebrew word *ʾĕlōhîm* refers neither to the true "God" nor to the false "gods" of the nations, but to heavenly creatures who do God's bidding—that is, to the angels.[13] Second, the Greek adverbial phrase βραχύ τι is semantically ambiguous. It can be read either as an adverb of degree—"a little"—or as an adverb of temporal duration—"for a little while."[14] The Septuagint translator undoubtedly intended

12 On the origins of the Septuagint and the history of its textual transmission (a pair of exceedingly complex topics), see Melvin K. H. Peters, "Septuagint," *ABD* 5.1093–1104; and Würthwein, *Text of the Old Testament*, 50–78.

13 W. O. E. Oesterley, *The Psalms: Translated with Text-Critical and Exegetical Notes* (London: SPCK, 1955), 140; Richard J. Clifford, *Psalms 1–72*, Abingdon Old Testament Commentaries (Nashville: Abingdon, 2002), 69. The translation "a little lower than God" (NRSV) does not give the ancient Israelite author much credit for understanding what the word "God" means. The incomparability of God is affirmed numerous times in the OT (e.g., Exod 15:11; Isa 40:17–18; Ps 89:7).

14 BDAG, 183.

βραχύ τι to express degree—"You made him *a little* less than angels"—for that is clearly the sense of the Hebrew adverb *mǝʿaṭ* in this context.[15] But later, when the Greek translation of Psalm 8 was read by Christians in a new salvation-historical context, this passage might as easily have been taken to mean, "You made him *for a little while* less than angels." Both of these features of Septuagint Psalm 8 factor into the interpretation it has been given in the second chapter of Hebrews, to which we now turn our attention.

HEBREWS 2:5–9

Taking his lead from the opening verse of Psalm 110—"Sit at my right hand, until I make your enemies a stool under your feet"—the author of Hebrews lays great stress on Christ's exaltation above the angels and session at the right hand of God. He concludes the exordium with these words, which contain the first of many allusions to Psalm 110:1: "Having made purification for sins, he took his seat at the right hand of the Majesty on high, having become so much greater than the angels as the name he has inherited is better than theirs" (Heb 1:3b–4). Then he quotes Psalm 110:1 directly as the final text in a catena of seven Old Testament passages (Heb 1:13).[16]

15 Strictly speaking, this semantic ambiguity may be present in the Hebrew text too. When *mǝʿaṭ* is used adverbially, the most clearly attested sense is "to a small degree" (2 Kgs 10:18; Zech 1:15; Ezek 11:16), but other senses, such as "for a short distance" (2 Sam 16:1), are also found. The only passages where *mǝʿaṭ* likely means "for a little while" are Job 10:20b and 24:24. This sense is often also assigned to Ruth 2:7b, but the clause in which *mǝʿaṭ* occurs is wholly obscure and almost certainly corrupt. In any case, in its original context in Psalm 8, *mǝʿaṭ* is certainly an adverb of degree, not of temporal duration.

16 By connecting Christ's exaltation above the angels to Psalm 110:1 via verbal echo and direct quotation, the author of Hebrews shows himself to be deeply rooted in dominical and apostolic tradition (cf. Mark 14:61–62; 16:19; Matt 26:63–64; Luke 22:67–70; Acts 2:32–36; 5:30–31; Rom 8:34; 1 Cor 15:24–25; Eph 1:19–21; Col 3:1; 1 Pet 3:22). He develops this tradition in an original manner by mingling his allusions to Psalm 110:1 with quotations of and allusions to v. 4 of the same psalm ("The Lord has sworn and will not repent, 'You are a priest forever, according to the order of Melchizedek'") and by connecting Christ's priestly self-offering to his exaltation to heaven (cf. Heb 1:3, 13; 5:6, 10; 6:20; 7:3, 11, 17, 21, 24–25, 28; 8:1; 10:11–14; 12:2). To suppose that the author of Hebrews refers Psalm 110:1 to Christ's "kingly office" and v. 4 to his high priesthood, as Simon Kistemaker does (*The Psalm Citations in the Epistle to the Hebrews* [Eugene, Ore.: Wipf & Stock, 1961], 86), is simplistic. Christ's session at the right hand of God is integral and vital to his high priesthood (see especially Heb 10:11–14). On the New Testament and early Christian use of Psalm 110, see Martin Hengel, *Studies in Early Christology* (Edinburgh: T&T Clark, 1995), 119–225; and David M. Hay, *Glory at the Right Hand: Psalm 110 in Early Christianity* (Nashville: Abingdon, 1973).

These references to Christ's session at God's right hand raise the question why the Son of God, who has already been described as "the reflection of [God's] glory and the imprint of his substance" (v. 3a), should need to be exalted at all. How and why did he descend to a status lower than that of the angels in the first place? It is to this question that the author of Hebrews turns in chapter 2, where he explains that, in order to become "a merciful and faithful high priest" and "to atone for the sins of the people" (v. 17), it was necessary for the Son to have a share in human "blood and flesh" (v. 14)—that is, to assume humanity in a mortal state.

It is in this context that the author quotes and comments on a few lines from Psalm 8 according to the Septuagint. We read:

> For it was not to angels that he subjected the world to come, of which we speak. But somewhere someone has testified, saying:
>
> What is man that you remember him,
> or the son of man that you look after him?
> You made him (for) a little (while) less than the angels,
> with glory and honor you crowned him;
> you subjected all things under his feet.
>
> In subjecting "all things," he left nothing that was not subjectable to him. Now we do not yet see all things subjected to him, but we do see Jesus, who "for a little while was made less than the angels," that by the grace of God he might taste death for everyone, [and who] on account of the suffering of death [has been] "crowned with glory and honor."[17]

The verb ὑποτάσσειν ("to subject") occurs five times in this short passage, binding together introduction, quotation, and comment. The introduction rejects a tenet that some of the author's intended audience must have held—namely, that God has subjected the eschatological kingdom, or "world to come," to angels. Next, the author has carefully delimited his quotation of Psalm 8 so that it concludes with the words "you subjected all things under his feet." The antecedent of "his" is clearly "man," who is also called "son of man." So, the author's first point is that, within God's master plan, man has a higher dignity and destiny than the angels, for God has "subjected" the whole creation ("all things") to him. Building on this point, the author makes a

17 The syntax of this long sentence is awkward. I have arranged the clauses in the translation to reflect the fact that ὅπως χάριτι θεοῦ ὑπὲρ παντὸς γεύσηται θανάτου must logically follow upon ἠλαττωμένον.

second point in the comment section. At present, when we look at the world around us, "we do not yet see all things subjected to him"—that is, to man in general.[18] "But we *do* see Jesus" already exalted and glorified over the whole creation. Note that here, for the first time in the homily, the author refers to Christ by his human name, Jesus. The implication is clearly that the incarnate Son represents the whole of humanity and has already lived out man's vocation and achieved man's destiny.

This identification of Jesus as the representative of humanity enables the author of Hebrews to give the anthropological Psalm 8 a Christological interpretation. In the few words quoted from the psalm, the author of Hebrews has discovered a précis of the Christ event and the beginning of an explanation for why the Son of God became "son of man." In the original Hebrew of Psalm 8, the words, "You made him a little less than gods," are reinforced by the words that immediately follow: "with glory and honor you crowned him." To be only a little less than gods is to occupy a position of honor. This is the echo parallelism characteristic of much biblical poetry. But as the author of the Epistle to the Hebrews reads the Septuagint version of Psalm 8, with its ambiguous adverbial phrase βραχύ τι, the same poetic couplet sounds more like contrast parallelism.[19]

> You made him *for a little while* less than the angels,
> [but afterwards] with glory and honor you crowned him.

18 The syntax, rhetorical structure, and logical argumentation of vv. 8b–9 require us to identify the antecedent of αὐτῷ ("to him") as ἄνθρωπος ("man") in v. 6. In summarizing the argument for this interpretation, Ellingworth correctly notes that the frontloading of τὸν δὲ . . . 'Ιησοῦν in v. 9 "strongly suggests a contrast with some other figure, namely 'man.'" See *Epistle to the Hebrews*, 150. Further on in his discussion, however, he rejects this interpretation, maintaining that "the balance of evidence" suggests that "the primary reference is to Christ" (151–52). Ellingworth's blind spot here is both hermeneutical and theological. He understands neither the relationship between literal sense and spiritual sense in the author's interpretation of Psalm 8, nor the relationship between anthropology and Christology in the author's theology. Albert Vanhoye, on the other hand, insightfully observes with regard to v. 5: "The author could have continued his sentence by saying, '*But it is to Christ* that God subjected the world to come.' He did not do so. Why? Because he wanted to give a more complete and more complex answer, based on a text from Scripture that speaks of humankind's calling." *The Letter to the Hebrews: A New Commentary* (New York: Paulist, 2015), 72. This comment gives the author of Hebrews his due for correctly understanding the literal-anthropological sense of Psalm 8, its spiritual-Christological sense, and the close, organic relationship between them.

19 Attridge, *Epistle to the Hebrews*, 72. The conventional terms—"synonymous parallelism" and "antithetical parallelism"—are misleading and have long outlived their usefulness. For a helpful introduction to Hebrew poetic parallelism, see Adele Berlin, "Parallelism," *ABD* 5.155–62.

Read Christologically, the two parts of the couplet now narrate the two poles of the Christ event. "You made him for a little while less than angels" refers to the Son's *temporary descent* in the incarnation, while "with glory and honor you crowned him" recounts his *permanent exaltation* in the resurrection and ascension.[20]

In his comment on this passage, the author of Hebrews has supplied the middle term between these two poles: the Lord's passion. He explains that the incarnation took place so that Christ "might taste death for everyone," and that the exaltation occurred "on account of the suffering of death." It is the burden of the next several chapters of the homily to explain further why Christ's passion was a fitting part of God's plan and what it accomplished. The long and short of it is that the Son of God "took a share of blood and flesh" (2:14) so that, as high priest and victim, he could make a definitive self-offering in expiation of human sins and inaugurate a new and better covenant in his blood, by which our consciences would be cleansed of "dead works" so that we might "worship the living God" (9:14).

Some scholars have assumed that this Christological interpretation of Psalm 8 entails an abandonment of the psalm's original anthropological meaning.[21] Others have correctly noted that in this context the author of Hebrews is concerned with Jesus Christ precisely *as man* and as "the true representative of humanity."[22] When we look at humanity generally, or even at God's chosen people Israel, "we do not yet see all things subjected" to man. Sin and the "fear of death," by which the devil holds man in bondage, have

20 Some commentators take v. 7a ("you made him for a little while less than the angels") to refer only to Christ's suffering, not to his incarnation: Aquinas, *In Heb.* c. 2, lect. 2; Ellingworth, *Epistle to the Hebrews*, 154; Craig R. Koester, *Hebrews: A New Translation with Introduction and Commentary*, AYB 36 (New Haven: Yale University Press, 2001), 216–17, 222. Others correctly recognize that, according to the descent-ascent schema operative in key NT passages (Rom 10:6–7; Phil 2:6–11; Eph 4:7–10), the Son's abasement begins with the incarnation, even if it is completed in his suffering and death: Vanhoye, *Letter to the Hebrews*, 73; Chris L. De Wet, "The Messianic Interpretation of Psalm 8:4–6 in Hebrews 2:6–9," part 2, in Human and Steyn, *Psalms and Hebrews*, 116.

21 E.g., Hans Windisch, *Der Hebräerbrief* (Tübingen: J. C. B. Mohr/Paul Siebeck, 1913), 22; Gerda de Villiers, "Reflections on Creation and Humankind in Psalm 8, the Septuagint, and Hebrews," in *Psalms and Hebrews*, ed. Human and Steyn, 80–82.

22 Bruce, *Epistle to the Hebrews*, 2nd ed., 74. Cf. Kistemaker, *Psalm Citations*, 102–7; Brevard S. Childs, "Psalm 8 in the Context of the Christian Canon," *Interpretation* 23, no. 1 (1969): 20–31; Dale F. Leschert, *Hermeneutical Foundations of Hebrews: A Study in the Validity of the Epistle's Interpretation of Some Core Citations from the Psalms* (Lewiston, N.Y.: Edwin Mellen, 1994), 115; De Wet, "Messianic Interpretation," 122–24; and, tentatively, Attridge, *Epistle to the Hebrews*, 75.

prevented man from living out his true identity and vocation (2:14). This is why the Son of God "had to be made like his brethren in all things" in the incarnation (2:17) and in the course of his life in the flesh was "tested like us in all things" but "without sin" (4:15). As our "forerunner" (6:20) and "the pioneer of our salvation," he has been "perfected" in his humanity through suffering (2:10; 5:8–9). And so, while we do not yet see all things subjected to man generally, "we do see Jesus," exalted above the angels in his humanity and "crowned with glory and honor" (2:9). Those who "approach God through him" (7:25) will likewise live out their true identity and vocation as human persons.

Finally, it is important to note that in Hebrews 2:5–9 the author adopts the perspective of realized eschatology. God has "subjected the world to come" to man in principle, and this subjection has already been realized in Jesus Christ, whom we "now" see (by the vision of faith) crowned with glory and honor at God's right hand. The author uses the phrase "the world to come" to refer to the eschatological kingdom as already present, just as he elsewhere says that the baptized have already tasted of "the powers of the age to come" (6:5).[23] Furthermore, he has gone out of his way to conclude his quotation from Psalm 8 with the clause "you subjected all things under his feet," which serves as the poetic echo and reinforcement of the clause "with glory and honor you crowned him" (2:7b–8a).[24] In the author's anthropological-Christological interpretation of Psalm 8, both clauses refer to the exaltation that has already taken place: of man (in principle) at creation, of Christ (in accomplished fact) at the resurrection and ascension.

Contrary to what some commentators hold, therefore, Hebrews 2:5–9 is not especially concerned with the fact that the subjection of all things to Christ is not yet complete and will not in fact be complete until all his enemies have been placed under his feet.[25] When the author of Hebrews wishes

23 A different perspective is found in 13:14, where Christians "seek" the city that is "to come," but in 12:22 the author says that Christians "have [already] come" to the heavenly Jerusalem. How exactly to understand the phrase "the good things to come" (10:1 and possibly 9:11) is a more complicated matter and involves a text-critical crux that we cannot discuss here.

24 The author has eliminated LXX Psalm 8:7a—"You established him over the works of your hands"—which did not serve his Christological interpretation. In this way he constructs a tricolon (a poetic line consisting of three segments or "cola") out of Psalm 8:6+7b. The relationship of the A-colon to the B-colon is contrast parallelism, but the relationship of the B-colon to the C-colon is echo parallelism. In other words, the C-colon reinforces the B-colon. It is incorrect to view the B-colon as the "already" and the C-colon as the "not yet."

25 Attridge, *Epistle to the Hebrews*, 70; Ellingworth, *Epistle to the Hebrews*, 146.

to focus on that fact, he does not quote Psalm 8 but rather adapts Psalm 110:1b—"*until* his enemies are made a stool under his feet" (Heb 10:13)—which he clearly understands to look toward the parousia.[26] The contrast at the heart of Hebrews 2:5–9 is not between two stages in the subjection of all things to Christ—incomplete and complete—but between the subjection of all things to man at creation and the subjection of all things to Christ at the resurrection. The former is not yet realized for man in general, but the latter has indeed been realized on man's behalf by Christ our representative.

PSALM 40 IN THE OLD TESTAMENT

We turn now to the citation of Psalm 40:7–9 in Hebrews 10:5–10, and we begin once again by looking at the psalm text according to the original Hebrew and in its Old Testament context.

Psalm 40 is a classic expression of *ʿănāwîm* piety.[27] The "afflicted one" (*ʿānî*) who speaks in this psalm has learned the secret of waiting upon Yahweh, humbly trusting in him in the midst of suffering and persecution (vv. 2–5, 12–16). Through the teaching of the prophets he has come to understand that Yahweh does not desire animal sacrifices and grain offerings for their own sake but has created man to hear and obey his word (vv. 7–8).[28] Though he lives under the old covenant, this worshipper of Yahweh has received the grace to internalize the Mosaic law to some extent and can honestly say that his desire is to do what is pleasing to God (v. 9). God has placed a "new song" of praise in his heart (v. 4).

The three verses of Psalm 40 to be quoted in Hebrews 10 read as follows according to the original Hebrew.

> Sacrifice and offering you have not desired,
> [but] ears you have dug for me.
> Holocaust and sin offering you have not required;

26 Paul quotes Ps 8:7b in conjunction with an allusion to Ps 110:1b in a context that requires both to be understood in terms of future eschatology (1 Cor 15:23–28), but this fact should not determine the interpretation of Heb 2:5–9. The author of Hebrews uses Ps 8:7b in a manner more akin to that found in Eph 1:22, where the perspective of the whole passage is decidedly that of realized eschatology.

27 See chapter 1 in this volume.

28 Cf. 1 Sam 15:22–23; Isa 1:10–20; Jer 7:21–23; Hos 6:6; Amos 5:21–24; Mic 6:6–8; Ps 50:7–23; 51:18–21.

> then I said, "Behold, I have come!
> In the scroll of the book it is written for me;
> to do your good pleasure, my God, is my desire;
> your law is deep within me."

Strange as it may seem, biblical Hebrew has no word to refer to the living human "body" as an organically unified whole. This is why the Old Testament authors, when referring to bodily actions and attributes, sometimes employ synecdoche, by which one part of the body represents the whole. For example, Proverbs 7:11 says of the adulterous woman that "her feet never stay at home." We are not, of course, to imagine two disembodied feet mincing seductively down the street, but to understand that the whole person does so. Not only is there is a charming concreteness in such *pars pro toto* figures of speech, but they sometimes convey profound anthropological truths. In the passage with which we are concerned, the statement "ears you have dug for me" means roughly, "you have designed me to hear and obey your word."

It is helpful to note how this affirmation factors into the poetic parallelism of the passage. In the contrast parallelism of the first couplet, the claim that God has not desired animal sacrifices or grain offerings is completed by the idea that he has created the human person to receive and respond to divine revelation. Is there not here already a hint that the pious Israelite who comes to the temple to offer sacrifice should in some sense present *himself* as an offering to Yahweh? This hint is confirmed as we move to the next couplet, where "sacrifice and offering you have not desired" finds its echo in "holocaust and sin offering you have not required," and "ears you have dug for me" is reinforced by "then I said, 'Behold, I have come!'" Quoting and commenting upon a statement made by Augustine of Hippo, Thomas Aquinas teaches us: "'Every visible sacrifice is a sacrament, or sacred sign, of the invisible sacrifice.' And the invisible sacrifice is that by which a man offers his spirit to God."[29]

The psalmist seems to have understood that Yahweh had in fact required of Israel the whole battery of temple rites, including sacrifices and offerings, holocausts and sin offerings. Like the authors of Psalms 50 and 51, he was influenced by the prophetic critique of sacrifice but did not understand the prophets to wish to undermine or abolish these ceremonies. The point was rather to insist that sacrifices be offered more authentically—that is, in

29 Aquinas, *STh* III, q. 22, a. 2, corp. Cf. Augustine, *De civitate Dei* 10.5.

conjunction with a life of justice and steadfast love.[30] Ultimately, these rites represent the fact that man has been made to receive creation from the hand of God and to render it back to him. As Thomas notes, "in the oblation of sacrifices man bore witness that God is the first principle of the creation of things and the last end to which all things are to be rendered back." In this regard Thomas aptly cites a prayer of King David: "For everything comes from you, and what we have received from your hand we give back to you."[31] But to receive creation from the hand of the Creator ultimately means to receive ourselves, even our bodies, from him and to make a suitable offering of ourselves back to him. Thus, the apostle Paul writes, "I exhort you . . . to present your bodies as a living sacrifice, holy and well-pleasing to God, which is your rational service" (Rom 12:1).

"A BODY YOU HAVE FURNISHED FOR ME"

The Septuagint translator of Psalm 40 (LXX Psalm 39), recognizing that Greek-speaking Jews might not readily grasp the Hebraic expression "ears you have dug for me," devised a fine paraphrase: "Sacrifice and offering you did not desire, but a *body* you furnished for me."[32] The Greek word σῶμα ("body") refers to man's fleshly dimension, not simply as so many members, but as a unified, organic whole. It is this whole that is designed for obedience. The body gives man, a rational creature made to the image of God, a way of

30 Pss 50:8; 51:18–19. The views of the various prophets and even of the Priestly School itself are more difficult to determine. For a brief treatment, see Gary A. Anderson, "Sacrifice and Sacrificial Offerings (OT)," *ABD* 5:881–82.

31 Aquinas, *STh* I-II, q. 102, a. 3, corp.; 1 Chron 29:14; cf. Deut 26:10.

32 The text of the three great LXX codices (Vaticanus, Sinaiticus, and Alexandrinus) reads σῶμα δὲ κατηρτίσω μοι, just as in Heb 10:5. The Gallican Psalter has *aures autem perfecisti mihi*, which presumably reflects a Greek *Vorlage* ὠτία δὲ κατηρτίσω μοι. Ellingworth considers it "most likely" that this was the original reading of LXX and that σῶμα δὲ κατηρτίσω μοι is the result of an inadvertent scribal error (*Epistle to the Hebrews*, 500). The retroverted reading ὠτία δὲ κατηρτίσω μοι is also given in the text of Alfred Rahlfs and Robert Hanhart, eds., *Septuaginta: Id est Vetus Testamentum graece iuxta LXX interpretes* (Stuttgart: Deutsche Bibelgesellschaft, 2006). But this hypothetical reconstruction of the text of LXX leaves unexplained the Greek translator's choice of the verb κατηρτίσω, rather than the expected ὤρυξας, as well as the absence of the reconstructed reading from all Greek witnesses to LXX, including the three great codices. The Gallican Psalter reading much more likely reflects a simple one-word adjustment on Jerome's part (*aures* in place of *corpus*) in the direction of the Hebrew (Proto-Masoretic) text with which he was familiar. Cf. his *Psalterium iuxta Hebraeos*: *aures fodisti mihi*.

acting concretely and meaningfully in the world of time and space. Before we consider how the author of Hebrews takes this Septuagint text up into his argument, it behooves us to reflect briefly on the theological significance of the body.

The human body has a special relation to the rational soul with its faculties of intellect and will. According to Gregory of Nyssa (as noted above in chapter 6), the human body differs from those of other animals insofar as the Creator has prepared it to be an apt "instrument" (ὄργανον) for the exercise of reason. For example, the mouths of beasts are designed primarily for feeding and so produce only inarticulate sounds such as a bleat or bark, but the human mouth is configured to produce the much more varied sounds that are necessary for intelligible speech.[33] In like manner, the suppleness and dexterity of human hands make them apt for every art of human ingenuity and to do the bidding of reason.[34] Thomas Aquinas teaches that "the body is proportioned to the soul as matter is to its own form" and that the human body is thus apt to be perfected by a rational soul.[35] According to John Paul II, man's body manifests his spiritual interiority and "expresses the human, personal 'I.'"[36]

The human body also has a special relation to the cosmos. The Old Testament presents the physical universe, the earth in particular, as God's singular *gift* to "the sons of men" (Ps 115:16). According to John Paul, "every creature bears within itself the sign of the original and fundamental gift" of existence, but *man* "appears in the visible world as the highest expression of the divine gift, because he bears within himself the inner dimension of the gift."[37] The human person discovers this interior dimension by discerning the "spousal meaning of the body," which is "the power to express love: precisely that love in which the human person becomes a gift and—through this gift—fulfills the very meaning of his being and existence."[38] The human body "has been created to transfer into the visible reality of the world the mystery hidden from eternity in God, and thus to be a sign of it." "In man, created in the image

33 Gregory of Nyssa, *De hominis opificio* 8:8–9:1 (PG 44:148–49).

34 *De hominis opificio* 8:2; 8:8 (PG 44:144, 148).

35 Aquinas, *STh* III, q. 5, a. 4, corp.; cf. q. 4, a. 1 ad 2.

36 John Paul II, *Man and Woman*, 176 (*TOB* 12.4).

37 John Paul II, 180, 203 (*TOB* 13.4; 19.3).

38 John Paul II, 185–86 (*TOB* 15.1).

of God, the very sacramentality of creation, the sacramentality of the world, was thus in some way revealed."[39]

John Paul's insights have a certain affinity to the venerable notion of man as microcosm. Each human person fulfills his vocation to receive the whole creation as a gift from the hand of God most essentially by receiving his or her concrete body-soul existence as God's gift. We consecrate creation to God by the way we live in the body, making rational use of the good things of creation out of love for God and neighbor. Finally, bodily death presents us with our optimal opportunity to render the gift of creation back to God, for it is only in death that we can make a definitive act of trustful self-surrender and love.

HEBREWS 10:5–10

The pertinence of these reflections on the body will become apparent when we examine precisely how the author of Hebrews introduces, cites, and comments on Psalm 40:7–9. The introduction and citation read as follows:

> Therefore, coming into the world [κόσμον] he says,
> "Sacrifice and offering you did not desire,
> but a body [σῶμα] you furnished for me.
> Holocausts and sin offering you took no pleasure in;
> then I said, 'Behold, I have come—
> in the scroll of the book it has been written concerning me—
> to do your will, O God.'" (Heb 10:5–7)

Remarkably, in these lines from an ancient Israelite prayer the author of Hebrews hears words that the Son spoke to the Father upon entering the created world in the incarnation. As the apostle Peter teaches us, the Holy Spirit who inspired the authors of the Old Testament was "the Spirit of Christ bearing witness in advance" concerning the Christ event (1 Pet 1:11). As in Psalm 8, here too in Psalm 40 the author of Hebrews finds a précis of the Christ event. The only difference is that in this case the psalmist is understood to speak not simply about Christ but *ex persona Christi*.[40]

39 John Paul II, 203 (*TOB* 19.4–5).

40 For a prosopological interpretation of this passage, see Matthew W. Bates, *The Birth of the Trinity: Jesus, God, and Spirit in New Testament and Early Christian Interpretation of the Old Testament* (Oxford: Oxford University Press, 2015), 85–87.

Of special importance is the way the author of Hebrews brings the words κόσμος and σῶμα into close correlation. The Son of God is furnished with a σῶμα in the Virgin's womb so that he can enter the κόσμος. Like σῶμα, the Greek term κόσμος has no real synonym in Biblical Hebrew. It designates the created "world" as a beautiful, well-ordered, and well-integrated whole. At the same time, in the New Testament it often denotes the "world" of human society, where God's good creation has been defiled by sin and stands in need of redemption. The conceptual similarity between σῶμα as integral whole and κόσμος as integral whole lends some credence to reading this passage of Hebrews in terms of man as microcosm. In the body-soul humanity furnished for him, the Son of God recapitulates the created cosmos even as he enters it.

There are thus deep connections between the Christological-anthropological-cosmological interpretation of Psalm 40 in Hebrews 10 and the Christological-anthropological-cosmological interpretation of Psalm 8 in Hebrews 2. But since major developments in the overall doctrinal argument of the epistle occur in the intervening chapters, we need to take cognizance of a couple of these developments in order to appreciate how the citation of Psalm 40 functions within this argument and may even represent its culmination.

In the first place, there is the notion that the paschal mystery constitutes a high-priestly self-offering. That Jesus Christ in his humanity is the definitive high priest who has taken his seat at the right hand of God is implied in the exordium (1:3), thematized near the end of chapter two (2:17), and carefully developed step by step in chapters three through ten. The author explicitly identifies this as the "main point" of his discourse (8:1). What can be easily overlooked, however, is the concurrent development of the idea that Christ is not only priest but sacrificial victim, and that his priestly act is a self-offering. Once we are alerted to this theme, however, we begin to see that this is the thread of the argument that leads us into the heart of the saving mystery.

This definitive self-offering can be made only by one who is both true God and true man. Because it is the Son who offers himself to the Father "through the eternal Spirit," his self-offering is the visible manifestation of the Trinitarian mystery (9:14). At the same time, this mystery can enter the world of time and space to be manifested in human history only if the Son assumes a human body and a rational soul. If John Paul is correct to say that the human body "has been created to transfer into the visible reality of the world the mystery hidden from eternity in God,"[41] this would be supremely true of the human flesh and blood of Jesus Christ. At the beginning of the Tertia Pars, when addressing the question of whether it was fitting for God to become incarnate, Thomas Aquinas says that "it would seem most fitting that by means of visible things the invisible things of God should be manifested; for to this end the whole world was made."[42]

But even with respect to the human operation of Christ, the Epistle to the Hebrews presents his self-offering as having an interior dimension as well as an exterior one. In other words, the interior or invisible dimension of Christ's high priestly service is by no means limited to the operation of the divinity properly speaking. It is located also and especially in the operation of his created rational soul as moved by the divine person. His self-offering was an offering made "in the days of his flesh" with "a loud cry and tears" (the exterior dimension), but it was at the same time an act of "prayer," of "reverence," and of "obedience" (the interior dimension). Indeed, though he is eternal Son, in his human soul Christ "learned obedience through the things he suffered, and having been perfected, became the cause of eternal salvation for all who obey him" (5:7–9). It is this dual aspect of our Lord's self-offering—interior and exterior—that the author of Hebrews develops more fully by way of his exegesis of Psalm 40.

The second major development of the author's argument to which we must attend is his teaching about the relationship between old covenant and new covenant. This theme, too, is announced in the opening lines of the homily (1:1–2) and developed step by step in the ensuing chapters. In the course of this development, the author explains why Christ's high priesthood according to the order of Melchizedek is superior to the priesthood instituted in accordance with the Mosaic law and how Christ's blood accomplishes what the blood of bulls and goats never could—namely, the perfecting of the worshipper through the cleansing of his or her conscience. This exposition culminates in chapter nine, where the most solemn of the Mosaic rites, that of Yom Kippur, is presented as a prefigurement of the paschal event.

Then, at the beginning of chapter 10, in the verses immediately preceding the passage with which we are concerned, this theme of the relationship between old and new receives a hermeneutical refocusing. Here the author tells us that the Mosaic law possesses "a shadow of the good things to come,

41 John Paul II, *Man and Woman*, 203 (*TOB* 19.4).

42 Aquinas, *STh* III, q. 1, a. 1, sc.

not the very image of the things" (10:1). It was in large part on the basis of this passage that Ambrose of Milan would later formulate his classic threefold distinction between *umbra, imago*, and *veritas*, whereby "shadow" refers to the old law, "image" refers to the new law as present in history—that is, in the Christ event and in the life of the Church on earth—and "truth" refers to that same life as we shall possess it in heaven.[43] In the present context we need only attend to the way the category "shadow" (σκιά) helps the author of Hebrews to express both the limitation of the Mosaic rites and their positive contribution to the divine economy. Their limitation lay in the fact that they were unable to take away sin and perfect the worshipper (10:1, 4). They were in that sense a *mere* shadow of that which was to come. At the same time and more positively, they provided for Israel a salutary annual "remembrance of sins" (10:3), even as they *foreshadowed* the definitive high-priestly self-offering by which Christ would deal effectively with sin.

In light of these two developments in the author's argument—namely, the notion of a high-priestly self-offering, and the relationship between old law and new law—we may now return to his citation of Psalm 40:7–9. And at this point we should take careful note of how the author has edited his source text. Where Septuagint Psalm 39:9 says, "to do your will, my God, I have desired," the Epistle to the Hebrews has written simply, "to do your will, O God." With the omission of the word ἐβουλήθην, "I have desired," the infinitival phrase "to do your will" must now be construed with what precedes it. As we shall see, the author wishes us to take the infinitive "to do your will" as the verbal complement of "Behold, I have come." The intervening clause—"in the scroll of the book it has been written concerning me"—is then understood as parenthetical.

Having quoted his text, the author of Hebrews now supplies a brief exegesis:

> Saying first, "Sacrifices and offerings and holocausts and sin offerings you neither desired nor took pleasure in"—which things are offered according to the law—he then has said, "Behold, I have come to do your will." He takes away the first in order to establish the second. (10:8–9)

43 "The shadow accordingly came first, the image followed, the truth is yet to be. The shadow is in the law, the true image in the gospel, the truth in heaven." Ambrose of Milan, *Enarratio in Psalmum* 38, no. 25; PL 14:1101 (*Primum igitur umbra praecessit, secuta est imago, erit veritas. Umbra in lege, imago vero in evangelio, veritas in coelestibus*).

Here the author of Hebrews has rearranged his poetic source text, transforming it into linear prose. By combining "sacrifice and offering" with its poetic echo, "holocaust and sin offering," the author creates a list of four types of sacrifice, a list that evokes the whole system of sacrificial rites under the Mosaic law. Further, by pluralizing the nouns—"sacrifices . . . offerings . . . holocausts . . . sin offerings"—he creates the impression of a great multitude of old covenant sacrifices over against the single and definitive self-offering of Christ. According to Paul Ellingworth, this procedure has the effect of "destroying the [poetic] parallelism, which does not seem to have been appreciated by the author."[44] I disagree. In fact, the author of Hebrews demonstrates that he has understood the parallelism and theology of Psalm 40 quite well.

In his paraphrase of the psalm text, the author of Hebrews also eliminates the parenthetical clause "in the scroll of the book it has been written concerning me." This omission enables him to join the verb "I have come" (ἥκω) directly to its infinitival complement, "to do your will." In this way he distills the prayer of the Israelite psalmist down to its very essence and, by presenting it as spoken *ex persona Christi*, gives us a remarkably succinct précis of the Christ event: "Behold, I have come to do your will, my God." According to this formulation, which has deep theological affinities to the Gospel of John, the Son of God has come into the world in the incarnation in order to do the will of the Father throughout his earthly life, culminating in his passion. This is the saving mystery. With the divine authority given to him as the incarnate Son, our Lord "takes away" the ceremonies of the old law in order to establish this new covenant in his body and blood.

Up to this point in his exegesis of Psalm 40, the author of Hebrews has made no reference to the clause, "a body you have furnished for me." He has held it in reserve for the passage's solemn conclusion: "By this 'will' we have been sanctified through the offering of the 'body' of Jesus Christ once and for all" (10:10). This summary statement highlights the dual aspect of the Lord's self-offering, interior and exterior, by reiterating two nouns from LXX Psalm 39: θέλημα ("will") and σῶμα ("body"). The θέλημα referred to here is the incarnate Son's fully human decision to do the divine will, which he accomplishes visibly, concretely, and historically in the σῶμα that he assumed in the Virgin's womb upon entering the κόσμος.

44 Ellingworth, *Epistle to the Hebrews*, 503.

THE FIRST SORROWFUL MYSTERY

To help us penetrate the mystery to which Scripture refers here, we may turn to Thomas Aquinas's teaching about Christ's human will in the Tertia Pars, question 18. The human *voluntas* in Christ, as in every man, is one rational power that performs two species of act. The first of these species of act is called the "simple will" or "will as nature." In this case the will is "borne along simply and absolutely" towards the end "as towards that which is good in itself." The second species of act is called the "counseling will" or "will as reason." In this case the will is directed towards the means not as that which is good in itself but as that which is good in relation to an end.[45] Since this second act, as well as the first, is in Christ, Thomas affirms that Christ had "free will" (*liberum arbitrium*) and could choose this or that means to an end.[46] In addition, Thomas notes that the "sensitive appetite" or "sensuality," which naturally obeys reason and is thus "rational by participation," may be considered "a will by participation." This too was in Christ, for "the Son of God assumed human nature together with all things that pertain to the perfection of that nature."[47]

Now, "in the days of his flesh" (Heb 5:7) the Son of God permitted the powers of his humanity to do what was proper to each of them. Thus, when he faced the prospect of being brutally tortured and executed, his "will of sensuality naturally [fled] from sensible pains and bodily injury," while his "will as nature," or "simple will," likewise rejected "those things which are contrary to nature and evil in themselves," including death. In these two respects, Thomas dares to say, Christ "was able to will other than God willed."[48] At the same time, even God did not will Christ's suffering and death "in themselves" (*secundum se*) but "as ordered to the end of human salvation" (*ex ordine ad finem humanae salutis*). And Christ in his counseling will, or will as reason, likewise willed these for the sake of our salvation. Indeed, "according as his will operated in the mode of reason, he always willed the same as God."[49]

Thus, in the garden of Gethsemane our Lord experienced a real conflict between the aversion to suffering and death that was good and natural to

45 Aquinas, *STh* III, q. 18, a. 3, corp.

46 *STh* III, q. 18, a. 4, corp.

47 *STh* III, q. 18, a. 2, corp.

48 *STh* III, q. 18, a. 5, corp.

49 *STh* III, q. 18, a. 5, corp.

his sensuality and simple will, on the one hand, and what the divine will proposed to him as the means ordered to the end of our salvation on the other hand. And so he prayed, "My Father, if it be possible, let this cup pass from me" (Matt 26:39a). But this conflict was resolved in his counseling will, by which, in perfect conformity to the divine will, he chose to drink the cup of suffering for the sake of our salvation. And so he completed his prayer, "Nevertheless, not as I will, but as you do" (26:39b).

What we glimpse here in the First Sorrowful Mystery is the very essence of prayer, which Thomas defines as "a certain unfolding of one's will before God."[50] Although Thomas does not regard prayer as the proper office of priests, and he hesitates to view Christ's prayer in the garden as a sacerdotal act on his own behalf, he recognizes that this is precisely how the author of the Epistle to the Hebrews views it. In a passage explicitly concerned with Christ's high priesthood, the author of Hebrews evokes the Gethsemane narrative, saying that our Lord "with a loud cry and tears *offered* petitions and supplications *to the one who was able to save him from death*" (Heb 5:6–7). Deferring to the authority of this passage, Thomas is willing to say that Christ "participated in the effect of his own priesthood," at least "according to the passibility of the flesh."[51]

In conclusion, and moving now beyond Thomas Aquinas's reflections, we may briefly consider why it is especially fitting that our Lord should accomplish our salvation by means of a prayer that places the good and natural human aversion to death in subordination to the divine will, and by means of an act of obedience in which he makes the handing over of his body to death a definitive priestly self-offering. And here we must consider a much earlier decision, made in another garden. The original temptation called into question God's motives by insinuating that his commandment was aimed at withholding godlikeness from man so as to jealously guard his own prerogatives (Gen 3:4–5). Succumbing to this temptation, our first parents allowed their trust in their Creator to die in their hearts and "conceived a distorted image of God" (*CCC* 397, 399). Now viewing godlikeness as "something to be grasped" (cf. Phil 2:6), they could no longer accept their status as creatures.

Indeed, man could no longer receive creation as a gift from the hand of the Creator and no longer receive his own body as the sign of the gift of existence. Instead, he experienced a tragic alienation from the physical

50 *STh* III, q. 21, a. 1, corp. (*oratio est quaedam explicatio propriae voluntatis apud Deum*).

51 *STh* III, q. 22, a. 4, ad 1.

world—including his own body and the bodies of others—now viewed as objects for appropriation and domination. This alienation involves what John Paul II calls "cosmic shame"—that is, fallen man's "awareness of being defenseless" in the presence of the rest of creation, a sense of the vulnerability of his body "in the face of the processes of nature that operate with an inevitable determinism."[52] Man now experiences his mortality as a sign of his alienation from God and his mortal body as a field of cosmic resistance to all his plans and choices, above all to his desire to "be like God," but "without God, before God, and not in accordance with God."[53] According to the Epistle to the Hebrews, it is by this fear of death that the evil one holds man in bondage throughout his life (Heb 2:14–15).

Coming into the κόσμος, the Son of God received the mortal σῶμα furnished for him in the womb of the Virgin not as the sign of alienation and divine opposition but as the sign of the gift of existence. Made "for a little while less than the angels," he accepted the creaturehood of his own humanity and the mortality of his body, and as the incarnate Son he received the whole of creation from the hand of the Creator on our behalf (John 3:35). He "did not deem equality with God something to be grasped at" but through a lifetime of humble obedience, even unto death, he offered himself, and thus creation, back to the Father (Phil 2:6–8). In his humanity he experienced a good and natural aversion to suffering and death, but with perfect trust in the Father he discovered in biological death man's unique opportunity to make a total self-offering to God.

52 John Paul II, *Man and Woman*, 242 (*TOB* 27.4).

53 *CCC* 398; citing Maximus the Confessor, *Ambiguum* 10; PG 91:1156c (δίχα θεοῦ καὶ πρὸ θεοῦ καὶ οὐ κατὰ θεόν).

CHAPTER NINE

The Goods of Grace and Glory: Filial Adoption in Romans 8

According to its mundane usage in the Greco-Roman world, the word υἱοθεσία denotes the "adoption of a son," especially in order to secure an heir and to provide for one's old age.[1] The apostle Paul seems to have coined the theological usage whereby υἱοθεσία denotes the grace by which God brings human beings into a filial relationship with himself.[2] In

1 In this sense the word occurs with some frequency in inscriptions, literature, and nonliterary papyri, beginning in the second century BC. See LSJ 794b–95a, 1846b; and James Hope Moulton and George Milligan, *The Vocabulary of the Greek Testament, Illustrated from the Papyri and other Non-Literary Sources* (Grand Rapids: Eerdmans, 1930), 648b–49a.

2 BDAG 1024; W. von Martitz and E. Schweizer, υἱοθεσία in *TDNT* 8:397–99. On the Old Testament background, see especially James M. Scott, *Adoption as Sons of God: An Exegetical Investigation into the Background of Huiothesia in the Pauline Corpus*, Wissenschaftliche Untersuchungen zum Neuen Testament 2/48 (Tübingen: Mohr-Siebeck, 1992). The twentieth-century debate over whether we should look to the Greco-Roman world or to the Old Testament for the background to Paul's use of this word is resolved in the recognition that both backgrounds are operative but are so on two different levels of discourse. Paul is using the term υἱοθεσία metaphorically, applying the Greco-Roman concept of one human being's adoption of another to the biblical reality of God's establishment of a covenant relationship with human beings, his "adoption" of sons and daughters. The Greco-Roman background is thus relevant to the term's literal semantics, while the Old Testament background is relevant to its metaphorical usage. Whether or not the Old Testament contains references to the practice of *literal* adoption comparable to what we find in the Greco-Roman world is therefore irrelevant. Nor is it really telling that the Old Testament itself never actually uses a word meaning "adoption" to refer to God's election of Israel or of the house of David. That Paul can metaphorically apply the Greco-Roman term υἱοθεσία to Yahweh's election of Israel in an intelligible manner is patently clear from his use of the term in Rom 9:4, which recalls a whole trajectory of Old Testament passages, beginning with Exod 4:22. A similar conclusion is reached, after a helpful sketch of the history of interpretation, in James I. Cook, "The Concept of Adoption in the Theology of Paul," in *Saved by Hope: Essays in Honor of Richard C. Oudersluys*, ed. James I. Cook (Grand Rapids: Eerdmans, 1978), 133–44.

Romans 9:4 Paul uses this term to refer to God's election of Israel to a covenant relationship, placing it at the head of a list of Israel's divinely bestowed prerogatives. The remaining four New Testament occurrences of υἱοθεσία, which are likewise in the Pauline corpus, refer to the new covenant grace by which God makes us his sons and daughters in Christ (Rom 8:15, 23; Gal 4:5; Eph 1:5).[3]

In Romans 8, Paul uses the word υἱοθεσία ("filial adoption") in two different contexts. In verse 15 he speaks of "the Spirit of filial adoption" (πνεῦμα υἱοθεσίας) as something Christians have already received and by which we cry out "Abba, Father," but in verse 23 he refers to υἱοθεσία as something that we still await and identifies it with "the redemption of our bodies."[4] Douglas Moo, an exegete in the Reformed tradition, explains that the Spirit of filial adoption to which Paul refers in verse 15 is received "at the moment of justification" but that "this adoption is incomplete and partial ... until the body has been transformed."[5] Moo further observes that Paul's double use of υἱοθεσία in Romans 8 is typical of "the 'already–not yet' tension that pervades his theology."[6] Thomas Aquinas's explanation is similar. Verse 15 refers to our filial

3 Etymologically, υἱοθεσία is a compound noun formed of two elements: υἱο-, which is the root of the word υἱός ("son"); and -θεσία (a modification of θέσις, derived from the verb τίθημι), which means "adoption." As Paul uses the term, both parts of the compound are important. The first element, υἱο-, associates our adoptive *sonship* with Jesus's status as "Son of God" (ὁ υἱός τοῦ θεοῦ). Paul is emphatic that Christians are "sons of God" (υἱοὶ θεοῦ) and "coheirs with Christ" (Rom 8:14, 17; Gal 3:26; 4:6–7). His use of the Aramaic word "Abba" (Rom 8:15; Gal 4:6) suggests that we are invited to share something of Jesus's intimacy with, trust in, and affection for God (cf. Mark 14:36). At the same time, the second element, -θεσία, is crucially important inasmuch as it distinguishes our *adoptive* sonship from the divine Sonship of Christ. According to the axiom, Christ is Son of God by nature, while we are sons and daughters of God by grace. The Vulgate consistently renders υἱοθεσία with the phrase *adoptio filiorum*, a translation that nicely captures both truths. We are *filii in Filio*, but ours is a *filiatio adoptiva*, to borrow a phrase that Thomas Aquinas sometimes employs (e.g., *STh* III, q. 23, a. 2, ad 3).

4 In v. 23 the word υἱοθεσίαν (accusative of υἱοθεσία) is missing from some Greek manuscripts and other textual witnesses, especially representatives of the Western Text. Joseph Fitzmyer would omit it on the grounds that, according to v. 15, "Christians are already [in this life] adopted children of God." See Joseph A. Fitzmyer, SJ, *Romans: A New Translation with Introduction and Commentary*, AB 33 (New York: Doubleday, 1993), 510. But this apparent contradiction is no doubt the reason for the omission of υἱοθεσίαν from some witnesses, whereas Fitzmyer himself admits that "it is difficult to explain how it got into the text of most of the other Greek MSS" (510). Cf. C. E. B. Cranfield, *A Critical and Exegetical Commentary on the Epistle to the Romans*, vol. 2, ICC (Edinburgh: T&T Clark, 1979), 419n1.

5 Douglas J. Moo, *The Epistle to the Romans*, NICNT (Grand Rapids: Eerdmans, 1996), 521.

6 Moo, 501. Similarly, Cook, "Concept of Adoption," 139.

adoption as "initiated by the Holy Spirit justifying the soul," whereas verse 23 indicates that this adoption "will be consummated by the glorification of the body itself."[7] There is, then, a two-stage realization of υἱοθεσία, since by adopting human beings God admits them "to the goods of grace and glory" (*ad bona gratiae et gloriae*).[8]

This final chapter will consider the nature of filial adoption, its relation to the infusion of grace and charity at justification, and the dynamics of the believer's progress from the initiation of adoption to its consummation. The first two sections of the chapter will examine the treatment of these issues in Douglas Moo's *Epistle to the Romans* and in Thomas Aquinas's *Super epistolam ad Romanos* respectively. While Moo will serve as something of a foil for Aquinas, he is not merely that. Moo brings the tools and methods of modern biblical scholarship to the service of a serious, theological attempt to grasp Paul's argument as an integral whole, thus avoiding the atomistic and superficial treatment of the biblical text that is characteristic of some historical-critical exegesis. He thus proves to be a more able dialogue partner for Thomas than even many Catholic exegetes might be. Thomas's commentary, for its part, sheds considerable light on Paul's teaching on filial adoption, especially with regard to its nature and its relation to the infusion of grace and charity, but leaves Paul's teaching on "sanctification" (ἁγιασμός) insufficiently illuminated. To begin to fill this lacuna, a third section will deal with Thomas's discussion of the increase of charity in *Summa Theologiae* II-II, question 24. Like all good exegesis and theology, Thomas's interpretation of Paul does not constitute an end in itself but sends us back to the sacred text with new insights and further questions. Accordingly, the fourth and final section of the chapter will take a fresh look at Paul's teaching on filial adoption in Romans 8, with reference also to other parts of the Pauline corpus. Here I wish to expound the dynamics by which the believer makes progress toward the consummation of filial adoption in glory, and in doing so to account for the particular accent that Paul places on the role of the body and the place of suffering in the Christian life. My purpose throughout is to illuminate not simply the *thought* of Thomas or of Paul but the *thing itself*—namely, the grace of filial adoption which has been bestowed on us in Jesus Christ.

7 Thomas Aquinas, *In Rom.* c. 8, lect. 5. All translations of Aquinas's works in this chapter are my own and are based on the Latin texts at www.corpusthomisticum.org.

8 Thomas Aquinas, *STh* III, q. 23, a. 1, corp. and ad 1.

DOUGLAS MOO'S *EPISTLE TO THE ROMANS*

As we have seen, Douglas Moo and Thomas Aquinas agree that Paul's references to υἱοθεσία in Romans 8:15 and 8:23 point to two distinct moments in the redemption of the human person: the initiation of filial adoption and its consummation. However, once we begin to consider the precise nature of filial adoption and its relation to other dimensions of redemption such as justification, moral transformation, and the hope of attaining heavenly glory, major differences emerge between these two exegetes, both in the interpretation of the Epistle to the Romans and in the overall understanding of the mystery of redemption. We can arrive rather quickly at the heart of these differences between Moo and Aquinas if we begin in each case with the interpretation of Romans 5:1–11, which anticipates and lays the groundwork for chapter 8.[9] In particular, we need to attend to how each exegete understands Paul's statement that "the love of God has been poured into our hearts through the Holy Spirit" (5:5) as well as his teaching on "the hope of the glory of God"—that is, the assurance we have in Christ of attaining final salvation (5:2, 9-10). Moving on from this starting point, we shall consider how each exegete interprets Paul's teaching on filial adoption in Romans 8.

In his comment on Romans 5:5, Moo notes that the phrase "the love of God" (ἡ ἀγάπη τοῦ θεοῦ) can denote either God's love for us (subjective genitive) or our love for God (objective genitive). Moo considers it "certain" that we should construe Paul's grammar in the former manner, and he by no means understands Paul to refer to divine love as an infused virtue. What we are given, rather, is "the subjective certainty that God does love us."[10] The Father has demonstrated his love for us "in the objective, factual event of Christ's death on the cross," and this love is "experienced 'in the heart' by the believer" by the action of the Holy Spirit.[11] While Moo does not deny that this gift includes an "intellectual recognition of the fact of God's love," he accents the "internal, subjective—yes, even emotional—sensation within

9 Modern commentators, including Moo, recognize a strong thematic and structural link between Rom 5:1–11 and 8:1–39, but this link is especially obvious in the Latin text upon which Thomas is commenting. In 5:2, where the Greek text says that we boast "in the hope of the glory of God" (ἐπ' ἐλπίδι τῆς δόξης τοῦ θεοῦ), the Vulgate reads: "in the hope of the glory of the sons of God" (*in spe gloriae filiorum Dei*), a phrase that anticipates 8:18–25 in particular. Not surprisingly, Thomas's commentary on chapter 8 refers back to 5:1–11 several times.

10 Moo, *Epistle to the Romans*, 304.

11 Moo, 309.

the believer."[12] This interpretation fits the context of Romans 5:1–11 tolerably well and also has the merit of harmonizing nicely with 8:15–16, where Paul identifies the Holy Spirit as "the Spirit of filial adoption" who "bears witness with our spirit that we are children of God," thus prompting us to "cry out, 'Abba, Father.'" It is important to note, however, that Moo does not attempt to relate the Holy Spirit's gift of "the love of God" to the same Spirit's work of delivering the regenerate believer from the power of sin, though he readily acknowledges that such deliverance takes place.[13] In Moo's reading of Paul these two components of the Christian life seem to be extrinsically related, even though they both come from the Holy Spirit.

Moo's interpretation of "the love of God poured into our hearts" correlates with his dual conviction that justification by faith is a strictly forensic matter (not to be confused with the transformative power of the Spirit that *accompanies* justification) and that the justified believer possesses the absolute certainty of attaining salvation. Justification is God's "past declaration of acquittal pronounced over the sinner who believes in Christ," and there is an "unbreakable connection between the believer's justification and his or her salvation from the wrath of God still to be poured out in the last day."[14] The "already–not yet" tension characteristic of Christian existence in this life derives from the fact that on the one hand the "believer's acceptance of salvation" is "absolute and final," while on the other hand "salvation is not complete until the body is redeemed and glorified."[15] The "love of God poured into our hearts" mediates between justification and final salvation only in the sense of providing the subjective assurance that one *has been* justified and *will be* saved. It is not an infused virtue or principle of moral progress that moves one qualitatively closer to one's goal. While a certain level of "holy living" is made possible by the Holy Spirit and is in fact a "precondition" for attaining salvation, it is not in any sense a ground or cause of salvation.[16] In other words, "justification" and "sanctification" are not only quite distinct but also extrinsically related.

As for filial adoption, Moo interprets the υἱοθεσία referred to by Paul in Romans 8:15 as a status of sonship conferred at the moment of justification,

12 Moo, 304–5.

13 Moo, 494.

14 Moo, 310–11.

15 Moo, 311.

16 Moo, 494–95.

a status that gives the believer subjective "peace and security," while the completion of adoption spoken of in 8:23 is nothing less than the redemption of the body and is thus tantamount to final salvation.[17] And just as Moo understands the Holy Spirit's work of pouring God's love into our hearts (5:5) in terms of "subjective certainty," so his exegesis of the phrase πνεῦμα υἱοθεσίας in 8:15 emphasizes the "comforting conviction that we are God's own children." He explains: "Paul stresses that our awareness of God as Father comes not from rational consideration nor from external testimony alone but from a truth deeply felt and intensely experienced."[18] While the justified believer is "sadly conscious" of moral failings, he or she has no anxiety about whether final salvation will be achieved, and so the inward "groaning" of which Paul speaks in 8:23 is only the "frustrated longing for final deliverance" from sin, death, and wrath. While Moo occasionally refers to salvation, or adoption, as a "process," it is so only inasmuch as it consists of two moments of transition—justification and glorification—with the latter in some sense "completing" the former.[19] Though the interim between these two moments may be characterized by moral and spiritual vicissitudes, it is a steady state with respect to one's eternal destiny. Moral progress or regress does not affect one's qualitative proximity to salvation, and still less is there any possibility of falling from grace or being restored to grace.

The exegetical strength of Moo's interpretation lies in the way it does justice to the accent Paul places, both in Romans 5 and in Romans 8, on the specific activity whereby the Holy Spirit touches the human "heart" or "spirit" in order to bestow upon the believer the subjective assurance of salvation and the confidence to call upon God as Father. A weakness in his interpretation, in my opinion, is that it does not adequately account for the way Paul closely relates this interior work of the Spirit both to the believer's death to sin and to his or her endurance of afflictions. Why does Paul choose to discuss filial adoption within that portion of the letter that is most intensely concerned with moral transformation and suffering (chapters 5–8)? That Paul perceives these dimensions of Christian existence to be linked organically is especially clear in 8:12–17, and this is precisely where Moo's exegesis runs into serious difficulties.

17 Moo, 501, 521.

18 Moo, 502.

19 Moo, 519–20.

Having exhorted the Roman Christians to consider themselves "dead to sin and alive to God" in chapter 6, and having established a diametric opposition between living "according to the flesh" and living "according to the Spirit" in the first part of chapter 8 (vv. 1–11), Paul now sternly warns his readers: "If you live according to the flesh you will die, but if by the Spirit you put to death the deeds of the body you will live" (8:13). Next, this reference to the mortification of disordered drives "by the Spirit" gives way to a more general reference to being "led by the Spirit," as Paul strongly asserts that those who are so led—and only they—are "sons of God" (8:14). By means of this statement, moreover, Paul's argument segues into the description of the Holy Spirit as the πνεῦμα υἱοθεσίας (8:15–16). It seems reasonably clear, therefore, that the mortification of sinful habits "by the Spirit" is one integral component of being "led by the Spirit." Moo grants as much. Further, since Paul specifies that "as many as [ὅσοι] are led by the Spirit of God are sons of God," the conclusion that death to sin is an intrinsic and essential dimension of filial adoption seems inescapable.

It is precisely this conclusion, however, that Moo fails to draw. According to him, death to sin is one aspect of being "led by the Spirit," and the latter is "a distinguishing sign" of filial adoption, but filial adoption is not per se a matter of dying to sin.[20] The two are extrinsically related. Those who enjoy the status of filial adoption *are the very same people* as those who put sin to death, but it is not one and the same grace that accomplishes both, even though Paul ascribes both to the activity of the Holy Spirit. Clearly Moo's concern is to guard against the idea that one's ongoing status as son or daughter of God—and thus one's prospects for attaining the completion of filial adoption in the glorification of the body—is in any respect determined by one's moral condition. Moo attempts to bolster this interpretation by resisting the idea that the theme of adoptive sonship is central to Romans 8. According to Moo, the discussion of filial adoption in verses 15–16 is "somewhat parenthetical," and the references to sonship in verses 19, 21, and 23 are "incidental" to Paul's argument.[21]

Moo's commitment to "the finality of justification" and to keeping moral sanctification extrinsic both to justification and to sonship leads to a rather strained exegesis of Romans 8:13, where Paul writes, "If you live according to the flesh you will die, but if by the Spirit you put to death the deeds of the

20 Moo, 499.

21 Moo, 496.

body you will live." Moo recognizes that Paul here is saying that "his readers will be damned if they continue to follow the dictates of the flesh," but insofar as Paul's readers are "regenerate believers," Moo must suppose that Paul's threat is merely theoretical. Damnation is not a real possibility for the justified, for "the truly regenerate believer" is "infallibly prevented from living a fleshly lifestyle by the Spirit within."[22] Further, Paul's teaching (as Moo understands it) that God's work in Christ is "the sole and final grounds for our eternal life" and Paul's insistence on "the indispensability of holy living as the precondition for attaining that life" are two things "we cannot finally synthesize in a neat logical arrangement."[23] Since Moo admits that "this problem is basic to Reformed theology,"[24] one might reasonably wonder whether it is not the elements of Paul's teaching so much as those of Calvinist doctrine that resist synthesis.

THOMAS AQUINAS'S *SUPER EPISTOLAM AD ROMANOS*

Turning now to the *Super epistolam ad Romanos* (supplemented by pertinent passages from the *Summa Theologiae*), we may observe how differently Thomas Aquinas deals with the same set of exegetical and theological issues. In taking up the question of whether "the love of God" (*caritas Dei*) in Romans 5:5 should be understood as God's love for us or our love for God, Thomas maintains that *both loves* are poured into our hearts. He explains that, since the Holy Spirit is the eternal "love [*amor*] of the Father and of the Son," the gift of the Spirit brings us "into a participation of the love [*amor*] who is the Holy Spirit," and that by this participation we are made "lovers of God" (*Dei amatores*). Further, he notes that "the love [*caritas*] by which we love [*diligimus*] God is said to be poured into our hearts" because "it reaches to the perfecting of all the moral habits and acts of the soul."[25] Four features of this richly illuminative comment deserve our special attention.

First, Thomas judges the grace of redemption to bestow upon the human person a real participation in God's inner life. The Holy Spirit is the eternal love of the Father and the Son, or as Thomas says elsewhere, the "bond"

22 Moo, 494.

23 Moo, 495.

24 Moo, 495n120.

25 Aquinas, *In Rom.* c. 5, lect. 1.

(*nexus*) between the Father and the Son.[26] Thomas is able to develop this point with particular clarity precisely in the context of explaining what is meant by filial adoption. By "grace and charity" the rational creature is "assimilated to the eternal Word according to the unity which the Word has with the Father."[27] Filial adoption is thus "a certain similitude of the eternal Sonship, just as all things which occur in time are certain similitudes of those things which have been from eternity."[28] It is evident from these passages that Thomas's interpretation of Paul's doctrine of filial adoption is grounded in metaphysical principles and in Trinitarian theology properly speaking (i.e., not simply in a vague economic Trinitarianism), a grounding that is absent from Moo's interpretation. While many biblical scholars and theologians might view this hermeneutical difference as a point in Moo's favor, I think that metaphysics and Trinitarian theology enable Thomas to give an interpretation of Romans that is, on balance, more penetrating and coherent than that offered by Moo.

Second, Thomas is able to hold that "both loves" are poured into our hearts because he understands that while these two infused loves are distinguishable, they are aspects of a single grace—namely, *gratia gratum faciens*, or "sanctifying grace." Indeed, the grace by which we are justified, sanctified, and glorified is numerically one,[29] such that moral transformation is an intrinsic component of redemption and may be seen to mediate, in a certain sense, between justification of the soul and glorification of the body, and therefore between the beginning of adoption (Rom 8:15) and its consummation (8:23). *Gratia gratum faciens* is the grace by which a rational creature is united to God "through the effect of love" (*secundum effectum dilectionis*) and is none other than "the grace of adoption."[30] One might say that to view the effects of sanctifying grace, from justification to glorification, under the aspect of filial adoption is to grasp something of their unity.

26 Aquinas, *STh* II-II, q. 1, a. 8, ad 3. Naturally, Thomas distinguishes between the Holy Spirit as eternal reality (*aliquid aeternum*) and grace as an effect in time (*effectus temporalis*), so that "the love of God poured into our hearts" signifies the latter insofar as it gives us a participation in the former (*STh* I-II, q. 111, a. 3, ad 1).

27 *STh* III, q. 23, a. 3, corp.

28 *STh* III, q. 23, a. 2, ad 3.

29 *STh* I-II, q. 111, a. 3, corp.

30 Aquinas, *In Rom.* c. 1, lect. 3.

Third, Thomas (like Moo) recognizes that Paul's references to the Holy Spirit's action upon the "heart" and "spirit" of the believer (Rom 5:5 and 8:16 respectively) point to an interior, affective dimension of Christian existence. This is suggested already in the way Thomas expounds the phrase *caritas Dei* (5:5) in terms of *amor* and *dilectio*, but it is all the clearer in his comment on the phrase *in quo clamamus Abba Pater* (8:15). We make this cry "not so much with the sound of the voice as with the intention of the heart," and the ardor of this intention proceeds "from the feeling of filial love" (*ex affectu filialis amoris*). Like the seraphim, whose name means "burning" (*ardentes*) and who "cried out" (*clamabant*) in the prophet's vision (Isa 6:3), we pray this way because we burn "as with the fire of the Holy Spirit."[31] The difference between Moo and Aquinas in this regard is that whereas the former is concerned with the believer's "comforting conviction" that he or she is loved *by* God, the latter accents the believer's love *for* God. These two emphases complement each other nicely, I think. Moo perceives, in a way that Thomas seems not to, the close correlation Paul is drawing between the objective historical demonstration of God's love for sinners in Christ's death on the cross (5:8) and the subjective appropriation of that demonstration which the Spirit works in the heart of the believer (5:5; 8:16).[32] Thomas, for his part, notes that the Spirit's interior testimony to God's love *for us* immediately produces affection *for God* in us. He goes as far as to say that the Spirit "speaks his testimony by the effect of filial love [*per effectum amoris filialis*] which he produces in us."[33] Apart from this effect, the believer might remain turned in on himself or herself in the "comforting conviction" of God's love.

Fourth, Thomas relates Paul's reference to the "heart" not only to our dilection of God but also to "all the moral habits and acts of the soul," thus indicating the intimate connection between love of God and love of neighbor.[34] The same grace by which God convinces us of his love for us and turns us away from ourselves to love him heals and perfects the powers of the soul for Christian charity. The *effectus amoris filialis*—the specific effect of infused grace by which we love God—is the crucial link between God's love for us and our love for neighbor, a link that is conspicuously missing between "justification" and "sanctification" in Moo's Reformed doctrine. It is

31 *In Rom.* c. 8, lect. 3.

32 Moo, *Epistle to the Romans*, 309.

33 Aquinas, *In Rom.* c. 8, lect. 3.

34 *In Rom.* c. 5, lect. 1.

not coincidental that Moo refuses to see any reference to our love for God in Romans 5:5 and that when he comes to Paul's undeniable reference to "those who love God" in 8:28, he merely offers the bland comment that this is a way of summing up "the basic inner direction" of Christians. Absent a robust notion of infused and inhering grace, love *for* God can hardly be more than "our response" to grace and thus can make no real contribution to the process of redemption.

When we turn to Thomas's commentary on Romans 8, we find that he discerns a greater coherence among the elements of Paul's discussion in that chapter than Moo does, and that his interpretation is closely linked to what he has already said about *caritas Dei* in Romans 5. The *gratia gratum faciens* by which "we have been justified" (5:1) and by which "the love of God has been poured into our hearts" (5:5) is the same grace by which we "walk according to the Spirit" (8:4), "mortify the deeds of the body" (8:13), are "led by the Spirit" (8:14), "cry out, 'Abba, Father'" (8:15), "suffer with" Christ (8:17), and finally attain "the freedom of the glory of the children of God" (8:21). Unlike Moo, Thomas does not treat Paul's discussion of filial adoption as "parenthetical" or "incidental" to the argument of Romans 8, and he is able to give full exegetical weight to the equation Paul makes between those who are "led by the Spirit" and those who qualify as "sons of God" (8:14). Thomas paraphrases Paul: "Only those who are ruled [*reguntur*] by the Holy Spirit are sons of God."[35] To be ruled by the Spirit is to be ruled by love, and love is the key to understanding how all the effects of grace, from justification to glorification, fit together.

To see why this is so, it is crucial to recognize that, according to Thomas, redemption essentially *is* the healing and perfecting of human nature. Commenting on Romans 5:6 ("when we were still weak [*infirmi*], at the right time, Christ died for the impious"), Thomas notes that here Paul compares sin to bodily illness. "For just as by bodily infirmity the due harmony of the humors is destroyed, so by sin the due order of the affections is excluded." [36] Now, since justice is "a certain rectitude of order in a man's interior disposition, namely, inasmuch as what is superior in man is subject to God, and the inferior powers of the soul are subject to the superior, namely, to reason,"[37] the

35 *In Rom.* c. 8, lect. 3.

36 *In Rom.* c. 5, lect. 2; cf. *STh* I-II, q. 82, a. 1.

37 Aquinas, *STh* I-II, q. 113, a. 1, corp. Cf. J. Mark Armitage, "A Certain Rectitude of Order: Jesus and Justification according to Aquinas," *The Thomist* 72, no. 1 (2008): 45–66.

justification of the ungodly cannot simply be God's "declaration of acquittal pronounced over the sinner," as Moo would have it, but requires an infusion of inhering grace if it is to restore man to the right order that is the essence of justice. That is why Thomas says that "the remission of guilt is meaningless unless it includes the infusion of grace."[38]

Commenting on Romans 8:19—"for the expectation of the creature awaits the revelation of the sons of God" (*nam expectatio creaturae revelationem filiorum Dei expectat*)—Thomas says that the word "creature" may be understood here to refer to human nature itself, "which is the substratum of grace," and which in the unjustified man is "not yet justified but as though without form."[39] If we read this statement from within the interpretive framework of modern New Testament scholarship (which has been determined to a significant extent by the agenda and categories of Protestant theology), it seems tautologous to say that the unjustified man is "not yet justified," and in any case a distortion of Paul's doctrine of grace to make human *nature* the proper object of justification. But if we remember that for Thomas justification is not only the remission of sins but also the infusion of grace, we see that he means that the grace of justification restores nature to that rectitude of order that *is* justice and that this justice is a kind of form. Thomas goes on to say that in those who have been justified human nature is "partially formed by grace but nevertheless still unformed with respect to the form which it will receive by glory."[40] Further, since the "expectation" of justified human nature is "the revelation of the sons of God," we may suppose that the "form" to which Thomas refers here is none other than "adoptive filiation" (*filiatio adoptiva*).

Recalling that adoptive sonship is "a certain similitude to eternal Sonship" inasmuch as "the creature is assimilated to the eternal Word according to the unity that the Word has with the Father," and that this assimilation "is accomplished by grace and charity," we may conclude that the *gratia gratum faciens* by which "the love of God has been poured into our hearts by the Holy Spirit" brings human nature to this intermediate state of being "partially formed" (*partim formata*). At this stage, which Paul elsewhere refers to as *sub gratia* (Romans 6:14), nature is *iustificata* and thus "formed" with respect to

38 Aquinas, *STh* I-II, q. 113, a. 2 corp. Cf. q. 110, a. 1, ad 3: "The remission of sins does not take place without some effect divinely caused within us."

39 Aquinas, *In Rom.* c. 8, lect. 4.

40 *In Rom.* c. 8, lect. 4.

its prior *iniusta* and "unformed" condition, but it is "not yet formed" (*adhuc informis*) with respect to the form that it will receive *per gloriam*. Thomas insists that while the rational creature is by nature *capax adoptionis*, only those who possess charity *are* adopted sons.[41] In his commentary on Romans, as we have seen, Thomas says that adoption "is initiated" (*inchoata est*) in justification and "will be consummated" (*consummabitur*) with the glorification of the body.[42] But in the *Summa Theologiae* he explains that the assimilation of the rational creature to the eternal Word, insofar as this is accomplished by the infusion of grace and charity, gives adoption a kind of formal completeness (*talis assimilatio perficit rationem adoptionis*) already in this life.[43] What is "inchoate" in one respect is already "perfect" in another respect. It is inchoate inasmuch as the transformation of human nature that filial adoption entails cannot really be complete short of the glorification of the body, but it is perfect inasmuch as the *caritas Dei* poured into our hearts at justification really is, already in this life, a participation in eternal love that "reaches to the perfecting of all the moral habits and acts of the soul."[44] Moreover, the grace by which charity and the other theological and moral virtues are infused is not simply one ingredient in a recipe but is sufficient to bring us all the way to our goal. As Thomas explains in another context, "Grace that is subsequent according as it pertains to glory is not numerically other than the prevenient grace by which we are now justified," and so "the charity of the way is not voided in the fatherland but perfected."[45] In still another place, Thomas makes this point even more plainly: "Grace is nothing other than a certain beginning [*inchoatio*] of glory in us."[46]

One ramification of this understanding of redemption—according to which *iustificatio* means the infusion of a grace that not only remits sin but heals and perfects nature—is that the justified believer can forfeit grace

41 Aquinas, *STh* III, q. 23, a. 3, ad 3.

42 Aquinas, *In Rom.* c. 8, lect. 5.

43 Aquinas, *STh* III, q. 23, a. 3, corp. Jeremy Holmes notes that in Thomas's works *perficit rationem* (or *perficitur ratio*) is a technical expression indicating that all the necessary elements of a form are made present, not that the form has been brought to its ultimate perfection (email communication to the author, March 18, 2010). Cf. Thomas Aquinas, *II Sent.* d. 1, q. 2, a. 5 expos. (*delectatio quae perficit rationem fruitionis*) and *STh* I-II, q. 73, a. 3, ad 2 (*in qua perficitur ratio mali*).

44 Aquinas, *In Rom.* c. 5, lect. 1.

45 Aquinas, *STh* I-II, q. 111, a. 3, ad 2.

46 *STh* II-II, q. 24, a. 3, ad 2.

and charity, and thus his or her salvation, through subsequent mortal sin. Thomas draws out this implication frequently and in no uncertain terms in *Super epistolam ad Romanos*. Glossing the phrase *spes autem non confundit* ("but hope does not confound us"; 5:5), he writes that hope "does not fail, unless a man fail it."[47] Similarly, in his comment on Romans 8:9, he explains that Paul appends the conditional clause *si tamen Spiritus Dei habitat in vobis* ("if nevertheless the Spirit of God dwells in you") because although his readers received the Holy Spirit in baptism, "they might have lost the Holy Spirit through an ensuing sin."[48] To cite but one further example, Thomas expounds Paul's argument in Romans 8:13–14 in the form of a syllogism. Major premise: "All who are sons of God attain the eternity of a glorious life." Minor premise: "But only those ruled by the Holy Spirit are sons of God." Conclusion: "Therefore only those ruled by the Holy Spirit attain the inheritance of a glorious life."[49] Douglas Moo would accept this conclusion, but only after entering the caveat that justified believers are *infallibly* ruled by the Holy Spirit and thus in no real danger of losing their salvation.

PROGRESS ALONG THE WAY

It will be obvious from the foregoing presentation that I find that Thomas Aquinas provides a more theologically cohesive account of Paul's doctrine of adoption than does Douglas Moo. In particular, Thomas's recognition that justification, which both commentators identify as the beginning of filial adoption, is not merely a declaration of acquittal but the infusion of sanctifying grace enables us to grasp the coherence of all the effects of grace and thus something of the inner logic of redemption. However, important aspects of Paul's thought and of the saving mystery to which he refers remain unilluminated to this point in our analysis. I am especially interested in the dynamics of the justified believer's "progress along the way" (*processus viae*).[50] This seems to be at the forefront of Paul's thinking in Romans 5–8 and generally throughout his corpus of letters. In 2 Corinthians, for example, he says that "we are being transformed from glory to glory" (3:18), that "our inner self is renewed day by day" (4:16), and that we "bring sanctification to

47 Aquinas, *In Rom.* c. 5, lect. 1.

48 Aquinas, *In Rom.* c. 8, lect. 2.

49 *In Rom.* c. 8, lect. 3.

50 Aquinas, *STh* II-II, q. 24, a. 4, corp.

perfection in the fear of God" (7:1). Apart from acknowledging in passing that "the saints progress daily in purity of conscience and in the understanding of divine things," Thomas does not give such expressions a great deal of attention in the commentaries on Romans and 2 Corinthians.[51] Because he binds justification and sanctification so closely together, his interpretation of Paul may seem at first glance to minimize the importance of making gradual progress in sanctity. And when we view redemption in terms of filial adoption, it is even more difficult to discern any room for "progress along the way" in Thomas's interpretation of Paul. If the infusion of grace and charity at justification already completes the *ratio* of adoption, what is left for the believer but to await the consummation of adoption in bodily glory?

In Paul's letters "righteousness" (δικαιοσύνη) and "sanctification" (ἁγιασμός) are clearly distinct *secundum intellectum* and are to a certain extent also distinct *secundum esse*. In 1 Thessalonians 4:1–8, for example, where the latter term occurs three times, it designates a moral quality of life (here with special reference to sexual purity) that clearly admits of increase or intensification in those to whom "God has given his Holy Spirit." Paul acknowledges that to some extent the Thessalonians are already living in such a way as to please God, but he exhorts them to "increase all the more" (ἵνα περισσεύητε μᾶλλον) in this way of life (v. 1). In Romans 6:19–22 ἁγιασμός seems to be a middle term between the δικαιοσύνη received at justification and the τέλος of eternal life. This is perhaps also true in 1 Corinthians 1:30, where Paul says that Jesus Christ has become our "righteousness and sanctification and redemption" (δικαιοσύνη τε καὶ ἁγιασμὸς καὶ ἀπολύτρωσις).[52] No doubt, Paul's distinction between δικαιοσύνη and ἁγιασμός has contributed to the Protestant doctrine of imputed righteousness. Commenting on Romans 6:19, Moo defines ἁγιασμός as "the process of becoming holy," whereas Thomas takes the corresponding Latin term (*sanctificatio*) to mean "the execution and increase of sanctity."[53] While both

51 Aquinas, *In II Cor.* c. 4, lect. 5. Cf. c. 6, lect. 3.

52 The word ἀπολύτρωσις would in that case refer to the consummation of salvation, as it does in Rom 8:23 and Eph 1:14 and 4:30. Modern commentators are generally dismissive of any attempt to find a systematic arrangement in this passage: "These are not three different steps in the saving process; they are rather three different metaphors for the same event (our salvation that was effected in Christ)." Gordon D. Fee, *The First Epistle to the Corinthians*, NICNT (Grand Rapids: Eerdmans, 1987), 86. Cf. Hans Conzelmann, *1 Corinthians: A Commentary on the First Epistle to the Corinthians*, trans. James W. Leitch, Hermeneia (Philadelphia: Fortress, 1975), 52.

53 Moo, *Epistle to the Romans*, 405; Aquinas, *In Rom.* c. 6, lect. 4.

commentators understand Paul to refer to a *processus*, the subtle but important difference is that Thomas speaks of putting into act (*executio*) a sanctity already possessed, whereas Moo implies that one *becomes* holy only subsequent to justification.

If we turn to Thomas's discussion of the increase of charity in *Summa Theologiae* II-II, question 24, we find that in fact he gave a great deal of thought to the dynamics of the *processus viae*, even if this is not always reflected in the commentaries on the Pauline epistles. Christians are called "wayfarers" (*viatores*) because they are on the way to God, to whom they draw near "not with bodily steps but by affects of the mind." Infused charity makes this approach to God possible, since it is by love that the mind is united to God, and so it is of the essence of the *caritas viae* that it should increase. Since charity is a virtue ordained to act, its increase is virtual (not dimensive) and consists in "the efficacy to produce an act of more fervent dilection."[54] Because charity is formally complete when it is infused, it increases not by addition but by an intensification of its form. And since charity is an accident, "its being is to be in" (*eius esse est inesse*) its subject, and so its essential increase or intensification of form is nothing other than a deeper radication in the subject.[55] Thomas explains:

> Thus charity increases only by way of the subject's greater and greater participation of charity, that is, the subject's being more reduced to its act and more subject to it.... Each act of charity disposes one to an increase in charity, inasmuch as by a single act of charity a man is rendered more ready to act again according to charity; and as this aptitude grows, a man breaks forth into a more fervent act of dilection.[56]

Citing 2 Corinthians 6:11—*cor nostrum dilatatum est* ("our heart is dilated")—Thomas explains that there is no limit to how much charity can increase in the subject in this manner since "whenever charity grows, the aptitude for a further increase grows," and so "the capacity of the spiritual creature is increased by charity, for by it the heart is dilated."[57]

Next, Thomas takes up the question of whether charity can be perfected in this life. Since God is infinitely good and therefore infinitely lovable, while

54 Aquinas, *STh* II-II, q. 24, a. 4, corp., and a. 4, ad 3.

55 *STh* II-II, q. 24, a. 4, ad 3, and a. 5, corp.

56 *STh* II-II, q. 24, a. 5, corp., and a. 6, corp.

57 *STh* II-II, q. 24, a. 7, corp. and ad 2.

no creature is capable of infinite love, the only absolutely perfect love is that by which God loves himself. Nevertheless, one can speak of "perfect charity" in the human subject when a person loves as far as he or she is able (*secundum totum suum posse*). This happens in three ways. First, there is the perfection common to all who possess grace and charity, whereby a person "habitually places his whole heart [*cor*] in God" and "neither thinks nor wills anything contrary to the dilection of God."[58] As this would apply even to the tepid soul who barely avoids mortal sin, it might seem a stretch to refer to it as "perfection" at all. But doing so is entirely consistent with and, in a sense, even required by Thomas's high view of infused charity as a participation of eternal love, his recognition that sanctifying grace is the *inchoatio gloriae*, and his affirmation that by grace and charity filial adoption is aleady formally complete at justification.[59] We might refer to this level as the *perfectio caritatis iustitiae* or *perfectio caritatis habitualis* since, strictly speaking, it implies no progress beyond the infusion of grace at justification (e.g., it is possessed by the baptized infant). A second and higher state of perfection is reached when "a man makes an earnest endeavor to devote himself to God and divine things, setting aside all else except insofar as the necessity of the present life requires." This perfection of charity is possible in this life but is not achieved by all who have charity. Thomas calls it the *perfectio caritatis viae*, and he notes that the apostle Paul evidences this perfection when he says, "I desire to be dissolved and to be with Christ" (Phil 1:23). Third, there is the *perfectio caritatis patriae*, by which "a man's whole heart [*cor*] is always actually borne to God." This occurs only in heaven (*patria*), since the infirmity of this life makes it impossible "always in act to think about God and to be moved by dilection for him."[60]

Finally, on the basis of the distinction between the first two modes of perfection—the *perfectio caritatis iustitiae* and the *perfectio caritatis viae*—Thomas specifies three degrees of charity according to the principal pursuits (*studia*) which are characteristic of three distinct stages in the *processus viae*. First, there is *caritas incipiens*, whereby the Christian is principally concerned to withdraw from sin and resist concupiscence. Second, once the onslaught of sin and concupiscence has become somewhat less violent, there is *caritas proficiens*, whereby one is primarily occupied with the more positive task of

58 *STh* II-II, q. 24, a. 8, corp.

59 Aquinas, *In Rom.* c. 5, lect. 1; *STh* II-II, q. 24, a. 3, ad 2; *STh* III, q. 23, a. 1, corp.

60 Aquinas, *STh* II-II, q. 24, a. 8, corp.

progressing in virtue. Third, there is *caritas perfecta*, whereby one's principal care is to be united to God and to delight in him.[61] Each of these degrees implies some progress beyond the sheer possession of infused charity. That the third degree is identical to the *perfectio caritatis viae* discussed in the previous article is apparent from the fact that Thomas once again cites Philippians 1:23: *Cupio dissolvi et esse cum Christo.*[62] Thomas recognizes that these three pursuits overlap (e.g., even the beginner has *some* concern to make progress in virtue and to be united to God), and he explicitly states that all of the many discernable advances in charity that one might make *sub gratia* are comprised within these three principal stages.[63]

Thomas's schema is thus quite compatible with Paul's notion of being "renewed day by day" (2 Cor 4:16), in light of which it is somewhat surprising that Thomas's understanding of the increase and perfection of charity plays such a minor role in his exegesis of Romans 5–8 and 2 Corinthians 3–6. With some justification, for example, Thomas might easily have found the three degrees of charity reflected in Romans 8:13–15. *Caritas incipiens* is primarily concerned to "mortify the deeds of the flesh by the Spirit." *Caritas proficiens* is "led by the Spirit" to ever-increasing virtue. And *caritas perfecta* expresses its desire to be united with God when it cries out in the Spirit, "Abba, Father!" Significantly, this very passage constitutes the heart of Paul's teaching about what filial adoption means for this life. And whether or not one accepts the specific correlation I have just drawn between Paul's words in Romans 8 and Thomas's teaching on the increase of charity in *Summa Theologiae* II-II, q. 24, the latter holds some promise for probing further the relationship between the beginning of adoption in justification and its consummation in glory, which is the central concern of this chapter.

What I find especially striking about both Thomas's treatment of filial adoption and his teaching on the increase of charity is the strong accent he places on affectivity. Naturally, no one supposes that his view of the Christian life, broadly speaking, shortchanges the role of faith as the perfection of the intellect or the role of the infused moral virtues. Still, when Thomas approaches the mystery of redemption under the aspect of filial adoption, he views the Christian primarily as *amator Dei* and describes prayer as proceeding *ex affectu filialis amoris*. Similarly, his explanation of how charity

61 *STh* II-II, q. 24, a. 9.

62 *STh* II-II, q. 24, a. 9, corp.

63 *STh* II-II, q. 24, a. 9, ad 1 and ad 3.

increases and comes to perfection is decidedly nonmoralistic. The perfection of charity is fundamentally a question of "a man's heart being borne to God" (*cor hominis feratur in Deum*), whether this be *habitualiter*, as is true of all those in the state of grace; or *actualiter* insofar as the limitations of this life permit, as is the case with those who have achieved *perfectio caritatis viae*; or *actualiter semper*, as is possible only in heaven.[64] In defending the position that charity can be perfect in this life (whether in the sense of *perfectio caritatis iustitiae* or in the sense of *perfectio caritatis viae*), Thomas is not at all troubled by the seemingly compelling objection that we can never be entirely free of venial sins prior to death. These, he explains, are not incompatible with *perfectio viae* since, though they are contrary to the act of charity, they do not touch the infused habit.[65] Charity is defined as "a certain friendship of man for God," which "has for its object the ultimate end of human life, namely, eternal happiness."[66] And the closer one comes to this end, the more one finds oneself saying with Paul: *Cupio dissolvi et esse cum Deo.*

This link back to Paul's letters is important. What still remains insufficiently illuminated in his understanding of redemption is the role of the body—its suffering, its dissolution in death, and its glory. The accent Paul places on the body throughout his epistles (not least in Romans 5–8 and 2 Corinthians 3–6) is truly remarkable and raises difficult questions that neither Moo nor Aquinas deal directly with in their commentaries. One such question, an important one for our purposes, is why Paul virtually identifies υἱοθεσία with "the redemption of the body" (Rom 8:23). It is fine to say, as both commentators do, that the glorification of the body is the consummation of filial adoption, but that merely raises the question why this should be so. If the υἱοθεσία that is received at justification is a status of sonship and an "awareness of God as Father" that gives the believer "peace and security," as Moo maintains, what does this have to do with the body?[67] Why should the glorification of the body be identified as the consummation of *this* aspect of redemption in particular?

Thomas's more cohesive understanding of the various effects of grace at least paves the way for an answer to this question. If the grace of filial adoption *is* the grace of justification, and if justification *is* the healing and

64 *STh* II-II, q. 24, a. 8, corp.

65 *STh* II-II, q. 24, a. 8, ad 2.

66 *STh* II-II, q. 23, a. 1, corp., and a. 4, ad 2.

67 Moo, *Epistle to the Romans*, 501–2.

perfection of human nature, it makes perfect sense to say that adoption is not complete in every respect until the entire human person, body and soul, rests in heavenly glory. Furthermore, if filial adoption is a participation of eternal love that makes the believer an *amator Dei*, filial adoption is perfect insofar as charity is perfect, and it is precisely the mortal condition of the body and the concomitant limitations of this life that prevent the human heart from being "borne to God" *actualiter semper*, which is the ultimate perfection of charity. The "groaning" of those who await the consummation of adoption is not merely "frustration at the remaining moral and physical infirmities" of this life, as Moo would have it, but something much more positive: "affliction due to the delay of what is anticipated with great desire"—namely, union with God—as Thomas explains.[68] In other words, the "groaning" referred to in Romans 8:23 is identical with the longing expressed in the words *cupio dissolvi et esse cum Deo* in Philippians 1:23. Once again, Thomas appreciates the importance of the Christian's love *for* God in Paul's doctrine of filial adoption, whereas Moo does not.

One should not, however, draw the conclusion that Paul views the mortal body merely as a hinderance to final beatitude. On the contrary, as we shall see momentarily, he looks upon the body, precisely in its weakness and mortality, as playing an integral role in the believer's union with Christ *already in this life*. While Thomas has laid the groundwork for appreciating this positive somatological dimension of the *processus viae*, it is not an aspect of Paul's thought to which he pays much attention in the commentaries on Romans and 2 Corinthians. Accordingly, I would like to devote the remainder of this chapter to a fresh look at Paul's teaching. By building on what we have learned from Thomas and attending carefully to Paul's anthropology, I hope to expound further some of the dynamics involved in the believer's progress from the present possession of the πνεῦμα υἱοθεσίας to the eschatological consummation of υἱοθεσία constituted by the redemption of the body. My focus will be on Romans 8, drawing other Pauline texts into the discussion insofar as this seems helpful.

68 Moo, 519; Aquinas, *In Rom.* c. 8, lect. 5.

ANOTHER LOOK AT PAUL'S TEACHING

Spirit and Body

Douglas Moo objects to those interpretations that "seek to relieve the tension" between Romans 8:15 and 8:23 by pressing the distinction between πνεῦμα υἱοθεσίας in the former verse and υἱοθεσία by itself in the latter. According to these interpretations, Christians now possess only the *Spirit* of filial adoption, whereas at the resurrection on the last day they will possess filial adoption itself.[69] Moo is right to resist any implication that the gift of the Holy Spirit is somehow insufficient or that the believer's cry of "Abba, Father!" expresses anything less than real adoption. Indeed, Paul makes it clear that the same indwelling Spirit by which υἱοθεσία is begun in us at justification brings this gift to its eschatological consummation: "If the Spirit of the one who raised Jesus from the dead dwells in you, he who raised Christ from the dead will give life also to your mortal bodies through his Spirit which dwells within you" (8:11). To say that we now possess "the Spirit of filial adoption" is to say that we possess exactly what we need to get us all the way to our goal: the consummation of filial adoption in glory.

On the other hand, Paul's choice of πνεῦμα υἱοθεσίας for verse 15 and υἱοθεσία by itself for verse 23 is not arbitrary. The terms are not simply interchangeable. He includes the word πνεῦμα in verse 15 not only to indicate the principle of our filial adoption—namely, the Holy Spirit—but also in order to suggest the specific mode in which we possess υἱοθεσία throughout the pilgrimage of *this* life. Ours is a filial adoption *on the way* to glory, lived by faith, love, and hope. Accordingly, Paul refers to our present possession of the Spirit as "first fruits" in verse 23, and elsewhere speaks of the gift of the Spirit as an ἀρραβών, a "deposit" or "first installment" (2 Cor 1:22; 5:5; Eph 1:14).

We must likewise note that the contrast between Romans 8:15 and 8:23 is not only in terms of the "already" and the "not yet" but also in terms of "spirit" and "body," or inner man and outer man. For the Holy Spirit is not the only πνεῦμα referred to in Romans 8. Paul also speaks of "our spirit" when he locates the specific activity of the divine Spirit in the interior core of the human person: "The Spirit itself bears witness with our spirit that we are children of God" (8:16). The work of the Spirit begins in the spiritual dimension of the human person and is completed in the glorification of the somatic dimension (8:11). The Christian must live out the rest of this life in

69 Moo, *Epistle to the Romans*, 521.

a body subject to mortality, which is the penalty of sin, but at the same time he possesses a new principle of life within: "If Christ is in you, though the body is dead on account of sin, the spirit is alive on account of righteousness" (8:10). As Paul puts it in 2 Corinthians: "Though our outer man is decaying, our inner man is being renewed day by day" (4:16). In other words, we experience the tension between the "already" and the "not yet" in large part as a tension between enlivened spirit and dying body. And it is this tension that prompts "groaning" within those who possess the firstfruits of the Spirit while they await the consummation of υἱοθεσία, the redemption of their bodies (Rom 8:23).

By granting a certain priority to the interior life of the believer, Paul neither denigrates the body nor suggests its relative unimportance. On the contrary, the precise tension to which he refers would not obtain at all if the body were not integral to the human person and to Christian redemption. Paul does speak in this context of redemption as *emancipation* from the "bondage to decay" (8:21), a condition that our mortal bodies share with all organic matter. But the "glorious freedom of the children of God" is by no means deliverance *from* the body or from the realm of matter. As Paul says elsewhere, "while we are in this tent we groan under its weight, not because we wish to be unclothed but further clothed, so that what is mortal may be swallowed up by life" (2 Cor 5:4).

Must the body, then, wait for the general resurrection before it can play a positive role in the mystery of redemption? Not at all. If we ask Paul how it is that one gets from here to there, from pilgrim υἱοθεσία to the consummation of υἱοθεσία in glory, he gives us an uncharacteristically straightforward answer: We must "suffer with" Christ "in order that we may also be glorified with him" (Rom 8:17). As we live with the tension between decaying body and enlivened spirit, the body, precisely in its mortality, is an important locus of union with Christ. "We always bear about in our body the dying of Jesus . . . in order that also the life of Jesus may be manifested in our mortal flesh" (2 Cor 4:10–11). Note that it is not simply his "death" (θάνατος) that we bear about in our bodies, but his "dying" (νέκρωσις).[70] Our whole Christian existence *usque ad mortem* is a process of dying with Christ. Note also that at the same time his life is to be manifest "in our mortal flesh"—that is, even in *this* life prior to glory.

70 BDAG, 668.

Death to Sin

Before developing those last two points, we need to consider more precisely what this "suffering with" Christ entails and how Paul's accent on the body might be compatible with the priority we have already seen him give to the "spirit" or "inner man." In Romans 8, Paul specifies two crucial dimensions of our suffering with Christ: death to sin, and the endurance of afflictions and persecution. The latter is highlighted within the magnificent crescendo in which the chapter culminates (8:31–39), and I shall touch on it near the end of this essay. But for the present I would like to develop the former aspect, death to sin. In 6:10–11, Paul makes the remarkable assertion that Jesus's own death was a death "to sin" and his risen life a life "to God," and on that basis he exhorts the Romans to reckon themselves dead to sin and alive to God. Later we shall briefly consider in what sense Christ's death was not only a death *for* sins but a death *to* sin. I mention this passage here to underscore the point that Paul views our death to sin as an integral aspect of our imitation of Christ.

The relationship between the inner man and the outer man with respect to the death to sin is illuminated especially in the first part of Romans 8, where Paul locates the power of sin in "the flesh" and speaks of habitual sin as "walking according to the flesh" (8:4). The claim is frequently made that Paul does not use the term σάρξ ("flesh") here to refer to man's material dimension as distinct from his mind or soul, but rather in a specialized sense to denote a basic attitude or disposition of the whole person as one opposed to God and dominated by sin.[71] The important grain of truth in this claim ought not, however, to obscure the fact that in several passages in Romans Paul explicitly locates sin and the power of sin in the physical body, as distinct from the inner man. For example, in chapter 7 he writes: "I take pleasure in the law of God according to the inner man, but I see another law in my members making war against the law of my mind and taking me captive by the law of sin which is in my members" (7:22–23). Whether this passage refers to regenerate or unregenerate man,[72] it is an expression of Pauline anthropology,

71 "Nevertheless, in many instances in Paul 'flesh' has a fuller meaning not found in the Old Testament. Then it designates man's being and attitude *as opposed to and in contradiction to God and God's Spirit*." Günther Bornkamm, *Paul*, trans. D. M. G. Stalker (Minneapolis: Fortress, 1995), 133. Bornkamm cites Rom 8:4 as his first example of this usage.

72 On the history of interpretation of the "I" in Rom 7:7–25, see Moo, *Epistle to the Romans*, 424–27; Fitzmyer, *Romans*, 463–65.

and in the epistle it is surrounded by similar statements. In chapter 6, Paul reminds us that "our old man was co-crucified that the body of sin might be nullified" (6:6) and exhorts us not to let sin "reign" in our "mortal bodies" and not to present our "members" as "weapons of unrighteousness for sin" (6:12–13). In chapter 8, as we have seen, he tells us that we must "by the Spirit put to death the deeds of the body," and he presents this practice as the opposite of living "according to the flesh" (κατὰ σάρκα, 8:12–13).

At the same time, it is clear from Paul's letters that the power of sin works upon the life of the mind and that moral transformation can only take place through the renewal of the mind.[73] The mind is the primary battleground between vice and virtue, and so it is the place where the grace of filial adoption must take deepest root if it is going to transform the whole person. As Thomas puts it, spiritual generation "comes about by spiritual seed transmitted to the place of spiritual generation, which is a man's mind or heart, for we are begotten sons of God by the renewal of the mind."[74]

Ground zero in the spiritual battle is what Paul refers to as the φρόνημα. This term designates the preoccupation of the mind, the set of concerns that dominate the conscious life of the mind.[75] According to Paul, "the φρόνημα of the flesh is death, but the φρόνημα of the spirit [πνεύματος] is life and peace" (8:6). Here πνεῦμα should probably be translated "spirit" (with a lowercase *s*), and we should understand the φρόνημα as mediating between "flesh" and "spirit." The word "spirit," in other words, can designate the deepest inner core of the human person (roughly equivalent to the "heart"), where the Holy Spirit intercedes "with inexpressible groanings" (8:26). I am not suggesting that Paul had a tripartite anthropology, nor that "spirit" designates an irrational element in man. The φρόνημα and the πνεῦμα are two aspects of a single rational soul (with faculties of intellect and will). But these terms represent "levels" of the soul's life. The φρόνημα lies nearer the surface, so to speak, near the soul's interface with the physical body. At this level the mind may be occupied with either speculative or practical concerns, though the latter tend to dominate, both because the needs of the body are so many and

73 Rom 12:2; Eph 4:17–24; Phil 1:9–11; 4:8; Col 1:21; 2:2–3; 3:10.

74 Thomas Aquinas, *In Gal*. c. 4, lect. 3.

75 BDAG, 1066. While this word is etymologically related and semantically proximate to φρόνησις, it does not mean precisely "prudence," despite the Vulgate translation of Rom 8:6. Paul's use of φρόνημα is closely related to his use of the verb φρονέω in 8:5 and elsewhere, especially Phil 2:5; 3:19; and Col 3:2.

so persistent and because this is precisely the level at which the thoughts of the mind, governed by the will, are translated into bodily actions.[76]

Now, when the drives of the body, disordered by sin, dominate the conscious life of the mind or φρόνημα, they press down into the deeper dimensions of the soul and suffocate the life of the spirit (lowercase *s*). This is what Paul means by saying, "the φρόνημα of the flesh is death"—spiritual death. He expands on this statement by indicating that "the φρόνημα of the flesh is enmity with God, for it does not submit to the law of God, nor can it" (8:7). But when the human πνεῦμα is enlivened by the divine πνεῦμα and *the will* allows the promptings of the Holy Spirit to inform, illuminate, and even preoccupy the conscious life of the mind in both its speculative and practical dimensions, the desires (so closely identified with the life of the body) are gradually purified, and the interior transformation of the personality manifests itself on the somatic level in concrete bodily-historical actions. This is what Paul has in mind when he speaks of the moral sanctification of the person "in perfect wholeness" (ὁλοτελεῖς), a sanctification that begins in the inner core of the personality and works its way outward: "spirit, soul, and body" (1 Thess 5:23).[77] The union of body and soul in the human person is so intimate that the presentation of one's body to God as a "living sacrifice" constitutes one's "rational worship" (Rom 12:1).[78]

The Love of God

In Romans 8, Paul refers to the manner of life that brings about this sanctification as "walking according to the Spirit" (8:4) or being "led by the Spirit of God" (8:14). These expressions, like the entire thrust of his paraenesis here and in chapter 6, presuppose that this mode of life is not forced upon the Christian. It is not inevitable that those who have received the quickening gift of the Holy Spirit will in fact cooperate with grace and experience transformation. That is why Paul exhorts the Galatians in these words: "If we live by the Spirit, let us also walk in step with the Spirit" (Gal 5:25).

The crucial question, then, is this: What exactly can induce the will to pursue this spiritual way of life? And it is this question that brings us back

76 Therein lies the aforementioned semantic proximity between φρόνημα and φρόνησις.

77 Naturally this is not a strictly linear progression. The process of sanctification also involves a dialectical or back-and-forth movement between inner man and outer man.

78 On the phrase λογικὴ λατρεία ("rational worship"), which is often dubiously translated "spiritual worship" (RSV, NRSV, NABRE), see Fitzmyer, *Romans*, 640.

to υἱοθεσία. Paul expounds what it means to be "led by the Spirit of God" by calling our attention to the specific character of sanctifying grace as filial adoption and by contrasting this grace with the dynamic that is operative under the Mosaic law. Under the old covenant, one might "delight in the law of God in the inner man," but this was not sufficient to emancipate fallen man from captivity to "the law of sin" that operates in one's "members" (7:22–24). The Mosaic law could not justify because it did not "vivify" (Gal 3:21). To the extent that it was effective in modifying behavior, it was so largely by means of fear, the fear of forfeiting a blessing or incurring a punishment. By contrast, the baptized "have received not a spirit of slavery back into fear, but a Spirit of filial adoption, by which we cry out, 'Abba, Father!'" (Rom 8:15).

Now, the grace described here in terms of υἱοθεσία is, as we have seen, identical to the grace spoken of earlier in the letter in terms of ἀγάπη: "The *love* of God has been poured into our hearts through the Holy Spirit who has been given to us" (5:5). The death of Jesus Christ for us "while we were still sinners" is the definitive historical demonstration of "God's own love for us" (5:8), while the interior gift of the Spirit bears personal witness to that demonstration of love and to the filial adoption that it brings about: "The Spirit itself bears witness with our spirit that we are children of God" (8:16). The "joint mission" of the Son and the Spirit is "manifested in the children adopted by the Father in the Body of his Son" (*CCC* 690).

The infusion of divine ἀγάπη into the inner man is the only force that can break the power of sin, and it does this not by means of servile fear but by means of a powerful attraction to the good. "The love of Christ compels us" not by violating our freedom, of course, but by means of the theological virtues, which enable us to recognize in Christ's passion God's love *for us* and to realize that the supreme good of our existence is "no longer to live for [ourselves] but for the one who died and rose for [us]" (2 Cor 5:14–15).[79] The enmity with God that is original sin consists in large part in a profound lack of trust in God and his goodness (*CCC* 397). The wound of sin begins to heal when Christ's merciful death for us sinners convinces us that God is, after all, a loving Father who can be trusted and who wants what is best for us. The Spirit's interior witness to this love begins a transformation of our

79 Thomas explains that a man "judges" (*diiudicat*) concerning what is to be done according to the habitual disposition of his mind, because a habit "makes what convenes to it appear good" (*STh* II-II, q. 24, a. 11, corp.). The theological virtues thus enable us to "judge" (κρίνω) rightly concerning Christ's death on the cross and the sort of life we should lead in response to it (2 Cor 5:14–15).

wounded personality by means of a reformation of our deeply disordered desires. According to Thomas, "We cry 'Abba, Father' when we are kindled affectively by the warmth of the Holy Spirit to desire God."[80] This purification of desire moves through the levels of the personality and manifests itself somatically in concrete, historical acts expressive of love of God and love of neighbor. This is the ἀγάπη that Paul identifies as the "fullness of law" (πλήρωμα νόμου, Rom 13:10). Love accomplishes what fear never could, so that "the righteous requirement of the law might be fulfilled in us who walk not according to the flesh but according to the Spirit" (8:4).

The process of sanctification that is driven by divine love cannot be completed prior to death, for only in death can one give oneself to God totally in reciprocal love. Our life is embedded in temporality, our freedom is realized in history, our soul acts through a body that is subject to death—and so the process of sanctification is determined (to some extent) by the structure of human life as life moving toward death. Our "obedience of faith" must imitate Jesus's obedience "even unto death" (Rom 1:5; 16:26; Phil 2:8; cf. Heb 5:8–9). Within such a structure, every authentic act of obedience and love *along the way* anticipates and prepares for the opportunity for self-oblation that biological death will present us with. Even at a merely human level, aging and the deterioration of the body constitute a kind of daily, proleptic participation in one's own death. Under the grace of filial adoption, this ineluctable experience of mortality serves as the material and occasion of our "suffering with" Christ. The daily reckoning of ourselves as dead to sin imitates Christ's once-and-for-all death to sin (Rom 6:10–11). The presentation of our members to God as instruments of righteousness constitutes a "living sacrifice" (6:13; 12:1). Note the oxymoron!

Power Perfected in Weakness

The recognition of this dynamic of "dying daily" (1 Cor 15:31) is even more illuminative when we turn from our consideration of death-to-sin in order to look at the other element of "suffering with" Christ that Paul highlights in Romans 8—namely, the endurance of afflictions and persecution. Jesus Christ "knew no sin" (2 Cor 5:21). The sin he "died to" was outside of himself. It was the sin of the world, which surrounded him and pressed in upon him (Rom 6:10; cf. 1 Pet 2:22–23). Therefore our "suffering with" Christ

80 Thomas Aquinas, *In Gal.* c. 4, lect. 3.

is more perfect to the degree that, having gained some level of victory over personal sin and having proclaimed the gospel with our life and words, we incur afflictions and persecution for the sake of the gospel. As Ignatius of Antioch puts it, "Christianity achieves its greatness when it is hated by the world" (*Rom.* 3.3). It is in this context especially that Paul speaks in terms of proleptic death and living sacrifice. To the Corinthians he writes: "We always bear about in our bodies the dying of Jesus ... we the living are always being handed over to death on account of Jesus" (2 Cor 4:10–11). And in Romans 8, he quotes the Psalter in reference to the Christian life: "For your sake we are put to death all the day; we have been reckoned as sheep for the slaughter" (Rom 8:36; cf. Ps 44:22).

In the context of his apostolic ministry, Paul experienced not only participation in the suffering and death of Jesus but also a paradoxical anticipation of bodily glory. Christ's risen life was manifest already in Paul's "mortal flesh" (2 Cor 4:10). When he was beaten down by afflictions, attacks, and infirmities of every sort, the power of Christ overshadowed him (2 Cor 12:9). He pummeled his own body and made it his slave (1 Cor 9:27); he worked with his hands indefatigably "night and day" (1 Thess 2:9); he traveled thousands of miles, often going without proper food, sleep, or shelter (2 Cor 6:5); he performed "signs and wonders and acts of power ... with all endurance" (12:12); and he carried on this way with indomitable energy for decades (Col 1:29). "Power is perfected in weakness ... when I am weak, then I am strong"—this was the mystery revealed to Paul by means of the "thorn in the flesh" (2 Cor 12:7–10). Living this mystery filled him with confidence that Christ would always be "magnified in [his] body, whether through life or through death" (Phil 1:20).

Paul, in other words, knew "Christ and the power of his resurrection," not only in the inner man, but also overflowing into his body. Far from providing Paul with a life of physical ease, however, this power flowed through him only in the midst of tireless apostolic labor and great affliction. Paul's experience of resurrection power was inextricably linked to his "communion" (κοινωνία) in the sufferings of Christ, while at the same time this mystery of power-in-suffering was a real anticipation of glory. Paul yearned to be "conformed to [Christ's] death, that [he] might somehow attain to resurrection from the dead" (Phil 3:10–11). This may explain why Paul speaks of glorification in the past tense in Romans 8:30: "Those he called he also justified, and those he justified he also glorified." That which takes us all the way to glory has already been conferred upon us in justification.

As we have seen, Paul refers to this grace in several ways in Romans. It is "the love of God poured into our hearts through the Holy Spirit" (5:5), "the law of the Spirit of life in Christ Jesus" (8:2), "the Spirit of filial adoption" (8:15), "the first fruits of the Spirit" (8:23), and "the love of God that is in Christ Jesus our Lord" (8:39). Still another phrase for the same reality—"newness of life"—is found in Paul's description of the sacrament of baptism: "We have been buried with him through baptism into his death, in order that, just as Christ was raised from the dead through the glory of the Father, we might walk in newness of life" (6:4). The parallelism between Christ's resurrection through the Father's glory and our newness of life suggests that the latter is a real participation in the former.

Paul reminds us that "we hope for what we do not see" (8:25). But this does not mean that Christian hope amounts to a blind leap of the will with no intellectual or experiential basis. On the contrary, "affliction produces steadfast endurance, steadfast endurance proven character, and proven character hope" (5:3b–4). This rhetorical *sorites* (or staircase device) expresses the truth that the infused virtue of hope is built up in us as part of a moral and intellectual transformation that finds its material and occasion in suffering. As Thomas puts it, "tribulation prepares the way for hope."[81] The ultimate basis for hope is, of course, the love of God. "Hope does not disappoint, because the love of God has been poured into our hearts" (5:5). But we know this love and grow in it through the mystery of "suffering with" Christ, with all the elements that this entails, including death to sin, the endurance of afflictions and persecution, and the experience of power perfected in weakness. The Christian who dares to imitate Paul in the appropriation of these graces will be "transformed into the image" of God's Son "from glory to glory" (2 Cor 3:18; cf. Rom 8:29).

81 Aquinas, *In Rom.* c. 5, lect. 1.

Bibliography

Aharoni, Yohanan. *The Land of the Bible: A Historical Geography*. Translated by A. F. Rainey. 2nd ed. Philadelphia: Westminster, 1979.

Alter, Robert. *The Art of Biblical Narrative.* New York: Basic Books, 1981.

Anderson, A. A. *Psalms 1–72*. New Century Bible Commentary. Grand Rapids: Eerdmans, 1981.

Anderson, Gary A. "Sacrifice and Sacrificial Offerings (OT)." In Freedman, *Anchor Bible Dictionary*, 5:870–86.

———. *Christian Doctrine and the Old Testament: Theology in the Service of Biblical Exegesis.* Grand Rapids: Baker Academic, 2017.

Aquinas, Thomas. *Basic Writings of Saint Thomas Aquinas*. 2 vols. Edited by Anton C. Pegis. New York: Random House, 1945.

———. *Commentary on the Epistle to the Hebrews.* Translated by Chrysostom Baer. South Bend, Ind.: St. Augustine's Press, 2006.

Armitage, J. Mark. "A Certain Rectitude of Order: Jesus and Justification according to Aquinas." *The Thomist* 72, no. 1 (2008): 45–66.

Athanasius. *The Life of Antony and the Letter to Marcellinus*. Edited and translated by Robert C. Gregg. Classics of Western Spirituality. New York: Paulist, 1980.

Attridge, Harold W. *The Epistle to the Hebrews*. Hermeneia. Philadelphia: Fortress, 1989.

Augustine of Hippo. *The City of God*. Translated by Marcus Dods. New York: Modern Library, 1950.

Balthasar, Hans Urs von. *The Dramatis Personae: Man in God*. Vol. 2 of *Theo-Drama: Theological Dramatic Theory.* Translated by Graham Harrison. San Francisco: Ignatius, 1976.

———. *The Word Made Flesh*. Vol. 1 of *Explorations in Theology.* Translated by A. V. Littledale and Alexander Dru. San Francisco: Ignatius, 1989.

Barr, James. *Old and New in Interpretation: A Study of the Two Testaments*. New York: Harper & Row, 1966.

———. *The Semantics of Biblical Language.* London: SCM, 1983. First published 1961.

Barton, John. "Form Criticism (OT)." In Freedman, *Anchor Bible Dictionary*, 2:838–41.

Bates, Matthew W. *The Birth of the Trinity: Jesus, God, and Spirit in New Testament and Early Christian Interpretation of the Old Testament*. Oxford: Oxford University Press, 2015.

Bauckham, R. J. "Sabbath and Sunday in the Post-Apostolic Church." In *From Sabbath to Lord's Day: A Biblical, Historical, and Theological Investigation*, edited by D. A. Carson, 251–98. Eugene, Ore.: Wipf & Stock, 1982.

Bauer, Walter, Frederick William Danker, William F. Arndt, and F. Wilbur Gingrich, eds. *Greek-English Lexicon of the New Testament and Other Early Christian Literature*. 3rd ed. Chicago: University of Chicago Press, 2000.

Beale, G. K., and Benjamin L. Gladd. *Hidden But Now Revealed: A Biblical Theology of Mystery*. Downers Grove, Ill.: InterVarsity Press, 2014.

Benedict XVI, Pope. "Christmas Address to the Roman Curia." December 22, 2005.

———. *Verbum Domini*. Post-Synodal Apostolic Exhortation. September 30, 2010.

———. *See also* Ratzinger, Joseph.

Berlin, Adele. "Parallelism." In Freedman, *Anchor Bible Dictionary*, 5:155–62.

Bieler, Martin. "The Mysteries of Jesus' Public Life: Stages on the Way to the Cross." *Communio* 29 (Spring 2002): 47–61.

Blenkinsopp, Joseph. *A History of Prophecy in Israel*. 2nd ed. Louisville: Westminster John Knox, 1996.

———. *Isaiah 1–39: A New Translation with Introduction and Commentary*. Anchor Bible 19. New York: Doubleday, 2000.

Blondel, Maurice. *Action (1893): Essay on a Critique of Life and a Science of Practice*. Translated by Oliva Blanchette. Notre Dame, Ind.: University of Notre Dame Press, 2004. First published 1893.

———. *The Letter on Apologetics and History and Dogma*. Edited and translated by Alexander Dru and Illtyd Trethowan. Grand Rapids: Eerdmans, 1994. First published 1897 and 1904.

Bobichon, Philippe. *Justin Martyr, Dialogue avec Tryphon, édition critique, traduction, commentaire*. 2 vols. Paradosis 47. Fribourg: Academic Press, 2003.

Bornkamm, Günther. *Paul*. Translated by D. M. G. Stalker. Minneapolis: Fortress, 1995.

Botterweck, G. Johannes. "Knowledge of God." In *Encyclopedia of Biblical Theology*, edited by Johannes B. Bauer, 2:472–75. London: Sheed & Ward, 1970.

Briggs, Charles A., and Emilie G. Briggs. *A Critical and Exegetical Commentary on the Book of Psalms*. Vol. 1. International Critical Commentary. Edinburgh: T&T Clark, 1906.

Brown, Peter. *Augustine of Hippo: A Biography*. 2nd ed. London: Faber & Faber, 2000.

Brown, Raymond E, SS. *The Sensus Plenior of Sacred Scripture*. Baltimore: St. Mary's University, 1955.

———. *The Gospel According to John*. 2 vols. Anchor Bible 29–29A. Garden City, N.Y.: Doubleday, 1966–1970.

———. *The Critical Meaning of the Bible*. New York: Paulist, 1981.

———. *Biblical Exegesis and Church Doctrine*. Mahwah, N.J.: Paulist, 1985.

———. "Addenda." In Neuhaus, *Biblical Interpretation in Crisis*, 37–49.

———. *The Death of the Messiah, From Gethsemane to the Grave: A Commentary on the Passion Narratives in the Four Gospels*. 2 vols. Anchor Bible Reference Library. New York: Doubleday, 1994.

———. *An Introduction to the New Testament*. Anchor Bible Reference Library. New York: Doubleday, 1997.

Brown, Raymond E., SS, Joseph A. Fitzmyer, SJ, and Roland E. Murphy, OCarm, eds. *The Jerome Biblical Commentary*. Englewood Cliffs, N.J.: Prentice Hall, 1968.

———, eds. *The New Jerome Biblical Commentary*. Englewood Cliffs, N.J.: Prentice Hall, 1990.

Bruce, F. F. *The Epistle to the Hebrews*. 2nd ed. New International Commentary on the New Testament. Grand Rapids: Eerdmans, 1990. First edition 1964.

Brueggemann, Walter. *The Land: Place as Gift, Promise, and Challenge in Biblical Faith*. 2nd ed. Minneapolis: Fortress, 2002.

Buchanan, George Wesley. *To the Hebrews: Translation, Comment and Conclusions*. Anchor Bible 36. Garden City, N.Y.: Doubleday, 1972.

Burge, Gary M. *Jesus and the Land: The New Testament Challenge to "Holy Land" Theology*. Grand Rapids: Baker Academic, 2010.

Buttrick, George Arthur, ed. *The Interpreter's Dictionary of the Bible*. 5 vols. New York: Abingdon, 1962–1976.

Carbajosa, Ignacio. *Faith, the Fount of Exegesis: The Interpretation of Scripture in Light of the History of Research on the Old Testament*. Translated by Paul Stevenson. San Francisco: Ignatius, 2013.

Carson, D. A., ed. *From Sabbath to Lord's Day: A Biblical, Historical, and Theological Investigation*. Eugene, Ore.: Wipf & Stock, 1982.

Cassiodorus. *Explanation of the Psalms*. Vol. 1, *Psalms 1–50*. Edited and translated by P. G. Walsh. Ancient Christian Writers 51. Mahwah, N.J.: Paulist, 1990.

Childs, Brevard S. "Psalm 8 in the Context of the Christian Canon." *Interpretation* 23, no. 1 (1969): 20–31.

———. *The Book of Exodus: A Critical, Theological Commentary*. Old Testament Library. Louisville: Westminster, 1974.

———. *Introduction to the Old Testament as Scripture*. Philadelphia: Fortress, 1979.

Clarke, W. Norris. *The One and the Many: A Contemporary Thomistic Metaphysics*. Notre Dame, Ind.: University of Notre Dame Press, 2001.

Clifford, Richard J. *Psalms 1–72*. Abingdon Old Testament Commentaries. Nashville: Abingdon, 2002.

Collins, John J. "Daniel, Book of." In Freedman, *Anchor Bible Dictionary*, 2:29–37.

Congar, Yves. *The Meaning of Tradition*. Translated by A. N. Woodrow. San Francisco: Ignatius, 2004.

Conzelmann, Hans. *1 Corinthians: A Commentary on the First Epistle to the Corinthians*. Translated by James W. Leitch. Hermeneia. Philadelphia: Fortress, 1975.

———. *Gentiles—Jews—Christians: Polemics and Apologetics in the Greco-Roman Era*. Translated by M. Eugene Boring. Minneapolis: Fortress, 1992.

Cook, James I. "The Concept of Adoption in the Theology of Paul." In *Saved by Hope: Essays in Honor of Richard C. Oudersluys*, edited by James I. Cook, 133–44. Grand Rapids: Eerdmans, 1978.

Coote, Robert B., ed. *Elijah and Elisha in Socioliterary Perspective*. Atlanta: Scholars Press, 1992.

Craigie, Peter C. *Psalms 1–50*. Word Biblical Commentary 19. Waco, Tex.: Word Books, 1983.

Cranfield, C. E. B. *A Critical and Exegetical Commentary on the Epistle to the Romans*. 2 vols. International Critical Commentary. Edinburgh: T&T Clark, 1979.

Cross, Frank Moore. *Canaanite Myth and Hebrew Epic: Essays in the History of the Religion of Israel*. Cambridge, Mass.: Harvard University Press, 1973.

Daniélou, Jean, SJ. *From Shadows to Reality, or Sacramentum Futuri: Studies in the Biblical Typology of the Fathers*. Translated by Wulstan Hibberd. London: Burns & Oates, 1960.

Davies, W. D. *The Gospel and the Land: Early Christianity and Jewish Territorial Doctrine*. Berkeley: University of California Press, 1974.

———. *The Territorial Dimension of Judaism, With a Symposium and Further Reflections*. Minneapolis: Fortress, 1991.

Dawson, Christopher. *The Age of the Gods: A Study in the Origins of Culture in Prehistoric Europe and the Ancient East*. Washington, D.C.: The Catholic University of America Press, 2012.

Day, John. "Canaan, Religion of." In Freedman, *Anchor Bible Dictionary*, 1:831–37.

Deissler, Alphonse. *Le Livre des Psaumes 1–75*. Verbum Salutis 1. Paris: Beauchesne, 1966.

Dentan, Robert C. *The Knowledge of God in Ancient Israel*. New York: Seabury, 1968.

Denzinger, Heinrich. *Compendium of Creeds, Definitions, and Declarations on Matters of Faith and Morals*. Revised and enlarged by Peter Hünermann. Edited by Robert Fastiggi and Anne Englund Nash. 43rd ed. San Francisco: Ignatius, 2012.

DeVries, Simon J. *1 Kings*. Word Biblical Commentary 12. Waco, Tex.: Word Books, 1985.

De Wet, Chris L. "The Messianic Interpretation of Psalm 8:4–6 in Hebrews 2:6–9," part 2. In Human and Steyn, *Psalms and Hebrews*, 113–25.

Diodore of Tarsus. *Diodori Tarsensis Commentarii in Psalmos*. Vol. 1, *Commentarii in Psalmos I-L*. Edited by Jean-Marie Olivier. Corpus Christianorum Series Graeca 6. Turnhout: Brepols, 1980.

Drazin, Israel, and Stanley M. Wagner, *Exodus: Onkelos on the Torah, Understanding the Bible Text*. Jerusalem: Gefen, 2006.

Dulles, Avery, SJ. "Mystery (In Theology)." In *New Catholic Encyclopedia*, edited by William J. McDonald, 10:151–53. New York: McGraw-Hill, 1967.

———. *Models of Revelation*. Garden City, N.Y.: Doubleday, 1983.

Ellingworth, Paul. *The Epistle to the Hebrews: A Commentary on the Greek Text*. New International Greek Testament Commentary. Grand Rapids: Eerdmans, 1993.

Farkasfalvy, Denis, O. Cist. *Inspiration and Interpretation: A Theological Introduction to Sacred Scripture*. Washington, D.C.: The Catholic University of America Press, 2010.

———. *A Theology of the Christian Bible: Revelation, Inspiration, Canon*. Washington, D.C.: The Catholic University of America Press, 2018.

Fee, Gordon D. *The First Epistle to the Corinthians*. New International Commentary on the New Testament. Grand Rapids: Eerdmans, 1987.

Feuer, Avroham Chaim. *Tehillim: A New Translation with a Commentary Anthologized from Talmudic, Midrashic and Rabbinic Sources*. 2 vols. Brooklyn: Mesorah Publications, 1985.

Fisher, Eugene J. "A Commentary on the Texts: Pope John Paul II's Pilgrimage of Reconciliation." In Pope John Paul II, *Spiritual Pilgrimage: Texts on Jews and Judaism, 1979–1995*, edited by Eugene J. Fisher and Leon Klenicki, xx–xxxix. New York: Crossroad, 1995.

Fitzmyer, Joseph A., SJ. *The Gospel According to Luke: Introduction, Translation, and Notes*. 2 vols. Anchor Bible 28–28A. Garden City, N.Y.: Doubleday, 1981–1985.

———. "Historical Criticism: Its Role in Biblical Interpretation and Church Life." *Theological Studies* 50, no. 2 (1989): 244–59.

———. *Romans: A New Translation with Introduction and Commentary*. Anchor Bible 33. New York: Doubleday, 1993.

———. *Scripture, the Soul of Theology*. New York: Paulist, 1994.

———. *The Biblical Commission's Document 'The Interpretation of the Bible in the Church': Text and Commentary*. Subsidia Biblica 18. Rome: Pontifical Biblical Institute, 1995.

———. *The Acts of the Apostles: A New Translation with Introduction and Commentary*. Anchor Bible 31. New York: Doubleday, 1998.

———. *First Corinthians: A New Translation with Introduction and Commentary*. Anchor Yale Bible 32. New Haven: Yale University Press, 2008.

———. *The Interpretation of Scripture: In Defense of the Historical Critical Method*. New York: Paulist, 2008.

Fowl, Stephen E., ed. *The Theological Interpretation of Scripture: Classic and Contemporary Readings*. Blackwell Readings in Modern Theology. Malden, Mass.: Blackwell, 1997.

———. *Engaging Scripture: A Model for Theological Interpretation*. Oxford: Blackwell, 1998.

Freedman, David Noel, ed. *Anchor Bible Dictionary*. 6 vols. New York: Doubleday, 1992.

Frei, Hans W. *The Eclipse of Biblical Narrative: A Study in Eighteenth and Nineteenth Century Hermeneutics*. New Haven: Yale University Press, 1974.

Gadamer, Hans-Georg. *Philosophical Hermeneutics*. Translated and edited by David E. Linge. Berkeley: University of California Press, 1976.

Gelin, Albert, PSS. *The Poor of Yahweh*. Translated by Kathryn Sullivan, RSCJ. Collegeville, Minn.: Liturgical Press, 1964.

Granados, José, Carlos Granados, and Luis Sánchez-Navarro, eds. *Opening Up the Scriptures: Joseph Ratzinger and the Foundations of Biblical Interpretation*. Grand Rapids: Eerdmans, 2008.

Grant, Robert M. *Irenaeus of Lyons*. The Early Church Fathers. London: Routledge, 1997.

Gray, John. *I & II Kings: A Commentary*. Old Testament Library. Philadelphia: Westminster, 1963.

Guéranger, Prosper, OSB. *The Liturgical Year: Advent*. Translated by Laurence Shepherd. Westminster, Md.: Newman, 1948.

Gunkel, Hermann. *Die Psalmen*. 5th ed. Göttingen: Vandenhoeck & Ruprecht, 1968.

Habel, Norman C. *The Land is Mine: Six Biblical Land Ideologies*. Minneapolis: Fortress, 1995.

Hahn, Scott W. *Letter and Spirit: From Written Text to Living Word in the Liturgy*. New York: Doubleday, 2005.

———. "Canon, Cult and Covenant: The Promise of Liturgical Hermeneutics." In *Canon and Biblical Interpretation*, edited by Craig G. Bartholomew, Scott Hahn, Robin Parry, Christopher Seitz, and Al Wolters, 207–35. Scripture and Hermeneutics 7. Grand Rapids: Zondervan, 2006.

———. *Covenant and Communion: The Biblical Theology of Pope Benedict XVI*. Grand Rapids: Brazos, 2009.

———. *Kinship by Covenant: A Canonical Approach to the Fulfillment of God's Saving Promises*. Anchor Yale Bible Reference Library. New Haven: Yale University Press, 2009.

———. "For the Sake of Our Salvation: The Truth and Humility of God's Word." *Letter & Spirit* 6 (2010): 21–45.

Hahn, Scott, and Curtis Mitch. *Exodus: Commentary, Notes, & Study Questions*. Ignatius Catholic Study Bible. San Francisco: Ignatius, 2012.

Hay, David M. *Glory at the Right Hand: Psalm 110 in Early Christianity*. Nashville: Abingdon, 1973.

Hayes, John H., ed. *Dictionary of Biblical Interpretation*. 2 vols. Nashville: Abingdon, 1999.

Hengel, Martin. *Studies in Early Christology*. Edinburgh: T&T Clark, 1995.

Heschel, Abraham J. *The Prophets*. New York: Harper & Row, 1962.

Hidal, Sten. "Exegesis of the Old Testament in the Antiochene School with its Prevalent Literal and Historical Method." In Sæbø, *Hebrew Bible/Old Testament*, 543–68.

Hobbs, T. R. *2 Kings*. Word Biblical Commentary 13. Waco, Tex.: Word Books, 1985.

Hoffman, Lawrence A., ed. *The Land of Israel: Jewish Perspectives*. Notre Dame, Ind.: University of Notre Dame Press, 1986.

Holmes, Jeremy. *Cur Deus Verba: Why the Word Became Words.* San Francisco: Ignatius, 2021.

Hübner, Hans. "New Testament Interpretation of the Old Testament." In Sæbø, *Hebrew Bible/Old Testament*, 332–72.

Human, Dirk J., and Gert J. Steyn, eds. *Psalms and Hebrews: Studies in Reception*. Library of Hebrew Bible/Old Testament Studies 527. New York: T&T Clark, 2010.

Irenaeus of Lyons. *On the Apostolic Preaching*. Translated by John Behr. Crestwood, N.Y.: St. Vladimir's Seminary Press, 1997.

———. *Saint Irenaeus Bishop of Lyons' Five Books Against Heresies*. Edited by W. Wigan Harvey. 2 vols. Rochester, N.Y.: St. Irenaeus Press, 2013. Reprint of 1857 edition.

Isserlin, B. S. J. *The Israelites*. Minneapolis: Fortress, 2001.

Janzen, Waldemar. "Land." In Freedman, *Anchor Bible Dictionary*, 4:143–54.

John Paul II, Pope. *Redemptionis Anno*. Apostolic Letter. April 20, 1984.

———. "Address on the Interpretation of the Bible in the Church," April 23, 1993. In Pontifical Biblical Commission, *Interpretation of the Bible in the Church*, 11–25.

———. *Spiritual Pilgrimage: Texts on Jews and Judaism 1979–1995*. Edited by Eugene J. Fisher and Leon Klenicki. New York: Crossroad, 1995.

———. *Dies Domini*. Apostolic Letter. May 31, 1998.

———. *Rosarium Virginis Mariae*. Apostolic Letter. October 16, 2002.

———. *Man and Woman He Created Them: A Theology of the Body*. Translated by Michael Waldstein. Boston: Pauline Books & Media, 2006.

———. *See also* Wojtyła, Karol.

Johnson, Luke Timothy, and William S. Kurz, SJ. *The Future of Catholic Biblical Scholarship: A Constructive Conversation*. Grand Rapids: Eerdmans, 2002.

Jordaan, Gert J. C., and Pieter Nel, "From Priest-King to King-Priest: Psalm 110 and the Basic Structure of Hebrews." In Human and Steyn, *Psalms and Hebrews*, 229–40.

Joüon, Paul, SJ. *A Grammar of Biblical Hebrew*. Translated and revised by Takamitsu Muraoka. 2 vols. Subsidia Biblica 14. Rome: Pontifical Biblical Institute, 1993.

Justin Martyr. *Writings of Saint Justin Martyr*. Translated and edited by Thomas B. Falls. Fathers of the Church 6. New York: Christian Heritage, 1948.

Kant, Immanuel. *The Critique of Judgment*. Translated by James C. Meredith. Oxford: Clarendon Press, 1952.

Keating, Karl. *What Catholics Really Believe—Setting the Record Straight: 52 Answers to Common Misconceptions about the Catholic Faith.* San Francisco: Ignatius, 1992.

Keener, Craig S. *The Gospel of John: A Commentary.* 2 vols. Peabody, Mass.: Hendrickson, 2003.

Kereszty, Roch, O. Cist. "God the Father." *Communio* 26 (Summer 1999): 260–65.

Kilian, Rudolf. "Ps 22 und das priesterliche Heilsorakel." *Biblische Zeitschrift* 12, no. 2 (1968): 172–85.

Kistemaker, Simon. *The Psalm Citations in the Epistle to the Hebrews.* Eugene, Ore.: Wipf & Stock, 1961.

Kittel, Gerhard, Gerhard Friedrich, and Geoffrey W. Bromiley, eds. *Theological Dictionary of the New Testament.* 10 vols. Grand Rapids: Eerdmans, 1964–1976.

Koehler, Ludwig, Walter Baumgartner, Johann Jakob Stamm, and M. E. J. Richardson, eds. *The Hebrew and Aramaic Lexicon of the Old Testament.* 5 vols. Leiden: Brill, 1994–2000.

Koester, Craig R. *Hebrews: A New Translation with Introduction and Commentary.* Anchor Yale Bible 36. New Haven: Yale University Press, 2001.

Kraus, Hans-Joachim. *Theology of the Psalms.* Translated by Keith Crim. Minneapolis: Augsburg, 1986.

———. *Psalms 1–59: A Continental Commentary.* Translated by Hilton C. Oswald. Minneapolis: Augsburg, 1988.

Kugel, James L. *The Bible as It Was.* Cambridge, Mass.: Belknap Press of Harvard University Press, 1997.

Kuntz, P. G. "Decalogue." In Hayes, *Dictionary of Biblical Interpretation*, 1:256–62.

Kysar, Robert. "John, The Gospel of." In Freedman, *Anchor Bible Dictionary*, 3:912–31.

Latourelle, René, SJ. *Theology of Revelation: Including a Commentary on the Constitution "Dei Verbum" of Vatican II.* Staten Island, N.Y.: Alba House, 1966.

Leschert, Dale F. *Hermeneutical Foundations of Hebrews: A Study in the Validity of the Epistle's Interpretation of Some Core Citations from the Psalms.* Lewiston, N.Y.: Edwin Mellen, 1994.

Levering, Matthew. *Participatory Biblical Exegesis: A Theology of Biblical Interpretation.* Notre Dame, Ind.: University of Notre Dame Press, 2008.

Lewis, Jack P. "Flood." In Freedman, *Anchor Bible Dictionary*, 2:798–803.

Liddell, Henry George, Robert Scott, and Henry Stuart Jones. *A Greek-English Lexicon.* Oxford: Clarendon Press, 1968.

Louth, Andrew, ed. *Genesis 1–11.* Ancient Christian Commentary on Scripture, Old Testament 1. Downers Grove, Ill.: InterVarsity Press, 2001.

Lubac, Henri de, SJ. *History and Spirit: The Understanding of Scripture according to Origen.* Translated by Anne Englund Nash. San Francisco: Ignatius, 2007. First published 1950.

———. *Medieval Exegesis: The Four Senses of Scripture*. 3 vols. Translated by Marc Sebanc and E. M. Macierowski. Grand Rapids: Eerdmans, 1998–2009. First published 1959–1964.

Martin, Francis. *Sacred Scripture: The Disclosure of the Word*. Naples, Fla.: Sapientia Press of Ave Maria University, 2006.

Martin-Achard, Robert. "Resurrection (OT)." In Freedman, *Anchor Bible Dictionary*, 5:680–84.

Martitz, W. von, and E. Schweizer. "Υἱοθεσία." In Kittel, Friedrich, and Bromiley, *Theological Dictionary of the New Testament*, 8:397–99.

Maurer, Christian. "Πρόσφατος." In Kittel, Friedrich, and Bromiley, *Theological Dictionary of the New Testament*, 6:766–67.

Mays, James L. *Psalms*. Interpretation. Louisville: John Knox, 1994.

McArthur, H. K., and R. F. Berkey. "Jesus, Quest of the Historical." In Hayes, *Dictionary of Biblical Interpretation*, 1:578–85.

McCann, J. Clinton, Jr. *A Theological Introduction to the Book of Psalms: The Psalms as Torah*. Nashville: Abingdon, 1993.

———. "The Book of Psalms: Introduction, Commentary, and Reflections." In *The New Interpreter's Bible*, edited by Leander E. Keck, 4:639–1280. Nashville: Abingdon, 1996.

McCarter, P. Kyle, Jr. *1 Samuel: A New Translation with Introduction, Notes & Commentary*. Anchor Bible 8. Garden City, N.Y.: Doubleday, 1980.

McKim, Donald K., ed. *Historical Handbook of Major Biblical Interpreters*. Downers Grove, Ill.: InterVarsity Press, 1998.

Meier, John P. "Matthew, Gospel of." In Freedman, *Anchor Bible Dictionary*, 4:622–41.

Mendenhall, George E., and Gary A. Herion, "Covenant." In Freedman, *Anchor Bible Dictionary*, 1:1179–1202.

Milgrom, Jacob. *Leviticus: A New Translation with Introduction and Commentary*. 3 vols. Anchor Bible 3–3B. New York: Doubleday, 1991–2001.

———. *Numbers*. JPS Torah Commentary. Philadelphia: Jewish Publication Society, 1990.

Millard, A. R. "Literacy (Israel)." In Freedman, *Anchor Bible Dictionary*, 4:337–40.

Miller, Patrick D. *Interpreting the Psalms*. Philadelphia: Fortress, 1986.

Mitchell, M. M. "Chrysostom, John." In McKim, *Historical Handbook*, 28–34.

Moberly, R. W. L. *At the Mountain of God: Story and Theology in Exodus 32–34*. Journal for the Study of the Old Testament Supplement Series 22. Sheffield: JSOT Press, 1983.

Montefiore, Hugh. *A Commentary on the Epistle to the Hebrews*. London: Adam & Charles Black, 1964.

Moo, Douglas J. *The Epistle to the Romans*. New International Commentary on the New Testament. Grand Rapids: Eerdmans, 1996.

Moulton, James Hope, and George Milligan. *The Vocabulary of the Greek Testament, Illustrated from the Papyri and other Non-Literary Sources.* Grand Rapids: Eerdmans, 1930.

Nelson, Richard. *First and Second Kings.* Interpretation. Louisville: John Knox, 1987.

Neuhaus, Richard John, ed. *Biblical Interpretation in Crisis: The Ratzinger Conference on Bible and Church.* Grand Rapids: Eerdmans, 1989.

Nickelsburg, George W. E. "Resurrection (Early Judaism and Christianity)." In Freedman, *Anchor Bible Dictionary*, 5:684–91.

Oesterley, W. O. E. *The Psalms: Translated with Text-Critical and Exegetical Notes.* London: SPCK, 1955.

Osborn, Eric. *Irenaeus of Lyons.* Cambridge: Cambridge University Press, 2001.

Paul, Shalom M. *Isaiah 40–66: Translation and Commentary.* Eerdmans Critical Commentary. Grand Rapids: Eerdmans, 2012.

Penchansky, David. "Barr, James." In McKim, *Historical Handbook*, 423–27.

Peters, Melvin K. H. "Septuagint." In Freedman, *Anchor Bible Dictionary*, 5:1093–1104.

Pfitzner, Victor C. *Hebrews.* Abingdon New Testament Commentaries. Nashville: Abingdon, 1997.

Piper, O. A. "Knowledge." In Buttrick, *Interpreter's Dictionary of the Bible*, 3:42–48.

Pius XII, Pope. *Divino Afflante Spiritu.* Encyclical Letter. September 30, 1943.

Polanyi, Michael. *Personal Knowledge: Towards a Post-Critical Philosophy.* Chicago: University of Chicago Press, 1962.

Pontifical Biblical Commission. *The Interpretation of the Bible in the Church: Address of His Holiness John Paul II and Document of the Pontifical Biblical Commission.* Boston: St. Paul Books & Media, 1993.

Pope, Marvin H. "Devoted." In Buttrick, *Interpreter's Dictionary of the Bible*, 1:838–39.

Potterie, Ignace de la, SJ. "Interpretation of Holy Scripture in the Spirit in Which It Was Written (*Dei Verbum* 12c)." In *Vatican II: Assessment and Perspectives Twenty-Five Years After (1962–1987)*, edited by René Latourelle, 1:220–66. New York: Paulist, 1988.

Preuss, Horst Dietrich. *Old Testament Theology.* 2 vols. Old Testament Library. Louisville: Westminster John Knox, 1995.

Propp, William H. C. *Exodus 1–18: A New Translation with Introduction and Commentary.* Anchor Bible 2. New York: Doubleday, 1999.

Quasten, Johannes. *Patrology.* Vol. 3, *The Golden Age of Greek Patristic Literature, From the Council of Nicaea to the Council of Chalcedon.* Utrecht: Spectrum, 1960.

Rad, Gerhard von. *Old Testament Theology.* Vol. 2, *The Theology of Israel's Prophetic Traditions.* London: SCM, 1965.

———. *Genesis: A Commentary.* Translated by John H. Marks. 3rd ed. London: SCM, 1972.

Rahlfs, Alfred, and Robert Hanhart, eds. *Septuaginta: Id est Vetus Testamentum graece iuxta LXX interpretes.* Stuttgart: Deutsche Bibelgesellschaft, 2006.

Rahner, Karl. *Theological Investigations*. Vol. 6, *Concerning Vatican Council II*. Translated by Karl-H. Kruger and Boniface Kruger. Baltimore: Helicon, 1969.

Rahner, Karl, and Joseph Ratzinger. *Revelation and Tradition*. Translated by W. J. O'Hara. Quaestiones Disputatae 17. New York: Herder & Herder, 1966.

Ramage, Matthew J. *Dark Passages of the Bible: Engaging Scripture with Benedict XVI and Thomas Aquinas*. Washington, D.C.: The Catholic University of America Press, 2013.

Rashi [Rabbi Shelomo Yitsḥaki]. *Rashi's Commentary on Psalms 1–89 (Books I–III) with English Translation, Introduction and Notes*. Edited by Mayer I. Gruber. South Florida Studies in the History of Judaism 161. Atlanta: Scholars Press, 1998.

Ratzinger, Joseph. *Principles of Catholic Theology: Building Stones for a Fundamental Theology*. Translated by Mary Frances McCarthy. San Francisco: Ignatius, 1987.

———. *Eschatology: Death and Eternal Life*. Translated by Michael Waldstein. 2nd ed. Washington, D.C.: The Catholic University of America Press, 1988.

———. "Biblical Interpretation in Crisis: On the Question of the Foundations and Approaches of Exegesis Today." In *Biblical Interpretation in Crisis*, ed. Neuhaus, 1–23.

———. "Schriftauslegung in Widerstreit: Zur Frage nach Grundlagen und Weg der Exegese heute." In *Schriftauslegung im Widerstreit*, edited by Joseph Ratzinger, 15–44. Quaestiones Disputate 117. Freiburg: Herder, 1989.

———. Preface to *The Interpretation of the Bible in the Church: Address of His Holiness John Paul II and Document of the Pontifical Biblical Commission*, by the Pontifical Biblical Commission. Boston: St. Paul Books & Media, 1993.

———. *'In the Beginning...': A Catholic Understanding of Creation and the Fall*. Translated by Boniface Ramsey. Ressourcement. Grand Rapids: Eerdmans, 1995.

———. *Many Religions—One Covenant: Israel, the Church and the World*. Translated by Graham Harrison. San Francisco: Ignatius, 1999.

———. *Jesus of Nazareth: From the Baptism in the Jordan to the Transfiguration*. Translated by Adrian J. Walker. New York: Doubleday, 2007.

———. "Biblical Interpretation in Conflict: On the Foundations and the Itinerary of Exegesis Today." Translated by Adrian Walker. In Granados, Granados, and Sánchez-Navarro, *Opening Up the Scriptures*, 1–29.

———. *God's Word: Scripture—Tradition—Office*. Translated by Henry Taylor. San Francisco: Ignatius, 2008.

———. *Jesus of Nazareth, Part Two: Holy Week, From the Entrance into Jerusalem to the Resurrection*. Translated by the Vatican Secretariat of State. San Francisco: Ignatius, 2011.

———. *See also* Benedict XVI, Pope.

Ratzinger, Joseph, Alois Grillmeier, SJ, and Béda Rigaux, OFM. "Dogmatic Constitution on Divine Revelation." In *Commentary on the Documents of Vatican II*. Vol. 3, *Declaration on the Relationship of the Church to Non-Christian Religions, Dogmatic Constitution on*

Divine Revelation, Decree on the Apostolate of the Laity, edited by Herbert Vorgrimler, 155–272. New York: Herder & Herder, 1969.

Rentería, Tamis Hoover. "The Elijah/Elisha Stories: A Socio-cultural Analysis of Prophets and People in Ninth-Century B.C.E. Israel." In Coote, *Elijah and Elisha*, 75–126.

Reumann, John H. "Psalm 22 at the Cross: Lament and Thanksgiving for Jesus Christ." *Interpretation* 28, no. 1 (1974): 39–58.

Reventlow, Henning Graf. *Problems of Old Testament Theology in the Twentieth Century*. Philadelphia: Fortress, 1985.

———. *Problems of Biblical Theology in the Twentieth Century*. Philadelphia: Fortress, 1986.

Roberts, J. J. M. *First Isaiah: A Commentary*. Hermeneia. Minneapolis: Fortress, 2015.

Robinson, Thomas A. *Ignatius of Antioch and the Parting of the Ways: Early Jewish-Christian Relations*. Peabody, Mass.: Hendrickson, 2009.

Rordorf, Willy. *Sunday: The History of the Day of Rest and Worship in the Earliest Centuries of the Christian Church*. Translated by A. A. K. Graham. London: SCM, 1968.

Russell, Brian D. *The Song of the Sea: The Date of Composition and Influence of Exodus 15:1–21*. Studies in Biblical Literature 101. New York: Peter Lang, 2007.

Sæbø, Magne, ed. *Hebrew Bible/Old Testament: The History of Its Interpretation*. Vol. 1, *From the Beginnings to the Middle Ages (Until 1300)*. Göttingen: Vandenhoeck & Ruprecht, 1996.

Sawyer, John F. A. *The Fifth Gospel: Isaiah in the History of Christianity*. Cambridge: Cambridge University Press, 1996.

Schnackenburg, Rudolf. *The Gospel According to John*. Vol. 1, *Introduction and Commentary on Chapters 1–4*. Translated by Kevin Smyth. New York: Herder & Herder, 1968.

Schulte, Raphael. "Sacraments." In *Encyclopedia of Theology: The Concise Sacramentum Mundi*, edited by Karl Rahner, 1477–85. New York: Seabury, 1975.

Schulz-Flügel, Eva. "The Latin Old Testament Tradition." In Sæbø, *Hebrew Bible/Old Testament*, 642–62.

Schüssler Fiorenza, Elisabeth. *Bread Not Stone: The Challenge of Feminist Biblical Interpretation*. Boston: Beacon, 1984.

Schütz, Christoph. "The Mysteries of the Life of Jesus as a Prism of Faith." *Communio* 29 (Spring 2002): 28–38.

Scott, James M. *Adoption as Sons of God: An Exegetical Investigation into the Background of Huiothesia in the Pauline Corpus*. Wissenschaftliche Untersuchungen zum Neuen Testament 2/48. Tübingen: Mohr-Siebeck, 1992.

Senior, Donald, CP. "Dogmatic Constitution on Divine Revelation *Dei Verbum*, 18 November, 1965." In *Vatican II and Its Documents: An American Reappraisal*, edited by Timothy E. O'Connell, 122–40. Wilmington, Del.: Michael Glazier, 1986.

———. *Raymond E. Brown and the Catholic Biblical Renewal*. New York: Paulist, 2018.

Smalley, Beryl. *The Study of the Bible in the Middle Ages*. Notre Dame, Ind.: University of Notre Dame Press, 1964.

Sokolowski, Robert. *Phenomenology of the Human Person*. Cambridge: Cambridge University Press, 2008.

Spencer, John R. "Golden Calf." In Freedman, *Anchor Bible Dictionary*, 2:1065–69.

Spicq, Ceslas, OP. *Theological Lexicon of the New Testament*. 3 vols. Translated and edited by James D. Ernest. Peabody, Mass.: Hendrickson, 1994.

Stallsworth, Paul T. "The Story of an Encounter." In Neuhaus, *Biblical Interpretation in Crisis*, 102–90.

Stendhal, Krister. "Biblical Theology, Contemporary." In Buttrick, *Interpreter's Dictionary of the Bible*, 1:418–32.

Sternberg, Meir. *The Poetics of Biblical Narrative: Ideological Literature and the Drama of Reading*. Bloomington, Ind.: Indiana University Press, 1985.

Taguchi, Paul Cardinal. "Sacred Scripture and the Errors of the 'New' Exegesis." *Letter & Spirit* 6 (2010): 383–400.

Tekippe, Terry J. *Scientific and Primordial Knowing*. Lanham, Md.: University Press of America, 1996.

Thiselton, Anthony C. *The Two Horizons: New Testament Hermeneutics and Philosophical Description*. Grand Rapids: Eerdmans, 1980.

Thompson, Thomas L. "Historiography (Israelite)." In Freedman, *Anchor Bible Dictionary*, 3:206–12.

———. *The Historicity of the Patriarchal Narratives: The Quest for the Historical Abraham*. Harrisburg, Pa.: Trinity Press International, 2002.

Timmer, Daniel C. *Creation, Tabernacle, and Sabbath: The Sabbath Frame of Exodus 31:12–17; 35:1–3 in Exegetical and Theological Perspective*. Forschungen zur Religion und Literatur des Alten und Neuen Testaments 227. Göttingen: Vandenhoeck & Ruprecht, 2009.

Todd, Judith A. "The Pre-Deuteronomistic Elijah Cycle." In Coote, *Elijah and Elisha*, 1–35.

Vall, Gregory. "Psalm 22:17b: 'The Old Guess,'" *Journal of Biblical Literature* 116, no. 1 (1997): 45–56.

———. "*Lucis Mysterium*: Ignatius of Antioch on the Lord's Baptism." *Nova et Vetera* 8, no. 1 (2010): 143–60.

———. *Learning Christ: Ignatius of Antioch and the Mystery of Redemption*. Washington, D.C.: The Catholic University of America Press, 2013.

Vanhoozer, Kevin J. *Is There a Meaning in this Text? The Bible, the Reader, and the Morality of Literary Knowledge*. Grand Rapids: Zondervan, 1998.

Vanhoye, Albert, SJ. "The Reception in the Church of the Dogmatic Constitution *Dei Verbum*." Translated by Adrian Walker. In Granados, Granados, and Sánchez-Navarro, *Opening Up the Scriptures*, 104–36.

———. *The Letter to the Hebrews: A New Commentary*. New York: Paulist, 2015.

Vatican Council II. *Lumen Gentium*. Dogmatic Constitution. November 21, 1964.

———. *Dei Verbum*. Dogmatic Constitution. November 18, 1965.

Vawter, Bruce, CM. *The Conscience of Israel: Pre-Exilic Prophets and Prophecy*. New York: Sheed & Ward, 1961.

Villiers, Gerda de. "Reflections on Creation and Humankind in Psalm 8, the Septuagint, and Hebrews." In Human and Steyn, *Psalms and Hebrews*, 69–82.

Viviano, Pauline A. "The Senses of Scripture." In *The Word of God in the Life and Mission of the Church: Celebrating the Catechetical Year 2008–2009*, 1–4. Washington, D.C.: United States Conference of Catholic Bishops, 2008.

———. "Fighting Biblical Fundamentalism." In *Vatican II: 50 Personal Stories*, edited by William Madges and Michael J. Daley, 140–43. Maryknoll, N.Y.: Orbis Books, 2012.

Wachterhauser, Brice. "Getting it Right: Relativism, Realism, and Truth." In *The Cambridge Companion to Gadamer*, edited by Robert J. Dostal, 52–78. New York: Cambridge University Press, 2002.

Waldstein, Michael Maria. "*Analogia Verbi:* The Truth of Scripture in Rudolf Bultmann and Raymond Brown." *Letter & Spirit* 6 (2010): 93–140.

Waltke, Bruce K., and Michael O'Connor. *An Introduction to Biblical Hebrew Syntax*. Winona Lake, Ind.: Eisenbrauns, 1990.

Watson, Francis. *Text and Truth: Redefining Biblical Theology*. Grand Rapids: Eerdmans, 1997.

Weinfeld, Moshe. *Deuteronomy 1–11: A New Translation with Introduction and Commentary*. Anchor Bible 5. New York: Doubleday, 1991.

Wenham, Gordon J. *Genesis 1–15*. Word Biblical Commentary 1. Waco, Tex.: Word Books, 1987.

Westermann, Claus. *Genesis 1-11: A Commentary*. Translated by John J. Scullion. Minneapolis: Augsburg, 1984.

———. *The Living Psalms*. Translated by J. R. Porter. Grand Rapids: Eerdmans, 1989.

Wigoder, Geoffrey, ed. *The Encyclopedia of Judaism*. New York: MacMillan, 1989.

Wilken, Robert L. *The Land Called Holy: Palestine in Christian History and Thought*. New Haven: Yale University Press, 1992.

Windisch, Hans. *Der Hebräerbrief*. Tübingen: J. C. B. Mohr/Paul Siebeck, 1913.

Witherup, Ronald D, PSS. *Scripture: Dei Verbum*. Rediscovering Vatican II. New York: Paulist, 2006.

Wojtyła, Karol. *The Acting Person: A Contribution to Phenomenological Anthropology*. Translated by Andrzej Potocki. Analecta Husserliana 10. Boston: D. Reidel, 1979.

———. *The Place Within: The Poetry of Pope John Paul II*. Translated by Jerzy Peterkiewicz. New York: Random House, 1982.

———. *See also* John Paul II, Pope.

Wolff, Hans Walter. *Hosea: A Commentary on the Book of the Prophet Hosea*. Translated by Gary Stansell. Hermeneia. Philadelphia: Fortress, 1974.

Worden, Thomas. "My God, My God, Why Hast Thou Forsaken Me?" *Scripture* 6, no. 1 (1953–1954): 9–16.

Wright, David P. "Day of Atonement." In Freedman, *Anchor Bible Dictionary*, 2:72–76.

Wright, N. T. *Jesus and the Victory of God*. Vol. 2 of *Christian Origins and the Question of God*. Minneapolis: Fortress, 1996.

Würthwein, Ernst. *The Text of the Old Testament: An Introduction to the Biblia Hebraica*. 2nd ed. Translated by Erroll F. Rhodes. Grand Rapids: Eerdmans, 1995.

Index of Biblical and Ecclesial Sources

OLD TESTAMENT

NEW TESTAMENT

FATHERS AND DOCTORS

MAGISTERIAL

Index of Hebrew, Greek, and Latin

HEBREW

GREEK

LATIN

Author Index

Subject Index